Ius Gentium: Comparative Perspectives on Law and Justice

Volume 128

Ius Gentium is a book series which discusses the central questions of law and justice from a comparative perspective. The books in this series collect the contrasting and overlapping perspectives of lawyers, judges, philosophers and scholars of law from the world's many different jurisdictions for the purposes of comparison, harmonisation, and the progressive development of law and legal institutions. Each volume makes a new comparative study of an important area of law. This book series continues the work of the well-known journal of the same name and provides the basis for a better understanding of all areas of legal science.

The *Ius Gentium* series provides a valuable resource for lawyers, judges, legislators, scholars, and both graduate students and researchers in globalisation, comparative law, legal theory and legal practice. The series has a special focus on the development of international legal standards and transnational legal cooperation.

Rahime Erbaş
Editor

Criminal Prosecution of Domestic Violence

A Comparative Analysis

Springer

Editor
Rahime Erbaş
Faculty of Law
Istanbul University
Istanbul, Türkiye

ISSN 1534-6781 ISSN 2214-9902 (electronic)
Ius Gentium: Comparative Perspectives on Law and Justice
ISBN 978-3-032-01201-2 ISBN 978-3-032-01202-9 (eBook)
https://doi.org/10.1007/978-3-032-01202-9

This Springer imprint is published by the registered company Springer Nature Switzerland AG
The registered company address is: Gewerbestrasse 11, 6330 Cham, Switzerland

Acknowledgements

I would like to express my profound thanks and gratitude to all contributors of the book for their hard work, commitment and passion. I must say that I am genuinely amazed every day by the commitment and excellence you have brought to this project.

I feel also fortunate that I have brilliant colleagues, and friends who gave me constant support and encouragement, as such provided me with external review and insights during this demanding book project. Therefore, I would like to extend my deepest gratitude to; Aleksandra Deanoska – Trendafilova ("Ss.Cyril and Methodius" University- Skopje Republic of North Macedonia), Anna Lorenzetti (The University of Bergamo, Italy), Annalisa Mangiaracina (Palermo University, Italy), Angioletta Sperti (Pisa University, Italy), Anu Sivaganesan (The University of Zürich, Switzerland), Barbara Herceg Pakšić (Josip Juraj Strossmayer University of Osijek, Croatia), Caterina Murgo (Pisa University, Italy), Chara Chioni-Chotouman (National and Kapodistrian University of Athens, Greece), Clara Rigoni (Affiliated Researcher at Max Planck Institute for the Study of Crime, Security and Law; The University of Lausanne), Cristina Ruiz López (University of Burgos, Spain), Erdem İzzet Külçür (Ibn Haldun University, Türkiye), Francesco Rossi (Universidad Carlos III de Madrid), Krisztina Karsai (The University of Szeged, Hungary), Liane Wörner (The University of Konstanz, Germany), Lucia Parlato (Palermo University, Italy), Pınar Bacaksız (Dokuz Eylül University, Türkiye), R. Murat Önok (Koç University, Türkiye), Selena Tierno Barrios (The University of Salamanca, Spain), Serena Vantin (The University of Bologna, Italy), Szomora Zsolt (The University of Szeged, Hungary) and Valentina Bonini (Pisa University, Italy). Massive thanks for always having my back!

I do thank my family for their support.

I would also like to thank Anja Trautmann for her guidance and precious help.

Istanbul, Türkiye
April 2025

Dr. Rahime Erbaş

Acknowledgements

Contents

About the Editor and Contributors

About the Editor

Rahime Erbaş is associate professor in criminal law at Istanbul University. She studied law at Selçuk University, pursued public law master with the topic 'the Mandatory Reporting Duty of Healthcare Providers from a Comparative Law Perspective' at Istanbul University and at Justus Liebig Universität Gießen in Germany (Erasmus Exchange) in 2012. In 2019, she completed her PhD with the title 'Legal Duty to Act in Crimes of the Omission *(delicta commissionis per omissionem)* in the Turkish Penal Code' at Istanbul University. Dr. Erbaş carried out a doctoral research at the Osnabrück University in Germany between 2016 and 2017 and has been a visiting scholar at the Max Planck Institut in Freiburg (2019), University of Zürich (2020) and Alma Mater Studiorum– University of Bologna (2023). Dr. Erbaş spent one year between September 1, 2023 and August 31, 2024, in Scotland where she carried out her postdoctoral research in Criminal Law and Criminal Justice in the Glasgow Law School as a fellow of the Scientific and Technological Research Council of Türkiye (TÜBİTAK). She has taken part in the workshops on intervention programmes for sexual offenders by the Department of Probation, the Ministry of Justice in Türkiye.

She has edited books on various topics: E. Johnston, R. Erbaş and D. Jasinski, A Comparative Analysis of Pre-Trial Procedure in Europe: The Search for an Ideal Model (Istanbul University Press, 2020), V. Bonini and R. Erbaş, The 10th Anniversary of the Istanbul Convention (Pisa University Press, 2022) and V. Bonini, R. Erbaş and S. Türkoğlu, Dangerousness and Criminal Justice: Dialogue Between Italy and Türkiye (Pisa University Press, 2023). Further, Global Problems in Sexual Offenses (Lexington, 2022), Combatting Violence against Women from a Criminal Law Perspective I, II, II, (Turkish: Adalet, 2022; 2023; 2024), Sexual Offenses from Legal and Criminological Perspective (Turkish and with S. Çakırhan: Adalet, 2023) and European Perspectives on Attrition in Sexual Offenses (Lexington, 2023). Dr.

Erbaş has recently published Restorative Justice Conversations with the Experts (Adalet, 2024). She is section editor at Journal of Penal Law and Criminology. Further, she serves as an Editorial Board Member of Women's Studies International Forum, an Elsevier journal.

Contributors

Besa Arifi Criminal Law and Criminology at the South East European University, Tetovë, North Macedonia

Büşra Hazel Ateş-Sarıdağ Public Prosecutor in Türkiye and PhD Candidate at Istanbul University, Faculty of Law, Istanbul, Türkiye

Raquel Borges Blázquez Department of Administrative and Procedural Law, Faculty of Law, University of Valencia, Valencia, Spain

Ena Kazić- Çakar Faculty of Law of the International University of Sarajevo, Sarajevo, Bosnia and Herzegovina

Vittorio Cama Criminal Law, Doctoral Programme in Comparative and European Legal Studies, University of Trento, Trento, Italy

Chara Chioni-Chotouman LLM National and Kapodistrian University of Athens, Athens, Greece

Rahime Erbaş Criminal Law and Criminal Procedural Law, Istanbul University, Faculty of Law, Türkiye

Lara Ferla Università Cattolica del Sacro Cuore, Faculty of Law, Milan, Italy

Arta Mero Civil Law and Family Law at the South East European University, North Macedonia

Marta Palmisano Criminal Law at the University of Palermo, Post-doc in Comparative Public Law at the University of Turin, Turin, Italy

Lucia Parlato Criminal Procedure at the University of Palermo, Palermo, Italy

Elisa Simó Soler University of Valencia, Valencia, Spain

University of Buenos Aires, Buenos Aires, Argentina

Selena Tierno Barrios FPU Predoctoral Researcher, Procedural Law Area, University of Salamanca, Salamanca, Spain

Ramazan Zeyrek Judge in Türkiye and PhD Candidate at Istanbul University, Faculty of Law, Istanbul, Türkiye

Mina Zirojevic Institute of Comparative Law, Belgrade, Serbia

List of Abbreviations

AI	Artificial Intelligence
Art./Arts.	Article/articles
B&H	Bosnia and Herzegovina
CCFBH	Criminal Code of Federation of B&H
CCBD	Criminal Code of Brčko District of B&H
CCRS	Criminal Code of RS of B&H
CEDAW	The Convention on the Elimination of All Forms of Discrimination Against Women of 1979
CJEU	The Court of Justice of the European Union
cf.	Compare
COVID-19	Coronavirus Disease 2019
e.g./eg	For example
DV	Domestic Violence
ECHR	European Convention on Human Rights of 1950
ECtHR	European Court of Human Rights
ed./eds.	Editor/editors
EHRR	European Human Rights Reports
et al.	And others
et seq.	And the following
EU	European Union
Fig.	Figure
GBV	gender-based violence
GPS	The Global Positioning System
i.e.	That is
ibid.	In the same place
NGO	Non-governmental organization
no.	Number
n.	Note
OSCE	Organization for Security and Co-operation in Europe
Para/s.	Paragraph/s
RJ	Restorative Justice

s./ss.	Section/sections
Istanbul C (IC)	The Council of Europe Convention on preventing and combating violence against women and domestic violence of 2011
Lanzarote C.	The Council of Europe Convention on Protection of Children against Sexual Exploitation and Sexual Abuse of 2007
U.S./ US/USA	United States of America
UDHR	Universal Declaration of Human Rights of 1948
UN	United Nations
v./vs.	Versus vol. Volume
VAW	Violence against women
WHO	World Health Organization

Introduction: A Comparative Approach to Domestic Violence

Rahime Erbaş

Abstract Domestic settings as a private/family life sphere have been abused as a criminal law immunity area by the perpetrators of domestic violence regarding various types of crime, such as injury, threat, sexual offences and defamation, etc. This sphere requires the particular attention of criminal justice authorities to prevent the perpetrators from enjoying impunity or receiving lenient punishment for their violence at home. Furthermore, those involved in criminal investigation and prosecution of domestic violence are not always sufficiently trained to cope with this type violence at home, as opposed to acts of violence by strangers in the public sphere, since violence at home demands special attention (e.g., evidence gathering) from judicial authorities. This book offers a micro-level comparative analysis to draw conclusions from different jurisdictions in Europe, as such, to offer holistic solutions on how to tackle the issue of ineffective criminal prosecutions. The contributions in this edited book fill the research gaps from a comparative perspective by proving the importance of learning from one another for every jurisdiction.

1 Introduction

Domestic violence does not typically manifest itself in the form of a separate crime type in the legal texts in every jurisdiction. Mostly, its relevant criminal law provisions are found dispersed in various crime types, ranging from injury, murder, rape, and defamation to threats, etc. Apart from that, generally, crimes against the family order is where the classic and simplest way of addressing domestic violence in

R. Erbaş (✉)
Faculty of Law, Istanbul University, Istanbul, Türkiye
e-mail: rerbas@istanbul.edu.tr

R. Erbaş (ed.), *Criminal Prosecution of Domestic Violence*, Ius Gentium: Comparative Perspectives on Law and Justice 128,
https://doi.org/10.1007/978-3-032-01202-9_1

penal codes comes in. Further, this type of violence does not always affect only a single victim, i.e., the partner or spouse; it may also impact others connected to the relationship, most importantly the child/children. This book, thus, considers domestic violence not as a disease that is attached to a body part, such as various heart diseases, ear-nose-throat disorders or pancreatic diseases. Rather, domestic violence, as a public health issue, is rather like a cancer disease or a contagious virus, which may affect the whole body. From a methodical point of view, on the one hand, the sort of struggles and challenges that may exist for cancer or contagious virus researchers, equally exist for domestic violence researchers. On the other hand, the kind of success and benefits likely to appear for cancer or virus researchers are equally likely to appear for domestic violence researchers. For example, even if this book deals particularly with the European context, the outcomes can be useful in a more universal sense. Eleven chapters, as team research, hailing from seven jurisdictions in Europe are united to walk together along this long and demanding road to obtain this reward, i.e., overcoming this public health issue.

The German scholar, Claus Roxin, aptly states that "a State under rule of law does not protect its citizens only through the criminal law, but it protects its citizens also against the criminal law."[1] Consequently, whether criminal law is the right place to deal with the domestic violence cases or not has been a controversial topic in Europe.[2] However, the fact that perpetrators of domestic violence (and violence against women) may enjoy impunity or receive lenient punishment, is still one of the main concerns of victims, as well their lack of protection.

The first source of inspiration behind this book project, thus, comes from the following statement by the ECtHR in 2020: "…violence against women was under-reported, under-investigated, under-prosecuted, and under-sentenced."[3] In conjunction with this, the second inspiration is that domestic violence just as with sexual violence becomes a legal transplant area in Europe through the role of the Council of Europe: The case law of the ECtHR and the Istanbul Convention. While this development has allowed a transnational cooperation between law enforcement in Europe, at the same time this urges us to comprehend and to retrace law enforcements in different societies in Europe with regard to the case law of the ECtHR and the Istanbul Convention. As a recent development, Directive (EU) 2024/1385 of the European Parliament and of the Council of 14 May 2024 on combating violence against women and domestic violence was taken in force. Directive (EU) 2024/1385 has taken the Istanbul Convention's approach one step further. That said, this book aspires to determine the core problems and to come up with common solutions and values on domestic violence from a criminal procedure law perspective by applying a comparative law methodology. Richard R. Peterson, however, argues that

[1] Roxin (2006), p. 138, rn. 1.

[2] See Elisa Simó Soler in this volume.

[3] *Tërshana v. Albania* (48756/14), 04.08.2020, par. 156.

comparing jurisdictions regarding domestic violence can be problematic.[4] Because considering some challenges and difficulties on doing a comparative study on domestic violence, the question arises as to whether a comparative approach to domestic violence is possible and sensible or not.

The challenges and difficulties that prevent a proper comparative study stem from the fact that domestic violence is a multi-faceted phenomenon and, as such, any penal policy turns out to be complex multi-variable process. Accordingly, this introductory chapter demonstrates some remarkable peculiarities of domestic violence in comparison with non-domestic cases and challenges to penal policies. As a matter of fact, this violence type appears an area that *legal formants*, a term referring social and cultural influence through the practice of law-makers, scholars, prosecutors or judges, meaning *a living law*,[5] as coined by Rodolfo Sacco,[6] may be much more powerful than the legal statutes in a given jurisdiction. This is already evident in the terminology.[7] How to understand "domestic violence": as identical with family or every long-term relationship? Indeed, terminologies used by jurisdictions for describing this violence reflect on their respective penal policies. This chapter demonstrates what this book understands by domestic violence and its inherent concepts such as gender-based violence or violence against women. In spite of these difficulties, doing a comparative study on domestic violence, first of all represents a scientific approach to legal issues. Second, it may lead to production of some highly important fruit, which makes this methodological attempt worthy of taking the risks of unpredicted limitations of such a comparative law methodology on this violence type. As such, this introductory chapter puts forward its comparative law methodology. Respectively, it displays the outlines of the chapters as well as the aims and scope of this edited book.

2 Impunity

This book finds its first source of inspiration from the statement by the ECtHR in 2020: "…violence against women was under-reported, under-investigated, under-prosecuted, and under-sentenced."[8] As a matter of fact, the perpetrators of domestic violence (and violence against women) may enjoy impunity or receive lenient punishment and this reflects simultaneously one of the main concerns of victims, as well as lack of their protection. There are many reasons leading to impunity. One of the core reasons, however, is that "domestic violence cases have their challenging features that bring out some obstacles for carrying out an effective investigation

[4] Peterson (2013), p. 473.

[5] Sacco (1991), p. 22.

[6] Ibid, pp. 21–23.

[7] See Lucia Parlato and Marta Palmisano in this volume.

[8] *Tërshana v. Albania* (48756/14), 04.08.2020, par. 156.

such as the victim's vulnerability, requiring a prompt response and taking reasonable and appropriate measures for protection of women victim and difficulties in obtaining evidence and the like."[9] The private/public life dichotomy has been a prescribed as an impediment to the prevention of human rights violations at home. Further, it is quite common that the victim may withdraw their complaint under the pressure of the perpetrators. Indeed, the victims mostly do not want their partners to be imprisoned, rather they simply seek for an ending to the violence. Therefore, these cases require a peculiar prosecutorial approach and as such a particular penal policy, unlike incident-based crime, as in cases such as burglary. Therefore, "a holistic approach to domestic violence cases is essential. Considering domestic violence cases" challenging features—also for procedural authorities in terms of evidence or qualification of violent act as unique or multiples, as expressed in the legal sense of criminal law concepts, with respect to the vulnerability of the victims.[10] It is aptly stated that "DV *[domestic violence]* cases are difficult to prosecute."[11] Indeed, the classical tools and approach of criminal law may fail to respond to these cases effectively, which may create either impunity for the perpetrators or constitute a lenient punishment.

3 A Legal Transplant Area in Europe: The Role of the Council of Europe

This book finds its second source of inspiration in an increasing recognition of non-State law in addressing domestic violence in national jurisdictions. As a matter of fact, international law or supranational law are becoming more and more decisive in handling of domestic violence cases through the Istanbul Convention and its monitoring system, GREVIO reports for a given jurisdiction. The pathway toward the creation of the Istanbul Convention in 2011 was shaped by the proactive role played in the case law by the ECtHR, starting essentially in 1985 (*X and Y v the Netherlands*), reaching the peak in 2009 (*Opuz v Türkiye*) and reinforcing the subsequent cases until today. The formation and, respectively, the adaptation of a State's positive obligation has been cornerstone in addressing domestic violence in Europe. Therefore, it can be concluded without any hesitation that domestic violence became an intense legal transplant area in Europe and the main source is the Council of Europe as pertaining both to the case law of the ECtHR since 1985 and the Istanbul Convention since 2011. From a comparative law perspective, it seems that the jurisdictions in the Council of Europe move toward the same point regarding domestic violence in terms of the legislation level.

[9] Erbaş (2020), p. 223.

[10] Erbaş (2021a), p. 12.

[11] Peterson and Bialo-Padin (2012), p. 107.

Considering the Istanbul Convention's influence, the Convention's definitions of domestic violence and gender-based violence and violence against women, respectively, are adopted by the contracted countries and, as such, the definitions turn out to be repetitions. Further, the Convention envisages a set of crime types as well as prosecutorial policies that have both shaped the contracted countries' jurisprudence. However, the provisions of the Conventions do not necessarily mean that common solutions and values on domestic violence from a criminal procedure law have been fully established. Indeed, the influence of the Convention urges us to retrace law enforcements in different societies in Europe to figure out both similarities and differences regarding the provisions of the Istanbul Convention. Because, from a comparative law perspective, it remains unanswered as to whether the jurisdictions in the Council of Europe move toward the same point or toward separate directions regarding domestic violence in terms of the law enforcement level.

4 Challenges on Penal Policy and Comparative Study on Domestic Violence

This book aspires to define core problems and to establish common solutions and values on domestic violence from a criminal procedure law by applying a comparative law methodology. However, the question arises whether a comparative approach to domestic violence is possible and sensible. The challenges and difficulties that prevent a proper comparative study stem from the fact that domestic violence is multi-faceted and, as such, any penal policy turns out to be a complex multi-variable process. Some remarkable peculiarities of domestic violence in comparison with non-domestic related cases and challenges on penal policies exist. Indeed, this violence appears an area where *legal formants*, the term coined by Sacco, may be much more powerful than the legal statutes in a given jurisdiction. This is already evident in the terminology.

Any decision on how to define domestic violence in criminal code or how to initiate and carry the criminal prosecution of a domestic violence case (violence against women, respectively), vary from one jurisdiction to another, e.g., no harmonization of EU law exists.[12] Because such a decision represents a jurisdiction's penal policy over particular features, complexities and challenges of this violence type as well as the jurisdiction's choice to deal with domestic violence in criminal law or in civil law.

First, as a matter of fact, domestic violence refers to a criminological concept, a violence type, which does not always appear as a separate crime type in penal codes in every jurisdiction, but is considered within the existing crimes such as murder, injury, rape, defamation and coercion, etc.[13] Traditionally, in civil- law systems,

[12] Nakane (2021), p. 151.

[13] Erbaş (2020), p. 235.

many jurisdictions, as a rule, cover maltreatment of family members, but it protects the order of family, not individual legal interest.[14] As such, in the case where domestic violence is not articulated as a separate crime type in a penal code for a given jurisdiction, imposing a general penal policy on domestic violence through the criminal procedure and law of penal execution is not an easy task. The law, as a rule, sees this violence as a crime of murder, injury and threat, etc., in many jurisdictions. Any study evaluation of any penal policy on domestic violence inevitably leads to discussing various crime types.[15] Overall, it is problematic as it pertains to definitions of domestic violence in terms of criminal law. Even if the UN Convention and the Istanbul Convention define domestic violence, there is no definition accepted by every jurisdiction in Europe in terms of criminal law.

Second, from a criminological point of view, DV, as *a relationship-based crime*,[16] has a repetitive nature,[17] as an *ongoing threat*[18] to a family member. It was conceptualized as *the cycle of violence.*[19] As compared to incident-based crimes, such as burglary, the victims face the violence in a repetitive manner by the same perpetrator at various times within the certain relationship circuit.[20] Thus, on the one hand, how the criminal justice authorities qualify every single occurrence of violence legally may fail to address the issue of domestic violence.[21] On the other hand, addressing this violence may be challenging to the judicial authorities for various reasons, such as lack of evidence or non-cooperative victims, etc.[22] As aptly articulated by Peterson and Bialo-Padin, "DV cases are difficult to prosecute."[23] The prosecution of domestic violence may require the use of enormous resources.[24]

Third, as this violence is committed within a certain relationship circuit,[25] right to privacy arguments are often made by the perpetrators. It is frequently argued that even victims may not want judicial authorities to intervene in their private sphere. Indeed, the private-public life distinction[26] has been an impediment to development of women's human rights. As such, the private sphere, home, stands as an area for impunity for perpetrators of domestic violence. In other words, when a crime is committed at home, then, the commission of crime remains unpunished under the

---

[14] Ibid, p. 5.

[15] See e.g. Nakane (2021), pp. 160–165.

[16] Peterson and Bialo-Padin (2012), p. 103.

[17] Nakane (2021), p. 162; Hanna (1996), p. 1889.

[18] Hanna (1996), p. 1889.

[19] Walker (2016), pp. 91 ff.

[20] Peterson and Bialo-Padin (2012), pp. 103–104.

[21] Erbaş (2020), pp. 234–235; Erbaş (2021a), pp. 5–6.

[22] See Hanna (1996), p. 1860; Erbaş (2021b); Erbaş (2021a), pp. 5–6.

[23] Peterson and Bialo-Padin (2012), p. 106.

[24] Hanna (1996), p. 1898.

[25] Peterson and Bialo-Padin (2012), p. 103.

[26] See more Hanna (1996), pp. 1868–1877.

argument of right to privacy,[27] because this violence is deemed a private issue. It was the feminist movement in the USA that paved the way for domestic violence cases in the criminal justice system.[28] The feminist movement is considered as the catalyst for the transitioning of this type of violence from a private issue to a public issue in the USA.[29] Clark argues that addressing this violence in the context of civil law means *punishing the victim*[30] by concluding that:

> The burdens and consequences of crime should fall as completely as possible upon the perpetrator of crime, not upon the already injured victim.[31]

There was debate over the issue of whether criminal law is the right place to deal with the domestic violence cases or not during this transition in the USA in the 1990s.[32] According to Clark, "Both philosophy and common sense suggest that criminal remedies are an appropriate societal response to domestic violence."[33] Because, from a philosophical approach to the deterring effect of punishment, the fruits of committing crime are to be eradicated. That being said, this fruit in DV is the power to control the women by their abusive partner through the commission of crime.[34] This approach is welcomed as an elimination of the power dynamic in domestic violence as a short-term benefit.[35] However, as a long-term benefit, it is still criticized.[36] Indeed, considering the long-term effects, some scholars view preventive measures as a missing part of combatting DV.[37] Excessive reliance on criminal law is another problematic of this matter.[38]

Ultimately, domestic violence is a widespread problem in the world and represents an epidemic, a public health issue, as the UN aptly defines it.[39] Addressing domestic violence in a case-based approach to justice does not solve the problem. Rather, it necessitates a proper penal policy.

---

[27] See e.g., Clark (1987), p. 268.

[28] Hanna (1996), p. 1855.

[29] Hanna (1996), p. 1869.

[30] Clark (1987), pp. 268 ff.

[31] Ibid, p. 293.

[32] Ibid, p. 268.

[33] Ibid, p. 280.

[34] Ibid, p. 268. See also Hanna (1996), p. 1888.

[35] Hanna (1996), p. 1888.

[36] Ibid.

[37] See Raquel Borges Blázquez and Elisa Simó Soler in this volume. Hanna (1996), p. 1890.

[38] See Vittorio Cama in this volume.

[39] "Violence against women (VAW) is a violation of human rights, is rooted in gender inequality, is a public health problem, and an impediment to sustainable development," World Health Organization. (2019). RESPECT women: Preventing violence against women. Geneva: World Health Organization. https://www.who.int/publications/i/item/WHO-RHR-18.19.

5 Terminology

The choice of terminology and determining the scope in reflecting on violence against women with gender-based discrimination within domestic settings implies itself a considerable challenge. This edited book opted for the term "domestic violence," as stated in its title, *Criminal Prosecution of Domestic Violence*. The Istanbul Convention defines *domestic violence* as "all acts of physical, sexual, psychological or economic violence that occur within the family or domestic unit or between former or current spouses or partners, whether or not the perpetrator shares or has shared the same residence with the victim." This is not a definition of a crime type. It is a definition of "violence" from a criminological point of view. These acts may fall under tort law as well as criminal law.

Although the term domestic violence is used throughout this book, it is used interchangeably with the term violence against woman, which implies also gender-based violence. This edited book adopts both the Istanbul Convention and the UN definitions of violence against women. Accordingly, the Istanbul Convention defines it mainly as the type of violent acts "as a violation of human rights and a form of discrimination against women and shall mean all acts of gender-based violence that result in, or are likely to result in, physical, sexual, psychological or economic harm or suffering to women, including threats of such acts, coercion or arbitrary deprivation of liberty, whether occurring in public or in private life." As for the UN, it defines it from the perspective of general consequences of such violence in a broader sense as "a violation of human rights, is rooted in gender inequality, is a public health problem, and an impediment to sustainable development." Both definitions complement each other. The book touches on all violent acts that constitute crimes, while considering domestic violence as a public health issue as illustrated in the introductory part of this chapter.

This book confines itself to domestic violence as addressing violence against women *in the family settings,*[40] *in a domestic setting,*[41] or in an intimate relationship circuit. Therefore, violence against descendant or ascendant or any relevant living together in the same domestic setting are not addressed in this book. Furthermore, the book considers this violence as including a gender-based discrimination, as the Convention defines "gender-based violence against women" as "violence that is directed against a woman because she is a woman or that affects women disproportionately" (Art. 3-d). Of course, the term gender does not only encompass women; however, this book takes on gender-based discrimination against women, since the cases elaborated throughout this book show a predominant concern for women being victims of violence. As a matter of fact, acknowledging of gender-based discrimination perspective in this violence type implies "the realisation of *de jure* and *de facto* equality between women and men" as the preamble of the Istanbul

[40] For the term "in the family setting" see Clark (1987), p. 274.

[41] Ibid, p. 284.

Convention recognizes. The book address the prosecution of crimes committed against women in domestic settings.

6 Chapter Outline: Methods and Structure of the Research

The first part of the book consists of the jurisdictional contributions to the main obstacles to effective criminal prosecution for domestic violence cases. This book includes nine chapters from seven jurisdictions: Bosnia and Herzegovina, Greece, Italy, North Macedonia, Serbia Spain and Türkiye. Taking into account the fact that domestic violence became a legal transplant area in Europe through both case law of the ECtHR since 1985 and the Istanbul Convention since 2011, the contributing authors to this part have been asked to choose one of the main obstacles in the prosecution of domestic violence. In so doing, each chapter is so designed to unveil a problematic issue on prosecution of domestic violence to provide a wide-ranging analysis. If every jurisdiction had been asked to address the same obstacles, the analysis would have been limited, as well as including a remarkable amount of repetition. Approaches to domestic violence by national jurisdictions have been intensely shaped by the Council of Europe.

Comparative law methodologies appear as an open buffet, indeed. In order to avoid having an overly ambitious law-in context, depending on the aim of this edited book and the inherent difficulties in applying comparative law methodologies to domestic violence, micro-level and analytical methods are chosen, enabling us to dive into presumptions, hidden ideas and concepts. In so doing, the book attempts to capture what lies behind the legal rules, as aptly put by *Sacco*: "it is wrong to believe that the first step toward comparison is to identify 'the legal rule' of the countries to be compared. That is the typical view of an inexperienced jurist."[42] As such, an analytic method at a micro level allows us to identify common problems and to reach core solutions. Although the scope of analysis of the book is firmly within a Europe context, some examples are drawn from outside of Europe, e.g., those from the US law are given by covering their peculiar approach in prosecution of domestic violence.[43]

Nine chapters cover seven jurisdictions' approaches to main obstacles of prosecuting a domestic violence case from initiation to finalization of the prosecution throughout its journey in the criminal justice system. However, the chapters, as listed below, are mostly focused on the pre-trial phase of criminal prosecution in which the police and public prosecutors are mainly competent authorities. This stems from peculiarities of domestic violence cases as is explained in this chapter under the headings of challenges on penal policy and comparative study on domestic violence.

---

[42] Sacco (1991), p. 21.

[43] Flannigan (2013), p. 481.

The first point is *how the prosecution of domestic violence case is initiated.* Second chapter, by Chara Chioni-Chotouman, raises the question on how to balance the public and the private interest in initiating prosecution. It provides a historical and philosophical background and presents a case study example of Greece. Third chapter, by Rahime Erbaş, Hazel Ateş Sarıdağ and Ramazan Zeyrek, takes on more legislative approach on whether domestic violence case is prosecuted *ex officio* or *ex parte*. It examines whether we need a dosage or impetus in selecting prosecutorial policies. After that, it analyzes constitutional debate by the case-law for Türkiye's choice for impetus on the matter. Consequently, second and third chapter complement each other on the question of how to initiate the criminal prosecution regarding domestic violence.

The second point relates to *risk assessment and analysis,* which represents novelty in addressing domestic violence at the early stage of criminal prosecution to avoid further harm by considering the escalating effects of violence in domestic settings. Fourth chapter, by Lara Ferla, examines punitive and preventive measures against domestic violence in Italy though a critical assessment. Fifth chapter, by Elisa Simó Soler, goes one step further and presents Integral Monitoring System for Gender-based Violence Cases (VioGén) as a technological progress which was established in Spain for proper risk predictions and management by police, judges, and other professionals involved in victims' protection.

The third point is focusing on *the attitudes of the police toward domestic violence victims* at the early stage of a criminal prosecution. This is an area that has been highly studied in the literature so far. Sixth chapter, by Mina Zirojevic, addresses the role of police and prosecutorial bodies in (re)solving cases of domestic violence. But, in order to come up with new contribution to the field, it also provides insights into the Serbian example with local aspects.

The fourth point is with respect to *the vulnerability of the victims of domestic violence* during the prosecution. This point has various ramifications for the criminal justice system. However, this book addresses vulnerability from two aspects: secondary victimization and right to access a lawyer. First, seventh chapter, by Selena Tierno Barrios, examines challenges and proposals against the phenomenon of secondary victimization in terms of vulnerability of domestic violence victims from a gender-based discrimination perspective in Spanish criminal proceedings. Second, eighth chapter, by Lucia Parlato and Marta Palmisano, analyzes the right to access to a lawyer for victims of domestic violence by considering the vulnerability of the victims. As such, it provides genuine insights into the case law of the Italian Constitutional Court.

Point five regards *the applicability of restorative justice* in domestic violence and violence against women, respectively. Whether this violence type is suitable to be addressed within the restorative justice framework or not has been a controversial topic and approaches by jurisdictions vary considerably. A remarkable number of works on this topic have been carried out in the literature to date. Ninth chapter, by Ena Kazić-Çakar, demonstrates the main discussions and solutions. The chapter provides a case study of Bosnia and Herzegovina in order to come up with new contribution to the field, as does in the eighth chapter.

Point six addresses how to obtain *effective co-operation* among all relevant agencies, institutions and organizations, as the Istanbul Convention calls for in Art. 7 and as such, there is a need for *a holistic approach.* This is another peculiarity in prosecuting domestic violence. Tenth chapter, by Besa Arifi and Arta Mero, displays this urgent need for a holistic approach and provides the case-study of the Republic of North Macedonia.

Considering the fact that it was the concept of positive obligation by the ECtHR that has fueled the improvements in combatting domestic violence in criminal justice system, the second part is dedicated to the role of the ECHR. That being said, one of the two main parts of the book is reserved to "The ECtHR's Perspective: Positive Obligation and State's Intervention in Domestic Violence." This part entails two chapters, one from Spain and one from Italy. It is structured so as to provide a solid foundation for the first part, the jurisdictional contributions to addressing various obstacles to effective criminal prosecution of domestic violence in Europe. Jurisdictional contributions refer to the case law of ECtHR only when the occasion arises. Under this part, the first chapter, by Raquel Borges Blázquez, gives a brief reference to the jurisprudential developments of the ECtHR on the State's duty for domestic violence from a gender perspective. Afterwards, Vittorio Cama, delves into a recent judgment by the ECtHR, the case of *Talpis v. Italy*, as the most recent judgment against Italy, in comparison with the other case law of the Court, as a comprehensive look from the inside of Italian law into Italy's capability to counter, investigate and prosecute domestic violence.

7 Conclusion

Domestic settings as private/family life sphere have been abused as a criminal law immunity area by the perpetrators of domestic violence regarding various types of crime, such as injury, sexual offences, defamation, etc. This sphere requires the particular attention of criminal justice authorities to prevent the perpetrators from enjoying impunity or receiving lenient punishment for their acts of violence at home. Furthermore, criminal investigation and prosecution of domestic violence have not yet fully developed to deal accordingly with this type violence at home, as opposed to violence by strangers outside of home, since violence at home demands special attention (e.g., evidence gathering) from judicial authorities.

This edited book is created in order to encourage and foster an evidence-based approach to domestic violence and violence against women in criminal law studies. This book covers theoretical thinking and practices of penal matters pertaining to this type of violence. Furthermore, preferential responses to female victims of domestic violence within criminal proceedings remain insufficient to reflect the structural and multifaceted realities underlying such violence.[44] Rather, this

[44] Cf. Dempsey (2007).

approach creates other obstacles and problematic issues in criminal law logic, as well as constitutional principles in the long term. Therefore, in a scale ranging from having an "evidence-based approach" to having a "victim-centered" one,[45] the book puts emphasis on the evidence-based approach part of the spectrum. As such, it promotes analytical and critical thinking throughout each contribution. That being said, the book adopts the principles of dealing with domestic violence and violence against women, in the criminal justice system with an: *analytical approach*, *critical thinking*, *equality* and *evidence-based approach.*

The scientific approach to legal issues can be acquired through comparative law methodologies.[46] This book provides a comparative analysis, highlighting European jurisdictions that remain underrepresented in English-language academic research, including Bosnia and Herzegovina, North Macedonia, Serbia and Türkiye, as such, to reach holistic solutions on how to tackle the issue of ineffective criminal prosecution. As such, it aims to prove the importance of learning from one another across jurisdictions, as well as it aims to witness, evaluate and foster the current developments in Europe regarding domestic violence and to influence national penal policies. Most importantly, it amplifies national perspectives—especially from Bosnia and Herzegovina, North Macedonia, Serbia and Türkiye—that are too often overlooked in academic research in Europe, as such, it places them in comparative dialogue with jurisdictions that have received greater scholarly attention to domestic violence, such as Italy and Spain. Ultimately, the book also situates these national experiences within the broader perspective of the case law of the ECtHR.

This edited book originates from the proposition that the development of the law through the comparison of jurisdictions in viewing domestic violence as a public health issue leads to the development of the individual human being. It is hoped that this edited collection will constitute a solid basis for advancing the understanding of criminal prosecution of domestic violence both in Europe and beyond, thereby promoting positive change for individuals and societies around the world.

References

Clark NL (1987) Crime begins at home: let's stop punishing victims and perpetuating violence. William Mary Law Rev 28(2):263–294

Dempsey MM (2007) Toward a feminist state: what does 'effective' prosecution of domestic violence mean? Mod Law Rev 70:908–935. https://doi.org/10.1111/j.1468-2230.2007.00670.x

Eberle EJ (2011) The methodology of comparative law. Roger Williams Univ Law Rev 16(1):51–72

Erbaş R (2020) Effective criminal investigations in combating domestic violence and the ECtHR: Prima Ratio v. Ultima Ratio? In: Stradella E (ed) Gender based approaches to the law and Juris dictio in Europe. Pisa University Press, Pisa, pp 221–240

Erbaş R (2021a) Effective criminal investigations for women victims of domestic violence: the approach of the ECtHR. Women's Stud Int Forum 86:1–12

---

[45] Peterson (2013), p. 474.

[46] See Kaiser (1978), pp. 132–133 and also Eberle (2011).

Erbaş R (2021b) Evidentiary challenges to an effective criminal investigation for domestic violence: An introduction. In: Bonini V, Erbaş R (eds) The 10th anniversary of the Istanbul convention: Italian – Turkish conference. Pisa University Press, Pisa, pp 101–117

Flannigan KR (2013) The importance of prosecution policies in domestic violence cases. Criminol Public Policy 12(3):481–490. https://doi.org/10.1111/1745-9133.12058

Hanna C (1996) No right to choose: mandated victim participation in domestic violence prosecutions. Harv Law Rev 109(8):1849–1910

Kaiser G (1978) Die vergleichende Methode in der Kriminologie. In: Jescheck H (ed) Deutsche strafrechtliche Landesreferate zum X. Internationalen Kongreß für Rechtsvergleichung Budapest 1978. De Gruyter, Berlin, pp 129–164. https://doi.org/10.1515/9783110900309-014

Nakane T (2021) Prosecution ex officio or following a complaint by the victim? An analysis on offences related to violence against women and sexual offences. N J Eur Crim Law 12(2):146–165

Peterson RR (2013) Victim engagement in the prosecution of domestic violence cases. Criminol Public Policy 12(3):473–490

Peterson RR, Bialo-Padin D (2012) Domestic violence is different: the crucial role of evidence collection in domestic violence cases. J Police Crisis Negot 12:103–121

Roxin C (2006) Strafrecht Allgemeiner Teil, Band I. Verlag C. H. Beck, Munchen

Sacco R (1991) Legal formants: a dynamic approach to comparative law (installment I of II). Am J Comp Law 39(1):1–34. https://doi.org/10.2307/840669

Walker LE (2016) The battered woman syndrome, 4th edn. Springer, New York

Jurisdictional Contributions: Main Obstacles to an Effective Criminal Prosecution

Prosecuting Domestic Violence: Balancing the Public and the Private Interest—The Example of Greek Legislation

Chara Chioni-Chotouman

Abstract The criminal prosecution of domestic violence is a complex issue that cannot be considered in isolation from its historical development. Despite renewed attention on the European scene, the clash between public and private interests still plays a significant role. Greek legislation serves as an example of how complex and multifaceted the relevant choices are. This chapter displays the historical and philosophical background of prosecuting domestic violence (1) that leads to the choices made at the supranational level (2) in an attempt to highlight the impasse to which the *ex parte/ex officio* prosecution dichotomy leads and the dangers for autonomy from enhanced State intervention (3). Greek legislation serves as an example of how complicated and multifaceted the relevant choices are (4).

1 Introduction

Addressing violence against women receives renewed attention on the European scene. Through excessive jurisprudence, the ECtHR via the notion of positive obligations has included domestic violence in the scope of the ECHR. It was, though, the Istanbul Convention that consolidated features of the response that States should adopt, with the Directive 2024/1385 on combating violence against women and domestic violence underlining their importance for the EU.

Domestic abuse constitutes a form of gender-based violence since it affects women disproportionately.[1] However, the following remarks also apply to men that are victims of this crime. Any uniform definition of domestic violence does not

[1] See indicatively The Istanbul Convention, preamble, Hague (2021), p. 2.

C. Chioni-Chotouman (✉)
Aristotle University of Thessaloniki, Department of Criminal Law and Criminology, Thessaloniki, Greece

R. Erbaş (ed.), *Criminal Prosecution of Domestic Violence*, Ius Gentium: Comparative Perspectives on Law and Justice 128,
https://doi.org/10.1007/978-3-032-01202-9_2

exist.[2] This chapter adopts the definition of the Istanbul Convention, also followed in the Directive,[3] which defines it as physical, sexual, psychological or economic violence committed within the family or household unit or between former or current spouses or partners, irrespective of whether the perpetrator cohabits or cohabited with the victim.[4] The focus of this chapter is on domestic violence as intimate partner violence, thus not including children that are subjected to violence. The main goal is to ascertain how relevant offences are to be prosecuted. To address this issue, it is not only necessary to analyze the legislative trend at the supranational level, but predominately to resort to the nature of the offensive behavior to identify possible limits to State intervention.

The following chapters explore how the public element of the offence emerged and how it is balanced with the private interest. The history of the relevant offences' recognition as well as key aspects of liberal criminal law theory will illustrate the issues that arise in relation to prosecution. The choices at the supranational level will also be analyzed to determine the current trends in prosecuting domestic abuse. Finally, it will be examined how Greece, a State that adheres to the Western legal tradition and is bound by choices at the European level, has chosen to balance the public and private interests in prosecution.

2 Historical and Philosophical Background

The history of treating domestic violence and the philosophical underpinnings of State intervention play an important role when dealing with prosecuting it. They reveal the roots of the issues arising in relation to prosecution and the context in which the private and public interests in prosecution interact. The following is by no means an extensive analysis of the complex history of domestic violence. The aim is to highlight the main aspects to examine whether they still have an impact on persecution today.

2.1 Non-Interference with the Institution of Marriage in History

According to an old topos, the institution of marriage and the family are the basis of the State.[5] A common feature of the law, from classical Athens until the Middle Ages, was the protection of marriage, either in the form of the "house" and the

---

[2] Singelnstein (2019), Rn. 122; Herring (2020), p. 19.

[3] Directive 2024/1385, Art. 2 (b).

[4] The Istanbul Convention, Art. 3 (b).

[5] Dilcher (1993), p. 189.

"family" or, after the prevalence of Christianity, of the institution that constituted for Christian morality the only framework in which individuals could legitimately develop their sexuality. The Greek "*οίκος*" and the Roman "*domus*" were constructed to safeguard the rights and interests of the patriarch under whose authority lived, among others, his wife. The latter's relationship with the head of the household was essentially proprietary.[6] Despite an effort in legislation to limit the absolute power of the "*pater familias*" to use corporal punishment, his authority was retained in the Middle Ages.[7]

This historically entrenched male authority continued to find expression in Christianity and other belief systems.[8] Even though the New Testament promotes respect between the sexes,[9] the superiority of the male over the female and the latter's subordination during the marriage is asserted.[10] For example, Christian ethics and particularly canon law are at the root of the marital exception, which until recently in some States gave the husband unlimited sexual access to his wife. According to *the Concordia discordantium canonum*, a seminal compilation of canon and secular law on the matter, intercourse in marriage cannot be punished based on the introduction of a complex theory of marital obligations.[11] In summary, relying on 1 Corinthians 7:4, *Gratian* argued that upon marriage the parties enter into a binding contract in the framework of which they agreed to perform their conjugal duties when the other party requests it.[12] As a result, it was impossible in this view to speak of rape between spouses.[13] Moreover, exercising control and punishing was considered not only a prerogative of the husband but also beneficial for women.[14]

In general, even as the relationship between the spouses progressively became less proprietary, the main concern being the preservation of the marriage, domestic violence was hardly conceivable as a crime or, more accurately, was condoned by the law, unless it considered an incident of particular cruelty causing a public scandal.[15] And even in these cases, there was firstly an attempt at reconciliation.[16]

---

[6] Dover (1973), p. 61; Pretorius (2017), pp. 57–58; Nguyen (2006), p. 76; Witherington (1990), p. 20.

[7] Salisbury et al. (2002), p. 4; Dossey (2008), pp. 5–6.

[8] Meyer and Frost (2019), p. 39.

[9] Ephesians 5:25, 1 Corinthians 7:3, Galatians 3:28.

[10] Ephesians 5:22-24, 1 Timothy 2:11-15.

[11] Brundage (1987), pp. 229, 241.

[12] Decretum magistri Gratiani, causa XXXIII available at https://geschichte.digitale-sammlungen.de/decretum-gratiani/online/angebot.

[13] See this rationale also in Sir Matthew Hale's Historia Placitorum Coronæ, Kennedy (2020), pp. 262–263.

[14] Herring (2020), p. 3.

[15] See indicatively Vanneau (2016), p. 307; Wiesner-Hanks (2020), p. 88; Herring (2020), p. 4.

[16] Wiesner-Hanks (2020), p. 88.

2.2 Liberal Theory and Domestic Abuse

When talking about the influence of liberal theory on domestic violence it must be noted that liberal tradition is quite complex and, in some respects, inconsistent, especially considering that its primary concern was not women and their rights, something extremely premature for the era in which these ideas were first formulated.[17] Yet the origins of most contemporary national criminal law systems in Western Europe can be traced back to the Enlightenment period, an era when the individual was seen as occupying the position of a free citizen with rights.[18] It is, therefore, necessary to explore how it affected the prosecution of the relevant offences.

Of particular importance when examining domestic violence is the distinction between the public and the private space, which is central to liberal theory. Incidents occurring in the private sphere are considered a less urgent problem, as the boundaries that maintain the liberal political order are not threatened.[19] On the contrary, it is the State interference in private matters that endangers it. This distinction led to the exclusion of State intervention in family affairs.[20] The family was seen as a sphere of privacy, immune from State interference.[21]

In liberal theory, personal autonomy is considered a key principle.[22] Adult members of the household are considered competent to make their own decisions and negotiate the terms of their relationship with each other.[23] Even in the liberal theory though, the husband retained precedence over his wife.[24] Despite this focus on individual liberty and personal autonomy, traditional gender roles and power dynamics persisted in liberal thought, thus perpetuating the idea that the husband is the dominant figure within the household and the wife is subservient to him.

Although the above views are no longer claiming validity in an absolute manner, they do affect the relevant offences. The public/private division affects prosecution in the sense that even though nowadays *ex officio* prosecution cannot be disputed in relation to severe physical harm, it can be contested for cases of less serious harm. Moreover, individual liberty and personal autonomy may be interpreted as dictating a greater ability of the victim to have control over the prosecution.

---

[17] Dworkin (2012), p. 115. See also Pateman (1988), p. 6 who links political freedom with masculinity. Cf. though the work of Mill JS (1869) The subjection of women. See also for the consolidation of the traditional view that women are inferior to men during the Enlightenment Wapler (2012), p. 38.

[18] Cleiren and Voorde (2019), pp. 121, 124.

[19] Buchan (2001), p. 43.

[20] Boyd (1997), pp. 9–10; McQuigg (2017), p. 19.

[21] See Erbaş (2022), p. 105 on the evidentiary difficulties and investigative issues caused by this approach.

[22] Roberts (2004), p. 337.

[23] Indicatively Gobetti (1992), p. 88.

[24] Locke J (1689) Two Treatises of Government II, chapter VII, para 82; Gobetti (1992), p. 91.

2.3 *Women's Movement*

While first-wave of feminism did not prioritize violence against women, second-wave feminism fueled changes in the family, mainly in the 70s and the 80s, to eradicate images of women as dependent wives and mothers in need of -mainly economic- protection.[25]

Feminism challenged the dichotomy between public and private spheres.[26] The rigid distinction between the public and the private, with the latter including, among other things, the family and personal relationships, resulted in women's lives and women's issues being included in a distinct field, which was not subject to regulation.[27] As a result, the violence suffered by women within the family was invisible to the State, which by its stance legitimized it.[28] The private sphere became the starting point for feminist demands and the role of discrimination in the oppression of women was highlighted.[29] The women's movement was instrumental in making social relations that were considered personal or private the object of analysis, also political, and an appropriate field for legal regulation, especially when violence was involved.[30]

Regarding mandatory prosecution, the literature appears divided. Some applauded it while others stressed the risks for autonomy.[31] Regardless of the stance of feminist literature towards compulsory prosecution, the women's movement highlighted the public element of the behavior that renders it a crime against the victim and the State.[32] Consequently, the public interest in prosecution was also strengthened, which in turn led to the adoption of mandatory prosecution or, in any case, policies that remove the burden of prosecution from the victim, thus resulting in limiting the victim's control over it.

---

[25] Finlayson (2016), pp. 54–55.

[26] Finlayson (2016), p. 102; Schneider (1991), p. 977.

[27] Boyd (1997), p. 10; Gilmour (2022), p. 19. However, the public/private distinction was purely ideological, with liberal states always regulating the so-called "private" sphere, Finlayson (2016), p. 123.

[28] Molloy (2018), p. 695; Markard (2017), p. 140.

[29] Wischermann (2004), p. 187; Boyd (1997), p. 8; Künzel (2012), p. 55. The main motto of the women's movement was that "private is political". For its objectives see indicatively Rudolph (2015), p. 111.

[30] Boyd (1997), p. 10; Wapler (2012), p. 50.

[31] Guzik (2007), p. 42.

[32] Mills (1998), p. 307.

3 The Supranational Framework for Prosecuting Domestic Abuse

The public nature of domestic violence was affirmed and formalized at the supranational level. Although it has long been considered a private matter, at the EU level it is now recognized as a serious violation of human rights.[33] In this part, the focus will be on the Council of Europe's stance. The case law of ECtHR will also be examined, as it is an important part of the development and concretization of States' obligations in the field of prosecuting domestic violence.

Even before the Istanbul Convention, the public character of domestic violence prevailed in the Council of Europe's policy.[34] Regarding the prosecution, initial emphasis was placed on easing the burden of prosecution from the victim.[35] This approach, combined with the case law of the ECtHR, was included in the Istanbul Convention. The Istanbul Convention represents the first legally binding text in the European area to address violence against women and domestic violence.[36] It entered into force in 2014 and was signed by the EU in 2017, with formal accession taking place in 2023.[37] In relation to the prosecution of domestic violence, for some behaviors, the prosecution should be *ex officio.*[38] According to Art. 55, prosecution for certain offences should not be wholly contingent upon the victim's complaint and may continue even if the victim withdraws the complaint or statement. This applies to incidents of physical violence and sexual violence. Thus, psychological and economic violence between spouses or partners can be prosecuted entirely *ex parte*. The wording of the provision with the words "wholly" and "may" is also ambiguous, leaving a margin of appreciation to States.[39] Moreover, States can opt for a reservation according to Art. 78 para 2 in case of minor offences. It is, thus, possible to opt for prosecution by complaint for cases of minor physical violence. What constitutes a minor offence isn't yet specified in the Convention.[40] According

---

[33] Council of Europe Resolution 1512 (2006), para 7; Pais (2015), p. 27. See also Judgment of the Court, 15 September 2011, *Gueye and Salmerón Sánchez*—C-483/09, par. 61.

[34] See Council of Europe Recommendation 1582 (2002), para 2.

[35] Rec 1582(2002), para 7.

[36] Steinl (2021), p. 820; Guney (2020), p. 132.

[37] McQuigg (2017), p. 1, EU accession to Istanbul Convention available at https://eur-lex.europa.eu/legal-content/EL/LSU/?uri=CELEX:32017D0865.

[38] Cf. Ad hoc Committee on Preventing and Combating Violence against Women and Domestic Violence (CAHVIO), Draft Convention on preventing and combating violence against women and domestic violence, CAHVIO (2009) 32 prov available at https://rm.coe.int/09000016809696b1, Art. 42 according to which *ex officio* prosecution was required for all the offences in the Convention.

[39] Niemi et al. (2020), p. 91. Cf. Explanatory Report to the Council of Europe Convention on preventing and combating violence against women and domestic violence, par. 280 where the use of the word "wholly" is explained by reference to procedural differences between states and it is clarified that states should be responsible for the prosecution. (also in the Montesinos García and Maravall-Buckwalter (2023)).

[40] McQuigg (2017), p. 149.

to the Explanatory Report, incidents of physical violence resulting in severe bodily harm or deprivation of life should be excluded.[41] As is evident, the threshold is quite high, with cases that do not result in severe bodily harm falling within the margin of appreciation.[42]

A narrower balancing act was followed in the framework of the Directive 2024/1385. According to Art. 15 para 5, only for the offence of rape the prosecution should not be made dependent on the report of the victim and criminal proceedings shall continue even if the report or accusation has been withdrawn. Even though the Directive does not include a specific provision on the criminalization of aspects of domestic violence *per se*, as part of a more general concern to tackle domestic violence, which results in provisions such as Arts. 11(a) and 15 paras 2 and 3, the nature of criminal prosecution could be also envisaged.[43]

Of decisive importance for breaking down the public/private distinction has been the development of positive obligations in ECtHR's case law. The ECHR at the time of its entry into force contained mainly negative obligations. In fact, most of the rights in the Convention are worded in negative terms. States were obliged to respect and not to interfere with the exercise of the rights and freedoms included in the Convention.[44] The Court has interpreted positive obligations of States under several Arts. of the ECHR, including Arts. 3 and 8 ECHR.[45] The ECtHR, through its case law, has extended their protective power by referring to an obligation to act and not merely to refrain from infringements. This obligation arises from Art. 1 ECHR, which provides for the need to respect the rights set out in the Convention, and from the need to ensure the effective protection of the rights guaranteed.[46]

Domestic violence falls into the scope of Arts. 3 and 8 ECHR, examined separately or in conjunction.[47] It has been held that interference with private and family

---

[41] Explanatory Report, ibid., par. 281.

[42] Niemi et al. (2020), p. 91; Nakane (2021), p. 150.

[43] See also Hahnkamper-Vandenbulcke and Bacian (2022), p. 40, where it is mentioned that it was among the Parliament's requests that were not followed.

[44] Mavronicola (2021), pp. 50, 52; Webster (2018), p. 33; Peršak (2020), p. 147. See also Pretty v. UK, 29.04.2002, par. 50.

[45] Lavrysen (2014), p. 162; Stoyanova (2020), p. 634.

[46] Ashworth (2013), p. 198; Mavronicola (2021), p. 129; Lavrysen (2014), p. 162. See also *Mahmut Kaya v. Turkey*, 28.03.2000, par. 115, P.M. v. Bulgaria, 24.01.2012, par. 63, *Đorđević v. Croatia*, 24.07.2012, par. 138, *Mudric v. The Republic of Moldova* (74839/10), 16.07.2013, par. 40, *O'Keeffe v. Ireland* (35810/09), 28.01.2014, par. 144, *Cestaro v. Italy*, 07.04.2015, par. 204, *V.C. v. Italy*, 01.02.2018, par. 89.

[47] Indicatively *A. v. Croatia* (55164/08), 14.10.2010, *Hajduová v. Slovakia* (2660/03), 30.11.2010, *Valiulienė v. Lithuania* (33234/07), 26.03.2013, *Ž.B. v. Croatia* (47666/13), 11.07.2017, *Volodina v. Russia*, 09.07.2019, par. 73, *Buturugă v. Romania*, 11.02.2020. As the concept of positive obligations becomes established, the more domestic violence seems to be addressed in the context of Article 3 ECHR. See for example *Tunikova and others v. Russia* (55974/16), 14.12.2021, par. 75, where the fear of further assaults was deemed sufficient to attain the minimum threshold of Article 3. See also for the stance of the Court to move between those two Articles when examining the States' positive obligations McQuigg (2016), p. 1015.

life may be deemed necessary to protect the health and rights of a person or to prevent criminal acts in certain circumstances.[48] Domestic violence is defined, alongside the Istanbul Convention, broadly, including physical and sexual assault, economic, emotional or verbal abuse.[49]

The particular vulnerability of domestic violence victims, which often experience acute psychological, physical and material insecurity,[50] and the public importance of the relevant crimes activate states' positive obligations, which include *inter alia* the obligation to conduct an effective investigation, which can lead to the identification and punishment of those responsible, thereby affording protection to the victims.[51] In the framework of this obligation, the prosecuting authorities should be able to pursue the proceedings as a matter of public interest, irrespective of the victim's complaint or its withdrawal.[52] This is not an absolute obligation.[53] However, the competent authorities should be able, under the legal framework, to act on their own initiative to investigate incidents of domestic violence, punish those responsible and protect victims, especially, but not by any means exclusively, in cases of severe physical violence.[54] It has also been held that despite the very diverse practice among Contracting Parties, in the case of serious offences or where there is a high risk of further offences, the balance of the public interest in prosecution may be considered to outweigh the withdrawal of the victim's complaint.[55] Generally, it can be inferred from the ECtHR's case-law that the possibility of initiating and continuing criminal proceedings despite the withdrawal of the victim's complaint or statement should be available to the competent authorities in cases where the public interest outweighs the private one.

In serious cases of physical and sexual violence, the prosecution should therefore be *ex officio*. For other forms of violence, it is left to States' discretion, which should, however, provide for the balancing of the two interests and not in absolute terms opt for *ex parte* prosecution. Moreover, competent authorities should ensure that all necessary evidence is promptly gathered so that the prosecution of at least

---

[48] *Eremia v. The Republic of Moldova* (3564/11), 28.05.2013, par. 52, *B. v. The Republic of Moldova*, 16.07.2013, par. 46.

[49] *Volodina v. Russia* (41261/17), 09.07.2019, par. 71, *Levchuk v. Ukraine* (17496/19), 03.09.2020, par. 78. See also *Valiulienė v. Lithuania*, 26.03.2013, par. 78.

[50] *Talpis v. Italy* (41237/14), 02.03.2017, par. 130.

[51] *Valiulienė v. Lithuania*, 26.03.2013, par. 69, *Bălşan v. Romania* (49645/09), 23.05.2017, par. 57, *Volodina v. Russia*, 09.07.2019, par. 77, *Buturugă v. Romania*, 11.02.2020, par. 60, *Volodina v. Russia* (No 2) (40419/19), 14.09.2021, par. 49. See for the positive obligations Kempees (2020), pp. 20, 27; Mavronicola (2021), p. 139; Ashworth (2013), p. 198.

[52] *Volodina v. Russia*, 09.07.2019, par. 84.

[53] Burton (2022), p. 29.

[54] *T.M. and C.M. v. The Republic of Moldova* (26608/11), 28.01.2014, par. 46–47, *Tunikova and others v. Russia*, 14.12.2021, par. 155.

[55] *Opuz v. Turkey* (33401/02), 09.06.2009, par. 139, *B. v. The Republic of Moldova* (61382/09), 16.07.2013, par. 54, *Tunikova and others v. Russia*, 14.12.2021.

serious forms of physical violence can continue even without the participation of the victim in the proceedings.[56]

4 Remarks on Balancing the Public and Private Interest in the Prosecution of Domestic Violence

The public interest in the prosecution of domestic violence became an important aspect. In cases where the wishes of both the victim and the State coincide, *ex officio* prosecution relieves the burden and protects the victim, while challenging a sense of impunity inherent even in modern societies.

It is, however, possible that the victim may not want the perpetrator prosecuted and convicted or may recant at some point in the process.[57] That may also lead to reconciliation with procedural consequences.[58] This observation can be attributed to the cycle of violence, which often leads victims back to their abusers, and to victims' dependence on the perpetrator.[59] It is also affected by the widespread fear of retaliation.[60] Therefore, it can be argued that the victim's freedom of choice in the context of abusive relationships is limited.[61] Nevertheless, autonomy, self-determination and individual decision-making for women should be respected and protected to avoid paternalism. This is an important aspect of the discussion. The main argument against mandatory prosecution is the avoidance of secondary victimization.[62] As a result, the adoption of protective measures appears to be a sufficient countervailing factor. However, when secondary victimization is broadly defined as including also the harm resulting from a process to which the victim opposes -even if it seems irrational to the outside observer- the discussion is put on a new footing.[63]

Trying to balance these considerations, *i.e.,* respecting individual autonomy while recognizing that there are behaviors in which the public interest in prosecution cannot be outweighed, is a difficult exercise. This is also reflected in the choices made at the supranational level.[64] Before coming to some conclusions though, it must be noted that several shortcomings in the criminal justice system prevent vic-

[56] Explanatory report, ibid., par. 280.

[57] See indicatively Hanna (1996), p. 1853.

[58] See for example the special mediation procedure in Greek law analysed in the next section. See also Steinl (2021), p. 831.

[59] Walker (2009), pp. 85 et seq.; Pais (2015), p. 32; Steinl (2021), p. 829; Abarbanel (2010), p. 472.

[60] Abarbanel (2010), p. 474; McQuigg (2017), p. 104. See also *Levchuk v. Ukraine*, 03.09.2020, par. 80.

[61] Hirschmann (1996), p. 133.

[62] Nakane (2021), p. 152.

[63] See also Nakane (2021), p. 154.

[64] See also McQuigg (2017), p. 104.

tims from seeking and achieving redress and even hinder the efforts of prosecutors, contributing to the attrition rates.[65] It is, therefore, vital to remove external barriers in prosecution. Substantive and procedural barriers should be lifted by establishing a coherent legal framework to be applied in practice. Firstly, the legal framework should be comprehensive and make the victim feel that it can be an effective remedy for their abuse. Moreover, given the particularities of the relationship between victims and their abusers, it is important that the relevant cases are dealt with timely and by specialized actors.[66] Only when all these barriers are lifted, can the victim's autonomy be balanced with mandatory and no-drop prosecution.

From a pragmatic point of view, it is difficult to prosecute domestic violence without the victim's cooperation.[67] In cases of physical violence, the State's obligation to conduct an effective investigation as formed in the ECtHR's case law may provide the prosecution with the necessary evidence to carry on with the prosecution. Physical violence, especially severe, thus may be easier to prosecute without the victim's cooperation and at the same time, the public interest also appears stronger in comparison to other forms of domestic abuse. Therefore, the intrusion into the victim's private sphere is limited, since the prosecution will be based on hard evidence, such as photos of the physical injuries or medical reports. On the other hand, cases of minor physical, psychological and economic violence pose several difficulties. Usually, hard evidence without the victim's cooperation is hard to get.[68] Moreover, the intrusion into the victim's private sphere to secure such material appears disproportionate (such as private messages or electronic devices). Also, any serious prosecutorial effort has to investigate the specifics of the relationship and examine witnesses close to the victim, a process that somehow devalues the victim's personality. In this situation, respect for the autonomy and the will and interests of the specific victim and of all women that are in abusive relationships renders mandatory prosecution an ill-adapted mechanism for dealing with the phenomenon. This conclusion is by no means absolute, as competent authorities should have a margin of appreciation, especially given the complex dynamics of abusive relationships. However, ultimately domestic abuse should not be substituted or compounded by the paternalism of the state.

In this framework, it appears that the dilemma of *ex parte* or *ex officio* prosecution has long constrained the discussion on how to address domestic violence. Both choices have advantages and disadvantages, especially given the very different nature and operation of the national criminal justice systems, which hardly allows for general considerations. Perhaps it is time to think beyond this dichotomy and consider ways to better support domestic violence victims and address the systemic alienation they often face. An attempt to combine the advantages of the two

---

[65] See by analogy for the offence of rape Chioni-Chotouman (2022), pp. 25 et seq. See also Hanna (1996), p. 1884 on the issue of mistrust towards the criminal justice system.

[66] See also Krizsán and Roggeband (2021), p. 197; Nakane (2021), p. 150.

[67] See also Pais (2015), p. 32.

[68] See Hanna (2009), p. 1465.

different approaches to prosecution would allow, for example, a form in which prosecution is initiated in a timely manner without burdening the victim along the lines of *ex officio* prosecution, whilst allowing for the possibility of respecting the different subsequent will of the victim. In such a model though, it is necessary to take into account the specific circumstances of each case, which may require the continuation of the prosecution due to, for instance, the seriousness of the offence or the repetitive nature of the conduct. Restorative justice in this framework that could lead to the imposition of conditions on the perpetrator without disturbing the domestic relationships that the victim themselves wish to maintain can, in cases of less serious offences, serve as an alternative to a trial. Yet this requires enhancing cooperation and communication between prosecuting authorities and victims and creating a flexible system that allows for balancing and diversion when necessary.

5 Prosecuting Domestic Violence in Greece: A Look at Current Legislation

Before reviewing the choices made by Greece in relation to the prosecution of domestic violence, some preliminary observations are necessary. Greece introduced a specific statute for domestic violence in 2006. Until then, the relevant incidents were covered by general provisions rather insufficiently.[69] Law 3500/2006 for combating domestic violence entered into force on 24 October 2006, being a significant step towards the acknowledgment of the issue and protection of the victims. This law has been also supplemented by Law 4531/2018, which incorporated the Istanbul Convention introducing significant changes[70] and recently by Laws 5090/2024 and 5172/2025.

In general, Greece's domestic violence legislation is situated along liberal egalitarian lines. As such, the relevant statutes are formulated in a gender-neutral way.[71] Concerning physical violence, all its forms are prosecuted *ex officio*.[72] Mandatory prosecution is also provided for psychological violence, entailing causing fear or distress by the threat of violence or other unlawful act, as well as coercion.[73] It is also provided for cases where the dignity of the victim is affected by a particularly degrading language or act relating to their sexual life.[74]

As a rule, minor physical violence as well as the offences of threat and insult are only prosecuted following a complaint by the victim. However, the legislator decided that in the context of domestic abuse, all forms of physical and

[69] See Ranjan (2020), p. 43.

[70] See the analysis of the changes in Chioni-Chotouman (2020), p. 211.

[71] See for example Law 3500/2006 or Art. 336 Penal Code on the offence of rape.

[72] Art. 17 Law 3500/2006.

[73] Art. 7 Law 3500/2006.

[74] Art. 9 Law 3500/2006.

psychological violence should be included in mandatory prosecution. It is a choice that relieves the victim from the onus to initiate prosecution. In addition, it takes into consideration the fact that domestic abuse victims often need time to process the abuse and resort to authorities, considering that in Greece for *ex parte* offences a victim must file a complaint within 3 months of the incident to initiate prosecution. However, as demonstrated in the aforementioned analysis, such a choice is never simplistic or free of consequences for the victims.

Apart from the aforementioned benefits of this option, it is questionable how the need to respect the victim's autonomy can be combined with mandatory prosecution, which can be initiated based on a third-party report, for acts falling within the scope of the victim's consent.[75] A vivid example is the use of degrading language, something that an individual should not only have the right to choose to tolerate but may also be desirable. Notwithstanding the fact that *ex parte* prosecution in Greece is problematic, mainly due to the tight time constraints, mandatory prosecution for all types of physical and psychological violence, even for those to which the victim can consent, in cases where the victim has a different will, raises issues with autonomy. A viable compromise could be a provision according to which prosecution for minor behaviors should not be initiated and continued against the express will of the victim, unless there is a public interest justified by the specific nature of the case, in the rationale of combining the two prosecution approaches presented above.

Finally, it should be stressed that in Greece, especially at the time of its introduction, mandatory prosecution was an absolute necessity. It was the only way for a very formal and law-abiding system to start responding to domestic violence and addressing it as a serious crime. Even after the provision of mandatory prosecution, the mobilization of the competent authorities has been a slow process. Moreover, practically the prosecution in Greece for domestic abuse cases not involving minor victims is seldomly initiated *ex officio* against the expressed will of the victim, and generally the victim's will plays an indirect and covert role in the prosecution and especially in the conviction. The investigation of even serious forms of physical or sexual abuse also relies heavily on the participation of the victim. For example, a victim who reports serious physical violence receives a referral from the police station and is then asked to undergo an examination at the forensic service, sometimes even 3 days after the incident if it took place outside the forensic service's opening hours.

For Greece it is, therefore, difficult -and even dangerous for victims- to advocate for *ex parte* prosecution for minor offences, even though doctrinally it is more rational and declaratively important that prosecution be organized in a way that protects victims without calling their autonomy into question.

---

[75] According to Greek law physical violence that doesn't risk the victim's life or is not serious is not punishable if the victim consents to it.

See also Symeonidou-Kastanidou (2006), p. 1013 (in Greek), who opposes compulsory prosecution for all offences in relation to the role that a third party may play in the prosecution by misinterpreting a situation or having other motives.

The detachment of mandatory prosecution from the victim's will is only mitigated in Greece by *the special mediation* proceeding[76] provided for all domestic abuse misdemeanors in Law 3500/2006 as part of restorative justice.[77] The aim was to introduce a process that would act as a sort of precursor to the criminal procedure, capable of dealing with less serious behavior with the help of an impartial third party.[78] As a result, the system would be made more victim-friendly and the number of complaints would be increased.[79] This is, however, only one aspect, with the special mediation proceeding functioning as a tool to restore and maintain family relations.[80] At a practical level, it allows prosecutors to confer much more discretion to victims of domestic abuse in deciding whether to continue prosecution than they do in other crimes. Nevertheless, the institution does not seem to produce sufficient results.[81]

Law 5172/2025 introduced a significant change to the special mediation procedure, reflecting the need to take into account the public interest in cases where power is conferred to victims regarding the prosecution.[82] According to the current legal framework, the prosecutor may in exceptional cases set aside the mediation agreement reached by the parties and proceed with the prosecution through a reasoned order. The aim is to protect the victim from further victimisation, especially in cases where their freedom of choice is limited. The victim's protection is thus elevated to a component of the pubic interest. The criteria to be considered by the prosecutor are indicatively set out. They may be grouped into four categories. The first refers to the criminal act itself, the second concerns the offender, the third relates to the victim and the fourth involves the risk of reoffending or causing harm to the children. This amendment represents a policy choice that appears to take into consideration the tension between respecting individual autonomy and the need for the state to intervene, even in cases of misdemeanors, to protect primarily the victim and also the children. If it indeed functions as an exceptional choice without undermining the application of the special mediation procedure, it may succeed in addressing situations in which the state, based on the available indicators, is obliged to act to prevent further harm. Thus, it can serve as a model policy which goes beyond the binary of *ex parte* and *ex officio* prosecution.

---

[76] Since there is not enough research on the specifics of its practical application, the author is not prepared to introduce it separately as specific data and research are needed.

[77] Art. 11 Law 3500/2006.

[78] Explanatory memorandum Law 3500/2006 available at https://www.hellenicparliament.gr/UserFiles/2f026f42-950c-4efc-b950-340c4fb76a24/g-oikovia-eis.pdf (in Greek).

[79] Explanatory memorandum, ibid., par. 6.

[80] For this aspect see Symeonidou-Kastanidou (2006), p. 1014; Eleftherianos (2018), p. 99 (in Greek).

[81] See Symeonidou-Kastanidou (2017), p. 502 (in Greek).

[82] See Chioni-Chotouman (2025), p. 207.

6 Conclusion

Domestic abuse was historically seen as a husband's prerogative. Liberal theory continued to perceive domestic violence as a private matter with state intervention remaining inadequate at best. Progressively, both the transformation of family law and the recognition of women as autonomous and independent individuals led to the aknowledgement of the phenomenon and to the recognition of the need to address it beyond its perception as a private matter at the sole disposal of the victim. The analysis demonstrated that besides the apparent private interest in prosecuting the offence, there is also a public one. And the latter is increasingly highlighted at the supranational level.

However, not only the absence but also the presence of state intervention affects women's lives and status, posing new challenges.[83] Respect for victim's autonomy should not be outweighed by the responsibility of the state to tackle the phenomenon. Nor should the public interest and the understanding of the complexity of abusive relationships result in paternalism. Ultimately, victims need not laws that try to address systemic deficiencies and gender imbalance at the expense of respecting their individuality and choices, but rather a versatile system capable of meeting their needs and balancing competing considerations when required.

References

Abarbanel J (2010) In light of Crawford v. Washington and the difficult nature of domestic violence prosecutions, Maryland should adopt legislation making admissible prior acts of domestic violence in domestic violence prosecutions. Univ Baltimore Law Rev 39(3):467–506

Ashworth A (2013) Positive obligations in criminal law. Hart, Oxford

Boyd S (1997) Challenging the public/private divide: an overview. In: Boyd S (ed) Challenging the public/private divide. University of Toronto Press, Toronto, pp 3–36

Brundage J (1987) Law, sex, and Christian society in medieval Europe. University of Chicago Press, Chicago

Buchan B (2001) Liberalism and fear of violence. Crit Rev Int Soc Polit Philos 4(3):27–48

Burton M (2022) Domestic abuse, victims and the law. Routledge, Abingdon

Chioni-Chotouman C (2020) Combating gender-based violence: Greek criminal law vis-à-vis European trends. In: Stradella E (ed) Gender based approaches to the law and Juris Dictio in Europe. Pisa University Press, Pisa, pp 201–220

Chioni-Chotouman C (2022) Substantive and procedural challenges impeding an effective response to rape: the example of Greece. In: Erbaş R (ed) Global problems in sexual offenses. Lexington Books, London, pp 25–44

Chioni-Chotouman C (2025) The legal framework on domestic violence in Greece: amendments to Law 3500/2006 introduced by Law 5172/2025. Poiniki Dikaiosini 2:201–208

Cleiren C, Voorde J (2019) Harmonising legal interests. Legal interests under criminal law in a multilevel legal order. In: Ouwerkerk J, Altena J, Oberg J, Miettinen S (eds) The future of

[83] See also Hanna (2009), p. 1460 for the elusive relationship between law and women.

EU criminal justice policy and practice: legal and criminological perspectives. Brill Nijhoff, Boston, pp 121–142
Dilcher G (1993) Religiöse Legitimation und gesellschaftliche Ordnungsaufgabe des Eherechts in der Reformationszeit. In: Prodi P (ed) Glaube und Eid. Oldenbourg Wissenschaftsverlag, Berlin, pp 189–198
Dossey L (2008) Wife beating and manliness in late antiquity. Past Present 199:3–40
Dover K (1973) Classical Greek attitudes to sexual behaviour. Arethusa 6(1):59–73
Dworkin R (2012) Liberalism. In: Hampshire S (ed) Public and private morality. Cambridge University Press, Cambridge, pp 113–143
Eleftherianos A (2018) The conciliation in criminal proceedings. In: Kaiafa-Gbandi M (ed) Administration of justice as a fundamental pillar of the well-governed state. Nomiki Bibliothiki, Athens, pp 99–106. (in Greek)
Erbaş R (2022) Evidentiary challenges to an effective criminal investigation for domestic violence: an introduction. In: Bonini V, Erbaş R (eds) The 10th anniversary of the Istanbul Convention. Pisa University Press, Pisa, pp 101–118
Finlayson L (2016) An introduction to feminism. Cambridge University Press, Cambridge
Gilmour FE (2022) Feminist criminology. In: Gibbs A, Gilmour FE (eds) Women, crime and justice in context. Routledge, Abingdon, pp 13–26
Gobetti D (1992) Private and public: individuals, households, and body politic in Locke and Hutcheson. Routledge, London
Guney G (2020) The Istanbul Convention: a genuine confirmation of the structural nature of domestic violence against women within a Human Rights Law Framework? In: Kewley S, Barlow C (eds) Preventing sexual violence: problems and possibilities. Bristol University Press, Bristol
Guzik K (2007) The forces of conviction: the power and practice of mandatory prosecution upon misdemeanor domestic battery suspects. Law Soc Inq 32:41–74
Hague G (2021) History and memories of the domestic violence movement: we've come further than you think. Policy Press, Bristol
Hahnkamper-Vandenbulcke N, Bacian I (2022) Violence against women and domestic violence: the new Commission proposal in light of European Parliament requests. European Parliament, Brussels
Hanna C (1996) No right to choose: mandated victim participation in domestic violence prosecutions. Harv Law Rev 109(8):1849–1910
Hanna C (2009) The paradox of progress: translating Evan Stark's coercive control into legal doctrine for abused women. Violence Against Women 15(12):1458–1476
Herring J (2020) Domestic abuse and human rights. Intersentia, Cambridge
Hirschmann N (1996) Domestic violence and the theoretical discourse of freedom. Frontiers J Women Stud 16:126–151
Kempees P (2020) "Hard Power" and the European Convention on Human Rights. Brill Nijhoff, Leiden
Kennedy C (2020) Defences: justification, excuse and provocation. In: Hill M, Doe N, Helmholz RH, Witte J (eds) Christianity and criminal law. Routledge, Abingdon, pp 253–268
Krizsán A, Roggeband C (2021) Politicizing gender and democracy in the context of the Istanbul Convention. Palgrave, Cham
Künzel A (2012) Feministische Theorien und Debatten. In: Foljanty L, Lembke U (eds) Feministische Rechtswissenschaft. Nomos, Baden-Baden, pp 52–73
Lavrysen L (2014) The scope of rights and the scope of obligations. In: Brems E, Gerards J (eds) Shaping rights in the ECHR. Cambridge University Press, Cambridge, pp 162–182
Locke J (1689) Two Treatises of Government II. London: Awnsham Churchill, chapter VII, para 82
Markard N (2017) Eheschließungsfreiheit im Kampf der Kulturen. In: Lembke U (ed) Regulierungen des Intimen. Springer, Wiesbaden, pp 139–158
Mavronicola N (2021) Torture, inhumanity and degradation under Article 3 of the ECHR. Hart, Oxford

McQuigg R (2016) Domestic violence as a human rights issue: Rumor v. Italy. Eur J Int Law 26(4):1009–1025
McQuigg R (2017) The Istanbul Convention, domestic violence and human rights. Routledge, London
Meyer S, Frost A (2019) Domestic and family violence: a critical introduction to knowledge and practice. Routledge, London
Mill JS (1869) The subjection of women. London : Longmans, Green, Reader, and Dyer
Mills L (1998) Mandatory arrest and prosecution policies for domestic violence: a critical literature review and the case for more research to test victim empowerment approaches. Crim Justice Behav 25(3):306–318
Molloy C (2018) The failure of feminism? Rape law reform in the Republic of Ireland, 1980–2017. Law Hist Rev 36(4):689–712
Montesinos García A, Maravall-Buckwalter I (2023) Article 55 ex parte and ex officio proceedings. In: De Vido S, Frulli M (eds) Preventing and Combating Violence Against Women and Domestic Violence, Elgar Pub, p 623
Nakane T (2021) Prosecution ex officio or following a complaint by the victim? An analysis on offences related to violence against women and sexual offences. N J Eur Crim Law 12(2):146–165
Nguyen N (2006) Roman rape: an overview of Roman rape laws from the Republican period to Justinian's Reign. Mich J Gender Law 13:75–112
Niemi J, Verdu A, Sanmartin AV (2020) The concepts of gender and violence in the Istanbul Convention. In: Niemi J, Peroni L, Stoyanova V (eds) International law and violence against women: Europe and the Istanbul Convention. Routledge, Abingdon, pp 77–94
Pais P (2015) Challenging the efficacy of ex officio prosecution of domestic violence offenses: a comparative analysis. In: Tomás J, Epple N (eds) Sexuality, oppression and human rights. Brill, Boston, pp 27–45
Pateman C (1988) The sexual contract. Stanford University Press, California
Peršak N (2020) Positive obligations in view of the principle of criminal law as a last resort. In: Lavrysen L, Mavronicola N (eds) Coercive human rights: positive duties to mobilise the criminal law under the ECHR. Hart, Oxford, pp 141–160
Pretorius J (2017) Rape and infidelity: threats to the Athenian Πόλις and Οίκος. Fundamina 23(2):39–61
Ranjan S (2020) Domestic violence legislation in Greece: analysis of penal mediation. Women Crim Just 30(1):42–68
Roberts P (2004) Criminal law theory and the limits of liberalism. In: Simester AP, du Bois-Pedain A, Neumann U (eds) Liberal criminal theory: essays for Andreas von Hirsch. Hart, Oxford, pp 327–360
Rudolph C (2015) Geschlechterverhältnisse in der Politik. Verlag Barbara Budrich, Opladen
Salisbury E, Donavin G, Price ML (eds) (2002) Domestic violence in medieval texts. University Press of Florida, Gainesville, pp 1–27
Schneider E (1991) The violence of privacy. Conn Law Rev 4:973–999
Singelnstein T (2019) Häusliche Gewalt. In: Hilgendorf E, Kudlich H, Valerius B (eds) Handbuch des Strafrechts Band 4. C.F. Müller, Heidelberg, Rn. 122–124
Steinl L (2021) Der Einfluss der Istanbul-Konvention auf das deutsche Strafrecht – Völkerrechtliche Vorgaben für den Umgang mit Gewalt gegen Frauen und häuslicher Gewalt. ZStW 133(3):819–839
Stoyanova V (2020) Common law tort of negligence as a tool for deconstructing positive obligations under the European Convention on Human Rights. Int J Human Rights 24(5):632–655
Symeonidou-Kastanidou E (2006) The draft bill on domestic violence. Poiniki Dikaiosini 8-9:1013–1014. (in Greek)
Symeonidou-Kastanidou E (2017) Restorative justice: an alternative to crime. Poiniki Dikaiosini 6:497–504. (in Greek)

Vanneau V (2016) L' Invention juridique des violences conjugales au XIXe siècle. Les Cahiers de la Justice 2:305–318
Walker L (2009) The battered woman syndrome. Springer, New York
Wapler F (2012) Frauen in der Geschichte des Rechts. In: Foljanty L, Lembke U (eds) Feministische Rechtswissenschaft. Nomos, Baden-Baden, pp 33–51
Webster E (2018) Dignity, degrading treatment and torture in human rights law. Routledge, London
Wiesner-Hanks M (2020) Christianity and sexuality in the early modern world, 3rd edn. Routledge, Abingdon
Wischermann U (2004) Feminist theories on the separation of the private and the public: looking back, looking forward. Women German Yearb 20:184–197
Witherington A (1990) Women in Roman settings. In: Witherington B (ed) Women and the genesis of Christianity. Cambridge University Press, Cambridge, pp 19–26

How to Initiate the Criminal Prosecution of a Domestic Violence Case, *ex officio* or *ex parte*? The Example of Turkish Law

Rahime Erbaş, Büşra Hazel Ateş Sarıdağ, and Ramazan Zeyrek

Abstract This chapter explores two main approaches, *ex parte* and *ex officio*, as to how to initiate criminal procedure for the crimes committed in domestic settings. Domestic violence cases hold some challenging features preventing an effective criminal investigation as inhibiting factors. Our chapter, thus, argues that an important aspect of the criminal and penal policy's response to domestic violence is to break the cycle of violence through a prosecution policy as *ex officio*. As such, it considers the Istanbul Convention's approach taking on the traumatizing nature of crimes which are committed in domestic settings which aims to ease the burden of the victim during criminal procedure as well as the ECtHR's case-law. Then it looks at Türkiye's choice of avoiding dosage and opting for impetus in prosecution of domestic violence, which has triggered a constitutional debate on the equality principle.

1 Introduction

The crime of injury, as a rule, is an *ex officio* investigated and prosecuted crime in Turkish law. However, where the injury can be remedied by a simple/quick medical intervention, it is investigated and prosecuted following a complaint by the victim. Albeit, if the victim is spouse or ex-spouse of the perpetrator, it is still an *ex officio* investigated and prosecuted crime. Furthermore, in this case, the punishment shall

R. Erbaş (✉)
Faculty of Law, Istanbul University, Istanbul, Türkiye
e-mail: rerbas@istanbul.edu.tr

B. H. Ateş Sarıdağ · R. Zeyrek
Faculty of Law, Istanbul University, Istanbul, Türkiye

R. Erbaş (ed.), *Criminal Prosecution of Domestic Violence*, Ius Gentium: Comparative Perspectives on Law and Justice 128,
https://doi.org/10.1007/978-3-032-01202-9_3

be increased by half. This is because the crime of injury is, in Turkish law, designed to protect both the physical and the psychological well-being of a human and has been considered as a key catalyst in combatting domestic violence and violence against women in Türkiye during the penal reforms in the 2000s. This provision requiring an *ex officio* prosecution of the injury committed against a spouse/ex-spouse, even if the injury can be cured through a simple/quick medical intervention, was brought to the Constitutional Court in 2008 and 2020; However, it was argued that the deviation based on victim's status violates the principle of equality ensured in the Constitution. The Court rejected the violation claim in both years by stating that the different features of the victims and perpetrators can be standpoints considered during penal policy. Considering as the positive obligation of the State in conjunction with the case law of the ECtHR, it is argued that this deviation aims at effectively combating domestic violence, and as such preventing *the impunity of perpetrators of domestic violence* since perpetrators may coerce the female victims to not complain or to withdraw their complaint. The dissenting opinion describes this penal policy as "injuring of private sphere."[1]

This represents the Turkish law's prosecutorial policy after 2005 regarding crime of injury within the context of domestic violence. The decision on how to initiate the criminal prosecution of a domestic violence case (respectively violence against women), *ex officio* or *ex parte*, vary from one jurisdiction to another, e.g., no harmonization in the EU law exists.[2] Because, such decision firstly represents a jurisdiction's penal policy over particular features, complexities and challenges of this violence type as well as the jurisdiction's choice to deal with domestic violence in criminal law or in civil law. Secondly, whether a given jurisdiction's criminal procedure is closer to the adversarial (Anglo-American-oriented) or inquisitorial (civil law-oriented) approach plays a significant role in shaping penal policy regarding domestic violence. Indeed, it is stated that civil law-oriented jurisdictions have a tendency toward *ex parte*, following a complaint by the victim, whereas Anglo-American-oriented jurisdictions have a tendency toward *ex officio*.[3] These differences are also reflected upon terminologies. In the investigation's terminology procedure, *ex officio* is a term used in the laws of the Council of Europe and Continental Europe, while *no-drop policies*, either as "hard" and "soft" no-drop policies,[4] in the United Nations and Anglo-American legal systems, meaning the investigation irrespective of the complaint of the victim.[5]

The Turkish criminal law, which is civil law-oriented and having a criminal procedure closer to inquisitorial ones, however, embraces a slight deviation from other

---

[1] Anayasa Mahkemesi, E: 2005/151, K: 2008/37, 03.01.2008. https://normkararlarbilgibankasi.anayasa.gov.tr/ND/2008/37?KararNo=2008%2F37. and Anayasa Mahkemesi, E.2019/2, K.2020/28, 11.06.2020. https://normkararlarbilgibankasi.anayasa.gov.tr/ND/2020/28?EsasNo=2019%2F2. See also: Erbaş (2021), p. 10.

[2] Nakane (2021), p. 151.

[3] Ibid, p. 146.

[4] Hanna (1996), p. 1863; Mills (1998), p. 307.

[5] Pais (2019), p. 28.

civil law-oriented jurisdiction after 2005. Although the Istanbul Convention promotes *ex officio* prosecution in Article 55 and that Article is one of those which mostly contained reservation for minor offences,[6] Türkiye had no reservation for excluding minor offences from *ex parte* prosecution when it signed it. Indeed, in 2009, *Opuz v. Türkiye*[7] substantially changed the criminal law's approach in domestic violence in Türkiye. Indeed, the case-law and State positive obligation established by the ECtHR as well as recognition of the prevalence of this violence type across the country by the Turkish Constitution Court brings the deviation as aptly articulated by Clark:

> One of the most effective ways to stop domestic violence is to make clear to abusers and potential abusers that society will not tolerate it.[8]

Whereas Clark argues a prosecution relying upon the complaint of the victim as *punishing the victims*,[9] some consider this as an *aggressive prosecution*[10] in addressing domestic violence within the criminal justice system only with short-term benefits.[11] The role of arrest has been a standpoint to measure the effectiveness of the criminal justice system response to domestic violence in the US.[12] As a matter of fact, from a criminological point, for example, mandatory arrest[13] of a domestic violence perpetrator for a short period (custody) as one of the ramifications of an *ex officio* prosecution creates "a moral dilemma between short-term victim interest and long-term control of domestic violence,"[14] in comparison with the full arrest (conviction).[15] Therefore, Sherman et al. warn of *the escalation effect* of any aggressive prosecution covering the short arrest may escalate the violence at home and, as such, it may be harmful in some sections of society such as the urban underclass.[16] Indeed, revictimization, the escalating effect of criminal persecution, has been a great concern in domestic violence cases.[17] As such, Sherman et al. argue "the difference that dosage apparently makes."[18] However, considering domestic violence inherently suffers from the public-private dichotomy and, as such, "home" serves as a premise for impunity from the criminal justice system, the question remains

[6] https://www.coe.int/en/web/conventions/full-list?module=declarations-by-treaty&numSte=210&codeNature=0.

[7] *Opuz v. Türkiye* (33401/02), 09.09.2009.

[8] Clark (1987), p. 279. See e.g., Hanna (1996), p. 1890.

[9] Ibid, pp. 268 ff.

[10] Hanna (1996), p. 1887.

[11] Ibid, p. 1888.

[12] Dobash (2003), p. 313; Peterson and Bialo-Padin (2012), p. 103.

[13] Mandatory arrest comes after a clinical trial by the US National Institute of Justice in 1984 with the Minneapolis Police Department. See more Sherman (1992), p. 2.

[14] Sherman et al. (1991), p. 844; Hanna (1996), p. 1888.

[15] Ibid, p. 844.

[16] Ibid, pp. 845–846.

[17] See Hanna (1996), p. 1894.

[18] Sherman et al. (1991), p. 846.

whether a dosage could break this dichotomy or not. Indeed, the role of feminist movements in the 1970s in some US states served as an impetus for law reform, and as such pro-prosecution policies have changed the police response toward DV.[19]

The question whether we need a dosage or impetus in prosecution of domestic violence will be the main thrust of this chapter which carries all arguments surrounding *ex officio* prosecution. It is observed that scholars have diverged over the questions regarding how to initiate the criminal prosecution of a domestic violence case, *ex officio* or *ex parte*. For a State, this turns out to be a burning question to be answered in penal policy: should we follow *an aggressive prosecution?*[20] Or, in the opposite case, should we seek *the legitimacy for prosecutorial policy?*[21]

In an attempt to provide a guidance to jurisdictions for an appropriate choice on prosecutorial policies in domestic violence cases, this chapter explores two main approaches, pro *ex parte* or pro *ex officio*, as to the how to initiate criminal procedure for the crimes committed in domestic settings as possible *prosecutorial strategies*[22] in addressing domestic violence within the criminal justice system. Domestic violence cases hold some challenging features preventing an effective criminal investigation as inhibiting factors. Our chapter, thus, argues that an important aspect of the criminal and penal policy's response to domestic violence is to break the cycle of violence through a prosecution policy as *ex officio* investigation. As such, it considers the Istanbul Convention's approach taking on the traumatizing nature of crimes which are committed in domestic settings as well and as such eases the burden of the victim during criminal procedure[23] as well as the ECtHR's case-law, avoiding being "strictly dependent on the pursuance of complaints by victim."[24] Then it looks at Türkiye's choice of avoiding dosage and opting for impetus in prosecution of domestic violence as a trigger of a constitutional debate on equality principle.

2 Prosecutorial Policies in Domestic Violence

Hanna articulated a thought provoking question: "are women purely passive victims, or are they blameworthy agents in their violent relationship?"[25] The answer is neither one of them nor "in-between."[26] The answer is rather complex. Therefore,

[19] Hanna (1996), p. 1885; Flannigan (2013), p. 481.

[20] Hanna (1996), p. 1887.

[21] Ibid, p. 1888.

[22] Ibid, p. 1885.

[23] Explanatory Report of the Istanbul Convention for Art. 55, para. 279. See https://www.coe.int/en/web/conventions/full-list?module=treaty-detail&treatynum=210.

[24] *Opuz v. Türkiye* (33401/02), 09.09.2009, par. 145.

[25] Hanna (1996), p. 1868.

[26] Nakane (2021), pp. 146 and 161.

different opinions and practices exist regarding whether prosecution of domestic violence relies upon the complaint of the victim or not.[27]

In Council of Europe member States such as Albania, Austria, Bosnia and Herzegovina, Estonia, Greece, Poland, Portugal, Spain, and Switzerland, and in the United Kingdom, Canada, and the United States, criminal prosecutions may continue prosecution despite the victim withdrawing his or her complaint.[28] In countries such as Germany, Czechia, Bulgaria, Italy, Hungary, Latvia, Australia, Brazil, and Scotland, the victim's complaint is deemed necessary for the investigation to continue.[29] However, as it will be explained below, no unique standard for all domestic violence cases exists, as they may vary according to the types and severity of crimes.

This part first demonstrates the *ex parte* by complaint-based prosecution approach and then the *ex officio* prosecution. Prosecution of domestic violence relying upon a complaint by the victim has been the norm as domestic violence was historically considered as a private issue between spouses/partners. In this regard, *ex officio* prosecution of domestic violence represents a novelty or a new tendency.[30] It, indeed, took history to reach the acceptance that domestic violence is not a private matter anymore. However, today we face the question whether we should characterize domestic violence as *a purely public phenomenon* or not, and whether there is still maneuvering space for privacy and autonomy of the victim?[31] Finally, this part demonstrates the stance of the Istanbul Convention.

2.1 An Ex Parte Prosecution: Victim Participation Models

> Many domestic violence advocates emphasize the importance of listening to women and their concerns before taking action against their batterers.[32]

It is argued that any pressure to the victim to decide whether to make a complaint or not may negatively affect the victim. That being said, if the case is to be an *ex officio* prosecuted, women may be deprived of the right to make decisions regarding their own futures.[33] Some argue that it is not appropriate for States to prosecute domestic violence despite of the fact that the victim dismisses her complaint, assuming that it was best for all women, without considering their individual needs and positions.[34] It is also argued that such an assumption violates the victim's rights to privacy and

---

[27] Hanna (1996), p. 1855.

[28] Erbaş (2020), p. 238; Pais (2019), p. 28.

[29] 15 out of the 27 EU countries seek the victim's complaint for investigation in injury and sexual crimes. See more: Nakane (2021), p. 148 and also Cf. *Opuz v. Türkiye*, par. 88.

[30] Ibid, p. 146.

[31] Hanna (1996), p. 1868.

[32] Ibid, p. 1863.

[33] Nakane (2021), p. 155; Hanna (1996), p. 1856.

[34] Ibid. and Mills (1998), p. 309.

autonomy.[35] The uncooperativeness of the victim, indeed, is a common concern as it is aptly stated that "most domestic violence victims don't want to testify against their batterers."[36] Because the aims of the criminal justice system and the victim may not correspond for every case,[37] as such, whereas the justice system seeks for punishing the wrongdoer, the victim may hold hope for a future with her batterer.[38]

Apparently, three main reasons why a victim's complaint may be sought in order to prosecute domestic violence appear in jurisdictions as follows; (1) in case of minor crimes; (2) mediation (restorative justice) by virtue of the close relationship between the victim and the suspect; and (3) the purpose of protecting the privacy of the victim.[39] Although these reasons vary from one jurisdiction to another, generally in case of a minor crime, the victim's decision to not complain ends the investigation in some countries.

While the draft of the Istanbul Convention was being prepared, it was discussed that crimes such as sexual harassment and stalking could be investigated *ex parte*, but no regulation was made.[40] For example, sexual harassment is investigated in Germany, Lithuania and Switzerland following a complaint.[41]

In cases of domestic violence that are subject to complaint in Germany, if the complaint is withdrawn, the prosecutor evaluates whether there is a special public interest in order to prosecute. It can be *ex officio* investigated if it is deemed necessary due to special public interest.[42] However, in cases where it is not reasonable to file a criminal complaint due to the relationship between the victim and the perpetrator, the investigation is terminated.[43] The special public interest must be reasoned and subject to review by the court.[44] For example, if the suspect has a criminal record for the same crime, if the action is serious, and if the victim abandons the complaint due to fear, it is considered to have a special public interest.[45]

In Scotland, pro-arrest policy is adopted. If there is sufficient evidence, the suspect may be arrested even if the victim does not complain.[46] However, unlike no drop-policy, in the absence of complaints, as in Germany, the prosecutor decides whether there is a public interest in prosecuting.[47] The victim has traditionally been

[35] Mordini (2004), p. 319.

[36] Peterson and Bialo-Padin (2012), p. 105.

[37] Ibid.

[38] Ibid, p. 106.

[39] Nakane (2021), p. 154.

[40] Ibid, p. 156.

[41] Ibid.

[42] GREVIO, Baseline Evaluation Report Germany (2022)21 published on 7 October 2022, para. 247. Hereinafter GREVIO Germany Report (2022). Meysen and Grafe (2019), p. 147; Hagemann-White (2017), p. 97.

[43] GREVIO Germany Report (2022).

[44] Nakane (2021), p. 157.

[45] Ibid.

[46] Friskney et al. (2021), p. 249.

[47] Wutz (2011), p. 78.

assumed to be the prosecution's main witness. Prosecutors must conduct a "sufficient evidence test" assessment before filing a public claim.[48] Due to the disappearance of the victim statement, which is the most important evidence, the prosecutor, who does not find it useful in filing a lawsuit, drops the charge.

In domestic violence cases, in Romania, the investigation is terminated if the prosecutor does not find it useful to initiate a prosecution in mediation and withdrawal of the complaint.[49] In Bulgaria, victim complaint is sought for prosecution in cases of domestic violence. Even court proceedings are initiated by the victim with a written petition containing the victim's personal statement.[50] It was criticized by stating that this situation poses a risk to the victim and imposes a burden of proof on the victim.[51] In Hungary, only qualified injuries are investigated *ex officio* in domestic violence, and to investigate other acts of violence, the victim must file a criminal complaint.[52]

2.2 An Ex Officio Prosecution: A New Tendency?

> Not only is the victim told that crime in the family setting is less serious than similar crimes against strangers, but the victim is also more likely than a stranger-victim to be in continuing danger from the criminal.[53]

Domestic violence is characterized by the unwillingness of the victim to cooperate.[54] According to a study, in domestic violence, women are more likely to withdraw or alter their statements to prevent their close partners from being involved in the crime than in other types of crimes.[55] In general, it is stated that between 50% and 90% of victims withdraw their initial complaints and do not support the prosecution.[56] A survey conducted in England and Wales found that 46% of victims of domestic violence stopped seeking justice.[57] It implies that the law enforcement and prosecutor's office did not proceed with the case without a collaborative victim, as Hanna states: "Abused women often will not cooperate and refuse to appear in

---

48 Ibid, p. 79.

49 Birzu (2019), p. 289; Erbaş (2021), p. 7; cf. *Opuz v. Türkiye*, par. 90.

50 Vassileva and Delpeuch (2021), p. 120.

51 Ibid, pp. 124–125.

52 Hera and Szego (2021), p. 203. In the Brazilian model, some cases of domestic violence, such as threats, require the consent of the victim to be prosecuted. However, if the victim withdraws her request to prosecute at the police station prior to the indictment, a judicial hearing is required to drop the case. After the indictment, it is not possible to withdraw the authority to prosecute. See Ávila (2018), p. 19.

53 Clark (1987), p. 268.

54 Hanna (1996), p. 1876; Erbaş (2021), p. 10; Ateş Sarıdağ (2022), p. 17.

55 Douglas and Fitzgerald (2021), p. 350.

56 Wutz (2011), p. 77.

57 Ellison (2002), p. 834.

court. Sometimes they change their stories to protect their batterers or to shield themselves and their families from outside intervention."[58]

In domestic violence cases, the victim does not complain for various reasons such as special vulnerability, economic dependence, or fear of being exposed to violence again. Accordingly, withdrawing the complaint does not reflect the victim's true intentions.[59] Furthermore, due to the repetitive nature of domestic violence, there is a risk of being pressured to give up the complaint and it is risky to bring the parties against each other.[60] The imbalance of power between the parties is also an important obstacle for the victim to file a complaint.[61] It is also stated that an *ex officio* prosecution does not only protect the victim, but also the other women who may be prospective partners of the perpetrator.[62] Further, the crime types are decisive. For example, marital rape or any sexual assault within an intimate relationship necessitates an *ex officio* prosecution as providing an effective criminal investigation is crucial.[63] Therefore, the Istanbul Convention stipulates an *ex officio* prosecution for sexual assault within Article 55.[64] In a similar vein, Directive (EU) 2024/1385 of the European Parliament and of the Council of 14 May 2024 on combating violence against women and domestic violence, stipulates in Article 15 that "Member States shall ensure that investigations into or the prosecution of acts of rape are not dependent on a victim or the victim's representative reporting the act, or on a complaint by a victim or the victim's representative, and that criminal proceedings are not discontinued solely because the report or complaint has been withdrawn".[65]

The victim's withdrawal of her complaint during the prosecution phase or her failure to participate in the trial largely destroys the perpetrator's chance of conviction, and this also affects the police's approach in domestic violence cases.[66] Some argue that the police act with an attitude to prevent them from wasting time and resources in such cases.[67] For all these reasons, the need for a model that does not seek the participation of the victim in the judicial process has emerged.[68]

First of all, the "mandatory arrest" policy as the first response to domestic violence in the USA should be mentioned. It is stated that, until this policy, there was a veil of privacy in domestic violence and the acts remained unpunished.[69] In

[58] Hanna (1996), p. 1853.

[59] Ibid, p. 1859; Pais (2019), p. 28.

[60] Thoennes et al. (1995), p. 7.

[61] Ibid.

[62] Hanna (1996), p. 1895.

[63] Leskinen (2020), p. 149; Sosa (2020), p. 37.

[64] See Niemi and Sanmartin (2020), p. 91; Leskinen (2020), p. 149.

[65] Directive 2024/1385, Art. 15/5.

[66] Ellison (2002), p. 838.

[67] Ibid.

[68] Ibid, p. 834.

[69] Krieger (2002), p. 236.

domestic violence cases, in some States, the police have the power to arrest the perpetrator, regardless of the victim's wishes, if there is a possible reason to believe that violence exists.[70] In a study conducted in the USA, it was stated that reconciliation of the victim and the perpetrator would not have a deterrent effect in domestic violence, and even direct detention after the action was more effective than alternative means such as mediation and suspension.[71] Regarding the effect of the victim's withdrawal of her complaint on the prosecution, it is stated that the most effective method is the "no-drop policy."[72] According to that policy, for the prevention of domestic violence, after accusations are made, the State, not the victim, becomes a part of the case.[73] In the model applied, an investigation is carried out without the participation of the victim, as is the case with intentional killings, and, if it cannot be provided, even the victim's statements are not consulted.[74] It displays that 70% of the cases filed as a result of the investigations carried out with this policy involve uncooperative or missing victims.[75]

Although no-drop policy does not mean mandatory prosecution, it emerges as different practices in the States in the form of prosecution independent of the victim's participation or active encouragement of the victim.[76] Those applications are divided into "hard" or "soft" no-drop policies.[77] In hard policies, although the victim withdraws her complaint, in cases where there is sufficient evidence, prosecution can be initiated by the decision of the prosecutor. In the soft no-drop policy, the victim is not forced to participate in the proceedings. Instead, the victim is provided with support services and encouraged to continue with the process.[78]

In England and Wales, in a domestic violence case, prosecutors do assessments in terms of two points for the prosecution phase. These relate to whether there is sufficient evidence for the possibility of conviction (evidential test) and whether there is a public interest test in the conduct of the prosecution.[79] If the prosecutor makes a positive assessment, it does not matter whether the victim withdrew her statement or not.[80] It is argued that, with this model, the police will shift from the "victim-based" investigation technique to "evidence-based" investigation.[81]

---

[70] Hanna (1996), p. 1860; Smith (1995), p. 369.

[71] Hanna (1996), p. 1859.

[72] Corsilles (1994), p. 882.

[73] Ibid, p. 858.

[74] Ibid, p. 835.

[75] Ibid, p. 843.

[76] Hanna (1996), p. 1863; Corsilles (1994), p. 859.

[77] Hanna (1996), p. 1863; Mills (1998), p. 307.

[78] Ibid.

[79] Ellison (2002), p. 836.

[80] Ibid, p. 834.

[81] Ibid, p. 840.

However, the victim's withdrawal of her complaint often results in the dismissal of the case due to insufficient evidence.[82]

Many acts of violence against women in Austria (such as murder, intentional injury, qualified threats, stalking, sexual assault/abuse, sexual harassment) are within the scope of *ex officio* investigation. However, it is stated that the obligation to investigate without seeking the victim's complaint lowers the threshold for the law enforcement to intervene in these crimes and reduces the importance of reporting.[83]

In Slovenia, domestic violence offences punishable by up to 5 years of imprisonment are foreseen to be *ex officio* prosecuted. However, in practice, due to the victim's reluctance to testify and the witnesses' reluctance to make statements, the criminal process does not continue due to lack of evidence. Therefore, *ex officio* investigation usually does not have an effective result when the only evidence is considered to be statements.[84] Likewise, in Canada, if the victim withdraws her complaint, the prosecutor examines whether there is sufficient evidence for the prosecution stage in terms of evidence.[85]

It is claimed that the aggressive prosecution models used in the *ex officio* have two main problematic points.[86] First, they focus only on the crime as if it was committed against the state, and, as a result, they do not consider the potential impact of the prosecution on the victim. Second, their focus is often short-term, thus ignoring the fact that victims of domestic violence need long-term safety. Negative aspects such as the use of subpoenas to force the woman victim to make a statement, and the threat of contacting the child protection services (in case where the partners have common child) if she does not make a statement, were also reported.[87] In a study conducted in Indiana, the USA, in the late 1980s, mandatory prosecution resulted in less violence on some victims, while there was an increase in violence in other cases.[88] Many women's rights advocates argue that the victim knows best what the perpetrator of violence can do, so the victim should have the right to choose.[89] As a result, it is the consensus of all opinions that the prosecutor's office makes an assessment on a case-by-case basis and decides whether to continue the investigation or not.[90]

---

[82] Ibid. Domestic Abuse Statutory Guidance (July 2022), https://assets.publishing.service.gov.uk/government/uploads/system/uploads/attachment_data/file/1089015/Domestic_Abuse_Act_2021_Statutory_Guidance.pdf, para. 337.

[83] Herbinger et al. (2021), p. 103.

[84] Hagemann-White (2019), p. 90.

[85] Pais (2019), p. 33.

[86] Epstein et al. (2003), pp. 466–468; Nilsson (2012), p. 30.

[87] Nilsson (2012), p. 30.

[88] Mordini (2004), p. 314.

[89] Nilsson (2012), p. 30.

[90] Ibid, p. 33.

3 The Stance of the Istanbul Convention as a Third Approach: "Wholly Dependent"?

The Convention defines domestic violence as "all acts of physical, sexual, psychological or economic violence that occur within the family or domestic unit or between former or current spouses or partners, whether or not the perpetrator shares or has shared the same residence with the victim" (Art. 3-b). For prosecutorial strategies, the Convention does not consider domestic violence as a reference concept under which prosecutorial strategies are stipulated. Indeed, for initiation of criminal procedure for these acts which constitute a crime, the Istanbul Convention, "with a view to empowering victims,"[91] promotes *ex officio* prosecution of domestic violence cases.[92] Further, it promotes such proceeding approach by adopting a *crime catalogue based approach* (Art. 55). This also calls for justice authorities on continued proceedings despite the withdrawal of the complaint by the victim.[93] The aims of the Convention can be extracted from the Explanatory Report of the Convention as[94] :

1. To ease the burden which lengthy criminal investigations and proceedings often place on the victims
2. To ensure that perpetrators are brought to justice
3. To encourage victims to go through with criminal proceedings
4. To empower the victims

As such, the Istanbul Convention stipulates proceeding approach in Article 55, titled as *ex parte and ex officio proceedings* as:

> Parties shall ensure that investigations into or prosecution of offences established in accordance with Articles 35, 36, 37, 38 and 39 of this Convention shall not be wholly dependent upon a report or complaint filed by a victim if the offence was committed in whole or in part on its territory, and that the proceedings may continue even if the victim withdraws her or his statement or complaint.

We deliberately used the verb "promote" above. It is true that the Convention promotes *ex officio* prosecution of domestic violence cases. In so doing, this provision indeed does not explicitly require a State to provide *ex officio* prosecution. Neither does it prohibit any *ex parte* prosecution. Rather, it does so implicitly by disallowing "be wholly dependent upon a report or complaint filed by a victim."[95] That

---

[91] Explanatory Report of the Istanbul Convention for Art. 55, para. 282.

[92] Council of Europe Convention on Preventing and Combating Violence Against Women and Domestic Violence (2011), Art. 55 (1). United Nations General Assembly 65/228 (21 December 2010) Strengthening crime prevention and criminal justice responses to violence against women, https://www.unodc.org/documents/commissions/CCPCJ/Crime_Resolutions/2010-2019/2010/General_Assembly/A-RES-65-228.pdf. Pais (2019), p. 28; Nakane (2021), p. 147.

[93] See Steinl (2021), pp. 829–830.

[94] Explanatory Report of the Istanbul Convention for Art. 55, paras. 279–282.

[95] See Steinl (2021), pp. 822, 828–829.

means a State can be dependent upon pursuance of a complaint either partially or to some degree. The Explanatory Report further elaborates that "the drafters decided to use the terms 'wholly dependent' in order to address procedural differences in each legal system, bearing in mind that ensuring the investigations or prosecution of the offences listed in this article is the responsibility of the state and its authorities."[96] This is criticized as an ambiguous rule because the term, "wholly dependent," is open to interpretation.[97]

Crime types listed in this article are as following: physical violence (Art. 35), sexual violence, including rape (Art. 36), forced marriage (Art. 37), female genital mutilation (Art. 38) and forced abortion and forced sterilization (Art. 39). Particularly, the first two crime types are committed in domestic settings. As a matter of fact, the Convention's Explanatory Report for Art. 55 states that "the fact that many of the offences covered by this Convention are perpetrated by family members, intimate partners or persons in the immediate social environment of the victim and the resulting feelings of shame, fear and helplessness lead to low numbers of reporting and, subsequently, convictions." The Explanatory Report of the Convention further states as follows:

> Conscientious of the particularly traumatising nature of the offences covered by this article, the drafters sought to ease the burden which lengthy criminal investigations and proceedings often place on the victims while at the same time ensuring that perpetrators are brought to justice. The aim of this provision is therefore to enable criminal investigations and proceedings to be carried out without placing the onus of initiating such proceedings and securing convictions on the victim.

It cannot be directly concluded that the approach of Istanbul Convention is toward *ex officio* prosecution of domestic violence cases.[98] Furthermore, the Convention follows a *crime catalogue-based approach* in regulating *ex officio/ex parte* proceedings (Art. 55). This can be one of deficiencies of the Convention. Because it does not adopt a holistic approach as to how the initiating criminal procedure for domestic violence by ignoring domestic violence cases' peculiarities and challenges as crimes committed in domestic settings, even if the Convention's Explanatory Report paid attention to that many of the offences listed in Article are *perpetrated by family members, intimate partners or persons in the immediate social environment of the victim.*[99] It rather considers a "traumatising nature of the offences."[100] Minor physical violence does not fall under this catalogue.[101] What about the complexities and peculiarities of domestic violence? To illustrate, considering the repetitive nature of domestic violence, psychological violence can be equally damaging for victims just as psychical violence can be. However, the crime catalogue for *ex officio*

[96] Explanatory Report of the Istanbul Convention for Art. 55, para. 280. See also Sosa (2020), p. 37.

[97] Niemi and Sanmartin (2020), p. 91. See also Leskinen (2020), p. 149.

[98] Cf. Pais (2019), p. 28; Nakane (2021), p. 147.

[99] Explanatory Report of the Istanbul Convention for Art. 55, para. 280.

[100] Ibid, para. 279.

[101] Burek (2020), p. 280.

prosecution does not cover psychological violence regulated in Article 33 of the Convention for *ex officio* prosecution in Art. 55.

What's more, the Convention, thus, is based on the seriousness of the crime. As such, we argue that it embraced a "middle ground" or "in-between" approaches by disagreeing with Nakane's argument that the existing CoE law does not suggest an "in-between" approach as opposed to Germany.[102] Indeed, Article 55 of the Convention is one of those articles which mostly contained reservation, such as from Armenia, Finland, Latvia, North Macedonia, Poland, Romania, Slovenia and Switzerland.[103] The main ground for reservation was to exclude "minor offences" from such *ex officio* prosecution and in so doing provide the prosecutor with a discretionary power on weight for *public interest*[104] as to whether to prosecute the case.[105] To determine what constitutes "*minor offences*" of physical violence is left to Parties.[106] Further, the Convention's understanding of minor offence is itself already broad, and as such it represents *a high threshold*[107] as the Explanatory Report states:

> The drafters wished to make a clear distinction between serious offences of physical violence resulting in severe bodily harm or deprivation of life which would be then excluded by this possibility of reservation and other, minor, offences of physical violence which do not lead to such consequences.[108]

Niemi and Sanmartin criticize this interpretation provided by the Explanatory Report as "going too far."[109] Indeed, the textual content of Article 55 did not reflect upon its title, *Ex parte and ex officio proceedings.* That being said, an exact inference that the approach of Istanbul Convention mandates an *ex officio* prosecution for every type of domestic violence cases cannot be drawn.

The Convention's broad understanding of minor offence and these reservations made by signature parties prove that jurisdictions seek for a dosage not an impetus in prosecution of domestic violence. The same applies to the Convention by virtue of its adaptation of a "middle ground" approach. Do we need a dosage to serve for public interest, a dosage to serve for right to have a privacy, a dosage to serve for autonomy and self-determination right, a dosage to mitigate the concerns for retaliation and escalating effects and a dosage to prevent victims from revictimization etc.? It is still worth to raise the question whether there is a linear relationship between the seriousness of crime and combatting domestic violence.

---

[102] Cf. Nakane (2021), p. 165.

[103] https://www.coe.int/en/web/conventions/full-list?module=declarations-by-treaty&numSte=210&codeNature=0.

[104] Steinl (2021), pp. 830–831.

[105] See also Burek (2020), p. 285.

[106] Explanatory Report of the Istanbul Convention for Art. 55, para. 281.

[107] Niemi and Sanmartin (2020), p. 91.

[108] Explanatory Report of the Istanbul Convention for Art. 55, para. 281.

[109] Niemi and Sanmartin (2020), p. 91.

Directive (EU) 2024/1385 of the European Parliament and of the Council of 14 May 2024 on combating violence against women and domestic violence has taken the Convention approach one step further by stipulating in Article 15/3 that "where the competent authorities have reasonable grounds to suspect that a criminal offence might have been committed, they shall, without undue delay, effectively investigate, upon receipt of a complaint or on their own initiative, acts of violence against women or domestic violence".[110] As such, this provision requires avoiding over-reliance on the victim complaint and in so doing it reserves the public authorities initiatives as a norm.

4 Prosecuting Domestic Violence in Türkiye: A Constitutional Debate

In a search for a dosage or an impetus in prosecution of domestic violence cases within some set of crime types, Türkiye opted for an impetus. Apart from this, simply curable injury committed against spouse or ex-spouse is regulated as *ex officio* prosecuted crime during the penal reforms in 2000s. As a matter of fact, Türkiye, in 2011, had made no reservation to Article 55 of the Convention.[111] In Turkish law, the crime of injury is so designed to protect both the physical and psychological well-being of a human. As a consequence, the *ex officio* prosecution covers not only minor physical violence, but also psychological violence.

4.1 An Overview

The rationale behind this impetus is that domestic violence remains a significant problem in Türkiye.[112] Indeed, national studies measuring domestic violence against women have found that the proportion of women experiencing violence is between 35% and 38%.[113] To combat domestic violence, a set of amendments have been made to the Penal Code of 2005. Firstly, the commission of certain set of crimes against the spouse/ex-spouse, or against the blood relatives by descent and ascendancy has been accepted as qualified forms that increases the penalty.[114] Secondly, special bureaus under the prosecutorial structure have been established to

[110] Directive 2024/1385, Art. 15/3. See also Art. 12/5.

[111] See introduction to this chapter.

[112] Kaptanoğlu et al. (2015), p. 31.

[113] Gülseren and Başterzi (2012) p. 200; Kaptanoğlu et al. (2015), p. 83.

[114] Law No. 7331 on Amendments to the Code of Criminal Procedure and Certain Laws was published in the Official Gazette of the Republic of Türkiye dated July 14, 2021 and numbered 31541.

investigate and prosecute these crimes committed in a domestic setting.[115] Thirdly, several additional measures, including protection orders that can be used in domestic violence, have been put into force with Law No. 6284 which represents the adaptation of the Istanbul Convention into the Turkish law in 2012. Therefore, all concepts and institutions of the Convention are in application in Türkiye, even if Türkiye withdrew from the Convention in 2021.

The Turkish Penal Code (TPC) adopts an *ex officio* investigation procedure for various types of crimes to ensure that domestic violence cases are not ignored and that victims are provided with the necessary protection and support. Many victims of domestic violence in Türkiye may refrain from reporting these cases to the competent authorities due to fear of the perpetrator's violence again or social stigma, or because they internalize violence as *Opuz v. Türkiye* (2009) revealed. Considering these issues, the importance of *ex officio* investigation should be particularly emphasized. As a matter of the ECtHR in the Opuz case stated:

> There are many barriers facing women who need access to justice and protection from violence. Police officers often believe that their duty is to encourage women to return home and "make peace" and fail to investigate the women's complaints. Many women, particularly in rural areas, are unable to make formal complaints, because leaving their neighborhoods subjects them to intense scrutiny, criticism and, in some cases, violence,[116]

Along with the important amendments to the TPC in terms of DV, it is necessary to evaluate some of crime types that can be applied on the matter. In Türkiye, Article 2 of the Law No. 6284 defines domestic violence as "any physical, sexual, psychological and economical violence between the victim of violence and the perpetrator of violence and between the family members and the people who are considered as a family member whether they live or do not live in the same house." Respectively, it defines violence against women as "the gender (sex)- based discrimination directed against a woman just because she is a woman or that affects women disproportionately and any attitude and behavior violating the human rights of women and defined as violence in this Law."[117] However, these definitions do not contain a useful structure in terms of criminal law because there are no crime types titled "domestic violence" and "violence against women" in the TPC apart from *the maltreatment of a family member* which has existed as classical and a substitute (general) crime type in continental European jurisdictions to protect family order.[118] Consequently, the acts included in the aforementioned definitions do not fully fall within the scope of criminal law in every instance.[119]

---

[115] These special bureaus were established by the following law: Law No. 6284 on the Protection of the Family and Prevention of Violence against Women [Ailenin Korunması ve Kadına Karşı Şiddetin Önlenmesine Dair Kanun].

[116] *Opuz v. Türkiye*, par. 102.

[117] Law No. 6284 on the Protection of the Family and Prevention of Violence against Women [Ailenin Korunması ve Kadına Karşı Şiddetin Önlenmesine Dair Kanun].

[118] Erbaş (2021), p. 5.

[119] Ibid.

4.2 *Relevant Crime Types Ex-Officio Prosecuted*

The acts which shall be considered within the domestic violence or violence against women definitions of Law No. 6284 may fall under some standard crime types such as murder, injury, sexual assault, threat or defamation, etc., because no crime provision as domestic violence or violence against women appeared in the TPC. Due to the absence of separate crime types titled "domestic violence" or "violence against women," it is challenging for researchers to find out whether a given case or file is related to domestic violence or violence against women.[120] It, thus, necessitates to demonstrate the possible crime types under which the violence in domestic setting falls and as such, to analyze their investigation procedures on whether they are *ex officio* investigated or not.

First of all, it would be appropriate to examine the crime of "maltreatment of a family member" (Art. 232, TPC), which stands as a traditional crime type under the title of "Crimes Against the Family Order." The act of maltreatment is so criminalized by stating that "any person who maltreats a person that they are living together within the same dwelling, shall be sentenced to imprisonments from two months up to one year." This crime is investigated *ex officio* as it is stated in the preamble of the article that what should be understood by the act of ill-treatment are acts that are incompatible with mercy, compassion, and pity.[121] To illustrate, leaving a person without food and water or forcing them to work under difficult conditions. In a case by the Court of Cassation, the imposition of a criminal sanction on the defendant who cut the hair of a sister who ran away from home to scare her was not found to be correct, and continuity was also required within the crime of maltreatment.[122]

Any other acts of domestic violence, such as psychological or economic violence, which may not fall under other crime types in TPC, such as injury, can be punished though the crime of maltreatment at this point. Because this crime serves as a substitute of (general) crime to protect family order. However, it should be reiterated that this crime type applies only to persons living together in the same dwelling. Although this crime type serves as a general crime type and it is investigated *ex officio*, this crime type has not been used effectively. It is observed that there is a striking point in the Judicial Statistics for 2021 published by the Ministry of Justice.[123] In 2021, only 5485 investigations were initiated across Türkiye on account of this type of crime, and only 1563 of them resulted in public prosecutions. When other types of crimes are analyzed based on Judicial Statistics, it is seen that this type of crime is not used effectively, both in terms of the number of investiga-

---

[120] Erbaş (2020), p. 233.

[121] Türkiye Büyük Millet Meclisi [Grand National Assembly of Türkiye] (2003) Draft Turkish Penal Code and Justice Commission Report (1/593). https://www5.tbmm.gov.tr/tutanaklar/TUTANAK/TBMM/d22/c059/tbmm22059119ss0664.pdf.

[122] Yargıtay [Court of Cassation], Ceza Genel Kurulu E:2016/1412, K: 2020/8, 16.01.2020. https://karararama.yargitay.gov.tr/.

[123] Ministry of Justice (2021), Judicial Statistics 2021, https://adlisicil.adalet.gov.tr/Home/SayfaDetay/adalet-istatistikleri-yayin-arsivi.

tions initiated for this crime and the number of cases filed in these investigations. A similar situation is observed in all crimes under the heading of "offences against the family order" in the Judicial Statistics.

After the withdrawal from the Istanbul Convention in 2021, a set of substantial changes regarding violence against women were introduced to the Penal Code. First, committing crime of injury against not only a spouse, but also an ex-spouse (divorce) became aggravated circumstance.[124] It is argued that violence against the spouse, committed against the person who lives in the marital union and is defenseless, involves more injustice than other types of violence.[125] At this point, even though they do not live in the same residence, their vulnerability continues due to reasons such as knowing the divorced spouse's life routines, having a common environment, and having joint children. The most fundamental source for the protection of ex-spouses as victims of violence against women is the Istanbul Convention. In Article 46 of the Istanbul Convention titled "aggravating circumstances," the ex-spouse is also listed.[126] The ECHR's judgment in *M.G. v. Türkiye* also emphasized the need to provide effective protection against ex-spouses.[127] Therefore, considering the statistically high number of cases of violence against divorced spouses,[128] this amendment is an important step toward the protection of women.

In 2022, a highly controversial amendment that *committing some crime types against women* is accepted as an aggravated form of a set of crime types which consist of intentional homicide, intentional injury, torture, and deprivation of liberty. As such, if the victims of these crimes are women, this requires the increase of the punishment and as such it is an *ex officio* prosecution. For injuries that can be remedied by simple medical intervention, if it is committed against a woman, the punishment shall not be lower than 6 months whereas it is a lower range of 4 months for an ordinary case. The same is applied to the crime of threat. If the crime of threat is committed against a woman, the punishment shall not be less than 9 months whereas it is a lower range of 6 months for an ordinary case. As for insult and stalking in domestic settings, these crime types are *ex parte* investigated just as out of domestic settings.

This amendment, at first glance, can be assumed as a comprehensive protection to women in terms of criminal law. At a closer look, it stands as *a populist attempt* in the aftermath of withdrawal from the Istanbul Convention. Indeed, the regulation that subjects the commission of certain types of crimes against women to a higher penalty is, in our opinion, incomplete for various reasons. What's more, this incomplete form brings a constitutional debate on the principle of equality. The amendment, which was considered to be introduced as a requirement of the principle of

[124] Law No. 7331 on Amendments to the Code of Criminal Procedure and Certain Laws was published in the Official Gazette of the Republic of Türkiye dated July 14, 2021 and numbered 31541.

[125] Dönmez (2021), p. 607.

[126] Ibid, p. 621.

[127] *M.G. v. Türkiye* (646/10), 22.03.2016, par. 76.

[128] Gülseren and Ünal (2020), p. 89.

equality, was criticized also in the parliamentary debates as it could lead to practice to the detriment of women.[129] It was argued that the phrase "against women" should be substituted with the phrase "gender-based violence against women and violence perpetrated against a woman because she is a woman or violence that disproportionately affects women."[130]

By virtue of the current provisions, the punishment in the aforementioned crimes where a woman stands as a victim of crime is automatically increased. Especially in non-gender-based acts against women, even if a woman commits these crimes against another woman without any gender-based discrimination motives, the punishment is still to be increased. This argument was raised also in the parliamentary discussions on the amendments to the law but was not taken into account. In the transcript of the meeting, the opinion on the current regulation is as follows: "I said that it would not provide the expected benefit and that it might increase the penalties to be imposed on women due to its sloppiness. Because it is so arranged that when women threaten women or cause injuries in a fight, they will be sentenced to harsher penalties than men. Thereupon, a deputy defending the bill responded to me half-jokingly and half-seriously by saying, "women are naive creatures, fighting and threats do not suit them. They don't fight and so on."[131]

The punishment's lower limits for threat and injury when they are committed against a woman was alleged unconstitutional as it breaches the equality principle ensured in Art. 10 of the Turkish Constitution. Therefore, it was brought before the Turkish Constitutional Court in 2022 and, on 5 January, 2023, the Court rejected the allegation and held these deviations *proportional*[132] by stating that:

> The discretion of the law-maker is wider, when it comes to penal policy. It is observed that the law-maker has adopted this deviations which is a matter of the allegation by parties in this case in order to solve the problem of violence against women, which the Court considers to have become widespread problem in our country, and in this context, it should be taken on that women are more vulnerable than men in terms of intentional injury and threat crimes.[133]

It is remarkable that the Court reasoned its judgment on the vulnerability of women which the State should take into account due to positive obligation and therefore it held:

> ...[T]he concept of violence against women has not been used in a technical and narrow sense. With these provisions, it is aimed to prevent all kinds of violence against women regardless of the perpetrator's motive,

not just because of the societal perception of gender.[134]

---

[129] Türkiye Büyük Millet Meclisi [Grand National Assembly of Türkiye] (2022), pp. 107, 108. https://www5.tbmm.gov.tr/sirasayi/donem27/yil01/ss323.pdf.

[130] Ibid, pp. 107, 108.

[131] Ibid, p. 23.

[132] Anayasa Mahkemesi, E: 2022/117, K: 2023/4, 05.01.2023, paras. 19, 20 and 21. https://www.resmigazete.gov.tr/eskiler/2022/12/20221206-6.pdf.

[133] Ibid, par. 19.

[134] Ibid.

The Court underpinned the deviations stemming from this impetus by holding the provision as constitutional. The reasoning of the Court for deviation in the punishment when women are victim does not represent a novelty. It was based on the main arguments in the previous case law in 2008 and 2020 for allegations that the minor injury against spouse/divorced spouse as an *ex officio* prosecuted act breaches the equality principle.

4.3 *Minor Injury as Ex-Officio Prosecuted Act Under the Constitutional Review*

As mentioned in the introduction, in regard to injuries that can be remedied by a simple medical treatment committed against the spouse or the divorced spouse, this incident is investigated *ex officio*, although it is prosecuted by complaint in other cases. Furthermore, in this case, the punishment shall be increased by half. This provision, which was part of TPC in 2005, was brought before the Constitutional Court first in 2008 and then 2020 through the concrete norm control by some first instance courts by claiming that it breaches the principle of equality in Art. 10. Further it is argued why the simple injury is *ex officio* prosecuted crime, while a heavier crime type, *marital rape* (Art. 102/2 of TPC), is an *ex parte* prosecuted crime. In both years, the Constitutional Court, held the *ex officio* prosecution of simple injury against spouse and divorced spouse in complying with the principle of equality in Art. 10. A such, it rejected the argument that Türkiye's choice that avoiding dosage and opting for impetus in prosecution of domestic violence is a trigger of a constitutional debate on equality principle.

The Court states: "Having considered the statistics prepared by national and international organizations, crimes committed in domestic settings and the consequences of these crimes are the common problem of all societies. It is observed that that States take some criminal, legal and administrative measures to prevent these crimes, taking into account their social background, traditions and psychological tendencies of their individuals. As such, some States adopted an *ex officio* prosecution, while some others opt for an *ex parte* prosecution policy. As for our country, the Court notes that the law-maker considered the probable pressure on victim to prevent the complaint, as such adopted an *ex officio* prosecution policy for simple injury against spouse/ex-spouse. The law maker took into account the comprehensive legal and administrative studies carried out in recent years for the prevention of domestic violence incidents and aimed the effective punishment of domestic violence offenders for injury which can be eliminated with simple medical intervention which is one of the most common manifestations of domestic violence."[135]

Some judges dissented to the judgment in both 2008 and 2020. The dissenting opinion argues that an *ex officio* prosecution for simple injury by a spouse breaches

[135] Anayasa Mahkemesi, E: 2005/151, K:2008/37, 03.01.2008 and Anayasa Mahkemesi, E.2019/2, K.2020/28, 11.06.2020.

not only principle of equality, but also it breaches the State's duty to protect the family ensured in Art. 41 in the Constitution. Accordingly, it considers that this prosecutorial policy does not provide a sphere of protection, but it *damages the private sphere* as it leads to incarceration of spouses, which is irreversible. That being said, an option for the victims to withdraw her/his complaint should have been reserved by law as well as restorative justice should have been allowed. After all, the right to private life was considered for *marital rape* (Art. 102/2 of TPC). What's more, according to dissenting opinion, this penal policy is based on that the presumption that any reconciliation or forgiveness among family members is not possible without any external pressure, which is contrary to the right to living in *a sense of justice* ensured in Art. 2 and *peace in society* ensured in Art. 5 in the Constitution. In a nutshell, it is argued that subjecting one of the spouses to sanction due to a "simple" incident that they may resolve between themselves and that the reflection of this domestic issue by the judicial authorities may have irreparable consequences, and finally that an *ex officio* investigation may serve to disrupt the family unity.

According to the Constitutional Court, in order to achieve a *peace in society* ensured in Art. 5 in the Constitution, firstly domestic violence cases have to be prevented because moral and physical well-being of individuals in the family, which forms the basis of society, depends on ensuring an environment of peace and security in society. The Court further elaborates that:

> The law-maker can distinguish between crimes that should be *ex officio* or *ex parte* prosecuted crimes by taking into account the gravity of the crimes, their importance in terms of public order, the right to private life and similar factors. Making this distinction, within the framework of constitutional principles, lies at the discretion of the law-maker by considering social needs. In order to reduce crimes in domestic settings and prevent crimes committed within the family to be covered up, the law-maker may envisage the introduction of ex officio prosecution for the case of family members who are most obliged to treat each other with compassion, intentionally injure each other.

The Constitutional Court further took into consideration past experiences, and evaluated the *ex officio* prosecution policy here as a requirement of the positive obligation of the State and as a result of the legislator's penal policy preference. The Constitutional Court agrees with the law maker's approach in 2005 that the crime of injury may serve as a key catalyst in combatting domestic violence and violence against women in Türkiye.[136]

What's more, it should be highlighted that simple medical intervention may not seem very serious in terms of its consequences; it may be degrading, especially when committed between spouses. As the cases of injuries that can be eliminated by simple medical intervention are ignored, this will lead to more severe and grave consequences both for the victim and for the families that make this situation a domestic issue with the motive of defending the family structure. This process and the grave consequences of this process have found their place in cases such as *Opuz*

---

[136] Ibid.

v. Türkiye and *Talpis v. Italy*,[137] which have been reflected on the agenda of the ECtHR. Considering the unfairness of the crime committed against the spouse, it is obvious that this crime involves a more severe unfairness than any ordinary simple injury and should be investigated *ex officio* by the positive obligation of the state.

4.4 Ex Officio Intervention in Terms of Cautionary Decisions: Prevention

Addressing both prevention and punishment is crucial in cases of domestic violence and respectively violence against women. Criminal law primarily focuses on post-violence punishment; however, it should be noted that "*prevention of violence is as important as its punishment.*"[138] In addition, since there are also measures that can be applied *ex officio* in our laws, this issue is also important for our subject.

Law No. 6284 introduces some important principles to combat violence against women and domestic violence. In this respect, important reforms include the fact that the women's statement shall be the basis for the issuance of a protective cautionary decision, since no evidence or documents shall be sought for the perpetration of violence, and *ex officio* decision-making in certain measures.[139] In this Law, prepared in parallel with the Istanbul Convention, measures are divided into two categories: protective and preventive measures. Protective measures are aimed at persons who have been subjected to violence or are in danger of being subjected to violence, while preventive measures are aimed at persons who have committed or are likely to commit violence. Protective measures are decisions that can also be taken by the local authority and law enforcement in cases where a delay is considered to be risky. Family courts can issue both protective and preventive cautionary decisions.

This law introduces significant changes to the Turkish legal system, allowing civilian authorities to take protective measures without evidence upon notification from relevant parties or *ex officio*.[140] This provision addresses situations where victims may be prevented from applying or forced to withdraw their application by the perpetrator or relatives.[141] Consequently, unless concrete proof of ceased violence and threats is provided, the victim's request to not issue or lift a cautionary decision will not affect the outcome. These measures include providing shelter, temporary financial assistance, and temporary protection in life-threatening situations. In urgent cases, even the chief of police can make decisions, subject to later approval by civilian authorities. This law's extension of power to law enforcement officers is seen as a positive

---

[137] *Talpis v. Italy* (41237/14), 02.03.2017.

[138] Ercoşkun Şenol (2019), p. 423.

[139] Law No. 6284 on the Protection of the Family and Prevention of Violence against Women [Ailenin Korunması ve Kadına Karşı Şiddetin Önlenmesine Dair Kanun].

[140] Şen (2018), p. 151.

[141] Ercoşkun Şenol (2019), p. 450.

development due to the urgency of decisions.[142] Judges may also order additional protective measures, such as workplace changes and identity alterations.

5 Conclusion

> To condemn and control violence against women, we have to make some hard choices-choices that challenge some assumptions about the nature of family violence and the role of domestic violence victims in the criminal process.[143]

This chapter is based upon a preposition that an important aspect of the criminal and penal policy's response to domestic violence is to break the cycle of violence through a prosecution policy as *ex officio* investigation. Domestic violence inherently suffers from the public-private dichotomy. As such, it considers the Istanbul Convention's approach taking on the traumatizing nature of crimes which are committed in domestic settings, which aims to ease the burden of the victim during criminal procedure as well as the ECtHR's case law. Further, the chapter brings to the light that Directive (EU) 2024/1385 of the European Parliament and of the Council of 14 May 2024 on combating violence against women and domestic violence has taken the Istanbul Convention's approach one step further by requiring avoiding over-reliance on the victim complaint and by reserving the public authorities initiatives as a norm (Art. 15). Considering the Directive (EU) 2024/1385 is the most recent legal action in Europe, the tendency in combatting domestic violence and violence against women is towards the acknowledging the need for impetus.

The chapter demonstrated two main approaches, *ex parte* and *ex officio*, as to how to initiate criminal procedure for the crimes committed in domestic settings. Furthermore, it shows Türkiye's choice that avoiding dosage and opting for impetus in prosecution of domestic violence has triggered a constitutional debate on equality principle. The Turkish Constitutional Court cannot ignore the underlying concept regarding the prevailing of patriarchy as a power imbalance based on gender in a given society. The Turkish examples demonstrate the need for impetus, rather than a dosage in approaching to prosecution of domestic violence because a dosage approach may fail in breaking down the public/private dichotomy.

References

Ateş Sarıdağ BH (2022) Kadına Karşı Şiddet Vakalarında Risk Değerlendirmesi ve Analizi. In: Erbaş R (ed) Ceza Hukuku Perspektifinden Kadına Yönelmiş Şiddetle Mücadele I. Adalet Yayınevi, Ankara, pp 11–44

Ávila TP (2018) Facing domestic violence against women in Brazil: advances and challenges. Int J Crime Justice Soc Democr 7(1):15–29

---

[142] Şen (2018), p. 151.

[143] Hanna (1996), p. 1909.

Birzu B (2019) Domestic violence in the Romanian law. In: Boldea I, Sigmirean C (eds) Identity and dialogue in the era of globalization social sciences. Arhipelag XXI Press, pp 288–292

Burek W (2020) Reservations and declarations under the Istanbul Convention. In: Niemi J, Peroni L, Stoyanova V (eds) International law and violence against women Europe and the Istanbul Convention. Routledge, New York, pp 277–295

Clark NL (1987) Crime begins at home: let's stop punishing victims and perpetuating violence. William Mary Law Rev 28(2):263–294

Corsilles A (1994) No-drop policies in the prosecution of domestic violence cases: guarantee to action or dangerous solution. Fordham Law Rev 63(3):853–882

Dobash RE (2003) Domestic violence: arrest, prosecution, and reducing violence. Criminol Public Policy 2:313–318. https://doi.org/10.1111/j.1745-9133.2003.tb00127.x

Dönmez E (2021) Kasten Öldürme Suçunun Eski Eşe Karşı İşlenmesi. Hacettepe Hukuk Fakültesi Dergisi 11:594–628

Douglas H, Fitzgerald R (2021) Proving non-fatal strangulation in family violence cases: a case study on the criminalisation of family violence. Int J Evid Proof 25(4):350–370

Ellison L (2002) Prosecuting domestic violence without victim participation. Mod Law Rev 65:834–858

Epstein D, Bell ME, Goodman LA (2003) Transforming aggressive prosecution policies: prioritizing victims' long-term safety in the prosecution of domestic violence cases. Am Univ J Gend Soc Policy Law 11(2):465–498

Erbaş R (2020) Effective criminal investigations in combating domestic violence and the ECtHR: Prima Ratio v. Ultima Ratio? In: Stradella E (ed) Gender based approaches to the law and jurisdiction Europe. Pisa University Press, Pisa, pp 221–240

Erbaş R (2021) Effective criminal investigations for women victims of domestic violence: the approach of the ECtHR. Women's Stud Int Forum 86:1–12

Ercoşkun Şenol HK (2019) Ailenin Korunması ve Kadına Karşı Şiddetin Önlenmesine Dair Kanun Üzerine Bir İnceleme. Uyuşmazlık Mahkemesi Dergisi 13:423–459

Flannigan KR (2013) The importance of prosecution policies in domestic violence cases. Criminol Public Policy 12(3):481–490. https://doi.org/10.1111/1745-9133.12058

Friskney R, Brooks-Hay O, Burman M (2021) Frontline responses to domestic abuse in Scotland. In: Lobnikar B, Vogt C, Kersten J (eds) Improving frontline responses to domestic violence in Europe. University of Maribor Press, Maribor, pp 239–256

Gülseren L, Başterzi AD (2012) Kadına yönelik aile içi şiddet: klinik uygulamada yaklaşım ve sorumluluklar. Psikiyatride Güncel Dergisi 2:199–209

Gülseren L, Ünal B (2020) COVID-19 pandemisinin görünmeyen yüzü: Aile içi kadına yönelik şiddet. Klinik Psikiyatri Dergisi 23:89–94

Hagemann-White C (2017) Responses to domestic violence in Germany in a European context. In: Buzawa ES, Buzawa C (eds) Global responses to domestic violence. Springer International Publishing, pp 87–105

Hagemann-White C (2019) Redress, rights, and responsibilities – institutional frameworks of domestic violence intervention in four countries. In: Hagemann-White C, Kelly L, Meysen T (eds) Interventions against child abuse and violence against women: ethics and culture in practice and policy. Verlag Barbara Budrich, pp 87–103

Hanna C (1996) No right to choose: mandated victim participation in domestic violence prosecutions. Harv Law Rev 109(8):1849–1910

Hera G, Szego D (2021) Frontline response to high impact domestic violence in Hungary. In: Lobnikar B, Vogt C, Kersten J (eds) Improving frontline responses to domestic violence in Europe. University of Maribor Press, Maribor, pp 201–214

Herbinger P, Neunkirchner M, Leonhardmair N (2021) Frontline response to high impact domestic violence in Austria. In: Lobnikar B, Vogt C, Kersten J (eds) Improving frontline responses to domestic violence in Europe. University of Maribor Press, Maribor, pp 95–116

Kaptanoğlu İY, Çavlin A, Ergöçmen BA (2015) Türkiye'de Kadına Yönelik Aile içi Şiddet Araştırması, Hacettepe Üniversitesi Nüfus Etütleri Enstitüsü, pp 31–45

Krieger S (2002) The dangers of mediation in domestic violence cases. Cardozo Women's Law J 8(2):235–260

Leskinen M (2020) The Istanbul Convention on sexual offences: a duty to reform the wording of national law or the way we think? In: Niemi J, Peroni L, Stoyanova V (eds) International law and violence against women Europe and the Istanbul Convention. Routledge, New York, pp 133–156

Meysen T, Grafe B (2019) Protection and self-determination. In: Hagemann-White C, Kelly L, Meysen T (eds) Interventions against child abuse and violence against women: ethics and culture in practice and policy, pp 134–150

Mills LG (1998) Mandatory arrest and prosecution policies for domestic violence: a critical literature review and the case for more research to test victim empowerment approaches. Crim Just Behav 25(3):306–318

Mordini NM (2004) Mandatory state interventions for domestic abuse cases: an examination of the effects on victim safety and autonomy. Drake Law Rev 52:295–329

Nakane T (2021) Prosecution ex officio or following a complaint by the victim? An analysis on offences related to violence against women and sexual offences. N J Eur Crim Law 12(2):146–165

Niemi J, Sanmartin AV (2020) The concepts of gender and violence in the Istanbul Convention. In: Niemi J, Peroni L, Stoyanova V (eds) International law and violence against women Europe and the Istanbul Convention. Routledge, New York, pp 77–94

Nilsson J (2012) Mandatory prosecution policies in cases of domestic violence-a state obligation under international human rights law? Master thesis, Lund University Faculty of Law, Lund

Pais P (2019) Challenging the efficacy of ex officio prosecution of domestic violence offenses: a comparative analysis. In: Tomás J, Epple N (eds) Sexuality, oppression and human rights. Brill, pp 27–45

Peterson RR, Bialo-Padin D (2012) Domestic violence is different: the crucial role of evidence collection in domestic violence cases. J Police Crisis Negot 12:103–121

Şen AA (2018) Türkiye'de Kadına Yönelik Şiddetle Mücadelede Kurumlar Arası İşbirliği Süreci ve 6284 Sayılı Yasanın Uygulanabilirliği. Motif Akademi Halkbilimi Dergisi 11:141–161

Sherman LW (1992) Influence of criminology on criminal law: evaluating arrests for misdemeanor domestic violence. J Crim Law Criminol 83(1):1–45

Sherman LW, Schmidt JD, Rogan DP, Gartin PR, Cohn EG (1991) From initial deterrence to longterm escalation: short-custody arrest for poverty ghetto domestic violence. Criminology 29:821–850

Smith DT (1995) We can settle this here or downtown: mediation or arrest for domestic violence calls Eagleston v. Guido. J Disput Resolut 2:369–382

Sosa L (2020) The Istanbul Convention in the context of feminist claims. In: Niemi J, Peroni L, Stoyanova V (eds) International law and violence against women Europe and the Istanbul Convention. Routledge, New York, pp 25–42

Steinl L (2021) Der Einfluss der Istanbul-Konvention auf das deutsche Strafrecht – Völkerrechtliche Vorgaben für den Umgang mit Gewalt gegen Frauen und häuslicher Gewalt. Zeitschrift für die gesamte Strafrechtswissenschaft 133(3):819–840. https://doi.org/10.1515/zstw-2021-0030

Thoennes N, Salem P, Pearson J (1995) Mediation and domestic violence. Fam Conciliation Courts Rev 33(1):6–29

Vassileva M, Delpeuch T (2021) Frontline response to high impact domestic violence in Bulgaria. In: Lobnikar B, Vogt C, Kersten J (eds) Improving frontline responses to domestic violence in Europe. University of Maribor Press, Maribor, pp 117–142

Wutz MC (2011) Evidentiary barriers to conviction in cases of domestic violence: a comparative analysis of Scottish and German criminal procedure. Aberdeen Stud Law Rev 2:76–98

Punitive and Preventive Measures Against Domestic Violence in Italy: A Critical Assessment

Lara Ferla

Abstract Domestic violence is a paramount and urgent issue in Italy. The latest statistics show a slight increase of reports and complaints about offences such as ill-treatment and stalking, as well as physical, psychological and sexual violence within the family and intimate personal relationships, which is a cause for concern. In this field, Law No. 69 of the 19th July 2019 (named "Red Code") implemented some important changes, both substantive and procedural, in the Italian criminal system. Recently, Law No. 168 of the 24th November 2023 has led to a strengthening of the relevant legislative tools in cases of domestic violence, including a tighten up of the preventive measures. However, a major obstacle to the application of the available laws and regulations exists, that is the difficulty of reliably predicting the dangerousness of the human behavior and the escalation of violent acts within personal relationships. As outlined by a series of judgments on this subject, considerable difficulties in ensuring prompt, proportionate and effective measures of protection for individuals exposed to violent contexts are related to the concrete possibility for public authorities to act at the most appropriate time.

1 Introduction

Statistical data collected by the Italian Ministry of Domestic Affairs updated in July 2025 indicate a growing trend in cases of ill-treatment and stalking as well as physical, sexual and psychological violence within intimate personal relationships.[1]

[1] Statistics published by the Ministry of Domestic Affairs show that the percentage of female victims of violent crimes is remarkable. In 2024, 314 murders were reported, with 111 female victims: 96 of them were murdered in a family context or in an intimate personal relationship; of

L. Ferla (✉)
Università Cattolica del Sacro Cuore, Facoltà di Giurisprudenza, Milan, Italy
e-mail: lara.ferla@unicatt.it

R. Erbaş (ed.), *Criminal Prosecution of Domestic Violence*, Ius Gentium: Comparative Perspectives on Law and Justice 128,
https://doi.org/10.1007/978-3-032-01202-9_4

Besides formal complaints, also the percentage of requests for help through the emergency phone number settled for the victims of such offences indicates a frequent phenomenon that cannot be ignored.[2] The available data do not indicate evidence of an upward trend in violent crimes, such as murders and sexual violence; however, the statistics constantly show that a high and disproportionate number of victims of these crimes are women.[3] The same information is highlighted in the final report of the Italian Parliament's Committee of inquiry on gender-based violence and femicide.[4] The report, published in November 2022, clearly illustrates the prevailing involvement of women as victims of violent crimes in the family context, which can therefore be regarded as an ongoing fact.

If caution should be paid towards general statistics, given the potential inaccuracy of the available data,[5] it is also important to consider that largely hidden nature of these phenomena suggests that the outlined results could have been underestimated.[6] These aspects explicitly highlight the urgency of addressing such forms of violence. The frequency of these crimes implies that domestic violence is a criminal phenomenon with a significant social impact, which has to be recognized.[7] Fundamental human rights—such as the right to life, to physical integrity and sexual freedom—are being threatened. Children are also involved as direct victims or witnesses of various forms of violence, with the risk of suffering long-term effects

these, 59 died at the hands of the partner or former partner. See https://www.interno.gov.it/sites/default/files/2025-07/report-ii-trimestre.pdf.

[2] ISTAT (National Statistical Institute) provides regularly up to date information regarding the requests for assistance logged through the public service's number from victims of domestic violence. The information collected by the 1522 service for the fourth quarter of 2023 provides evidence relating to the phenomenon of domestic violence, in particular regarding the trend of requests for help. Analyzing the percentage of valid calls by reason for calling, there has been an unprecedented number of help requests: from 9.796 in the first quarter to 21.132 in the fourth quarter of 2023. Data for the fourth quarter of 2024 confirm what was previously analyzed, that is, when victims contact 1522, more frequently they report physical violence as the main violence they experience; however, when considering all forms of violence, psychological violence is the most frequent. See https://www.istat.it/tavole-di-dati/il-numero-di-pubblica-utilita-1522-dati-trimestrali-al-iv-trimestre-2023-2.

[3] Despite some fluctuations from year to year, criminal justice statistics on violent crimes show a constant and high incidence of violence against women. See ISTAT (2020), pp. 58–64, and ISTAT https://www.istat.it/statistiche-per-temi/focus/violenza-sulle-donne/. On this topic, see also Merzagora (2009) and Merzagora (2023), p. 43–44.

[4] See the report "Relazione finale sull'attività della Commissione" (*Commissione parlamentare di inchiesta sul femminicidio, nonché su ogni forma di violenza di genere*), in https://www.senato.it/service/PDF/PDFServer/BGT/1361120.pdf.

[5] For a specific analysis in the field of intimate partner violence in Italy, see Capecchi (2019), pp. 2635–2645. See also Forti (2000), pp. 394–400, and Merzagora (2009)

[6] Regarding statistical data, it is necessary to consider a certain discrepancy between the offences actually committed and those detected or reported. See Parlato (2021), pp. 133–134, and Erbaş (2022), pp. xvii–xviii.

[7] See Mantovani (2013), pp. 59–62, Merzagora (2015), Gino et al. (2019), pp. 132–135.

of this exposure to harmful contexts.[8] With regard to these risks, there should always be a clear response of disapproval and condemnation by the legal system, and by the criminal law in particular. In addition to punitive actions, however, there is a growing recognition that a specific form of intervention is needed to address the root causes of such violent behaviors.[9] Only by identifying these risk factors and the psychological motivations of the individuals who commit violent acts, it will be possible for the most appropriate law enforcement measures to be arranged.[10] The protections for victims of crime need to be complemented by legislative tools for those responsible of such offences. Despite the diversity of legislative instruments available, including criminal law, there is a widespread perception that the law enforcement system is not effective.[11] On the one hand, penalties, however severe, do not seem to have a sufficient deterrent effect on the perpetrators of such offences; on the other hand, the particular harmfulness of these forms of crime does not appear to be tackled only through legal instruments.[12]

The following analysis will address some of the critical aspects of this system. Firstly, it will be provided an overview on the existing legislation on domestic violence, which is mainly regulated by the Penal Code. Then, the critical profiles of the available legislative instruments and their practical application will be discussed. In the light of these considerations, emphasis will be placed on one of the most challenging aspects of the theme, namely the possibility of formulating a reliable and effective prediction of dangerousness with respect to the offender and their behavior.

2 The Italian Criminal Law System Against Domestic Violence: An Overview

In order to outline the Italian system of measures aimed at combating domestic violence, a more precise identification of the meaning of that term is necessary. The concept of domestic violence was expressly fixed in the 2011 Istanbul Convention, which provides under Art. 3, para. b), that domestic violence includes "all acts of physical, sexual, psychological or economic violence that occur within the family or domestic unit or between former or current spouses or partners, whether or not the perpetrator shares or has shared the same residence with the victim". This broad definition is intended to allow for the identification of the various forms in which domestic violence could be expressed.

---

[8] Regarding the long-term effects experienced by minors witnessing abusive behaviors, see Di Blasio (2000), pp. 5–8.

[9] See Giulini and Xella (2011), Zara (2018).

[10] See Merzagora (2015), p. 20.

[11] See Vitarelli (2020), pp. 477–478.

[12] See Pulitanò (2017), p. 12.

With regard to the Italian legislation, conduct that can be described as "domestic violence" may have criminal relevance on the basis of various figures of crime provided in the Italian Penal Code: ill-treatment (Art. 572), sexual violence (Art. 609-*bis*), bodily harms (Arts. 582 and 583), stalking (Art. 612-*bis*), threats (Art. 612) and further crimes characterized by abusive behavior in the sphere of honor, dignity and personal freedom of the victim. Some of these figures of crime were already included in the 1930 Penal Code, the "Code Rocco" (*Codice Rocco*), as originally written.[13] In the social and cultural environment of the early decades of the twentieth century, consideration was already given to the need to fight against forms of violence that occur in a family relationship.[14] The social and cultural transformation that happened over time has led to a change in this regulatory framework, through both the introduction of new figures of crimes and the revision of those already existing.[15]

In regards to the first aspect, it is worth noting the introduction by the Law No. 38 of the 23rd April 2009 of the crime of persecutory acts (*Atti persecutori*), designed to fight the phenomenon of stalking.[16] This legislative provision, disciplined by Art. 612-*bis* of the Italian Penal Code, attributes criminal relevance to the behavior of those who, with repeated acts, harass or threaten the victim in a way that causes a serious and long-lasting state of anxiety or fear. The same provision is also applicable in cases where the victim is forced to significantly change their life habits, as a result of harassing behavior. This crime also occurs when the victim is subjected to a serious and enduring fear for his or her safety or that of a family member. Continuous subjection to forms of psychological violence is, therefore, the main characteristic of the crime of persecutory acts.[17]

To counteract the forms of domestic violence, some legal provisions already existing in the Italian penal system have been amended. In this regard, the offence of ill-treatment plays a pivotal role.[18] The term "ill-treatment", in fact, refers to a wide spectrum of acts of physical or psychological violence, which intentionally provoke a condition of suffering in the victim. This crime is regulated by Art. 572 of the Italian Penal Code (*Maltrattamenti contro familiari e conviventi*). In its original terms, this provision was intended to incriminate abusive behaviors committed within the family and against children.[19] Considering how the rule was perceived in the early decades of the twentieth century, the purpose of this crime was to protect the family in the form of a public institution, a social entity. In light of this approach,

---

[13] See Bertolino (2015), pp. 1710–1715.

[14] See Spena (2012), pp. 25–35.

[15] See Pezzini and Lorenzetti (2020), Vitarelli (2020), p. 464.

[16] See Marandola (2009), pp. 947–952.

[17] See Merzagora and Pettorossi (2009), pp. 548–560.

[18] See Bertolino (2021) and Bartoli (2022), p. 3.

[19] Under the 1930 Penal Code, Art. 572 regulated the offence of "Maltreatment in the family or against children" (*Maltrattamenti in famiglia o verso fanciulli*). In this context, the term "family" referred only to persons bound by a lawful marital relationship.

the "family order", rather than the individual's rights, was the legal interest worthiest of protection.

Currently, this rule shows a different terminology and a more complex content. The most recent formulation is the result of two legislative reforms: the first one was implemented by Law No. 172 of the 1st October 2012, which ratified the 2007 Lanzarote Convention in Italy; the second one concerns the legislative reform called "Red Code", that is the Law No. 69 of the 19th July 2019.[20] The effect of these two legislative reforms is an extension of the scope of the ill-treatment offence, with regard to the victims of the crime. Indeed, this discipline also applies to behaviors committed in the family context, even if the relationship is based on cohabitation. Therefore, even members of *de facto* family are intended to be protected against the physical and psychological violence that takes place within personal relationships. With this amendment, the profound social renovation that the family, as an institution, has undergone in recent decades has been incorporated into the legislative text.[21]

The Italian society has gradually accepted cultural models of family lacking legal recognition and has also given importance to families founded on spontaneous personal relationships.[22] Together with the traditional family model based on marriage, therefore, new forms of family are also perceived as deserving of protection. The extension of criminal protection is for individuals linked by intimate personal relationships in the absence of marriage, and it is consistent with this more recent approach.

At the same time, this legislative amendment also corresponds to the decisions of the Italian Constitutional Court. The Court was repeatedly solicited to express judgments on the legitimacy of various provisions of Italian legislation, which introduced different regulations for spouses legally married and for *de facto* family members. The main critics outlined a discriminating approach in the protection accorded to the individual, in relation to their personal status as a spouse or a partner. In the light of these doubts concerning Italian legislation and its capacity to guarantee equal protection to the rights of the person, the Court held that *de facto* families also have constitutional consideration on the basis of Art. 2 of the Italian Constitution.[23] While emphasizing the difference between this family model and that based on the legal recognition of marriage, the Court affirmed that the *de facto* family has its own dignity and socio-cultural relevance.[24] Indeed, the legal concept of *de facto* family falls within the scope of those "social communities" (*formazioni*

---

[20] For a comprehensive analysis of this legislative reform, see the Report of the Italian Supreme Court of Cassation (specifically, of the *Ufficio del massimario e del ruolo*) in https://www.portaledelmassimario.ipzs.it/frontoffice/studiPubblicazioni.do. See also Romano (2021), pp. 132–160.

[21] See Bartoli (2022), pp. 7–12 and Bertolino (2022), pp. XIX–XXVIII

[22] See Spena (2012), pp. 15–25.

[23] See Corte costituzionale, judgment No. 8 of the 18th January 1996; judgment No. 237 of the 18th November 1986.

[24] See Corte costituzionale, judgment No. 6 of the 12th January 1977.

sociali) in which the individual develops their personality (Art. 2 Constitution).[25] Through these statements, the Italian Constitutional Court affirmed the necessity for the rules that counteract violence committed within the family to be applied also to the contexts of cohabitation and intimate personal relationships.

A further significant structural change can be observed in the Art. 572, namely the provision of an aggravating circumstance in cases where the conduct of maltreatment is committed "against" or "in the presence of" a minor. The purpose of this norm is to attribute serious gravity to the crime when a child is exposed to a violent context. Based on psychological researches on the negative consequences for children who have experienced violent family situations,[26] Art. 572 of the Penal Code provides a more severe penalty whether the violent act was directly committed against a minor or in a manner that the minor involved is able to understand its harmful effects.[27] A further statement under the Art. 572 is that the child who witnesses the acts of ill-treatment "is regarded as a victim of the crime".[28] In Italy, the legal implications of this statement are a matter of discussion. According to some scholars, the crime is a unique and sole event, and the presence of the child has a functional role as aggravating circumstance. In other scholars' opinion, maltreatment committed against the adult victim and that committed against the child give rise to two different crimes.[29] This matter is currently being debated by criminal law scholars, not just in theory, but also in the light of the consequences on sentencing and convictions of the accused person. At the same time, it is noteworthy that the legal provision is aimed at affirming the seriousness of the fact, when the abuse involves minors in the role of direct victims or witnesses.

The system of repression of domestic violence can also count on the provisions designed to combat sexual violence. This matter is regulated by Art. 609-*bis* and the following of the Italian Penal Code. These rules criminalize behaviors such as forcing a person to commit or undergo sexual acts without their consent or by means of violence or threat. In the original version of the 1930 Penal Code, these regulations were included amongst the crimes against "public morality", namely according to a conception that did not recognize adequate relevance to the person and their rights in the sexual sphere. Subsequently, on the basis of a renewed consideration of human rights, in accordance with the constitutional principles, Law No. 66 of the 15th February 1996 was enacted, transferring sexual offences within the Title concerning crimes against the personal freedom. As a result of this different position in the Penal Code, the characteristic of sexual offences has been revealed as a violation of the victim's sexual freedom.

Currently, sexual crimes pose a complex system in which offences committed by adults or minors, with adult or minor victims, are differentiated. In that context, in

[25] See Martines (2020), p. 652.

[26] See, among others, Cirillo and Di Blasio (1989).

[27] See Spena (2012), Bartoli (2022) and Bertolino (2021).

[28] Art. 572, para. 4, of the Italian Penal Code.

[29] For a reconstruction of this doctrinal discussion, see Morelli (2022), pp. 415–430.

fact, it is very important to identify those aspects of the victim's particular vulnerability that make the crime more harmful. Especially in relationships of knowledge or kinship, sexual violence is particularly offensive, because it represents a betrayal of the trust, care and protection that the victim expected. As a result of the amendments introduced by the above-mentioned "Red Code", sexual crimes are also punished more harshly.[30] Under the same provisions, the Law No. 172 of the 1st October 2012 established an amendment to the statute of limitations for the offence, which takes now place over a much longer period of time.[31] This rule, in combination with the procedure of the complaints' submission, enables the victim to achieve a more effective criminal protection.[32]

All this stated, it can be inferred that the Italian penal system is articulated and, as such, provides various legislative instruments to fight the different forms of domestic violence. On paper, therefore, Italian legal system provides legal rules and disciplines which seem appropriate to respond to the different acts of aggression committed in the family context or within intimate personal relationships. Furthermore, the 2019 GREVIO report on Italy highlighted the existence of a "solid legislative framework" consisting of various regulatory provisions aimed at combating domestic violence.[33]

3 Critical Issues in Prosecuting Domestic Violence Outlined by the Italian Case-Law

The focus on the critical issues outlined in prosecuting domestic violence seems to be essential for a reflection on the aspects that need improvement to better protect the individuals involved. As a matter of fact, the analysis of the criminal case-law concerning domestic violence delivered by the Italian Courts outlines the widespread nature of this phenomenon. At the same time, the difficulties in combating these forms of violence can be explained by its heterogeneous and multifaceted characteristics, linked to its forms of manifestation, its agents, the relationship between offenders and victims, and the specific circumstances in which they occur.[34] In accordance with the definition of "domestic violence" established in the Istanbul Convention, the criminal act includes physical and sexual abuse, but also psychological threats and offences to the victim's freedom or dignity, even through the deprivation or control of economic resources. This multiplicity of possible offences

[30] See Art. 609-*bis*, para. 1, of the Italian Penal Code. The penalty of imprisonment from five to ten years was increased from six to twelve years by Art. 13, para. 1, of the Law No. 69 of the 19th July 2019.

[31] See Art. 157, para. 6, of the Italian Penal Code.

[32] On this topic, see Triggiani (2020), p. 456.

[33] See 2019 GREVIO Baseline Evaluation Report on Italy, published on 13th January 2020, p. 7.

[34] See Bartoli (2022), pp. 1–13.

leads to the application of many criminal rules, which have been upheld in the judgments of the Italian Courts.[35]

Many of these judgments pointed out the difficulty of dealing with the persons exposed to the risk of violence. Even in the cases where the victims have shown their willingness to react to the violence suffered and to invoke the protection of the criminal justice system, a critical point of the effectiveness of the legal protection is still in the identification of the appropriate time in which public authorities should get involved.[36] Domestic violence, in fact, is frequently perpetrated through conducts of physical and psychological ill-treatment, mainly charged under the above-mentioned Art. 572 of the Italian Penal Code. This crime is characterized by repeated behaviors that may occur in different forms, more or less serious, joint by their suitability to cause a condition of physical or psychological suffering to the victim.[37] When these forms of offence do not take place continuously nor throughout a long period of time, the victim may not clearly perceive a climate of oppression or imminent risk.[38] Without explicit signs of danger, it is difficult to determine whether such conducts could abruptly become more aggressive and violent. The degree of danger to the person exposed to violence, in other words, could be quite difficult to assess from the perspective of both the victim and the public authorities. Other difficulties lie in reliably predicting if habitual aggressive behaviors can reach the point where they threaten the victim's physical integrity or life. In this regard, judicial cases show that offences such as murder and serious physical injuries often result from an increase, in the offender's previous violent conduct, of harmful behaviors towards the victim.[39]

The same issues are related to criminal offences such as stalking. Criminal judgments referring to this offence confirmed that acts included in this criminological definition could be quite different. Even actions that do not involve a physical contact between the offender and the victim may be classified as stalking, such as harassment, repeated and intrusive requests for a more intimate relationship and other behaviors demonstrating a unilateral interest in the person concerned or a persecutory approach towards the same.[40] Even apparently innocuous behaviors could be signs of a conduct of stalking and could rapidly degenerate in aggressive

[35] See the data collected by the Italian Ministry of Justice in https://www.giustizia.it/cmsresources/cms/documents/codicerosso_rapporto_24nov2020.pdf.

[36] See Mantovani (2013), pp. 59–65.

[37] See, among others, Corte di cassazione, judgment No. 13067 of the 12th February 2021; judgment No. 19778 of the 26th February 2019; judgment No. 10433 of the 15th February 2018. See also Spena (2012).

[38] See Roia (2017), pp. 25–32.

[39] See, among others, Corte di cassazione, judgment No. 48945 of the 4th October 2022; judgment No. 6238 of the 29th September 2021; judgment No. 31003 of the 25th September 2020.

[40] See, in this regard, Corte di cassazione, judgment No. 20861 of the 17th March 2021; judgment No. 34757 of the 26th November 2020.

and harmful acts against the victim.[41] The Art. 612-*bis* of the Italian Penal Code (*Atti persecutori*) aims to surround with criminal relevance a large number of illicit conducts. In fact, very heterogeneous situations are described in the judgments taken under this legislative provision. Even in this case-law, it emerges that it is necessary to evaluate each case with regard to its own specificities, in the view of a particular assessment of the risk factors.

Similar difficulties are observed also in relation to criminal behavior like sexual violence (Art. 609-*bis*) and other serious psychical injuries (*Lesioni*) (Arts. 582 and 583). When these offences are perpetrated within the family or intimate personal relationships, the conduct could be hidden, as the victim may have tolerated this illicit behavior for many reasons, included the importance subjectively attributed to that relationship. Thus, the severity of violence that the offender involved is able to express could have been underestimated. Case-law concerning sexual violence outlined that the criminal conduct could appear both as an isolated act, expressed in a unique occasion, or as a usual way of living. In many cases, the sexual violence represents the final expression of an increasing aggressive behavior.[42]

In relation to these facts, many difficulties are linked to the understanding of the pathway of development of violent behavior, which could gradually increase or suddenly explode. Furthermore, difficulties of an intervention on these criminal conducts are linked to the fact that the family and intimate personal relationships take place within a private dimension characterized by feelings of affection, trust and care.[43] The confidential nature of such relationships could be an obstacle to the protection of the person exposed to violence, especially in cases where the person concerned is unwilling or unable to end the relationship or leave the family context.[44] In addition, largely held cultural conceptions perceive the family as a "private matter", a "realm of privacy",[45] protected from external interferences,[46] even if an intervention is carried out in accordance with the law and in the exclusive interest of the victim. Economic, social and cultural conditions are in some cases barriers to breaking out of the so-called "cycle of violence",[47] even if legal tools are available to facilitate this change. In cases of domestic violence, anti-violence centers' workers, psychologists, health professionals and police officers are figures with a fundamental role. They have the professional competence to interpret signs of danger and prevent them from escalating. As highlighted in the 2019 GREVIO report on Italy,

---

[41] See, among others, Corte di cassazione, judgment No. 32615 of the 14th June 2022; judgment No. 50178 of the 8th October 2019.

[42] See, among others, Corte di cassazione, judgment No. 36323 of the 26th May 2021; judgment No. 16543 of the 21st February 2017; judgment No. 24124 of the 18th February 2021.

[43] See Merzagora (2015), p. 19, Maugeri (2021), p. 77–78, Taylor and Gassner (2010), p. 241.

[44] See Corte di cassazione, judgment No. 55833 of the 18th October 2017. The Court stated that even the victim's decision to withdraw the criminal complaint showed "a condition of inferiority, psychological submissiveness and fear towards her husband".

[45] Fletcher (2020), p. 11.

[46] See Erbaş (2021), p. 105.

[47] For a detailed analysis of this topic, see Walker (1979). See also Merzagora (2009).

the continuous training of these qualified professionals is a fundamental element for the development of effective strategies against domestic violence.[48]

4 Dangerousness and Difficulties in Predicting Violent Behavior

Considering the offender's point of view in cases of domestic violence is therefore useful to identify criticisms of the Italian criminal system in its main aspects: preventive, punitive and inherent to treatment. The right approach to the personal and relational sphere, where each individual expresses their own existential condition, together with the availability of legal instruments influence the possibility to achieve concrete results in the fight against previously described behaviors. Considering the judgments of the Italian Court of Cassation, it is undeniable that certain offensive conducts are conditioned by the connotation that each person gives to human relationships and roles and how these are integrated into a specific social, cultural and moral system. Legal measures providing protection, and competences granting improved knowledge of the accused person, undoubtedly need to better coordinate, especially when it comes to crimes within the family context.[49]

An interdisciplinary approach is needed, as an appropriate response to this type of violence cannot be identified with the simple application of a criminal sanction.[50] However, the objective of improving knowledge of the offender must be compared with the tools that the legal order provides to the judicial authority and with the requirements of the proceedings.[51] During various stages of the criminal proceedings, there are occasions to investigate the personality and attitude of the individual who committed the crime.[52] In addition, with respect to domestic violence cases, the most recent reforms have introduced precise measures,[53] which can be assured via the implementation of specific psychological pathways. In this respect, it is worth mentioning Art. 165 of the Italian Penal Code, which regulates the conceding of conditional suspended sentences. Indeed, this provision subordinates the suspension of the sentence to the offender's undertaking a rehabilitation process.[54] In such manner, the less severe penalty treatment is accompanied by a commitment that can

[48] See 2019 GREVIO Baseline Evaluation Report on Italy, especially pp. 38–40. On this topic, see also Chinnici (2022), pp. 14–17.

[49] Merzagora (2015), pp. 20–22.

[50] See Garbarino and Giulini (2020), pp. 185–190.

[51] On this topic, see di Martino (2022), pp. 11–19. See also Bonini (2023), pp. 65–67.

[52] See Moscarini (2006), pp. 929–932.

[53] See Marandola (2021), pp. 161–175.

[54] See Art. 169, para. 5, of the Italian Penal Code.

allow the offender to become aware of the harmful nature of their behavior.[55] This path implies a critical review of the fact and its motivation—at a psychological level—in order to facilitate, in the future, a refusal of the offensive behavior.[56]

However, a prognostic assessment of the development of criminal behavior remains a crucial issue in order to address forms of violence in family and intimate personal relationships. This assessment implies the feasibility of a specific "prognosis" on the future behavior of offenders, their dangerousness, the risk of committing acts of equal gravity or more.[57]

During the first decades of the twentieth century, at the time of the enactment of the Italian Penal Code, this assessment assumed a strict and predefined profile, through the identification and classification of certain "types" of socially dangerous offenders.[58] In the current constitutional approach to criminal law, this conclusion is totally unacceptable.[59] It is indeed necessary that the probabilistic assessment inherent in the repetition of criminal behavior are anchored in objective elements that can then be controlled by judiciary authorities, with regard to the individual offender concerned.[60]

In the criminal law literature, specific attention has been paid to the assessment of dangerousness and the evaluation of the probabilistic elements on which this assessment could be established. If there is an agreement on the need to verify the *probability*—not the mere *possibility*—of the commission of further criminal conducts,[61] it is still difficult to give to such category a rigorous scientific ground. The characterization in terms of "dangerousness" of the offender, in fact, is not obtained "in the light of a rigorous sociological or anthropological investigation",[62] but by assuming that it is possible to refer to a pattern of behavior corresponding to a generic assessment of social expectations.[63] This assessment, however, seems to be "irreducible to a sufficiently circumscribed dimension".[64]

The emerging difficulties in providing a scientifically reliable basis for a category such as the dangerous nature of the offender are under discussion. Jurists highlight, in particular, the evident subjectivity of the assessment's foundation with respect to the probability of committing criminal behavior. These assessments are mainly based on the criterion regulated by Art. 133 of the Italian Penal Code, concerning the parameters that are applied by the judge at sentencing. Among these

[55] With regard to the importance of the link between suspended penalty and acceptance of a rehabilitation path, see the remarks of Bertolino (2021), pp. 77–78.

[56] See Garbarino and Giulini (2020), pp. 200–207. See also Forti (2021), p. 33, Giulini and Scotti (2013), pp. 1882–1883, Zara et al. (2020), p. 167, and Xella (2013)

[57] See Aliquò (2020), pp. 49–50, Paonessa (2020), pp. 1–28 and Bonini (2023), pp. 59–64.

[58] For a comprehensive analysis of this issue, see Pelissero (2008).

[59] See Bertolino (2016), p. 1377.

[60] See Art. 203 and the following of the Italian Penal Code.

[61] See Fiandaca, Musco (2024), p. 882; Marinucci et al. (2022), p. 913.

[62] See Martini (2017), p. 8.

[63] See Ibid.

[64] See Ibid.

parameters, the "criminal capacity", the "character", the "conduct" and the "condition of personal, family and social life" of the accused person are of notable importance. The critical aspect of this discipline is that these requirements are commonly interpreted without reliable scientific reference, in accordance with a generic *intuitus personae.*[65] The reference to a scientifically based framework for the relevant prognostic evaluation is all the more justified as the legal measures to be taken consist of unfavorable provisions (*in malam partem*), involving restrictions of the agent's rights and freedoms.[66] Given these uncertain premises, it becomes difficult to make a decision about a person's dangerousness. In this context, a doctrinal debate has been launched on the usefulness of the tools of artificial intelligence, and on their capacity to predict further aggressive acts that might be committed by the same offender.[67] However, while scientific expertise could provide valuable assistance in this area, the assessment of the dangerousness of human behavior involves a judgement about human personality. This assessment requires specialistic competences in behavioral sciences, a field of study focused on understanding and explaining human conduct, and it is ultimately left to the discretion of a public judicial authority, which is responsible for the decision of the offender's personal freedom.[68]

5 The Empowerment of Preventive Measures in the Italian Strategy Against Domestic Violence

Intervention based on prevention must be strengthened, especially when it comes to crimes involving acts of violence. In relation to behaviors which unequivocally express their harmful character and their risk of evolution in a more serious form, it is essential that legal regulations are allowed to develop based on a preventive strategy. This type of intervention seems to be effective, especially in cases of offensive or threatening behaviors that, even without constituting a crime, are expressed in ways that suggest a criminal progression.[69]

Even the EU statements underline the need for effective preventive action against domestic violence. The Istanbul Convention itself, which represents a considerable reference in this field,[70] expressly states the need to combine punitive tools with more comprehensive actions, including preventive measures relating to the

[65] Paonessa (2020), pp. 2–5.

[66] For further remarks, see Balbi (2017), pp. 506–507.

[67] For a comprehensive analysis of the main issues discussed, see Maugeri (2021), pp. 187–207. See also Bonini (2023), pp. 65–67.

[68] See Maugeri (2021), pp. 187–207, Bonini (2023), pp. 65–67.

[69] See Garbarino and Giulini (2022), pp. 48–51.

[70] See Bonini (2021).

offenders.[71] Recently, Directive 2024/1385/EU on combating violence against women and domestic violence is consistent with this approach, emphasizing the importance of preventive measures.[72]

Precautionary measures play an important role in this aspect. The Italian criminal justice system has indeed provided for a broad spectrum of measures, both civil and criminal. Such measures may be issued on the basis of objective and subjective requirements relating to situations in which a crime has been committed and there are indications that the offender is dangerous.[73] These measures can be applied in cases where there is evidence that a crime has actually been committed and whether there is a concrete risk that the offender may reiterate their criminal conduct.[74] The most serious precautionary measures concern restrictions of personal freedom, but other measures appear to be equally important, such as ordering the offender to leave the victim's house;[75] other measures are also useful as they provide for the prohibition of all contact with the victim of the crime.[76]

The need for timely and effective protection measures that cannot be met by the adoption of precautionary measures are at the fundaments of the orders that can be taken by the public security official, namely the *Questore*.[77] As an administrative public security authority, which has recently been entrusted with a specific role of social prevention,[78] this officer may intervene at any time before a criminal offence has been committed, at the request of the person who claimed to have suffered violence or harassment. The *Questore*'s intervention was initially planned with regard to stalking.[79] Thereafter, by Law No. 119 of the 15th October 2013, the possibility of recourse to the public safety authority was extended to cases of domestic violence.[80] Lately, Law No. 168 of the 24th November 2023 has strengthened the role of this public official by increasing the number of offences for which his intervention can be requested.[81]

---

[71] See Art. 16, para. 1 of the 2011 Istanbul Convention: «Parties shall take the necessary legislative or other measures to set up or support programs aimed at teaching perpetrators of domestic violence to adopt non-violent behavior in interpersonal relationships with a view to preventing further violence and changing violent behavioral patterns».

[72] See Art. 34 of Directive 2014/1385/EU. On this Directive, see Braschi (2024), pp. 1367–1379 and Massaro (2025), pp. 107–143.

[73] See Art. 282-*bis* and 283-*ter* of the Italian Code of Penal Procedure.

[74] On this topic, see Triggiani (2020), p. 456, Nascosi (2021), pp. 1189–1200 and Bonini (2018), pp. 117–137.

[75] See Art. 282-*bis* of the Italian Code of Penal Procedure.

[76] See Art. 282-*ter* of the Italian Code of Penal Procedure.

[77] See Marandola (2009), pp. 962–964; see also Bonini (2018), pp. 100–117, Catena (2021), pp. 851–852.

[78] See Aliquò (2020), p. 46.

[79] See Art. 8 of Law No. 38 of the 23rd April 2009.

[80] See Art. 3 of the Law No. 119 of the 15th October 2013.

[81] See Art. 1 of the Law No. 168 of the 24th November 2023.

A further important aspect of this discipline is the definition of the subject who is entitled to present a case to the *Questore*. In the event of stalking, a complaint from the victim is required to initiate this preventive measure, whereas in the case of domestic violence a non-anonymous report is sufficient. The complaint should be provided with factual and objectively verifiable information,[82] which would allow the precise cognizance of the claim's merits.[83] The warning measure, in fact, must apply "that demonstrative logic based on circumstantial and probabilistic elements that [...] informs the entire administrative law of prevention".[84]

The assessment of the facts by the public safety authority has the advantage of taking place in a shorter period of time than ordinary achievement, which results in the gathering of evidence within the criminal proceedings. In that regard, even if this measure does not provide the formal guarantees required for the application of precautionary measures, it still wouldn't imply any specific restriction of the offender's rights.[85] These measures maintain the efficiency and effectiveness of a public intervention, which has the potential to deter the accused from engaging in further harmful behavior.[86] In those aspects of this regulation, there appears to be a balance between conflicting requirements: on one hand, to ensure that the adoption of the administrative measure is justified by reliable and verifiable information which clearly indicates that an unlawful act has been committed; on the other hand, to facilitate the conduct of procedural investigations, so as to avoid that the course of an excessively long period frustrates the need to protect people exposed to violence.[87] The preventive aim of this administrative warning operates with regard to personal relationships that manifest "degenerative signals",[88] in order to avoid more serious consequences. Otherwise, if this measure does not explain any deterrent effects, the administrative official has the power to initiate criminal proceedings *ex officio* based on the information and the evidence gathered.[89]

From the accused person's point of view, the specificity of the measure and its correlation with precise and verifiable facts may allow an awareness of the illegality of their conduct. In the meantime, the public official's intervention could opportunely suggest that the acts perpetrated have been considered harmful according to the counterpart's perspective.[90]

Within the framework of the organizational competences assigned to the *Questore*, coordination initiatives with the institutions in charge of reporting

---

[82] See Consiglio di Stato, judgment No. 3493 of the 31st May 2018. On this point, see also Fiandaca and Musco (2024), p. 934.

[83] See Aliquò (2020), p. 45.

[84] See Consiglio di Stato, judgment No. 1085 of the 7th February 2019.

[85] On this topic, see Fiandaca and Musco (2024), pp. 943–947.

[86] See Consiglio di Stato, judgment No. 1085 of the 7th February 2019.

[87] See Bonini (2018), pp. 103–107 and Catena (2021), p. 851.

[88] See Consiglio di Stato, judgment No. 2545 of the 16th April 2020.

[89] See Marandola (2009), p. 966.

[90] See Consiglio di Stato, judgment No. 2545 of the 16th April 2020.

offences are of notable importance. Where the dissuasive objectives of the measure have not been achieved, the public official may independently promote initiatives in order to protect the victim against more serious events.

Statistics on the number of warnings issued by the *Questore* are significant as they highlight the recognition and increase the importance of this instrument.[91] On the other hand, the case-law shows that, in certain cases, the administrative measures did not achieve the preventive effects sought. The primary problem lies in the fact that sometimes the person who has been warned does not understand the dissuasive effect of this measure. In other words, there are cases where the offender has responded to the public authority's warning with more serious behaviors than previously perpetrated. While it is true that in such cases the offender will be subject to criminal proceedings and a more severe penalty, on the other hand this would result in a more dangerous situation for the victim. Therefore, the actual reaction of the warned person is one aspect of the great uncertainty which persists even after the public safety authority's intervention. A series of judgments regarding violent crimes show indeed an aggravated criminal liability for the condemned person, as a result of previous criminal acts and aggressive conducts committed against the same victim.[92]

6 Concluding Remarks

Punitive sanctions, preventive and precautionary measures and individual treatment appear as significant elements of strategies focused on combating domestic violence. These measures are part of an integrated response to the needs for protection raised by the crimes of ill-treatment, sexual crimes and other violent offences committed in family contexts and within intimate personal relationships.[93] The Italian criminal justice system currently relies on a variety of laws and regulations, that enable public authorities and professionals with specific expertise to intervene and provide protection to the victims and their rights. In this field, however, recourse to the instruments of criminal law must not divert attention from the need to "design a broader preventive strategy of a political-criminal nature, to be traced through

[91] See ISTAT (National Institute of Statistics), www.istat.it. Statistics show that the overall amount of warning requests addressed to the Italian *Questore* is arising. In 2014, this public official issued 420 warnings related to domestic violence: in 2014, 428. The overall number of measures has increased significantly in recent years. In 2018, 897 warnings were issued; in 2019, 1247; in 2020, 1115 and in 2021, 1403.

[92] For examples of violent behavior on the part of offenders after the *Questore*'s warning, see especially Corte di cassazione, judgment No. 27886 of the 24th March 2021; see also Corte di cassazione, judgment No. 3019 of the 9th October 2019.

[93] See Bertolino (2021), p. 82 and Aliquò (2020), pp. 50–51.

primary prevention".[94] The focus on early intervention reflects a recognition that insisting on the introduction of tougher sanctions is not an effective strategy against these violent crimes. This action is to be designed involving other sectors of the legal system which should effectively integrate the criminal law action. Only through a social policy oriented towards an approach that is not merely repressive but, above all, culturally and educationally aligned, can stronger premises be laid for the fight against violence in family and intimate personal relationships.[95] As the Italian Court of Cassation clearly stated in one of its judgments, domestic violence seems to be a manifestation of power, an attempt to exercise "dominance" and oppression over a partner or a family member.[96] This attitude, as an expression of psychological and behavioral models and cultural concepts about gender roles, do not respect fundamental human rights and therefore cannot be endured: that is the issue that mainly needs to be addressed.

References

Aliquò G (2020) La violenza domestica. L'ammonimento del Questore. Pacini giuridica, Pisa

Balbi G (2017) Le misure di prevenzione personali. Rivista italiana di diritto e procedura penale 3:521–525

Bartoli R (2022) La famiglia, le famiglie. In: Bertolino M (ed) Reati contro la famiglia. In Trattato teorico-pratico di diritto penale, Palazzo F, Paliero CE, Pelissero M (eds). Giappichelli editore, Torino, pp 1–13

Bertolino M (2015) Violenza e famiglia: attualità di un fenomeno antico. Rivista italiana di diritto e procedura penale 4:1710–1742

Bertolino M (2016) Il "crimine" della pericolosità sociale: riflessioni da una riforma in corso. Rivista italiana di medicina legale 4:1371–1397

Bertolino M (2021) La violenza di genere e su minori tra vittimologia e vittimismo: notazioni brevi. Rivista italiana di diritto e procedura penale 1:65–82

Bertolino M (2022) Reati contro la famiglia. In: Palazzo F, Paliero CE, Pelissero M (eds) Trattato teorico-pratico di diritto penale. Giappichelli editore, Torino

Bonini V (2018) Il sistema di protezione della vittima e i suoi riflessi sulla libertà personale. Wolters Kluwer, Milano

Bonini V (2021) The Istanbul Convention's values and its implementation in Italy. In: Bonini V, Erbaş R (eds) The 10th Anniversary of the Istanbul Convention. Pisa University Press, Pisa, pp. 69–84

Bonini V (2023) Protezione della vittima e valutazione del rischio nei procedimenti per violenza domestica tra indicazioni sovranazionali e deficit interni. Sistema penale 3:47–67

[94] See Eusebi (2018), p. 248. See also Eusebi (2016), pp. 285–301, Eusebi (2021), pp. 823–854 and Romano (1985), pp. 426–429.

[95] For further remarks, see di Martino (2022), p. 25, Mantovani (2013), p. 67, Petrini (2013), p. 1834, Bonini (2021), p. 80 and Garbarino and Giulini (2022), pp. 43–48.

[96] See Corte di cassazione, judgment No. 27166 of the 30th May 2022. Ruling on a case of maltreatment, the Court concluded that "the perpetrator's aggression was instrumental in preserving his dominance over the victim". The angry outbursts and violence were linked to the wife's behavior, which was perceived as a violation of "specific cultural patterns in the social assignment of gender roles". On this topic, see Milani and Grumi (2023), pp. 31–45.

Braschi S (2024) La nuova direttiva sulla lotta alla violenza contro le donne e alla violenza domestica e le sue ricadute nell'ordinamento nazionale. Diritto penale e processo 10:1367–1379
Capecchi S (2019) The numbers of Intimate Partner Violence and femicide in Italy: methodological issues in Italian research. Qual Quant 53:2635–2645
Catena R (2021) Profili processuali del reato di atti persecutori e nuove misure. In: Fidelbo G (ed) Diritto penale della famiglia. Giappichelli editore, Torino, pp. 823–865
Chinnici D (2022) La legislazione in materia di reati di "violenza domestica" e sessuale. Un itinerario lento e, ancora oggi, lacunoso. Archivio penale (web) 2:1–17
Cirillo S, Di Blasio P (1989) La famiglia maltrattante. Diagnosi e terapia. Raffaello Cortina editore, Milano
Di Blasio P (2000) Psicologia del bambino maltrattato. Il Mulino, Bologna
di Martino A (2022) Immagini e metodi del sistema penale di fronte ai delitti c.d. di genere (Fra sollecitazioni internazionali ed esperienza interna). Archivio penale 2:1–26
Erbaş R (2021) Evidentiary challenges to an effective criminal investigation for domestic violence: an introduction. In: Bonini V, Erbaş R (eds) The 10th Anniversary of the Istanbul Convention. Pisa University Press, Pisa, pp 101–117
Erbaş R (ed) (2022) Global problems in sexual offenses. Lexington Books, Rowman & Littlefield, Lahnam
Eusebi L (2016) Prevenzione e garanzie: promesse mancate del diritto penale o paradigmi di una riforma penale «umanizzatrice»? Criminalia:285–301
Eusebi L (2018) «Gestire» il fatto di reato. Prospettive incerte di affrancamento dalla pena «ritorsione». In: Paliero CE, Viganò F, Basile F, Gatta GL (eds) La pena, ancora: fra attualità e tradizione, I. Milano, Giuffrè editore, pp 223–250
Eusebi L (2021) La pena tra necessità di strategie preventive e nuovi modelli di risposta al reato. Rivista italiana di diritto e procedura penale 3:823–854
Fiandaca G, Musco E (2024) Diritto penale. Parte generale. Zanichelli, Bologna
Fletcher GP (2020) With justice for some. The rights of victims in criminal trials. Mazo Publishers, Jerusalem
Forti G (2000) L'immane concretezza. Metamorfosi del crimine e controllo penale. Raffaello Cortina editore, Milano
Forti G (2021) Il trattamento. In: Giarda A, Forti G, Giunta F, Varraso G (eds) Manuale di diritto penitenziario. Wolters Kluwer, Milano, pp 31–142
Garbarino F, Giulini P (2020) La violenza nelle relazioni strette. L'esperienza di giustizia riparativa del CIPM (Centro Italiano per la Promozione della Mediazione). In: Pezzini B, Lorenzetti A (eds) La violenza di genere dal codice Rocco al codice rosso. Giappichelli editore, Torino, pp 185–218
Garbarino F, Giulini P (2022) L'approccio multidisciplinare nel contrasto alla violenza di genere: il trattamento degli autori. Maltrattamento e abuso all'infanzia 3:37–60
Gino S, Freilone F, Biondi E, Ceccarelli D, Veggi S, Zara G (2019) Dall'intimate partner violence al femminicidio: relazioni che uccidono. Rassegna italiana di criminologia 2:131–148
Giulini P, Scotti A (2013) Il campo del trattamento del reo sessuale tra ingiunzione terapeutica e controllo benevolo. Rivista italiana di medicina legale 4:1863–1883
Giulini P, Xella CM (eds) (2011) Buttare la chiave? La sfida del trattamento per gli autori di reati sessuali. Raffaello Cortina editore, Milano
ISTAT (2020) Delitti, imputati e vittime dei reati. La criminalità in Italia attraverso una lettura integrata delle fonti sulla giustizia. ISTAT, Roma
Mantovani F (2013) La violenza di genere sotto il profilo criminologico e penale. Criminalia, pp 59–72
Marandola A (2009) I profili processuali delle nuove norme in materia di sicurezza pubblica, di contrasto alla violenza sessuale e stalking. Diritto penale e processo 8:947–962
Marandola A (2021) Codice rosso (profili processual-penalistici). Dig. disc. pen. Agg., 161–175
Marinucci G, Dolcini E, Gatta G L (2022) Manuale di diritto penale. Parte generale. Giuffrè editore, Milano

Martines T (2020) Diritto costituzionale. Giuffrè editore, Milano
Martini A (2017) Essere pericolosi. Giudizi soggettivi e misure personali. Giappichelli editore, Torino
Massaro A (2025) La Direttiva UE 2024/1385 sulla lotta alla violenza contro le donne e alla violenza domestica: il possibile impatto sull'ordinamento italiano. Sistema penale 3:107–143
Maugeri AM (2021) I reati sessualmente connotati e diritto penale del nemico. IUS/Pisa University Press, Pisa
Merzagora I (2009) Uomini violenti. I partner abusanti e il loro trattamento. Raffaello Cortina editore, Milano
Merzagora I (2015) La violenza in famiglia. Jus-online 1:1–22
Merzagora I, Pettorossi R (2009) Stalking e danno psichico. Rassegna italiana di Criminologia 3:547–562
Merzagora I (2023) Introduzione alla Criminologia. Raffaello Cortina Editore, Milano
Milani L, Grumi S (2023) Psicologia della violenza di genere. Vita e Pensiero, Milano
Morelli A (2022) La "violenza assistita": brevi riflessioni sulla complessa "traduzione" giuridica di un fenomeno sociale. Rivista italiana di medicina legale 2:409–430
Moscarini P (2006) La perizia psicologica e il "giusto processo". Diritto penale e processo 8:929–932
Nascosi A (2021) Gli ordini di protezione civili contro gli abusi familiari a vent'anni dalla loro introduzione. Famiglia e diritto 12:1189–1200
Paonessa C (2020) Ripercorrendo i "luoghi" della prognosi "personologica": alcuni spunti di riflessione. Archivio penale 3:1–28
Parlato L (2021) Domestic violence in light of the Istanbul Convention: some procedural issues. In: Bonini V, Erbaş R (eds) The 10th Anniversary of the Istanbul Convention. Pisa University Press, Pisa, pp 129–143
Pelissero M (2008) Pericolosità sociale e doppio binario. Giappichelli editore, Torino
Petrini D (2013) Il trattamento del delinquente sessuale, tra esigenze securitarie e controllo delle recidiva. Rivista italiana di medicina legale 4:1823–1836
Pezzini B, Lorenzetti A (2020) La violenza di genere dal Codice Rocco al Codice rosso. Un itinerario di riflessione plurale attraverso la complessità del fenomeno. Giappichelli editore, Torino
Pulitanò D (2017) Misure di prevenzione e problema della prevenzione. Rivista italiana di diritto e procedura penale 2:637–660
Roia F (2017) Crimini contro le donne. Politiche, leggi, buone pratiche, Franco Angeli, Milano
Romano B (2021) Codice rosso (profili penali sostanziali). Dig. disc. pen. Agg., 132–160
Romano M (1985) Legislazione penale e consenso sociale. Jus 3:413–429
Spena A (2012) Reati contro la famiglia. In: Grosso CF, Padovani T, Pagliaro A (eds) Trattato di diritto penale italiano. Giappichelli editore, Torino
Taylor SC, Gassner L (2010) Stemming the flow: challenges for policing adult sexual assault with regard to attrition-rates and under-reporting of sexual offences. Police Pract Res 3:240–255
Triggiani N (2020) L'ultimo tassello del percorso legislativo di contrasto alla violenza domestica e di genere: la legge 'Codice Rosso', tra effettive innovazioni e novità solo apparenti. Processo penale e giustizia: 2
Vitarelli T (2020) Violenza contro le donne e bulimia repressiva. Diritto penale contemporaneo – Rivista trimestrale 3: 461–484
Walker LE (1979) The Battered Woman. Harper Collins, New York
Xella CM (2013) La valutazione del rischio di recidiva per gli autori di reati sessuali. Rivista italiana di medicina legale 4:1885–1903
Zara G (2018) Il diniego nei sex offender. Dalla valutazione al trattamento. Raffaello Cortina editore, Milano
Zara G, Farrington DP, Freilone F, Lösel F (2020) Assessment, management, and treatment of sex offenders: what is known, what is controversial, what needs further investigation. Rassegna italiana di criminologia 3:166–185

Domestic Violence in Spain from A Gender Perspective: Risk Assessment and Analysis

Elisa Simó-Soler

Abstract Organic Act 1/2004 was a milestone in the effort to eradicate gender-based violence but has not fully achieved its objectives, primarily due to an overreliance on criminal law. Gender-based violence is a multifaceted issue influenced by various factors beyond the patriarchal context, necessitating a comprehensive approach to risk prediction and management. The roles of police, judges, and other professionals involved in victim protection are crucial for ensuring risk assessments are based on relevant information. Technological advancements, such as the predictive models used by VioGén System, can also contribute to a preventive approach. However, it is essential to recognize that criminal prosecution alone is insufficient and indicative of systemic failure. The goal is to enhance a more interdisciplinary preventive strategy to protect women and reduce victimization.

The chapter was carried out within the framework of the Margarita Salas grants for the training of young doctors of the program for the requalification of the Spanish university system, funded by the Ministry of Universities of the Spanish Government and the European Union (Next Generation EU). Likewise, the research is part of the Knowledge Generation Project "Keys to a digital and algorithmic justice with a gender perspective" (PID2021-123170OB-I00) of which the author of this chapter is a member.

E. Simó-Soler (✉)
University of Valencia, Valencia, Spain
e-mail: elisa.simo@uv.es

R. Erbaş (ed.), *Criminal Prosecution of Domestic Violence*, Ius Gentium: Comparative Perspectives on Law and Justice 128,
https://doi.org/10.1007/978-3-032-01202-9_5

1 A Critical Overview of the Gender-based Violence Approach in Spain

Organic Act 1/2004 of 28 December on Integrated Protection Measures against Gender Violence[1] (Act 1/2004), which introduced measures to prevent, punish and eradicate violence against women, constitutes a milestone in gender-based violence (GBV) eradication. Despite being a pioneering Act in the European Union,[2] more than twenty years after its enactment, there are two main critical points in its development: the restricted concept of GBV and the preference for a criminal law approach.

Spanish State regulated GBV as intimate partner violence (IPV) as follows: "the violence that, as a manifestation of discrimination, inequality and power relations of men over women, is exercised against women by those who are or have been their spouses or by those who are or have been linked to them by similar relationships of affection, even without cohabitation." (Article 1.1). Although GBV is understood as a typology separated from domestic violence,[3] defined as that which takes place in the home and family and encompasses a multiplicity of phenomena,[4] has a clear gender component, with the majority of victims being women and the aggressors being men.[5]

The legal concept set out in Article 1.1. neither is in accordance with the definition present in the Preamble of the Act, which refers to "violence directed against women for the very fact of being women, because their aggressors consider them as lacking the minimum rights of freedom, respect and decision-making capacity",[6] nor is a definition closer to the one in the Istanbul Convention (May 2011, ratified by Spain in 2014) which would make it possible to extend protection to other women outside the intimate partner relationship (Article 3).[7]

Following the structure of Act 1/2004, it consists of five titles with different areas of action defined. Awareness, prevention, and detection in education, health, and media measures are in Title I. The second is dedicated to the rights of women victims. Institutional attention is found in the third Title. And the fourth and fifth Titles contain the criminal aspects and judicial protection.

The deployment of Act 1/2004 has been carried out mainly from the criminal law, ignoring the potential of bringing together the spheres of education, health,

---

[1] According to Article 81 of the Spanish Constitution, the "Organic Act" is a special type of Act to regulate specific matters such as the development of fundamental rights and public freedoms and whose approval, modification or repeal shall require an absolute majority of the Congress.

[2] Laurenzo Copello (2015), p. 785.

[3] Gimeno Reinoso and Barrientos Silva (2009). http://ve.scielo.org/scielo.php?script=sci_arttext&pid=S1316-37012009000100004&lng=es&tlng=es.

[4] Alberdi and Matas (2002), p. 90.

[5] Cantera Espinosa (2002), p. 71.

[6] Añón Roig and Merino Sancho (2019), pp. 73–74.

[7] Doğan (2021), p. 20.

media, and justice to achieve a substantial transformation.[8] The development of the Act in its criminal aspect involved imposing harsher penalties only for less severe cases of GBV (occasional mistreatment by a partner, coercion, or minor threats)[9] and establishing the Courts for Violence against Women to deal with criminal and civil law matters (by way of an amendment of Article 87 ter in Organic Act 6/1985, of July 1st, 1985, of the Judiciary).

Without ignoring the need for the law to criminalize these behaviors, it is necessary to reflect on the consequences of this approach. First, the "4P policy" based on crime prevention, protection, prosecution and punishment[10] is utterly unbalanced in favor of the latter. In Spain, the criminal code continues to be an instrument susceptible to electoral games. This is why some issues that cause a certain amount of social alarm are addressed through criminal law. Moreover, reforming an article generates an immediate impact, giving the impression that the state has acted decisively. However, structural transformations require long-term projects and strategies (not individual approaches like penalties), the effects of which can be perceived and evaluated over time, making them much less advantageous in the electoral arena.

Consequently, all attention has been focused on the criminal process, and reporting is established as the best and sometimes the only option against GBV.[11] Thus, in the collective imagination there is a prevailing idea that finding a way out of GBV necessarily involves repression and increased penalties, a manifestation of populism and punitive paternalism.[12] However, the Spanish penal policy to combat GBV through the punitive approach has not yielded the desired results,[13] with 1.317 deaths recorded since January 1, 2003, to date (a figure that, sadly, is constantly being updated).[14]

Secondly, the sole use of criminal law as the only tool to eliminate GBV has blocked other means of access to the justice system and has forced the creation of a prototype of the "real" victim that serves the retributive criminal process.[15] The ideal pattern of a victim is fed with gender stereotypes that determine who deserves protection and redress,[16] those women who desperately need the assistance of justice to escape violence so that they are unable to discern their best interest, this being a matter for the state to decide. The consolidation of this unidirectional model turns women into victims always in need of judicial protection (even against their

[8] Observatorio Estatal de Violencia sobre la Mujer (2007), p. 9.

[9] For a critical analysis see: Laurenzo Copello (2015), pp. 783–830.

[10] Bonini (2019), p. 74.

[11] Villacampa (2021), p. 2.

[12] Villacampa (2021), p. 13 and Barona Vilar (2019), p. 36.

[13] Simó Soler (2019), p. 88.

[14] The relative invariability in the number of victims is evidenced by the fact that there are no major differences in the annual figures indicating that prioritising punishment does not address and prevent GBV. Statistics Portal of Government Office against Gender-based Violence (August 2025). Data are available at: https://violenciagenero.igualdad.gob.es/.

[15] Cubells and Calsamiglia (2018), pp. 120 and 122.

[16] Casado-Neira and Martínez (2016), pp. 889–890.

will),[17] neglects the risk of secondary victimization[18] and institutional violence that some women suffer when they access the courts,[19] and disregards other support measures such as psychological assistance, economic incomes or alternative housing. It also jeopardizes access to justice for those women who are not recognized as "real" victims in the first place.

While prosecution and punishment are seen as contributing to securing and redressing women's rights, it would be beneficial to examine the tools available to anticipate and try to prevent potential threats. The question then arises: can a proactive, *ex ante* assessment of the victim's situation be carried out to safeguard their well-being?

2 Intimate Partner Violence Risk Assessment

Risk assessment in cases of GBV is crucial for understanding this complex issue and should consider the heteropatriarchal macrostructure that enables abuse. The police have relied on a technological tool, better known as the VioGén System, to measure recidivism risk when a woman reports an incident. The use of predictive algorithms, given their objectivity, represents a significant advance to ensure victims are protected from the beginning of the criminal process. However, it presents some limitations such as operational opacity that compromises its predictive accuracy, and the lack of interdisciplinary inputs, which can result in inconsistent risk evaluations. This highlights the complexity of using algorithmic models in decision-making processes.

2.1 GBV and Risk factors

After offering a consolidated set of means to assist women (016 Telephone Service for Attention and Protection, Office for the Assistance to Victims of Crime, 24-hour Women's Center, and VIOPET a program for the temporary sheltering of animals of women victims of GBV)[20] and protect them, there seems to be a consensus that GBV, despite having a heteropatriarchal basis, is a multivariable phenomenon.

Just as *Lorente Acosta* states: "If all the factors and elements that act on people and the circumstances that affect them and can influence them were known, all subsequent behaviors could be foreseen. Nevertheless, this deterministic and

[17] Goldscheid (2014), pp. 640–641. On many occasions, the linearity of the criminal process does not adjust to the circularity or fragmentation of the emotional process that the victims go through. Dalia (2020), p. 21.

[18] Bonini (2019), p. 78.

[19] Villacampa (2021), p. 12 and Bodelón (2014), p. 142.

[20] Public resources can be checked in: https://violenciagenero.igualdad.gob.es/.

mechanistic approach is unrealistic and nowadays even more distant due to the complexity of social, individual, and criminal circumstances. We cannot know what can happen from a specific cause or factor in the face of the different possibilities that the interaction of different elements can produce. Everything is more complex and independent as it is influenced by individual circumstances, which makes linearity and prediction difficult.".[21]

This finding complicates the approach to risk prevention and makes it necessary to identify possible risk factors that could help to predict fatal outcomes. Risk factors can be structural (heteropatriarchal system), contextual (pandemic, or poverty, among others), and circumstantial (psychopathological elements); dynamic and static, depending on whether they can be modified during the person's life; and following an ecological model, four levels of risks are identified: individual, relationship, community and societal.[22]

A scientific literature review in Spain confirms the multi-causality of GBV. Researchers from the University of the Basque Country and the University of Burgos conduct a literature review of recent risk factors for IPV meta-analyses. The results affirm that on a community level, factors such as low economic development and democracy, lack of social rights, a culture of honor, and a masculine culture are risk factors. On a contextual and individual level, being younger, having low income and education, having more than one child, engaging in reciprocal violence with one's partner, depression, fear, and alcohol consumption increase the risk of being a victim of IPV.[23]

Complementary, it is possible to refer to studies that specifically examine some of the risk factors mentioned above in depth. For example, in a paper on a cognitive restructuring of convicted aggressors concerning sexist attitudes as a risk factor, *Barreiro Maceira* points out the incidence of the internalization of gender roles and mandates in mistreatment. The social imposition of his role as a male-bread winner and the consequent frustration and threat to his masculinity and identity, when expectations are not met, is a potent stressor that can lead to aggressive behavior to maintain his authority. It also refers to pathological jealousy, derived from attitudes of control, and to the belief in stereotypes and the reproduction of "micromachismos", very subtle daily behaviors that maintain in force traditions and customs that limit the autonomy, independence, and freedom of women.[24] Controlling behaviors significantly increase the risk of psychological and physical violence for adult women in Spain, especially among young couples and migrant women.[25]

The harmful use of alcohol has been defined as one of the most intensely and consistent risk factors associated with IPV by WHO.[26] According to *Catalá-Miñana,*

[21] Lorente Acosta (2012), p. 199.

[22] Lorente Acosta (2012), p. 197 and WHO (2010), p. 19.

[23] Aizpurua et al. (2021), pp. 303–304 and Rodriguez Martinez (2019).

[24] Barreiro Maceira (2018), pp. 56–58.

[25] Aizpurua et al. (2021), pp. 234, 248–249.

[26] WHO (2010), p. 27.

Lila, and Oliver, alcohol consumption is linked to other individual and contextual variables so that risky alcohol consumers manifest more significant psychopathological symptoms, show more problems with the consumption of other substances, are more impulsive, display lower levels of self-esteem, suffer a greater accumulation of stressful life events and more easily attribute the blame for the events that have occurred to the personal context, perceiving both greater social rejection for reporting and lower levels of support from their immediate environment. The findings highlight the importance of considering alcohol as a risk factor for recidivism.[27]

The risk of experiencing GBV increases in situations of exclusion. *Damonti's* study demonstrates how different dimensions of exclusions affect different types of GBV. A close link exists between the status and social level of the neighborhood and the probability of experiencing GBV: a situation of moderate exclusion increases by 70.0% the probability of facing physical violence.[28]

It is important to emphasize two key points: (1) the multifactoriality, complexity and even unpredictability of GBV;[29] and (2) the idea that risk factors only explain the potential for violence and not its root cause. *Damonti* suggests that if risk factors operate as they do, it is only because they act in the presence of a necessary precondition external to them: a structural background of unequal gender relations based on male power and women's subordination.[30] Therefore, to effectively address and reduce the risk of GBV, a comprehensive approach must be taken that includes and addresses the specific risk factors and the underlying systematic inequalities that perpetuate GBV.

2.2 Police Risk Assessment: The Case of VioGén

According to *Lorente Acosta's* definition, risk assessment is the procedure for predicting the probability of occurrence of a given violent behavior.[31] Tools for risk assessment play a decisive role in the prevention and response to GBV as they help identify women at risk of experiencing violence, allowing for targeted intervention and support.

The Comprehensive Monitoring System in cases of GBV, VioGén System, is a risk assessment tool based on predictive algorithms to categorize risk levels and recommend protective measures. Developed by the Secretary of State for Security of the Ministry of the Interior in 2007 based on the provisions outlined in Articles 31.3 and 32 of Act 1/2004, it was designed to be used by police officers after a

[27] Catalá-Miñana et al. (2013), pp. 24 and 26.

[28] Damonti (2019), p. 487.

[29] Escudero Nafs (2005), p. 104 and López-Ossorio et al. (2019), p. 57.

[30] Damonti (2019), p. 487.

[31] Lorente Acosta (2012), p. 197.

complaint is reported, to prevent revictimization.[32] Since 2020 it can be used by the staff in the Institutes of Legal Medicine and Forensic Sciences to conduct forensic assessments requested by a Judge.[33] As of June 30, 2024, the latest official data shows that there were 92,134 active cases, those with police monitoring.[34]

The approach taken is based on the understanding that it is impossible to eliminate the risk of violence.[35] A predictive model is therefore proposed, utilizing simple valuation algorithms, both additive and weighted,[36] excluding, for the moment, the use of machine learning (ML) techniques.[37]

Its ongoing performance is based on completing two forms with different indicators grouped into various analysis factors: Police Risk Assessment ($VPR_{5.0}$) and Police Risk Evolution Assessment ($VPER_{4.1}$) Ministerio del Interior (2019).[38] The former is divided into five dimensions (history of IPV; perpetrator characteristics; indicators of victims' vulnerability; circumstances related to children; and aggravating circumstances) which integrate 35 dichotomously coded risk factors (present/absent, allowing coding with Boolean elements for the development of predictive algorithms).[39] These dimensions result in five risk levels (not-appreciated, low, medium, high, and extreme) each of which automatically entails a set of mandatory protective measures.[40]

The second one, comprised of 37 indicators, is split into 6 dimensions of analysis and is designed for periodic assessments during victim follow-up by specialized police officers, enabling the monitoring of changes and continuous updating of risk estimates. This second form has two modes: "without incident" to be completed at specified intervals (extreme level, within 72 h; high level, within 7 days; medium level, every 30 days; and low level, every 60 days); and "with the incident" to be filled out in the event of a new act of violence or when a significant circumstance is revealed, or at the request of the court or Public Prosecutor's Office.[41]

---

[32] Excluding Catalonia and the Basque Country, where this application is not used.

[33] Martínez Garay et al. (2022), p. 21.

[34] Ministerio del Interior (2024), p. 10.

[35] González Álvarez et al. (2018b), pp. 18–19.

[36] Ibid., p. 50.

[37] Eticas Foundation (2022), pp. 6–7.

[38] In January 2025, the Spanish government introduced VioGén 2, featuring refined indicators and recalibrated algorithms to improve risk assessment and reduce prediction errors. At the same time, the 2025 Protocol was adopted, eliminating the 'not appreciable' risk level and subdividing the 'low' level based on judicial protection measures. A new category of 'supervised case' was also established for extended monitoring. Information available at: https://www.interior.gob.es/opencms/eu/detalle/articulo/Interior-disena-un-nuevo-modelo-derespuesta-policial-a-la-violencia-de-genero/

[39] The factors listed in Article 16 of the Directive (EU) 2024/1385 of the European Parliament and of the Council of 14 May 2024 on combating violence against women and domestic violence are included in the five dimensions.

[40] López-Ossorio et al. (2021), pp. 50–51 and González Álvarez et al. (2018a), p. 60.

[41] Ibid., pp. 52 and 61.

A precaution highlighted by *Martínez Garay et al.* must be considered: there is a notable lack of transparency in the algorithms underlying the VPR and VPER forms, preventing the public and external audit by third parties who are not involved in the design or daily operation of the system. Information about VioGén's functioning is limited, while the factors taken into consideration are known, the methods of their combination and the relative weight of each factor remain undisclosed, so the specific risk allocation process is unknown.[42]

2.2.1 Human Supervision

Regarding the required supervision of the results, although the police can increase the risk score assigned automatically, they maintain it in 95.0% of the cases.[43] In this point, it is interesting to review Judgment 2350/2020 of the National Court, dated 30th September 2020, the only one related to VioGén, which declared the patrimonial liability of the Public Administration for an inaccurate risk assessment in a case of GBV.

The facts include the complaint of a woman for assaults by her husband, who requested a protection order from the Civil Guard. The VioGén assessment gave her a "low risk." However, without further investigation, the agents qualified the risk as "not appreciated." The Magistrate of the Court of First Instance agreed to deny the protection order based on the information sent by the Civil Guard and the report of the Public Prosecutor's Office, which requested the dismissal of the measure. However, one month later, the victim was murdered by her husband.

The Chamber for Contentious Administrative Proceedings considers that "[t]he police response to violence against women requires that the system is able to prevent violence and reevaluate the risk, that is, beyond the collection of automated data, prediction, and prevention are the primary purpose of the evaluation system that requires specialized agents in its treatment and sensitization in its monitoring.".[44] The action of the Civil Guard is not limited to the mere formality of filling out a form, as the agents can actually modify the assessment upwards if they consider that the result obtained by the VPR form does not reflect the actual situation of risk as assessed by them.

According to the Ministry of the Interior's report on VioGén, "[i]t is important to point out that, in all cases, the risk estimation does not rely on a simple machine, but rather the system allows police officers, who are the ones who know the cases best because they have investigated them in depth, to correct the automatic result of the risk assessment protocol when they have information that makes it advisable to do so. [...] Thus, at the end of each police risk assessment, the VioGén System summarizes the answers given and asks for the police's agreement with the automatic

[42] Martínez Garay et al. (2022), pp. 15 and 29.

[43] González-Álvarez (2018), p. 37.

[44] Sentencia 2350/2020, p. 21.

result, allowing the user to express their disagreement and assign the level of risk that they consider most appropriate, providing their reasons, thus allowing the System to be improved.".[45]

Consequently, the magistrates held that "[i]t is clear that, had the above factors required by the aforementioned protocol been sufficiently assessed, especially if the aggressor's history of gender-based violence in his country of origin had been confirmed, the Civil Guard would have had very relevant information to consider the real situation of risk in which the victim was and, consequently, its assessment of the risk would have been, not "medium," but "high" or "extreme."". Having the capacity to detect the risks associated with GBV is crucial so that cases such as the one in this judgment do not happen again. In this context, one of the main concerns raised in the report on the *External Audit of the VioGén System* conducted by the Eticas Foundation in 2022, is that about 45.0% of cases are assessed as having "no risk." However, they note that simply filing a police report against the aggressor can be risky behavior and prompt retaliation. In addition, the failure of institutions to recognize the risk may result in the victim feeling discredited and increase the risk of revictimization if she goes forward with the complaint.[46]

2.2.2 Data Collection

The VioGén questionnaire can be completed with information from a variety of sources, including the victim, the perpetrator, witnesses, neighbors, family members, and available police and other complementary technical reports. Since this is a rapid risk assessment carried out by a police officer at the time of the complaint, in practice and in most cases, the information is only obtained from the victim, which means that if the woman does not want to report it, she gets less or no protection at all.[47] However, to ensure a comprehensive risk assessment, the Integral Forensic Assessment Units, formed by a multidisciplinary team with at least one forensic doctor, one psychologist, and one social worker to assess victim and aggressor, becomes an essential source of information and should be involved.[48] As pointed out by *González Álvarez et al.*, penitentiary and forensic psychologists can evaluate indicators related to the presence of psychopathology or beliefs, attitudes, or cognitive distortions of aggressors and victims to justify this violence that are beyond the professional scope of a police officer.[49] In that sense, the Guide to the Application of the $VPR_{5.0}$ in the forensic risk assessment, published by the Ministry of Interior,

[45] González Álvarez et al. (2018a), p. 56.

[46] Eticas Foundation (2022), p. 33.

[47] Martínez Garay et al. (2022), p. 23.

[48] CGPJ (2013), p. 150.

[49] González-Álvarez (2018), p. 37.

gives Integral Forensic Assessment Units the role of reducing the false positive rate by making use of their complementary expertise in forensic medicine.[50]

If VioGén is designed to predict recidivism, the requirement to incorporate all the information about the alleged offender is understandable.[51] The study by *Santos-Hermoso et al.* on risk factor interaction in Spanish GBV cases, which includes a typology of abusers profiles (normalized, violent, pathological, pathologically violent) shows that the pathological and above all the normalized types (representing 42.1% of the perpetrators of femicide in Spain), do not display the factors that best predict the death of the partner when tools of police risk assessment of recidivism are used. This has two significant implications. On the one hand, it means that VioGén cannot detect risk factors that involve a high percentage of perpetrators because they do not have a criminal record or previous complaints, so it will be necessary to find methods to include them in the risk assessment systems or to complement the evaluation with factors outside the police and judiciary frame. On the other hand, it reinforces the idea that femicide is not always the end of a history of battering, but that there may be convergent drivers that complicate the prediction of an act of violence.[52]

VioGén's predictive capacity is effective in identifying low-risk, but less reliable for high-risk cases. To address this, the H-Scale was developed in 2019 as part of the $VPR_{5.0}$ form to handle cases where the system indicated a not-appreciated or low risk assessment, but the case actually resulted in homicide. The H-Scale performs a monitoring function on cases with initial risk levels of not appreciated, low, and medium. Further analysis shown that this monitoring can detect those cases with more severe risk of violence and automatically reclassify them into higher risk levels.[53] When the H-Scale detects a high risk of homicide, it triggers an automatic "case of special relevance" warning and includes specific alerts for "minors in a situation of vulnerability".[54]

In summary, VioGén exhibits a good result distinguishing between risk and no risk. However, regarding the femicide prediction, it is not possible to conclude that the system is classifying correctly, even if it has a low number of false negatives, as the false positives are high. Without the raw data nor the algorithm details, it is difficult to know whether its inefficiency is due to the parameters chosen, to the input collected, or to the classification process itself.

---

[50] López-Ossorio et al. (2016), p. 16. For a discussion on VioGén's predictive accuracy and false positives, see: Martínez Garay et al. (2022), pp. 26–28.

[51] Fernández Teruelo (2017), p. 14.

[52] Santos-Hermoso (2022), p. 19.

[53] López-Ossorio et al. (2016), p. 25.

[54] Martínez Garay et al. (2022), pp. 16 and 45.

2.2.3 Judge Risk Assessment

As reaffirmed by the National Court in Judgment 2350/2020, the risk identified by VioGén is not binding. The Court recalls "that there is no regulatory provision that considers the risk assessment by the State Security Forces and Corps as binding for the criminal judge.".[55] Article 282 of Criminal Procedure Act regarding the functions of the judicial police, stipulates that notwithstanding the police assessment of the particular circumstances of the victims to determine what protective measures should be adopted provisionally, the final decision must be taken by the judge or court. In the same sense, Article 544 ter of the same Act attributes the decision to the Instructing Court to issue a protection order in case of an objective situation of risk.

Just as police officers' ability to assess specific aspects of the perpetrator's and victim's behavior is seen as beyond their scope, the judiciary's ability is viewed similarly. Judges are professional experts in law but lack adequate training in psychology, sociology, and forensic medicine.[56] Making an objective and comprehensive risk assessment would require that their judgment was complemented and reinforced by the expert knowledge they can obtain by requesting an urgent report from the Integral Forensic Assessment Units.[57] That information is of great value and usefulness for modulating the measures that a judge may dictate (e.g., a restraining order or the interruption of visits with a minor) and its duration.

As a result, to assess GBV risk, the judge takes into account not only the police risk assessment report but also the following sources: the victim's and perpetrator's declaration; forensic risk assessment; medical assistance, Offices for the Assistance to Victims of Crime reports, Women's Centers and Family Meeting points reports; incidents reported by the Comet Center,[58] and any other relevant evidence that can shed light on the risk situation being present. In this way, the judge can have a global and complete vision of the situation and make an adequate and well-founded decision on the necessary protection of the victim.

3 How can we Reduce the Risk of Suffering GBV?

Given that GBV is a multi-causal problem, it is crucial to adopt a holistic approach. This means that various interventions must be implemented to address the issue effectively, from changes in the risk perception in society to adopting judicial measures to protect victims from avoiding revictimisation. Finally, technological advances can help protect women and open the door to predictive models to anticipate violence.

---

[55] Sentencia 2350/2020, p. 12.

[56] Ortega Lorente (2018), p. 3.

[57] Ministerio de Justicia (2021), p. 5.

[58] Larrosa Ibáñez (2022), pp. 180–181.

3.1 Social and Political Measures

GBV is a public problem that affects fundamental rights and requires collective action to prevent and react to it. Consequently, knowing society's perception of the violence suffered by women can be a piece of useful information to design public measures. Although the study conducted by the Government Office for Gender-Based Violence in 2018 is limited to sexual violence, there are some data worth highlighting connected with the risk factors analyzed.

To the question about what is the main reason some men sexually assault women, the surveyed population answers: (1) "Having mental problems" quoted by 34.1% of the people interviewed; (2) "Consumption of alcohol and/or drugs" (25.3%); (3) "They cannot control their sexual impulses" (19.7%); and (4) "They do not identify their actions as sexual aggression" (14.3%). According to the report, which includes the question in a section on stereotypes and false beliefs towards sexual violence, these are reasons that justify the aggressor's behavior and at least partially exculpate him.[59] Moreover, the responses demonstrate the confusion between causes and risk factors in GBV cases.

Following the 2024 first quarter's data from the General Council of the Judiciary and the Observatory against domestic and gender violence, out of the total number of filed complaints, 71.26% were made by the victim at the police station and 16.16% by the direct intervention of the police. Of the complaints, 7.23% corresponded to injury reports from medical personnel and 2.66% to reports from welfare service personnel. Only 0.15% of the reports were filed directly by family members.[60]

The figures show the importance of police action, which requires protocols and training with an intersectional gender perspective,[61] as they are the first point of reference for victims directly or indirectly in over 87.0% of cases. The other professionals with whom the victim may have relatively continuous contact (doctors, social workers, teachers) represent a meager percentage, being a privileged space for detecting violent situations, especially in health centers. Families and friends are usually the first point of contact for victims; nevertheless, they remain at minimum thresholds, reflecting the low awareness of the risk of GBV, the lack of objective benchmarks to identify it and even the private consideration of the problem.

Stereotypes regarding GBV can make it difficult to appreciate the risk. As mentioned before, these preconceived ideas could permeate the administration of justice,[62] acting as cognitive biases in evaluating the evidence to determine the victim's credibility and to dictate the judgment.[63] Directive (EU) 2024/1385 of the European Parliament and of the Council of 14 May 2024 on combating violence

[59] Delegación del Gobierno para la Violencia de Género (2018), pp. 110–115.

[60] CGPJ (2024), p. 6.

[61] Peroni (2016), p. 52.

[62] Cusack (2014), p. 2.

[63] For an in-depth analysis of this issue, please consult: Arenas (2022).

against women and domestic violence, stipulates in Article 21 that Member States may issue guidelines for law enforcement and prosecutorial authorities on how to identify and avoid gender stereotypes. The aforementioned Guide to the Application of the $VPR_{5.0}$ in the forensic risk assessment also emphasizes the need for the police to debunk stereotypes about the "real" victim.[64]

Likewise, it seems essential to focus institutional attention and resources on the perpetrators. Specialized doctrine considers that intervention programs fulfill very beneficial objectives in terms of preventing GBV: "protecting victims who continue to maintain contact or live with their aggressors, preventing violent behavior in future victims, avoiding the victimization of children, avoiding the intergenerational transmission of violence and observational learning by children or allowing aggressors to change their attitudes and behavior.".[65] However, *Lila* emphasizes a controversial aspect: participation in the program may generate an expectation of transformation in the victim. If the effectiveness of these programs is not guaranteed, this fact may imply a substantial risk for these women.[66]

3.2 Judicial Measures

Judges can prevent the risk of recidivism by implementing security measures (precautionary measures or protection orders) or imposing a restrictive measure as a penalty in a judgment. In that sense, according to experts, one of the possible explanations for the high rate of false positives is the effectiveness of the measures adopted.[67]

Article 544 bis of the Criminal Procedure Act provides for four prohibitions (of residence, of going to certain places, of approach, and of communication) to be adopted as a precautionary measure in the case of an investigation of one of the crimes of article 57 of the Criminal Code (among which are homicide, abortion, injuries, against sexual freedom and indemnity, privacy).

Article 544 ter of the Criminal Procedure Act regulates the protection order, which may include criminal measures (any of those provided by the criminal law) and civil measures (a list detailed in the Article). In this case, if the judge considers an objective risk for the victim, he/she could dictate these measures. The judge may have had more sources of information to make the decision, so the risk level may differ from that generated by the VioGén system due to the limitations already mentioned. In any case, the risk factors for the breach of a protection order coincide with

---

[64] López-Ossorio et al. (2016), p. 3.

[65] Lila (2013), p. 82.

[66] Ibid.

[67] Martínez Garay et al. (2022), pp. 27 and 28.

those detected for recidivism, with the aggressors' attitudes based on jealousy, harassment, and control being particularly relevant.[68]

Once a conviction has been handed down, Article 57 of the Criminal Code requires issuing a restraining order.[69] However, this mandatory protection measure has faced criticism. *González Collantes* argues that it disregards the woman's voice and agency, treating her as unable to make decisions for herself. Prioritizing the woman's safety at all costs, even above herself, could lead to her being punished as an inducer or necessary cooperator of a crime under Article 468.2 of the Criminal Code.[70]

3.3 Technical Measures

The measure or penalty of the prohibition of approach to the victim agreed by court order may be controlled by installing a surveillance device with GPS and Radio Frequency technology.[71] The VioGén protocol establishes as a mandatory measure the monitoring of the aggressor through electronic devices in case the risk is determined to be high.[72] A GPS-based movement alert device sounds an alarm, provides a visual indication, or vibrates to warn if the man under investigation/conviction is within the specified range. Additionally, it features a panic button that the woman in emergencies can activate.[73] According to the latest records for May 2024, 17,469 devices of the System for telematic monitoring of restraint measures have been installed since 2009. As of May 31, 2024, the number of active devices was 4,775, an increase of 28.7% compared to May 2023.[74]

In the 2015 Macro Survey, women were asked what kind of help they would prefer to receive. The use of electronic devices to monitor and contain the abuser was the second least preferred option (with a percentage of 14%), only above telephone information on GBV. Obtaining psychological support, financial aid, legal support, medical help, facilities at work, sheltered accommodation, and a telephone that directly connects the victims with specialized care, in that order, were much more relevant for them.[75]

One of the reasons it is mentioned in such a low position may be due to the revictimizing effect. The use of GPS-moving warning devices has been controversial, as some experts argue that it undermines the freedom and autonomy of women. In

[68] Caballé-Pérez et al. (2020), p. 70.

[69] Magro Servet (2016).

[70] Gónzález Collantes (2019), p. 712.

[71] Sainz de Baranda Andujar (2022), p. 59.

[72] González Álvarez et al. (2018a), p. 56.

[73] Sainz de Baranda Andujar (2022), p. 59.

[74] Ministerio de Igualdad (2024), p. 3.

[75] De Miguel Luken (2015), pp. 202–203.

addition, the constant alarms and police visits associated with wearing the device result in constant surveillance, and the perpetrator might use the device to intimidate the victim further. While it may decrease the perception of crime, it does not necessarily reduce actual vulnerability, making it potentially counterproductive.[76]

The field of justice is benefiting from advancements in Artificial Intelligence. Predictive ML algorithms are used in the criminal justice system to aid decision-making and resource management. A Spanish engineering team has applied ML techniques to model and forecast the incidence of GBV over a six-month period. The possibility of predicting the number of complaints could let governments better plan their policies, optimizing and maximizing strategies.[77] In addition, a subsequent 2021 study on VioGén concluded that the use of ML would improve the predictive capability of the system.[78]

4 Conclusion

The invariability of rates of GBV in Spain indicates that the legal system is not always effective in protecting such victims. The legal process can be lengthy and cumbersome, and victims may not always receive the answer they need due to institutional paternalism that homogenizes all victims. Although the 1/2004 Act holistic approach would enable decision-makers to make informed and appropriate decisions that prioritize the safety and protection of the victim in a more effective and egalitarian transformative way, it has lost strength by giving too much space to criminal law. However, GBV is revealed as a complex problem influenced by a range of factors that do not obtain an adequate response in the form of punishment.

The multi-causality of GBV places risk prediction and management as fundamental axes. Recognizing the importance of the patriarchal context is essential, but many other aspects must be considered. This question becomes fundamental: monocausal analyses of GBV need to be overcome if incomplete responses that place women in positions of greater vulnerability are to be avoided. This does not mean adopting a more complacent position toward the patriarchy, but rather paying attention to the macro and micro structures that foster violence.

Therefore, the role of the police, judges and other professionals involved in the victims' protection is crucial in ensuring that risk assessments are comprehensive. They should not solely rely on technological tools but also consider all relevant information out of stereotyping, especially about the "real" victims. The intersectional gender perspective constitutes an imperative methodological instrument for activating interpretative warnings of the facts and laws that may be formulated using gender stereotypes that entail a violation or restriction of women's rights.

[76] Sainz de Baranda Andujar (2022), p. 67.

[77] Rodríguez-Rodríguez et al. (2020), pp. 2 and 19.

[78] González-Prieto et al. (2021).

The prediction of GBV risk should not only focus on second offenses. Public institutions must take proactive measures to prevent GBV and empower the population to identify potential incidents, discarding the conceptualization of GBV as a private matter. However, the priority of protecting women should not compromise their ability to make their own decisions. Paternalistic treatment of women reinforces their agency's limitations and limits their capacity for self-determination.

Ultimately, it is worth noting that a criminal justice-only approach to addressing GBV seems doomed to failure. Structural problems call for transformative action, directly addressing the causes and involving a community commitment of the whole of society as a matter of state. Women's lives depend on it.

References

Aizpurua E, Copp J, Ricarte JJ, Vázquez D (2021) Controlling behaviors and intimate partner violence among women in Spain: an examination of individual, partner, and relationship risk factors for physical and psychological abuse. J Interp Viol 36(1-2):231–254. https://doi.org/10.1177/0886260517723744

Alberdi I, Matas N (2002) La violencia doméstica. Informe sobre los malos tratos a mujeres en España. Fundación La Caixa, Barcelona. https://ibdigital.uib.es/greenstone/collect/portal_social/import/flacaixa/flacai0007.pdf

Añón Roig MJ, Merino Sancho VM (2019) El concepto de violencia de género en el ordenamiento jurídico español: balance crítico y propuestas de un concepto holista e integral. Ars Iuris Salmanticensis 7(1): 67–95

Arenas FJ (2022) Manual sobre los efectos de los estereotipos en la impartición de justicia. Suprema Corte de Justicia de la Nación, Ciudad de México

Barona Vilar S (2019) Justicia penal desde la globalizacion y la postmoderidad hasta la Neomodernida. Revista Boliviana de Derecho 27:20–53

Barreiro Maceira JM (2018) Una visión de la intervención sobre las actitudes sexistas como factor de riesgo en la violencia de género. Intervención psicoeducativa en la desadaptación social 11:55–63

Bodelón E (2014) Violencia institucional y violencia de género. Anales de la cátedra Francisco Suárez 48:131–155. https://doi.org/10.30827/acfs.v48i0.2783

Bonini V (2019) The Istanbul Convention's values and its implementation in Italy. In: Bonini V, Erbaş R (eds), The 10th Anniversary of the Istanbul Convention. Italian-Turkish Conference Pisa, 18th June 2021, Pisa University Press, pp 69–84

Caballé-Pérez M, Villalba García D, Santos-Hermoso J, López-Ossorio JJ, González-Álvarez JL (2020) El quebrantamiento de las órdenes de protección en violencia de género: análisis de los indicadores de riesgo mediante el formulario VPR4.0. Anuario de Psicología Jurídica 30:63–72. https://doi.org/10.5093/apj2019a17

Cantera Espinosa LM (2002) La violencia doméstica. Lectora: revista de dones i textualitat 8:71–77

Casado-Neira D, Martínez M (2016) La víctima simulada. Identidades forzadas en la violencia de género. Política y sociedad 53(3):879–896. https://doi.org/10.5209/rev_POSO.2016.v53.n3.49719

Catalá-Miñana A, Lila M, Oliver A (2013) Consumo de alcohol en hombres penados por violencia contra la pareja: factores individuales y contextuales. Adicciones 25(1):19–28. https://doi.org/10.20882/adicciones.68

CGPJ. Consejo General del Poder Judicial (2013) Guía de criterios de actuación judicial frente a la violencia de género. Madrid. https://www.poderjudicial.es/cgpj/es/Poder_Judicial/En_Portada/Guia_de_criterios_de_actuacion_judicial_frente_a_la_violencia_de_genero

CGPJ. Consejo General del Poder Judicial Sección Estadística Judicial (2024) Informe Trimestral sobre Violencia de Género 1° Trimestre de 2024. Madrid. https://www.poderjudicial.es/cgpj/es/Temas/Estadistica-Judicial/Estudios-e-Informes/Violencia-sobre-la-Mujer/

Cubells J, Calsamiglia A (2018) Do we see victims' agency? Criminal justice and gender violence in Spain. Crit Criminol 26:107–127. https://doi.org/10.1007/s10612-017-9379-2

Cusack S (2014) Eliminating judicial stereotyping. Equal access to justice for women in gender based violence cases. Final paper submitted to the United Nations Office of the High Commissioner for Human Rights

Dalia G (2020) La risposta del sistema processuale penale per la tutela delle vittime di violenza di genere. Archivio penale 1:1–30

Damonti PS (2019) Exclusión social como factor de riesgo de violencia de género en la pareja. Papers 104(3):485–523. https://doi.org/10.5565/rev/papers.2570

De Miguel Luken V (2015) Macroencuesta de Violencia contra la Mujer 2015. Ministerio de Sanidad, Servicios Sociales e Igualdad. Centro de Publicaciones. https://violenciagenero.igualdad.gob.es/violenciaEnCifras/estudios/colecciones/pdf/Libro_22_Macroencuesta2015.pdf

Delegación del Gobierno para la Violencia de Género (2018) Percepción social de la violencia sexual. Ministerio de Sanidad, Consumo y Bienestar Social. Centro de Publicaciones https://violenciagenero.igualdad.gob.es/wp-content/uploads/Libro_25_Violencia_Sexual.pdf

Doğan S (2021) Turkey's withdrawal from Istanbul Convention: demanding confessional, one-dimensional and homogenous society. In: Bonini V, Erbaş R (eds) The 10th Anniversary of the Istanbul Convention. Italian-Turkish Conference Pisa, 18th June 2021. Pisa University Press, pp 19–45

Escudero Nafs A, Polo Usaola C, López Gironés M, Aguilar Redo L (2005) La persuasión coercitiva, modelo explicativo del mantenimiento de las mujeres en una situación de violencia de género: I: Las estrategias de la violencia. Revista de la asociación española de neuropsiquiatría 95:85–117

Eticas Foundation (2022), Autoría externa del sistema VioGén, Fundación Ana Bella-Red de Mujeres Supervivientes. https://eticasfoundation.org/wp-content/uploads/2022/04/ETICAS-_-Auditori%CC%81a-Externa-del-sistema-VioGe%CC%81n-_-20220308.docx.pdf

Fernández Teruelo JG (2017) Diagnóstico del sistema de protección y propuestas de intervención para la predicción y prevención de feminicidios en contexto de pareja o expareja. Revista electrónica de ciencia penal y criminología 19–23:1–24

Gimeno Reinoso B, Barrientos Silva V (2009) Violencia de género versus violencia doméstica: La importancia de la especificidad. Revista Venezolana de Estudios de la Mujer 14(32):27–42. http://ve.scielo.org/scielo.php?script=sci_arttext&pid=S1316-37012009000100004&lng=es&tlng=es

Goldscheid J (2014) Gender neutrality, the "violence against women" frame, and transformative reform. Univ Missouri-Kansas City Law Rev 82:623 662

González Álvarez JL, López Ossorio JJ, Muñoz Rivas M (2018a) La valoración policial del riesgo de violencia contra la mujer pareja en España — Sistema VioGén, Ministerio del Interior. https://www.interior.gob.es/opencms/pdf/archivos-y-documentacion/documentacion-y-publicaciones/publicaciones-descargables/seguridad-ciudadana/La_valoracion_policial_riesgo_violencia_contra_mujer_pareja_126180887.pdf

González Álvarez JL, López Ossorio JJ, Urruela C, Rodríguez Díaz M (2018b) Integral monitoring system in cases of gender violence VioGén System. Behav Law J 4(1):29–40. https://doi.org/10.47442/blj.v4.i1.56

Gónzález Collantes T (2019) Violencia de género, protección, sobreprotección o paternalismo. A propósito de las órdenes de alejamiento no deseadas. In Políticas públicas en defensa de la inclusión, la diversidad y el género. Universidad de Salamanca, pp 710–720

González-Álvarez JL (2018) Sistema de seguimiento integral en los casos de violencia de género (Sistema VioGén). Cuadernos de la Guardia Civil 56:83–102

González-Prieto Á, Brú A, Nuño, JC y González Álvarez JL (2021) Machine learning for risk assessment in gender-based crime. Available at: https://arxiv.org/abs/2106.11847

Larrosa Ibáñez IM (2022) La protección de las víctimas de violencia de género. La valoración judicial del riesgo. Revista del Centro de Estudios Jurídicos y de Postgrado CEJUP 3:176–187
Laurenzo Copello P (2015) ¿Hacen falta figuras género específicas para proteger mejor a las mujeres? Estudios penales y criminológicos 35:783–830
Lila M (2013) La intervención con hombres condenados por violencia de pareja contra la mujer en España: Investigación y avances en intervención. Psychosoc Interv 22(2):81–85. https://doi.org/10.5093/in2013a10
López-Ossorio JJ, González-Álvarez JL, Andrés-Pueyo A (2016) Eficacia predictiva de la valoración policial del riesgo de la violencia de género. Psychosoc Interv 25(1):1–7. https://doi.org/10.1016/j.psi.2015.10.002
López-Ossorio JJ, Loinaz I, González-Álvarez JL (2019) Protocol for the police gender violence risk assessment (VPR 4.0): review of its performance. Spanish J Leg Med 45(2):52–58. https://doi.org/10.1016/j.remle.2019.01.004
López-Ossorio JJ, González-Álvarez JL, Loinaz I, Martínez-Martínez A, Pineda D (2021) Intimate partner homicide risk assessment by police in Spain: The Dual Protocol VPR 5.0-H. Psychosoc Interv 30(1):47–55. https://doi.org/10.5093/pi2020a16
Lorente Acosta M (2012) Violencia contra las mujeres: peligrosidad y valoración del riesgo. Revista europea de derechos fundamentales 19:185–214
Magro Servet V (2016) ¿Es preceptiva la pena de alejamiento en los casos de violencia doméstica y de género? Diario La Ley 8880
Martínez Garay L, Boix Palop A, Briz Redón Á, Flores Giménez F, García Ortiz A, Molina Sánchez M, Montes Suay F, Palma Ortigosa A, Peris Manguillot A, Soriano Arnanz A (2022) Three predictive policing approaches in Spain: Viogén, RisCanvi and Veripol. Assessment from a human rights perspective. Universitat de València. https://regulation.blogs.uv.es/files/2024/05/Three-predictive-policing-perspectives-web-17.06.24.pdf
Ministerio de Igualdad (2024) Principales datos sobre violencia de género. Mayo 2024. https://violenciagenero.igualdad.gob.es/wp-content/uploads/Principales_datos_mayo_2024.pdf
Ministerio de Justicia (2021) Carta de Servicios 2021-2024. Unidades de Valoración Forense Integral (UVFI). https://www.mjusticia.gob.es/es/ElMinisterio/OrganismosMinisterio/Documents/CartaServicios_UVFI.pdf
Ministerio del Interior (2019). Guía de Procedimiento VPR5.0 y VPER4.1. Protocolo de valoración policial del riesgo y gestión de la seguridad de las víctimas de violencia de género. https://violenciadegenerotic.wordpress.com/wp-content/uploads/2019/05/instruccion-4-2019.pdf
Ministerio del Interior (2024) Sistema de seguimiento integral en los casos de Violencia de Género (Sistema VioGén). Datos estadísticos Junio 2024. https://www.interior.gob.es/opencms/pdf/servicios-al-ciudadano/violencia-contra-la-mujer/estadisticas/2024/Junio-2024.pdf
Observatorio Estatal de Violencia sobre la Mujer (2007) Informe anual del observatorio estatal de violencia sobre la mujer. Año 2007. Ministerio de Trabajo y Asuntos Sociales. Secretaria General de Politicas de Igualdad. Delegacion Especial del Gobierno contra la Violencia sobre la Mujer. http://www.violenciagenero.igualdad.gob.es/violenciaEnCifras/observatorio/informesAnuales/docs/I_Informe_anual_Observatorio_Estatal_VMujer_Junio_2007_CASTELLANO.pdf
Ortega Lorente JM (2018) Breves reflexiones sobre necesidades formativas de juezas y jueces. Juezas y Jueces para la Democracia 10:3–6
Peroni L (2016) Violence against migrant women: the Istanbul convention through a postcolonial feminist lens. Fem Leg Stud 24:49–67. https://doi.org/10.1007/s10691-016-9316-x
Rodriguez Martinez P (2019) Intimate Partner Violence against Women in Scandinavia and Southern Europe. Comp Sociol 18(3):265–289. https://doi.org/10.1163/15691330-12341500
Rodríguez-Rodríguez I, Rodríguez JV, Pardo-Quiles DJ, Heras-González P, Chatzigiannakis I (2020) Modeling and forecasting gender-based violence through machine learning techniques. Appl Sci 10(8244):1–22. https://doi.org/10.3390/app10228244

Sainz de Baranda Andujar C, De Lamo Velado I, Nieto Rojas P (2022) Use of technological devices and (re) victimization in gender-based crimes in Spain: a qualitative study on professionals' perceptions. Sociología y Tecnociencia 12(1):56–72. https://doi.org/10.24197/st.1.2022.56-72

Santos-Hermoso J, González-Álvarez JL, Alcázar-Córcoles MÁ, Carbonell-Vayá EJ (2022) Intimate partner homicide against women typology: risk factor interaction in Spain. Eur J Crim Policy Res 1–23. https://doi.org/10.1007/s10610-022-09517-7

Simó Soler E (2019) Feminizar el derecho: cuándo, cómo y por qué. In: Barona Vilar S (ed) Claves de la justicia penal: feminización, inteligencia artificial, supranacionalidad y seguridad. Tirant lo Blanch, Valencia, pp 83–104

Villacampa C (2021) Spanish criminal policy and the state pact on gender violence: a critical assessment. SN Soc Sci 1:129. https://doi.org/10.1007/s43545-021-00141-6

WHO. World Health Organization/London School of Hygiene and Tropical Medicine (2010) Preventing intimate partner and sexual violence against women: taking action and generating evidence. Geneva. https://apps.who.int/iris/bitstream/handle/10665/44350/9789241564007_eng.pdf;jsessionid=DF7797EE08311856DFB581F5078625AF?sequence=1

The Role of Police and Prosecutorial Bodies in Resolving Cases of Domestic Violence: The Example of Serbia

Mina Zirojevic

Abstract The phenomenon of domestic violence is present in all countries of the world and all cultures. This problem can be considered a psychological, sociological, philosophical and theological one, but this chapter analyzes its practical side, *i.e.*, the role of the police and law enforcement agencies in Serbia because of their utmost importance in preventing and removing social anomaly. Domestic violence is often analysed as physical violence only. Little attention is paid to other types of violence. The chapters mainly focus on intimate partner violence only. The relevance of the subject comes from the fact that the number of cases, of domestic violence in Serbia, is still on the high level, and this number grows from year to year. Using the comparative law method, it is analyzed the legal and organizational solutions in Serbia in comparison with other parts of the world, especially the EU and the regional countries. Taking into account the research findings that point to organizational weaknesses, it is proposed to improve, the work of the relevant services, especially the police and prosecution authorities.

1 Introduction

One of the worst crimes from the spectrum of domestic violence, which was committed with the permission of State institutions, happened on July 12, 2017 in Belgrade, Serbia. The image and scene of a unhuman act is embodied in the act of murdering an innocent child and his mother Maja.[1] Marko Nikolić is a person who was convicted for illegal possession of weapons and robbery, while the trial for domestic violence was yet to begin. They did not make it to the courtroom, even the

[1] Ekspres net (2017).

M. Zirojevic (✉)
Institute of Comparative Law, Belgrade, Serbia

R. Erbaş (ed.), *Criminal Prosecution of Domestic Violence*, Ius Gentium: Comparative Perspectives on Law and Justice 128,
https://doi.org/10.1007/978-3-032-01202-9_6

date for the hearing was on schedule but he killed his ex-wife and son just the day before. Despite the expertise of psychiatrists from the Clinic for Psychiatric Diseases, who diagnosed Nikolić with as many as six personality disorders and determined that he could see his son for two hours a week, under controlled conditions, the Court, based on the opinion of the Center for Social Work, decided that Nikolić could see his son longer, even six and a half hours a week, without any supervision.[2] The mother prevented him from seeing her son, and because of this, the Serbian judiciary fined her 600,000 dinars (cc 5500 US Dollars), which is why she had to take out a loan.[3]

She called the police countless times, but they did not take any action and the trial never came. When the child came to him on the order of the center, the father suffocated the child with his bare hands, put him in the car, went to the Center for Social Work, passed security carrying his dead son, threw the son at the feet of the mother, who started to run away, and stabbed her more than 50 times.[4] None of the people employed in State institutions were held accountable and no law was changed despite public pressure.

"One third of women in Serbia have experienced certain combination of different forms of violence, and 3.4% of women have experienced, all four forms of violence, during the life".[5] In the past few years, more research shows an increase of the number of gender-related killings, particularly because of lockdowns, fear of death in global pandemic, and the economic impact of these.[6] The approach to this problem has changed not only in modern but also traditional society, in which a complex set of measures was implemented aiming victims' protection from domestic violence crimes.[7,8] The irreplaceable role of the court has been unquestionable, but the role of the police, prosecutor and social institutions has become more significant, meaningful, responsible and precisely defined. This approach comes from the fact that broad theoretical and scholars' discussions and examinations in this area show that the repressive measures have importantly bigger preventive effects than preventive measures as they are.[9] Facing this reality, decision makers in societies that adopted the advanced approach to the issue of domestic violence give the police and the prosecution bodies along with other state institutions a new role and authority in this matter by implementing them in specialized laws dedicated to domestic violence victim's protection.

[2] N1 (2017).

[3] RTS (2017).

[4] Blic (2017).

[5] Peščanik (2018).

[6] Politika (2022).

[7] Zirojević and Marković (2021), pp. 311–329.

[8] For example, see some information's on stable internet address of Istanbul Convention https://www.coe.int/en/web/istanbul-convention/key-facts.

[9] We can see a very good presentation of comparative solutions and comparisons between repressive and preventive measures at the Internet address: https://iskljuci-nasilje.rs/prevencija-2/.

This chapter aims to light up the current situation, certain obstacles and potential solutions. The first part of the article, attempts to explain the historical overview of the approach of the police to victims of domestic violence. The chapter investigates the role of the police of the Republic of Serbia in cases of domestic violence. Even though the new role and the authority resulted in positive end results in this issue, many obstacles remain whose solving is necessary to be done in order to reach the full harmonization in this matter in a modern society, so that will be the point of the conclusion.

2 Historical Overview of the Police Approach to Domestic Violence Victims

Police approach to the cases of domestic violence crimes in Serbia has considerably developed in previous years, but there are still many things that need to be improved. Inter-sectoral cooperation between the police, prosecution and the court, data collection and the treatment of the persistent domestic violence cases are among the set of improvement measures made as a result of comprehensive research done in this area.[10] Until the 1960s and 1970s, the prevailing understanding was that "a man's home is his castle",[11] that violence against women committed within the family is a private matter and that conflicts if they do not involve serious injury or loss of life, should be resolved exclusively between spouses within the family.[12] The right to privacy was guaranteed as one of the universal human rights, which excluded the action of State institutions in cases of all forms of violence committed within the family.[13]

Firstly, the police had no role in the prevention or any active role in cases of domestic violence.[14] The main problems was the passive behavior of State institutions, but also of tolerant attitudes of the community towards violence against women.[15] The police is not willing to prevent and investigate domestic violence, including the investigation into the violent death of women. Prosecutors refuse to open domestic violence investigations or order protective measures for women who are in danger from their families or communities. Police and courts fail to ensure that men comply with all court documents (court orders, protection orders). They are given an unjustified leniency in sentencing, based on "provocation" by their victim and based on the insubstantial evidence. Also in Opuz case art. 96–97 it was well noted that one of the most difficult obstacles towards victims of domestic violence is the negative attitude of police officers in their stations. Namely, police officers still

[10] Hall (2015), p. 394.

[11] Hafetz (2002), p. 175.

[12] Preventing and responding to Domestic Violence-Trainee's Manual (2011), p. 28.

[13] Erez (2002), p. 7.

[14] IACP (2000).

[15] It is specifically described in Articles 100-102 of the *Opuz v. Turkey* case (33401/02), 09.06.2009.

believe that domestic violence is a private family matter in which they are reluctant to interfere.[16] Neither the victims nor the witnesses reported the cases because there was no crime. Later, despite being punishable, the police were only a mediator.

The breakthrough was made precisely by the case *Opuz v. Turkey.*[17] According to the Opinion of the Women's Shelter Foundation, which is stated in Articles 91-93 of the Opuz case,[18] the laws are not fully implemented. In recent years, because of the influence of the Opuz case, in family courts there has been an increase in issued injunctions, but some courts, in response to petitions from women in danger, still schedule hearings two or more months in advance. Under these circumstances, prosecutors and judges act according to the procedure as per Law no. 4320 like it is a form of divorce action, while the point of the law is, to take prompt action to protect lives of the women. Also, the issue of status in society and influence on state bodies is of particular importance. Why do we only refer to the Opuz case here? Turkish and Serbian society share a large part of their common history, so family problems are the same. women still have a lower status and social position than men. As a rule, a man has more ways to influence social and state institutions.

However, if we talk about the police response, which is the first, together with social work centers, in the chain of interventions in cases of domestic violence, then we must mention that in literature we have three basic types of police response: (1) *mediation* when the police play the role of "peacemaker"; (2) *arrest* which is optional, and (3) *mandatory arrest* in cases of domestic violence specified by law.[19] These three types of police reactions are used depending on the specific situation and depend on the type and degree of violence.[20] In our opinion, the *mediation* is the relict of the past time when the police had bigger discretion in assessing the reported domestic violence crime case, actually during the time when domestic violence crimes were not in the focus of the community as it is the case now.[21] However, today, that discrete role of the police disappeared.[22] These days it is mandatory for the police to follow the second or the third way of conducting its duties, so the *arrest* or the *mandatory arrest* remained the only two options that limited the police discretion in the case of domestic violence.

It is interesting to mention the results of a study published in 1984, called the "Minneapolis Experiment", in which it was shown that arrest is a far more effective measure than counselling and separation to reduce the number of repeated spousal abuse leading to increased number of prisoners, is not supported in the current doctrine.[23]

---

[16] See: *Kurt v. Australia* (62903/15), 4.07.2019, *Tkhelidze v. Georgia* (33056/17), 08. 07. 2021, *Tërshana v. Albania* (48756/14), 04.08.2020.

[17] *Opuz v. Turkey* (33401/02), 09.06.2009.

[18] The opinion of the Purple Roof Women's Shelter Foundation (Mor Çatı Kadın Sığınağı Vakfı – "the Mor Çatı Foundation") on the implementation of Law no. 4320, dated July 7, 2007.

[19] Golubovic (2016), p. 32.

[20] Hoyle and Sanders (2000), p. 18.

[21] See IACP (2000).

[22] Hoyle (2000), p. 3.

[23] Egan (1999), p. 1.

Official institutions do not adequately monitor the prevalence and frequency of domestic violence against women.[24] The field of condition monitoring in Serbia is insufficiently regulated by law, even though the institutions have obligation to collect data, there is no separate record of gender- and sexually-based violence.[25]

Official statistics register the following: the number of reports of cases of violence in the Ministry of Interior, the number of lawsuits initiated and who initiated them (prosecutor or victim), the number of verdicts pronounced, the record of the person against whom domestic violence was committed and the record of the person against whom is a specific measure of protection against domestic violence (Center for Social Work).

According to the data of the Republic Institute of Statistics, in the period from 2004 to 2022, there was an increase in the number of reported adults for domestic violence. While in 2004, 1009 cases of domestic violence were reported, in 2022 a total of 8531 persons were reported in Serbia.[26] In 94.4% of cases the abuser was a man.[27]

3 The Role of the Police in Cases of Domestic Violence

The role of the police in situations of "domestic violence" has many dimensions. The first dimension comes from special criminal-law regulations that provide for the actions of certain State authorities in cases of criminal acts of domestic violence, as well as from the general role of the police in preventing the commission of criminal acts and misdemeanors.[28] The role of the police is essential and irreplaceable in cases of prevention and detection of crimes of "domestic violence" and their perpetrators.

3.1 Prevention of "Domestic Violence"

The prevention of domestic violence is a primary responsibility of law enforcement and other societal bodies, with the police playing a crucial role in this effort. This is an essential procedure in the activity known in the theory and practice of criminal law as prevention.[29]

---

[24] Komatina (2022).

[25] Peščanik (2018).

[26] Announcement number 194, year LX, 01.07.1010, Republic of Serbia, Republic Institute of Statistics. Also, see stable internet address https://birn.rs/porodicno-nasilje/.

[27] Republic Institute of Statistics. Republic of Serbia.

[28] Hoyle and Sanders (2000), pp. 14–36.

[29] Spasic (2013), p. 95.

Prevention in these cases, as well as in cases of other illegal actions, did not occupy a significant place in the past and its role in the repressive activity was secondary, less organized and therefore significantly neglected.[30] However, in recent decades, with the growing awareness of the need to suppress "domestic violence", legislators have attached much greater importance to the institution of prevention. In addition, the Ministerial Committee of the Council of Europe adopted several recommendations aimed at crime prevention, including crimes of "domestic violence", namely: Recommendation no. R(87)19 on the organization of crime prevention, Recommendation no. R(96)8 on creating a policy to fight crime in the time of major political changes and Recommendation no. R(2000)20 on the role of early psychosocial intervention for crime prevention, while the Council of the European Committee of Experts on Police Ethics adopted the European Code of Police Ethics by Recommendation REC (2001)10.[31]

In modern society, and especially in cases of "domestic violence", the police do not have exclusive competence. On the contrary, it is necessarily directed to cooperation with other bodies whose importance and effect of prevention are significantly greater.[32] These are primarily the media, educational and health institutions and the non-governmental sector, which again provides the greatest contribution in the field of education of the widest number of citizens, especially vulnerable categories of citizens, as well as legislative, detection and prosecution authorities and judicial institutions.[33] Therefore, the cooperation of the police and prosecution authorities and courts with these subjects of preventive action is of particular importance and it is necessary to maintain it continuously.[34]

However, despite the importance of these bodies in the prevention of "family violence" cases, the role of the police and its preventive activities is still irreplaceable.[35] The fact from the research done by OSCE in Serbia in 2012. showed that from all other institutions the domestic violence victims reported these cases to the police in 60% of cases. The first other institution is medical service that only 43% of domestic violence victims use for reporting domestic violence cases. This is primarily because the police are perceived in all modern societies as the most trained and capable state body that can provide personal security protection to vulnerable citizens.[36] It is for these reasons that citizens in all societies turn to the police in principle with the aim of reporting cases of "domestic violence", but also to prevent further threats to the personal safety of citizens in cases where such crimes are reported. Only after the primary and initial actions of the police authorities, do other prevention entities undertake measures within their jurisdiction. Prosecuting

[30] Ibid, pp. 444–445.

[31] Ibid., pp. 365; European Code of Police Ethics, Recommendation REC (2001)10.

[32] See Gasmi (2019).

[33] Ibid.

[34] Zirojević and Marković (2021), pp. 311–329.

[35] Survey on violence against women in Serbia conducted by the OSCE.

[36] Ibid.

authorities and judicial authorities do so by timely and efficient action, which is important in the field of general or general and special or special prevention as the basic types of preventive action of judicial authorities provided for by positive legislation.[37] The remaining subjects of prevention do so only at the end, i.e., only when the activity of the police and prosecuting authorities and judicial authorities is over, the media, educational and health authorities and the non-governmental sector undertake measures within their jurisdiction. They are commensurate with the character and place and role that these subjects occupy in society, so that they convey a general message in the case of the media, educate in the case of educational and health institutions and work with vulnerable categories or the widest citizenry in the case of non-governmental organizations.

Given that the main part of prevention is still in the hands of the police, the area with the greatest possibilities for preventive action is precise with this state body. Aware of its role and importance, the police in Serbia have undertaken several measures to improve its preventive role and activities. In the past period, the police authorities have adopted several by-laws whose goal was precisely the prevention of crime, and thus also cases of domestic violence. These are: "Instructions on how organizational units work to combat crime",[38] "Instructions on how to organize and carry out internal affairs in the security sector"[39] and "Mandatory instructions on the operational work of the police".[40] The results of the application of these by-laws are significant and evident, although there are no quantitative indicators of their contribution to the preventive role of the police. Their main contribution consists precisely in the fact that they regulate the organization of police actions in a fundamentally different way, which has a great general preventive importance on crime as a whole, and thus on cases of family violence.[41]

While the existing preventing activities of the police are important, there is still ample opportunity for them to expand their efforts in this area, which we will present in a separate chapter.

Detection of domestic violence is of particular importance in the system of repressive actions against these crimes. The relevance of detecting domestic violence related crimes stems from the fact that there is still a large dark figure in domestic violence in all societies.[42] The essence of the dark figure lies in the non-reporting of these cases by injured family members for different reasons. In a certain number of cases, these are traditional cultural values in some conservative societies where violence is an integral part of the generally accepted culture of the

[37] Ibid., p. 55.

[38] Instructions on how organizational units work to combat crime, dated March 8, 2002.

[39] Instructions on how to organize and conduct internal affairs in the security sector, dated April 8, 1997.

[40] Mandatory instruction on the operational work of the police.

[41] Ibid.

[42] Serra et al. (2022), p. 5.

community of life,[43] while in developed modern societies the presence of dark figures is related to completely different causes.[44] In a scientific study conducted in USA,[45] the following key reasons for not reporting criminal offences in this area are cited:[46] "belief that the police cannot do anything (99.7%)", that the police would not believe the victim's allegations (61.3%), "fear of abusers (11.7%)", the absence of the victim's desire to involve other institutions in solving these problems (32%) and the presence of the victim's desire to protect children or their partner relationship with the abuser (34.8%).[47]

In a study published in Serbia 2023, it is written that for 73% of women, a situation in which a woman suffers severe physical injuries is a justified reason to report violence. For the second most frequently cited situation when it is justified to report violence, the respondents cited violence against children—64%. In the sample we can see 3% of respondents who say that in no case is it justified for a woman to report violence.[48] The largest percentage (75%) of the surveyed respondents chose the answer that fear of a person who commits violence is the most common reason why they do not report violence.

The answer that shame and embarrassment due to the violence they are exposed to is the main reason, was given in slightly more than half of the cases (51%), while half opted for the answers that they did not they report violence because they have nowhere to go or feel the fear of condemnation and rejection by their family and surroundings (50%).

For almost a third of women (31%), understanding and support from the environment (family and friends) is the key thing that would help them feel empowered to report violence. In another place there was support from institutions (understanding of the problem, professional representation, protection), which 27% of the respondents opted for, and that financial support was something that would helped them feel empowered to report the abuser, 15% of women said.

3.2 *Legal Framework of "Domestic Violence"*

Although Serbia is a signatory to the Istanbul Convention, there are some differences.[49] The definition of rape in the Serbian Criminal Code is not completely harmonized with the provisions of Art. 36 of the Istanbul Convention, since it does not

---

[43] Zirojević and Marković (2021), p. 320.

[44] Mc Quigg (2017), p. 88.

[45] Canadian data is similar. to see: Prochuck (2018).

[46] Marković (2018b), pp. 446–447.

[47] Ibid., pp. 422–423.

[48] Antović (2023), p. 11.

[49] For more about Istanbul Convention see: Gasmi (2019).

contain the lack of free consent, as one of the constituent elements of rape.[50] In Serbia, "a criminal offence is categorized as a rape only if it includes the use of force or threat of use of force, which implies that the victim should physically resist."[51] The criminal offense of rape is regulated by Article 178 of the Criminal Code, which stipulates that "Whoever forces another to commit rape or an act equivalent to it by using force or by threatening to directly attack the life or body of that person or a person close to him", commits the crime of rape.[52] Therefore, in Serbian legislation, two basic elements are necessary for the existence of this criminal offense, and they are the use of coercion and the performance of sexual assault (penetration).

New Gender Equality Law of 2021 in its Art. 6 introduces the legal concept of gender-based violence and defines violence against women as separate categories:

> Gender-based violence is any form of physical, sexual, psychological, economic and social violence committed against a person or groups of persons due to belonging to a certain gender or gender, as well as threats to such acts, regardless of whether they occur in public or private life, as well as any form of violence that mainly affects persons belonging to a certain gender;
>
> Violence against women means a violation of human rights and a form of discrimination against women and all acts of gender-based violence that cause or may lead to: physical, sexual, psychological or financial injury or suffering for women, including threats of such acts, coercion or arbitrary deprivation of liberty, either in public or in private life.[53]

Those definitions of Gender Equality Law, which include also sexual violence, are harmonized with provisions of the Convention of the Istanbul Convention. Gender Equality Act is the first code after the Istanbul Convention dealing comprehensively with gender equality.[54]

Domestic violence as illegal behavior, as a crime that protects the interest of victims in cases of domestic violence was introduced into the criminal legislation of the Republic of Serbia by amendments to the Criminal Code of the Republic of Serbia in 2002.[55] However, it would be naive to assume that the phenomenon of domestic violence, and the prevention of violence against married partners became the subject of protection of criminal law provisions only with Criminal Law. As a matter of fact, the protection of parental couple was also provided by earlier criminal law regulations through other foreseen criminal acts, while with these

[50] Council of Europe (2021). The Mid-term Horizontal Review of GREVIO of all 17 baseline evaluation reports, Secretariat of the monitoring mechanism of the Council of Europe Convention on Preventing and Combating Violence against Women and Domestic Violence Council of Europe.

[51] Gasmi and Nikač (2022), p. 138.

[52] https://www.paragraf.rs/propisi/krivicni-zakonik-2019.html.

[53] Official Gazette of Serbia No 52/2021 of May 2021.

[54] Gasmi and Nikač (2022), p. 131.

[55] Criminal Code of the Republic of Serbia, Law on Amendments to the Criminal Code of the RS.

amendments it was only specified and harmonized with the current international and regional conventions with which Serbia harmonized in the period after 2000.[56]

Article 194 of the Criminal Code of the Republic of Serbia in the group of offences dedicated to the domestic violence provides for five forms of this criminal offence.[57] The first form of this criminal offence represents its basic form by which this criminal offence is defined: (1) "anyone who, by the use of violence, threats to attack life or body, insolent or reckless behavior endangers the tranquility, physical integrity or mental state of a member of his family". This new definition protects member of the family as individual. The remaining three forms provide for the use of certain means of implementation and the occurrence of serious bodily injury or death, while a special form of this criminal offence foresees a sanction for violating the protection measures imposed on persons declared responsible for these crimes.

Nevertheless, the formal legal protection of family members is provided not only by the CC but also by other positive legislation, primarily by the Law on Public Order and Peace of the RS, 2016.[58] The provisions of Articles 7, 8 and 9 provide for "argument, shouting, noise, indecent, insolent and reckless behavior, insults, acts of violence, threats and fights" which can be carried out both against third parties and against family members whose protection has been raised to a higher level.[59]

In terms of procedural law, with the amendments to the Law on Criminal Procedure, the role of the police has been changed to the previous decisions of this law.[60] According to current procedural solutions, the role of the prosecutor is defined as primary in criminal prosecution, while the role of the police is subsidiary. The police participate in criminal proceedings by undertaking measures and actions entrusted to it by the public prosecutor, while it can undertake certain actions independently. What is provided by the amendments to the procedural law in a qualitatively different way compared to the previous legal solutions is the supervision and control of the police in undertaking the measures and actions provided for by the CPC by the prosecutor.[61]

Finally, the Law on Police prescribes the powers of the police in pursuing domestic violence crimes defined in the Republic of Serbia Criminal Code.[62] That regulation defines and explains the powers and as such represents the obligation of the police in their actions. As part of the authority of the police refers precisely to taking measures and actions against family members who appear as victims or perpetrators of criminal acts of domestic violence, this formal legal act appears as one of the

[56] Marković (2018a), pp. 113–117.

[57] The name of the Chapter Nineteen is Criminal Offenses against Marriage and the Family, Arts. 187–197.

[58] Law on Public Order and Peace. https://www.paragraf.rs/propisi/zakon_o_javnom_redu_i_miru.html.

[59] Ibid.

[60] Law on Criminal Procedure from 2011, Amanded on 2011, 2012, 2013, 2013, 2014, 2019, 2021 2021.

[61] Law on Criminal Procedure.

[62] Law on Police, Art. 28.

regulations that controls the type of individual powers that the police can undertake in suppressing crimes of domestic violence. In addition, the Law on Police foresees the possibility of additional specifications of the manner of exercising these powers. As a result of such a possibility, the following by-laws are foreseen, which more precisely specify and elaborate the ways of undertaking or exercising individual powers of the police, namely: “Regulations on police powers”, “regulations on the manner of performing police duties”, “regulations on the manner of exercising control and immediate regulation of traffic on roads and keeping mandatory records on the application of special measures and authorizations” and “regulations on technical features and methods of use of means of coercion”.[63]

The previously described normative provisions envisage three basic roles of the police in cases of criminal offences in the field of domestic violence, namely their prevention, detection and participation in the prosecution of perpetrators of criminal offences under the authority of the prosecutor.

4 The Role of State Authorities in Preventing Domestic Violence

In accordance with its primary role of preventing criminal acts and misdemeanors, cases of domestic violence are usually reported mainly to the police.[64] When it comes to the police, the head of the regional police administration appoints a police officer, whom the Law calls a “police officer for the prevention of domestic violence”.[65] This police officer is responsible for performing all police duties related to the prevention of domestic violence and the implementation of measures to protect victims from domestic violence. Certainly, in Serbia, the most important authority that this police officer has is the authority to issue emergency measures.[66]

As for the public prosecutor’s office, in all prosecutor’s offices, except the special jurisdiction prosecutor’s office, the public prosecutor is compelled to appoint deputy public prosecutors to perform tasks within the jurisdiction of the public prosecutor’s office in connection with the prevention of domestic violence and criminal prosecution for criminal offences referred to in Article 4 of this law. The number of deputies to be determined will be decided by each public prosecutor, considering the needs and specifics of each prosecution.[67]

In the courts, the president of the court appoints the judges who will judge cases of prevention of domestic violence and criminal acts specified in Article 4 of the Law. Procedures for the extension of an emergency measure, procedures for

[63] Marković (2018b), pp. 446–447.

[64] OSCE (2012), p. 52.

[65] See the Law on Prevention of Domestic Violence.

[66] Hanna (1996), p. 1853.

[67] The Law on Prevention of Domestic Violence.

determining protection measures against domestic violence provided for by the Family Law and misdemeanor procedures for offences provided for by this law are considered cases of prevention of domestic violence.

In each center for social work, a team of experts has to be appointed, who have completed the specialized training prescribed by this law, to prevent and provide support in cases of domestic violence and other forms of gender-based violence.

In today's legal systems, when it comes to crimes of domestic violence, certain important roles are entrusted not only to the police, which has retained its primary role in detecting these crimes, but also to other state bodies, such as institutions of the educational and health systems and the media.[68]

With the new Law on Prevention of Domestic Violence, the role of the police takes on importance primarily in the area of professionalization and the formation of specialized internal organizational units entrusted with the role of suppressing domestic violence. A special "central database" of persons convicted of crimes of domestic violence appears as an integral part of the sub-law on the prevention of violence.[69]

What appears as a problem in the police's actions in suppressing domestic violence crimes is the discretionary right of the police to decide whether a certain action is a criminal offense or some other punishable behavior. One of the ways in which this potential problem is solved is the formation of internal organizational units and special training of police officers who deal with cases of domestic violence.[70]

The police play an active role in prosecuting perpetrators of domestic violence crimes, both in criminal and misdemeanor proceedings. The police will make a (current) report on the violence on the spot, take statements, describe or record the injuries, and if necessary, call an ambulance where the victim will receive a medical report (not a medical certificate).[71] According to this law, created on the basis of the Istanbul Convention, the police have the right to bring the violent person to the station and to assess the risk immediately after receiving notification of violence (Articles 15 and 16, 17) and can issue a written order on emergency measures to the perpetrator of violence.[72]

The public prosecutor's office is primarily responsible for prosecuting offences related to domestic violence in criminal and misdemeanor proceedings. Upon receipt of the report, the prosecutor is obliged to examine the above-mentioned reports and evaluate the risk assessment, which practically means that the prosecutor reassesses the risk. This is of the utmost importance as the risk is constantly changing. Also, because the risk the risk assessment is repeated by another person, precisely because of the possible negative attitudes of police officers. In addition to

[68] Zirojević and Marković (2021), p. 313.

[69] The Law on Prevention of Domestic Violence.

[70] Bjelajac (2022), p. 49.

[71] Law on Prevention of Domestic Violence, Arts. 10–14.

[72] See Gasmi (2019).

the reassessment of the risk by the competent police officer, the prosecutor can obtain preliminary reports from the competent center for social work on whether the family is in the center's files and since when, on what basis, i.e. whether domestic violence has been established in that family, with the obligation to submit its risk assessment; to obtain a report from a specialist doctor on possible injuries to the victim if this has not already been provided, and a report from a health institution if the person who committed the violence was previously treated for addiction or other mental illness in the institution where the person was treated.

In a study we aforementioned we descover that in Serbia if they were victims of domestic violence, the largest number of women (38%) would first turn to family members for support. 28% would turn to the police, while 9% of respondents would seek support from friends. Almost every tenth participant in the research said that in case of experienced domestic violence, she would not turn to anyone—8%.[73]

The existence of family support (parents, siblings and children) is something that would generally encourage women to report violence the most—this was the first choice for one third of respondents (33%). 17% of the participants in our research see the feeling of safety as the most important factor when reporting violence, as well as the fact that there is a person in the environment who will understand and be supportive.[74] The police (29%), the closest environment (24%) and internet portals and websites (18%) are the first places where Serbian citizens would look for information on where they can report violence.[75]

5 Proposals for Improving the Policy of Suppressing Cases of Domestic Violence

Research in Serbia shows that women who have been victims of partner violence are not sufficiently informed about which services they can ask for help and what this help entails.[76] On the Ministry of the Interior's website, there is a page with advice for potential and actual victims of domestic violence, both about their legal rights and whom they can turn to for help. However, the survey also shows that only about one-third of the respondents are unemployed, i.e. more than half of the respondents are in a poor financial situation and that one-third of the respondents have no schooling or the lowest level of education.[77] Therefore it is necessary to find more appropriate ways to inform these institutions and the victims about the possibilities of protection against domestic violence. Also, in the qualitative description of the attitude of the police towards the respondents who reported domestic vio-

[73] Antović et al. (2023), p. 17.

[74] Ibid.

[75] Ibid.

[76] Zirojević and Marković (2021), p. 322.

[77] Peščanik (2019).

lence, there are a considerable number of statements expressing distrust towards the police because often there was no adequate response or the police officers were unpleasant and told them that they had to solve the problem themselves, they asked why they had come again and, in some situations, it turned out that they were friends with the perpetrator. The results of some studies in other countries can be practically transferred to the situation in Serbia, so it is fair to say that family violence and the main solutions to this problem are universal.

A detailed study of police work in domestic violence cases carried out in two police stations showed that traditional attitudes towards domestic violence remained unchanged, although the rules had changed. It was obvious, as the author states, that the law "symbolically served to institutionalize domestic violence, highlighting the principles of non-interference in family life and patriarchal authority as inviolable principles above the principle of wife protection".[78] On the other hand, the protagonists of cultural theories held that legal and police rules have no influence on the actual direction of police action and that legal reforms cannot significantly change the "culture" of the police. There is a significant gap between legal rules and police practice, which Gasmi and Prlja argues that it is due to the existence of such laws that create a flexible and permissive structure within which the police operate.[79]

There are numerous reasons why the police fail to apply certain provisions of the law in practice: the so-called "loopholes" in the law, failure to regulate certain specific situations that arise in practice, application of the provisions of the law in situations other than those foreseen, misinterpretation, discretionary and enabling decisions, disregard for the spirit of the law and certain guidelines, etc. Effective implementation of domestic violence laws should provide victims of violence with comprehensive protection from this form of crime. However, Edwards believes that there is a "public-private split" of the law into theory and practice that affects the different levels of police response to priorities in action. Although the law does not state it, police treat domestic violence as a lower priority when intervening. Police officers are very strict in enforcing the law, except in cases of domestic violence where they rarely intervene, and when they do, they generally try to calm the situation down and keep the peace.[80]

The role of the police, as understood by these authors, is to provide services and maintain order, which is generally not achieved through law enforcement alone. The work of the police includes crime prevention and prosecution, but there are also other functions such as administrative procedures, traffic regulation, emergency response, crime prevention, conflict resolution and more. The police deal with many issues and provide various services to citizens. Research has shown that police officers believe that providing services to citizens distracts the police from the "real" work of fighting crime. Reiss,[81] for example, after conducting interviews with police

[78] Edwards (1989), p. 10.

[79] See McBarnet (1983).

[80] Edwards (1989), p. 15 and Palmiotto (2000), p. 225.

[81] See Reiss (1971) and Goldstein (2000), p. 11.

officers, stated that the role of the police is divided between law enforcement and law and order maintenance. When the police intervene in cases of domestic violence, they generally tend to keep the peace, taking on the role of mediator rather than the prosecutor.

Edwards also criticized this policy of responding to the police, stressing that they should not take on the role of social workers and counsellors. The police should resolve the conflict, apply criminal law and not just mediate. The decision whether or not to apply the law is rarely made based on an invitation alone, but usually after a discussion with the actors in the event. Police officers in most cases do not use their legitimate right to use force to resolve a conflict because their authority is protected by the fact that it is common knowledge that the police often use force when necessary. In this way, the use of the law becomes a means to achieve social order and peace. The attitude of the police towards domestic violence, the social and organizational perception of this phenomenon, depends on how the police respond to the perpetrator and the victim and how and how effectively they apply the law.

The scope for improving the actions of the police and prosecutors in suppressing cases of domestic violence is wide and full of multiple opportunities for improvement. Among them, the following measures stand out, and a particularly important place belongs to the improvement of police training and the training of prosecutors for more efficient handling of domestic violence cases.

6 Conclusion

In the Republic of Serbia, domestic violence was criminalized as a separate offence only in 2002, after a process of several years of public advocacy and lobbying by women's groups. There is no doubt that the police play an extremely important role in the prosecution of domestic violence, as the quantity and quality of data collected on the violent act, the victim and the perpetrator depend on their work. On the other hand, the way the police act and intervene has an impact on the victim's safety, the perpetrator's future behavior, the victim's willingness to testify, etc.

Research on comparative police practice, the results of which are presented in this paper, shows that because of the extremely heavy responsibility and complexity of the tasks that the police have in preventing the recurrence of domestic violence and prosecuting violent acts that have been committed, it is extremely important to establish specific rules of conduct in cases of reported family violence, the application of which ensures that police intervention is efficient and effective and does not have undesirable consequences. Moreover, research shows that the way police react, act and behave depends to a large extent on the personal attitudes, prejudices and stereotypical views of police officers, as the rules of operational work, even if strict, give the police a wide margin of discretion. The experience of comparative foreign police practice, which is continuously improved under the influence of reasoned criticism, is a useful guide for developing the operational strategy of domestic state authorities to improve the way police respond and act in domestic violence cases.

Accordingly, two tasks are of paramount importance for future work to improve police action and work in the field of domestic violence: the development of appropriate protocols on police behaviour and the training of police officers to ensure that they become familiar with the characteristics, structure and dynamics of domestic violence to overcome their prejudices and stereotypes and acquire the necessary communication skills.

If we look at the work of prosecutors, we will see that the main problem is the inadequate selection of cases. The real victims of domestic violence are easily dismissed and inadequately traced because many perpetrators report false victims, and the prosecutors are not trained enough to recognize and protect the real victim. This leaves the perpetrator free to further intimidate the victim. In many cases, the same people file false charges for years. The result is dismissed cases and long-term abuse of the victim, involving the system that is supposed to protect them.

References

Antović T et al (2023) Why do women not report domestic violence?: research results, Commissioner for the Protection of Equality: United Nations Development Program (UNDP) in Serbia. Proof, Belgrade

Bjelajac Ž (2022) Profil nasilnika: rani znaci za detekciju [Abuser Profile: Early Signs for Detection]. Kultura polisa 19(1):37–54. https://doi.org/10.51738/Kpolisa2022.19.2

Blic (2017) https://www.blic.rs/vesti/hronika/sest-godina-od-ubistva-maje-djordjevic-i-njenog-sina-ispred-centra-za-socijalni-radu/82zgdgt

Edwards SSM (1989) Policing 'domestic' violence women, the law and the state. Sage, London

Egan N (1999) The police response to spouse abuse: a selective, annotated bibliography. Law Libr J 91:499–576

Ekspres net (2017) In front of the murder counter: Who is responsible for tragedies in social work centers. https://www.ekspres.net/drustvo/pred-salterom-za-ubistvo-ko-je-odgovoran-za-tragedije-u-centrima-za-socijalni-rad

Erez E (2002) Domestic violence and the criminal justice system: an overview. Online J Iss Nurs 7(1):1–24. http://www.nursing world.org/oj/n/topic17/tpc173htm

Gasmi G (2019) Global Significance of European Standards of Women Human Rights Protection in Domain of Gender Based and Domestic Violence, Fiat Iustitia No 1/2019: 125–139

Gasmi G, Nikač Ž (2022) Sexual and gender-based violence in Serbia: after the istanbul convention. In: Erbas R (ed) Global problems in sexual offenses. Lexington Books, New York, pp 127–152

Gasmi, G, Prlja, D. (2024), Violence against women in international law, Institute of Comparative Law, Belgrade

Goldstein H (2000) Toward community-oriented policing. Potencial Basis Requirement and Threshold Questions, USA

Golubović, Z (2016) Violence in the family and police reaction (Nasilje u porodici I policijska reakcija) Partenon, Serbia

Hafetz JL (2002) A man's home is his castle?: Reflections on the home, the family, and privacy during the late nineteenth and early twentieth centuries. William Mary J Women Law 8(2):175–242

Hall RJ (2015) Feminist Strategies to End Violence Against Women. The Oxford Handbook of Transnational Feminist Movements Edited by Rawwida Baksh and Wendy Harcourt, https://gbvaor.net/sites/default/files/2019-07/Feminist%20Strategies%20to%20End%20VAW%20OXFORD%20Handbook%202015.pdf

Hanna C (1996) No right to choose: mandated victim participation in domestic violence prosecutions. Harv Law Rev 109(8):1849–1910
Hoyle C (2000) Negotiating domestic violence, police, criminal justice and victims. Oxford University Press, Oxford
Hoyle C, Sanders A (2000) Police response to domestic violence: from victim choice to victim empowerment? Br J Criminol 40(1):14–36
IACP (2000) What do victims want? Effective strategies to achieve justice for victims of crime. From the IACP Victims Summit. Recommendations Released. The International Association of Chiefs of Police, New York
Komatina S (2022) Female victim of violence from the point of view of statistics (Žena žrtva nasilja iz ugla statistike). Republic Institute of Statistics, Belgrade
Marković S (2018a) Prevention and suppression of domestic violence, JP Official Gazette
Marković S (2018b) Sprečavanje i suzbijanje nasilja u porodici [Prevention and suppression of domestic violence] Službeni glasnik, Belgrade
Mc Quigg RJ (2017) The Istanbul convention, domestic violence and human rights. Routledge
N1 (2017) He killed a woman and a five-year-old son in the Center for Social Work. https://n1info.rs/vesti/a282855-ubio-zenu-u-centru-za-socijalni-rad-u-rakovici/
Palmiotto M (2000) Community policing, a policing strategy for the 21 century. Jones & Bartlett Learning, Maryland
Peščanik (2018) Mapping domestic violence against women in Central Serbia. https://pescanik.net/wp-content/uploads/2018/05/Mapiranje_porodicnog_nasilja_prema_zenama_u_Centralnoj_Srbiji.pdf
Peščanik (2019) Prikaz preliminarnih rezultata istraživanja o nasilju prema ženama u porodici i partnerskom odnosu u seoskim područjima [Presentation of the preliminary results of research on violence against women in the family and partner relationship in rural areas]. Udruženje žena [Association of women] "Peščanik", Kruševac, Serbia. https://udruzenjepescanik.org/izvestaji/prikaz-preliminarnih-rezultata-istrazivanja-o-nasilju-prema-zenama-u-porodici-i-partnerskom-odnosu-u-seoskim-podrucjima/
Politika (2022) 200 murders were reported in Serbia last year. https://www.politika.rs/scc/clanak/512836/U-Srbiji-je-prosle-godine-prijavljeno-200-ubistava
Preventing and Responding to Domestic Violence-Trainee's Manual (2011) General Department of Anti-crime Police, MPS Administrative-Criminal Law Department, Edition 2. MOJ For Law Enforcement and Justice Sectors in Vietnam, Hanoi
Prochuck A (2018) We are here: women's experiences of the barriers to reporting sexual assault. Vancouver West Coast LEAF. http://www.westcoastleaf.org/wp-content/uploads/2018/10/West-Coast-Leaf-dismantling-web-final.pdf
Reiss AJ Jr (1971) The Police and the Public. Yale University Press, New Haven
RTS (2017) A man killed a woman and a child in the Center for Social Work in Rakovica. https://www.rts.rs/page/stories/sr/story/135/hronika/2801736/muskarac-ubio-zenu-i-dete-u-centru-za-socijalni-rad-u-rakovici.html
Serra L et al (2022) Analysis of the geographic pattern of the police reports for domestic violence in Girona (Spain). BMC Public Health 22:552. https://doi.org/10.1186/s12889-022-12916-4
Spasic D (2013) Community policing and domestic violence, PHD Dissertation. University of Belgrade, Faculty of Security Studies, Belgrade
Survey on violence against women in Serbia conducted by the OSCE (2012). https://www.unodc.org/e4j/en/crime-prevention-criminal-justice/module-14/key-issues/2%2D%2Dgeneral-issues%2D%2Dpublic-prosecutors-as-the-gate-keepers-of-criminal-justice.html.
UNODC, www.unodc.org/roseap/uploads/archive/documents/vietnam/publication/Trainee_manual_in_English_6-5-11_.pdf
Zirojević MT, Marković DM (2021) Silence between love and fear - Why victims of violence remain silent. In: Kuburić Z, Zotova A, Ćumura LJ (eds) Love and fear in interdisciplinary research: collection of papers from the scientific conference, Belgrade, pp 311–329

The Vulnerability of Domestic Violence Victims from a Gender Perspective in Spanish Criminal Proceedings: Challenges and Proposals Against the Phenomenon of Secondary Victimization

Selena Tierno Barrios

Abstract Although the protection of victims is one of the essential functions of criminal proceedings, its inadequate fulfilment is the main cause often associated with the crisis of the Spanish criminal justice system. In this sense, notwithstanding the special relevance of the access to justice right as a guarantee of the effectiveness of citizens' rights, there are remarkable obstacles traditionally faced by certain vulnerable groups, including victims of gendered violence. Thus, the aim of this chapter is to analyze the difficulties which are faced by victims of gendered violence in Spanish criminal proceedings, focusing on the tendency to revictimize them as a result of stereotypes embedded within the judicial system. Further, the chapter discusses the reform of the criminal justice system proposed by the current of restorative justice, as well as the practice of criminal mediation.

This chapter has been made in the framework of a contract obtained through the FPU (training for university teachers) programme from Ministerio de Universidades of Gobierno de España as Predoctoral Researcher within the Procedural Law Area of Universidad de Salamanca. This chapter has also been carried out within the framework of the Research Project "Agenda 2030 y acceso igualitario a la justicia de personas vulnerables desde una perspectiva de género" (PIC-2022-06) from Universidad de Salamanca, whose Principal Investigator is Dr. Adán Carrizo González-Castell.

S. Tierno Barrios (✉)
University of Salamanca, Salamanca, Spain
e-mail: selenatierno@usal.es

R. Erbaş (ed.), *Criminal Prosecution of Domestic Violence*, Ius Gentium: Comparative Perspectives on Law and Justice 128,
https://doi.org/10.1007/978-3-032-01202-9_7

1 Introduction

The protection of the rights and interests of the victim of a criminal offence is and should be an essential function of criminal proceedings. This is, indeed, an indisputable truth in the framework of a democratic State. Albeit, what it is not so clear is whether the exercise of this function has always been carried out effectively. In fact, the inadequate fulfilment of this function, which results in so-called secondary victimization,[1] is one of the causes that is frequently associated with the crisis of the Spanish criminal justice system to which other factors are added, such as the ineffectiveness of punishment in its preventive function of the criminal act, the failure to comply with the principle of resocialization or the stigmatization of the convicted person.[2]

This has meant focusing attention on the proposal for reform of the current model of the criminal procedural system represented by the current of restorative justice —and, within it, the practice of criminal mediation— in which the movement that advocates the revaluation and prominence of the victim in the solution of conflicts of a criminal nature is framed.[3] This occurs because the victim has been denied, from the outset of the criminal justice system, the leading role that he/she really has in criminal proceedings with the expropriation of his/her own conflict by the State[4] and being neutralized by the institutions themselves, hence this is why for centuries he/she has been the "great forgotten one" of the criminal procedural system, and even ignored.[5]

It was understood that the competence to react to the commission of a criminal act corresponded to the State, which had to play the main role in criminal protection. In this regard, it was accepted that the crime was committed against the State and society, so that the victims could not interfere in the reaction to the criminal offence, removing then any possibility of revenge.[6] In this sense, the exposure of the victim to the effects of the phenomenon of secondary victimization —translated into the impossibility of the criminal justice system to offer an adequate response to the protection of his/her rights and needs— has recently led to reflection on the role of the victim within the criminal process, acquiring a greater prominence in the framework, as I have said, of the current of restorative justice as one of the main trends in criminal justice and which is shaping the criminal process in recent times.[7]

In this order of things, it must be highlighted the basic foundations that sustain restorative justice, mainly, the active prominence of the parties in the solution of

[1] On the secondary victimisation, see García-Pablos de Molina (2014), pp. 126–130.

[2] In this regard, see Rodríguez-García (2017), pp. 275–277.

[3] Along this line of thought, see Carrizo González-Castell (2017), p. 251.

[4] On this issue, see Christie (1977), pp. 7–9.

[5] Barona Vilar (2019), pp. 64–65.

[6] Of this opinion is Pérez Rivas (2017), pp. 6–11.

[7] Flores Prada (2015), pp. 11–12 and 18.

conflicts of a criminal nature and the integral reparation of the victim that favors his/her *rediscovery* and revaluation within the criminal justice system.[8]

In fact, that allows me to dazzle with a diaphanous clarity the perfect fit of this current in the Goal 16 of the 2030 Agenda for Sustainable Development,[9] adopted by the United Nations Summit through Resolution of 25 September 2015 with the firm purpose of transforming our world, entitled "Peace, Justice and Strong Institutions" in the sense of facilitating equal access to justice for all people, promoting then peaceful and inclusive societies, being precisely one of its goals (Goal 16.3) that one to ensure equal access to justice for all people.[10] This reflects the concern of world leaders about the access to justice right, whereby encouraging the adoption of public policies aimed at guaranteeing the effective exercise of this right by particularly vulnerable groups.[11]

On the road to achieving the desideratum pursued through this Goal 16 of the 2030 Agenda —justice and social peace— the access to justice right[12] acquires a maximum relevance in the sense that it constitutes the most basic human right in the framework of a legal system that claims to be modern and egalitarian, and whose objective is not only to recognize, but also to guarantee the rights of all people,[13] since the simple fact of having a recognized right is completely useless if there are no instruments that allow its effective vindication.[14] However, notwithstanding this special relevance of the access to justice right, deficiencies in this area can still be observed today within judicial systems. This is because of a lack of response by countries, which are generally not implementing public policies which would eliminate the obstacles and difficulties that certain vulnerable population groups have traditionally faced. Such policies would be aimed not only at promoting, but also at guaranteeing that all people can access justice under equal conditions.[15] That is, without any kind of barrier that would limit, restrict or prevent certain groups from enjoying and exercising their rights because they are particularly vulnerable.[16]

Thus, one of the factors that stands out as the main cause of vulnerability, and on which this chapter focuses is gender, insofar as discrimination against women in certain areas constitutes an impediment that restricts the access to justice right, and this situation can be aggravated in those cases in which any other cause (e.g. age, disability, poverty or migration) is present —what is known as the intersectionality

[8] In this regard, see Montesinos García (2017), pp. 25–26; Alonso Salgado (2018), p. 63.

[9] On the Goal 16 of the 2030 Agenda, see Rodríguez-García and Pahul Robredo (2022), pp. 35–39.

[10] See Quispe Remón (2018), pp. 239–240.

[11] I do share the view expressed by Carrizo González-Castell (2021), pp. 191–192.

[12] On this issue, see Carrizo González-Castell (2019), p. 293; Añón Roig (2018), p. 31.

[13] Of this opinion are Cappelletti and Garth (1978), pp. 184–185.

[14] In that sense, see the definition of American Bar Association (2012), p. 1.

[15] Along this line of thought, see Carrizo González-Castell (2019), pp. 295–296.

[16] On this issue, it must be highlighted Cumbre Judicial Iberoamericana (2018). Brasilia Rules on access to justice for people in vulnerable situations. https://capacitacion.jusmisiones.gov.ar/files/material_curso/2019/Reglas_de_Brasilia_Centro_actualizadas.pdf.

phenomenon—.[17] Therefore, the claimed objective is the implementation of public policies and measures that contribute to eradicating discrimination against women in access to the judicial system for the protection of their rights and legitimate interests, and thus, obtaining effective equality of conditions. This is an objective that is aligned not only with Goal 16 aimed at promoting access to justice, but also with Goal 5 on "Gender Equality" which seeks to "achieve gender equality and empower all women and girls," including among its targets "end all forms of discrimination against all women and girls everywhere."[18]

In that way, the aim of this chapter will be to analyze the difficulties which are faced by victims of gendered violence in Spanish criminal proceedings, focusing on the tendency to revictimize them as a result of stereotypes embedded within the judicial system —as in cases where the victim's testimony constitutes the only incriminating evidence—. Further, to supplement this analysis, this chapter will study the reform of the criminal justice system proposed by the current of restorative justice, as well as the practice of criminal mediation as an instrument aimed at the revaluation and empowerment of the victim of gendered violence in the criminal justice system.

2 Gender as a Vulnerability Factor: The Phenomenon of Secondary Victimization

As I have highlighted at the beginning of this chapter, there are remarkable obstacles traditionally faced by certain groups of people who see their access to justice right under conditions of equality limited in its exercise because they are in a context of particular vulnerability. For instance, economic difficulties, the complexity of regulations or the cultural factor. In this line, it must be brought up the text of the Brasilia Rules on access to justice for people in vulnerable conditions, recently reformulated in 2018, which highlights what has been pointed out previously, namely, the simple fact of having a recognized right is completely useless if the holder of that right has restricted access to the justice system in order to obtain its protection.[19] In other words, although the difficulty of guaranteeing the effectiveness of rights is of a general nature, it is even more serious in the case of vulnerable groups, hence the importance of eliminating any obstacle that prevents the effective exercise of a genuine right to equal access to justice.[20] Thus, one of the factors that

---

[17] This can be read in Rule 17 which is set out in the text of the Brasilia Rules referred to above.

[18] On this issue, see UN Women (2018). Turning promises into action: Gender equality in the 2030 Agenda for Sustainable Development. https://www.unwomen.org/sites/default/files/Headquarters/Attachments/Sections/Library/Publications/2018/SDG-report-Gender-equality-in-the-2030-Agenda-for-Sustainable-Development-2018-en.pdf.

[19] In that way, see the Explanatory Memorandum to the Brasilia Rules on access to justice for people in vulnerable conditions.

[20] On the Brasilia Rules, see Álvarez Alarcón (2021), pp. 25–50.

stands out as the main cause of vulnerability is gender as referred to in Rule 4 of the Brasilia Rules text.

In this regard, the aforementioned regulatory text pays special attention to this factor insofar as discrimination against women in certain areas constitutes an impediment that restricts the access to justice right. Furthermore, this situation may be aggravated in those cases in which any other cause is present because of the intersectionality phenomenon,[21] for instance, victimization, on which I focus my research by considering this block of study, particularly, on victims of gendered violence. In that way, pursuant to Rule 18, discrimination against women encompasses any "exclusion or restriction made on the basis of sex which has the effect or purpose of impairing or nullifying the recognition, enjoyment or exercise by women, irrespective of their marital status, on a basis of equality of men and women, of human rights and fundamental freedoms in the political, economic, social, cultural, civil or any other field." Therefore, it coheres with the definition provided by Article 1 of the Convention on the Elimination of All Forms of Discrimination against Women, adopted by the United Nations General Assembly through Resolution 34/180 of 18 December 1979; and the Organic Law 3/2007, of 22 March, for the Effective Equality of Women and Men, in Spain.

Furthermore, pursuant to Rule 19, violence against women is defined as "any act or conduct, based on the fact of the female sex belonging, which results in, or it is likely to result in, death or physical, sexual or psychological harm or suffering to women, or property damage, including threats of such acts, coercion or arbitrary deprivation of liberty, whether in the public or the private sphere". Therefore, this coheres with the provisions of the Council of Europe Convention on Preventing and Combating Violence against Women and Domestic Violence, made in Istanbul on 11 May 2011, and the Directive 2024/1385 of the European Parliament and of the Council, of 14 May 2024, on combating violence against women and domestic violence.

Moreover, in cases of gendered violence there is also another cause of vulnerability such as the factor of victimization which is expressly referred to in Rules 10 to 12 of the text of the Brasilia Rules and which dedicate special mention to those people who have a double condition of vulnerability such as women who are victims of this kind of violence. As far as victimization is concerned, the main objective is the adoption of measures aimed both at reducing the negative effects caused by the commission of the crime suffered directly by the victim —which is known as primary victimization— and at preventing the harm that the victim may suffer as a consequence of their relationship with the criminal justice system (secondary victimization).[22]

In this sense, the phenomenon of secondary victimization or "double victimization" is especially frequently observed in the context of criminal proceedings for crimes of gendered violence, in which women victims perceive that justice does not

[21] On the intersectionality phenomenon, see Crenshaw (1989), pp. 139–167.

[22] García-Pablos de Molina (2014), pp. 126–130.

adequately attend to their needs to the extent that on many occasions what they demand is to be listened to, to receive support and assistance. Thus, this results in an increase in the intensity of the psychological-emotional damage that generates a sense of lack of protection and a feeling of guilt, vulnerability and insecurity. All of this, together with the existence of stereotypes, prejudices and discrimination within the judicial system, ends up causing gendered violence to become an impossible obstacle to overcome, preventing the survival of the situation of violence created by the aggressor.[23]

2.1 The Statement of the Victim as the Only Incriminating Evidence in Criminal Proceedings for Gendered Violence Crimes

In this line, it will be in the field of evidence in which I will delve in more detail into the effects generated by the phenomenon of secondary victimization in the framework of gendered violence through, on the one hand, the assessment of the victim's statement as the only incriminating evidence and, on the other hand, the so-called "legal exemption from the duty to testify" which has caused so much ink to flow not only in doctrine but also in case law. On this issue, the proposed modification and, finally, effective reform in 2021 of the limitation of this legal dispensation in the event that the witness exempted is a victim of gendered violence when certain procedural circumstances are present represents nothing more than one more legal stereotype within the legal system whereby the legislator presupposes that the woman victim of gendered violence is a helpless and defenseless person. That is, a person which is unable for decision-making and discernment who permanently needs a paternalistic tutelage by the State, showing a total lack of confidence in her decision-making capacity and the irrelevance of her true will. In short, this is another of the measures which has been adopted that shows a legislative patriarchy in this matter by creating a criminal system that reproduces the structural context of domination against which it is proposed to fight and tackle.[24]

As a starting point, it should be noted that one of the aspects that generates most debate and concern in criminal proceedings for gendered violence crimes is indeed the one related to evidence.[25] This happens because, in these cases, the victim of the offence is not only a victim but also a witness, and the evidentiary material available to the judge is often particularly scarce as, generally, it is only made up of the woman's statement due to the commission of such offences in a private

---

[23] Gil (2018), pp. 241–245.

[24] In this sense, I do share the view expressed by Ortiz Pradillo (2016), pp. 2–5. Along this line of thought, see also Hanna (1996), p. 1853; Sanz Mulas (2019), pp. 63–74; Beltrán Montoliu (2018), p. 20.

[25] Fuentes Soriano (2018), p. 4.

environment. Thus, the victim of the criminal act herself will often be the only one who may relate the sequence of events without any other evidence in the criminal process than her own statement. This makes her a main character not only by the simple fact of being able to become a private prosecutor in criminal proceedings, but also by subordinating the obtaining of a conviction or a guilty judgement to her statement at the oral trial phase on the basis of the exercise of the right not to testify against the defendant, in other words, the exemption from the duty to testify.[26]

In this regard, the main evidentiary problems that may arise in this type of proceedings due to the force of the right to the presumption of innocence revolve around two axes: (i) the scarce evidentiary material which has been mentioned above, reduced in most cases to the statement of the victim of gendered violence as the only incriminating evidence; (ii) changes in statements which are made by victims during the course of criminal proceedings, which will largely lead to the annulment of the evidentiary value, and besides that, it cannot be forgotten that, in connection with this previous point, there is the possibility to opt in of the exemption from the duty to testify, regulated by the Spanish Criminal Procedure Act[27] (from now on, LECrim), which I will examine below.[28]

Beginning with the evidentiary issue raised by the statement of the victim of gendered violence as the only incriminating evidence, it should be noted that this is by no means a futile issue because, in line with what has been explained in this chapter, the statement of the woman "witness-victim" is not generally understood, generating a certain amount of mistrust on the part of legal operators based on prejudices and preconceptions about the archetype of the victim.[29]

Thus, the recognition of the victim's statement in criminal proceedings as the only incrimination evidence with the power to undermine the presumption of innocence of the defendant has been widely accepted by Spanish jurisprudence (both by the Supreme Court and the Constitutional Court) for several decades. However, always and in any case, it has been subject to the concurrence of certain circumstances that would allow its plausibility to be extracted, especially in the framework of gendered violence, as these acts are committed in an intimate space and the statement of the woman victim constitutes the only existing evidential material. Hence, the establishment of certain parameters or criteria that should allow the judge to form his/her conviction and to attribute evidentiary value to the statement given, considering subjective credibility, objective credibility and persistence in the incrimination. All of this without constituting necessary requirements for the validity of the testimony, nor should they be cumulative, and they also have a relative value. This means that, in the event that any of them are missing, the testimony should not necessarily be considered invalid, but in the event that all of them are

[26] On this issue, see González Monje (2020), p. 1630.

[27] Royal Decree of 14 September 1882 Approving the Criminal Procedure Act (Official State Gazette no. 260, of 17 September 1882).

[28] This is the view expressed by Fuentes Soriano (2018), pp. 3–4.

[29] Along this line of thought, see Laurrari (2022), p. 155.

present, this does not mean that the presumption of innocence is automatically undermined, as it will depend on the free assessment of the jurisdictional body. Thus, the parameters established and reiterated by the Spanish Supreme Court in this regard are: (i) lack of subjective unbelievability of the victim; (ii) verisimilitude of the testimony; and (iii) persistence in the incrimination.[30]

Nevertheless, these parameters have recently been qualified in the latest line of case law pointed out by the Supreme Court in this area, and specifically in the context of gendered violence, indicating up to eleven factors that must be taken into account in the process of assessment by the judge of the victim's statement in order to confer credibility and verisimilitude on it,[31] namely (i) *security in the statement before the Court by the interrogation of the Public Prosecutor Service, the lawyer of the private prosecution and the defense*; (ii) *specific account of the events which are the subject of the case*; (iii) *clarity of exposition before the Court*; (iv) *convicting "gestural language". This element is of utmost importance and it is characterized by the way whereby the victim expresses herself in terms of the "gestures" with which she accompanies herself in her statement before the Court*; (v) *seriousness of exposition that distances the Court's belief from a figurative, fabricated or not very credible account*; (vi) *descriptive expressiveness in the account of the events that took place*; (vii) *absence of contradictions and concordance of the iter narrated of the facts*; (viii) *absence of gaps in the exposure story that could lead to doubts about its credibility*; (ix) *the statement must not be fragmented*; (x) *a full and unbiased account of the facts must emerge, not a piecemeal account of what is in her interest to testify and to conceal what is beneficial to her about what has happened*; and (xi) *she must tell what benefits her and her position as well as what harms her*.[32]

Many of these factors are largely reminiscent of the parameters previously reiterated by the Supreme Court, such as the absence of contradictions and gaps, or the specific nature of the account of the events that took place, that is, those relating to what is has been called "persistence in the incrimination". However, many others refer to characteristics that are intrinsic to the victim's own personality whose appreciation acquires a subjective nature —see, for example, the importance of gestural language— which seem to be identified with the traditional stereotypes that exist about women victims of gendered violence. Thus, this leads to an even greater increase in the effects of re-victimization and it generates a feeling of insecurity and mistrust in the victim which will eventually lead her to abandon the process and to end with the case being closed or with an acquittal.[33]

In fact, the Supreme Court itself goes on to recognize the effect of re-victimization that may be generated in the victim by having to relive what happened when recounting it before the Court in the plenary session after having done so, not only in police

[30] Supreme Court Judgments no. 238/2011, 21 March 2011 (Legal Ground 2°); no. 964/2013, 17 December 2013 (Legal Ground 2°); and no. 717/2018, 17 January 2018 (Legal Grounds 2°, 3°, 4° and 6°).

[31] On this issue, see Magro Servet (2020), pp. 4–5.

[32] Supreme Court Judgment no. 119/2019, 6 March 2019 (Legal Ground 3°).

[33] González Monje (2020), pp. 1646–1648 and 1653–1655.

custody, but also in the pre-trial phase. In so doing, it lists another series of factors that must be taken into account in the assessment process and which qualify the previous ones.[34]

2.2 *The Exemption from the Duty to Testify in Criminal Proceedings for Gendered Violence Crimes*

Continuing in the following paragraphs with the evidentiary problems associated with the exemption from the duty to testify, it should first be noted that all witnesses are under the obligation to testify everything that they know about what they were asked, as per Article 707 LECrim, with the exception of the people set out in Articles 416, 417 and 418 LECrim, in their respective cases. Thus, following the provisions of Article 416.1 of the criminal procedure text before the latest reform in 2021, this obligation was waived for: (i) *family members of the defendant in direct ascendant or descendant lines*; (ii) *his/her spouse or person linked to him/her by a de facto relationship similar to marriage*; and (iii) *his/her whole or half blood brothers and sisters and blood lines up to the second civil degree*.[35]

In this sense, the relevance of the exemption from the duty to testify is at least of utmost importance in the context of gendered violence in which women victims of this kind of violence, being at the same time witnesses to the facts, frequently avail themselves of this provision to avoid having to testify against their aggressor whom they may even have initially reported in their case, which ends up leading to the case being closed or with an acquittal. This occurs because despite the fact that Organic Law 1/2004, of 28 December, on Integrated Protection Measures against Gendered Violence, proceeded to reform multiple precepts and legal texts, it forgot to modify the provisions on evidence necessary for the application of measures of a criminal and criminal procedural nature, among them, Article 416 LECrim on the exemption from the duty to testify. Thus, the lack of a specific provision on this precept in matters of gendered violence led to its disparate application by the courts, which resulted in a broad debate on issues ranging from the very discussion on the applicability of the precept in this area to whether it could be applied in those cases in which the parties were no longer partners at the time of the trial, and whether the victim could avail herself of this right in the case of having reported the facts.[36]

In this order, with the aim of limiting the interpretation of the precept and putting an end to the contradiction between the different jurisdictional bodies, the Spanish Supreme Court adopted a first non-jurisdictional agreement establishing that "the exemption from the obligation to testify provided for in Art. 416.1 LECrim extends to people who are or have been linked by one of the ties referred to in the precept.

[34] Supreme Court Judgment no. 119/2019, 6 March 2019 (Legal Ground 3°).

[35] De la Herrán Ruiz-Mateos (2020), pp. 47–49.

[36] See Fuentes Soriano (2018), pp. 9–10; Rodríguez Álvarez (2019), p. 264.

The following are excepted: (a) testimony for events occurring after the dissolution of the marriage or the definitive cessation of the analogous situation of affection; (b) cases in which the witness appears as a prosecutor in the process."[37] However, new questions were not long in coming, among them, whether the victim who appeared as a prosecutor at an earlier stage, but he/she withdrew before the oral trial, can benefit from the exemption.[38]

The Supreme Court had occasion to rule on this issue in Judgment 449/2015, of 14 July, when it declared that a victim who, although initially appearing in the process as a private prosecutor during the pre-trial phase, waived the subsequent exercise of criminal and civil actions before the oral trial act, appearing therein as a "witness-victim", could not avail him/herself of the exemption from the duty to testify. In this sense, the interpretative problems continued to flood the debates about the controversial precept 416 LECrim insofar as, after the Supreme Court's pronouncement in this latest decision, it was not so clear what should be understood by the exercise of the private prosecution in an "active" manner.[39]

In this succession of jurisprudential milestones and in a *plot twist*, the Supreme Court adopted a second non-jurisdictional decision[40] establishing that "the possibility of availing oneself of this exemption (416 LECrim) is not excluded for those who, previously having been constituted as private prosecutor, have ceased in that capacity."[41] Thus, this paragraph established a new interpretative line on the validity of the exemption throughout the process that contradicted the previous position contained in Judgment 449/2015, of 14 July, aligning itself with the majority position of the Provincial Courts that had been kept up to the date of that decision.[42]

Nevertheless, far from a harmonious solution —and a *happy ending*— which seemed to be in sight as a result of the Supreme Court Agreement, the Plenary of the Criminal Chamber of the High Court changed its jurisprudential doctrine once again in Judgement 389/2020, of 10 July,[43] by declaring that victims, once they have been constituted as private prosecutors and have previously reported the facts, do not recover the right to the legal exemption from the duty to testify in those cases in which they waive the exercise of this procedural position and cease to do so, being obliged to testify, therefore, in the act of the oral trial. A development that responds to the imperative need to promote the protection of victims and, in particular, victims of gendered violence.[44]

---

[37] Agreement of the Non-Jurisdictional Plenary of the Second Chamber of the Supreme Court of Spain of 24 April 2013.

[38] On this point, it can be seen the view of Herrero Álvarez (2020), p. 4.

[39] In this regard, see Fuentes Soriano (2018), pp. 10–12; Rodríguez Álvarez (2016), p. 3. See also Supreme Court Judgment no. 449/2015, 14 July 2015 (Legal Ground 3°).

[40] Agreement of the Non-Jurisdictional Plenary of the Second Chamber of the Supreme Court of Spain of 23 January 2018.

[41] Castillejo Manzanares (2020), pp. 7–8.

[42] Rodríguez Álvarez (2019), pp. 267–270.

[43] Supreme Court Judgment no. 389/2020, 10 July 2020 (Legal Ground 11°).

[44] Marí Farinós (2020), p. 2.

Ultimately, this doctrine has been translated into legislation through the reform introduced by Organic Law 8/2021, of 4 June, on Integrated Protection of Childhood and Adolescence against Violence, which has modified one of the most controversial precepts and the one that has given rise to most debate, namely Article 416 LECrim.[45] Thus, a number of exceptions to the exemption from the duty to declare are introduced, among them, "when the witness appears or has appeared as a private prosecutor in the process" (Article 416.1.4° LECrim) and "when the witness has agreed to testify in the course of the process after having been duly informed of his/her right not to testify" (Article 416.1.5 LECrim).

In this sense, and in view of the legislative amendment which has finally been made to the controversial exemption from the duty to testify, I must point out that, although I recognize that its application in the framework of criminal proceedings for gendered violence crimes means eliminating all the material of evidence available in a large number of cases insofar as in most cases only the victim's statement is available,[46] I can only express my absolute opposition to the reform.[47] That is, it does not take into account the will of the woman victim of gendered violence, with the legislator deciding —once again— for her what is most convenient in the interests of her protection with the ultimate and main objective of obtaining a guilty verdict against the defendant that does not lead to his acquittal or to the case being closed. There is no doubt that I essentially share the same sentiment as the legislator, which is to provide the victims of this kind of violence with absolute protection through all the public policies which are necessary to eradicate this social scourge. However, what I do not agree with is that in order to put an end to the widespread impunity that occurs in these cases, the victim must be forced to testify against her will because this is only a reflection of another prejudice whereby the legislator assumes that the woman victim of gendered violence is a helpless and defenseless person. In short, this is another case in which the true will of the victim is clearly irrelevant.[48]

3 Proposals Against the Phenomenon of Secondary Victimization in the Framework of Gendered Violence

Against a justice system that could be based on an androcentric model that resolves conflicts from a patriarchal and stereotypical point of view, and in an attempt to prevent the harmful effects of the phenomenon of secondary victimization,[49] first of

[45] See number four of the first Final Provision of Organic Law 8/2021.

[46] In that way, see Fuentes Soriano (2018), pp. 9–10.

[47] Along this line of thought, see Rodríguez Álvarez (2021), p. 5; Castillejo Manzanares (2020), pp. 10–11. Against this opinion are Ortiz Pradillo (2016), p. 16; Fuentes Soriano (2018), pp. 12–13.

[48] I do share the view expressed by Rodríguez Álvarez (2019), p. 276.

[49] Martínez García (2018), pp. 16–17.

all, I do believe that it is absolutely and completely necessary to train all legal operators in gender perspective in order to eliminate all stereotypes, prejudices and biases that prevent victims from obtaining the protection which they seek.

Furthermore, bearing in mind that the Spanish legislator limits the definition of gendered violence to that which is exercised against women by their husband or ex-husband, their partner or ex-partner, even if they do not live together, it is absolutely necessary —and it is about time since the Convention's ratification in 2014— to extend the concept of gendered violence to all the cases which are covered by that Convention and expand the legal framework, instead of remaining confined within the narrower definition of current Spanish law, which runs the risk of turning a blind eye towards certain kinds of gendered violence that also require legal protection. In this line, the incorporation of new measures and the amendment of existing ones, such as the criminal prosecution by victims' associations or the strengthening of the protection order, are to be welcomed.[50]

However, beyond the necessary training in gender perspective of all legal operators, if there is a proposal that I understand, and I have firmly defended it in previous papers,[51] that represents an instrument aimed at the revaluation and empowerment of the victim of gendered violence in the criminal justice system, avoiding her re-victimization within the criminal process, it is the current of restorative justice. Specifically, one of its main methodological bastions, namely, criminal mediation, insofar as it represents a complementary instrument to the judicial process in the criminal field, which cannot be understood otherwise due to the State's right to punish.[52] This one is forbidden by the Spanish legislator to apply precisely in the context of gendered violence in section 5 of Article 87 *ter* of the Organic Law 6/1985, of 1 July, on the Judiciary, but without being systematically regulated in the criminal legal system.[53]

In this sense, the justification put forward is based on the fact that, if gendered violence is understood as the most brutal symbol of the existing inequality in society, this presupposes the lack of a situation of equality between victim and aggressor necessary to be able to reach an agreement within a mediation procedure.[54]

Notwithstanding that justification, it can be argued, firstly, that the victim of gendered violence is not always and in all cases in a position of imbalance or inferiority in comparison to the perpetrator, even in the case of this kind of violence which, as has been said in the sentence just before this one, constitutes the most brutal symbol of the existing inequality in society.[55] That is, it does not imply that,

---

50 Carrizo González-Castell (2018), pp. 105–121.

51 Tierno Barrios (2022), pp. 23–24 and 28.

52 In this sense, I do share the view expressed by Carrizo González-Castell (2017), pp. 264–266.

53 See Arangüena Fanego (2014), pp. 145–146.

54 Álvarez Suárez (2019), pp. 1089–1090.

55 Huertas Martín (2017), pp. 395–400.

in each and every particular case, the woman is subjected to the aggressor in such a way that she cannot assert her dignity or defend her interests.[56]

This argument leads to another one in favor of allowing the use of mediation in cases of gendered violence on the grounds that the justification of the prohibition based on a protective measure adopted by the State with respect to the woman may go against her own will by demonstrating a lack of trust in her decision-making capacity.[57] In this line, the legislator's starting point of assuming that in crimes of gendered violence the victim is always in a situation of inferiority with respect to the aggressor denotes a paternalistic attitude,[58] based on a stereotype which conveys the image of the woman victim of gendered violence as an incapable person in need of protection.[59]

Therefore, we can only consider that allowing women to decide to access restorative justice services and to submit crimes of gendered violence to mechanisms such as criminal mediation, in the terms provided for in Law 4/2015, of 27 April, on the Statute of the Victims of Crime —free and informed consent to participate in this type of practice—, contributes firstly to their empowerment.[60] In other words, it does not reduce or annul their decision-making capacity as independent and autonomous people capable of making their own decisions on whether they want to participate in this type of practice which, due to its consequences, also favors their empowerment.[61] There are two main reasons for this: on the one hand, women play a leading role in the solution of the conflict which allows them to leave behind their condition of victim and to position themselves on an equal footing with respect to the position of the male aggressor; and on the other hand, by facilitating their integral reparation,[62] with the consequent provision of support, understanding and explanation that is usually required.[63]

4 Conclusion

Through these pages I have sought to highlight the various problems that victims of gendered violence often face in criminal proceedings against this type of crime. Firstly, I would like to express my absolute rejection of this social scourge and my desire, shared with the legislator to implement as many public policies as are necessary for the total and adequate protection of women victims on access to justice —for

[56] Along this line of thought, see Vall Rius (2019), pp. 717 and 723.

[57] Carrizo González-Castell (2018), p. 124.

[58] On this issue, see Sanz Mulas (2021), pp. 169–172.

[59] Castillo Roldán (2020), pp. 3–5 and 8–10.

[60] Álvarez Suárez (2021), p. 185.

[61] Guardiola Lago (2009), pp. 14–15.

[62] On the "integral reparation", see Carrizo González-Castell (2017), p. 253.

[63] Álvarez Suárez (2019), pp. 1092–1093.

instance, the protection order or the criminal prosecution by victims' associations can be considered—, but also for the defence of their interests and the satisfaction of their needs.

It is the lack of this adequate protection in some cases which is clearly a worrying situation in the field of criminal justice, however. Indeed, one of the most visible effects is the dreaded phenomenon of secondary victimization, which particularly affects victims of gendered violence. This coheres with the generalized framework of a legal and judicial system that is permeable to prejudices and stereotypes that end up limiting the exercise of women's access to justice right, as has been made clear in the analysis of this research. In this sense, I have noted the preconceived ideas present in legislation and in case law on the victim of gendered violence which, in short, translate into a paternalistic vision of guardianship and lack of confidence in her decision-making capacity. In that way, I understand that these ideas only intensify her re-victimization and reproduce what society is effectively trying to combat: the structural inequality that hangs over women.

An absolute mistrust is also observed in the prohibition of criminal mediation in cases of gendered violence, the possibility of which I defend as a mechanism to reduce the effects of secondary victimization in these cases and to contribute to the empowerment of women in line with Goal 5 of the 2030 Agenda.

References

Alonso Salgado C (2018) La mediación en el proceso penal. Tirant lo Blanch, Valencia

Álvarez Alarcón A (2021) La recepción de las 100 Reglas de Brasilia en los ordenamientos jurídicos iberoamericanos. In: Álvarez Alarcón A (ed) Justicia y personas vulnerables en Iberoamérica y en la Unión Europea. Tirant lo Blanch, Valencia, pp 25–50

Álvarez Suárez L (2019) La mediación penal y su prohibición en supuestos de violencia de género: modelo español. Revista Brasileira de Direito Processual Penal 5(2):1075–1106

Álvarez Suárez L (2021) La mediación penal como manifestación del denominado "principio de oportunidad": ¿Debería replantearse el legislador su veto a las víctimas de violencia de género? Revista de Estudios Jurídicos y Criminológicos 3:171–204

American Bar Association (2012) Access to justice assessment tool: a guide to analysing access to justice for civil society organizations. American Bar Association Rule of Law Initiative, Washington

Añón Roig MJ (2018) El derecho de acceso como garantía de justicia: perspectivas y alcance. In: García-Pascual C (ed) Acceso a la justicia y garantía de los derechos en tiempos de crisis: de los procedimientos tradicionales a los mecanismos alternativos. Tirant lo Blanch, Valencia, pp 19–75

Arangüena Fanego C (2014) La mediación penal en el ámbito de la violencia de género ¿ha llegado el momento para replantearse su prohibición? In: Abel Lluch X (ed) Las medidas preventivas de conflictos jurídicos en contextos económicos inestables. J. M. Bosch Editor, Barcelona, pp 145–162

Barona Vilar S (2019) Mirada restaurativa de la justicia penal en España, una bocanada de aire en la sociedad global líquida del miedo y de la securitización. In: Soleto Muñoz H, Carrascosa Miguel A (eds) Justicia restaurativa: una justicia para las víctimas. Tirant lo Blanch, Valencia, pp 55–94

Beltrán Montoliu A (2018) Víctima de violencia de género y la dispensa del art. 416 LECrim: evolución jurisprudencial. Revista de Derecho Penal y Criminología 3ª Época 19:13–46

Cappelletti M, Garth B (1978) Access to justice: the newest wave in the worldwide movement to make rights effective. Buffalo Law Rev 27(2):181–192

Carrizo González-Castell A (2017) Reparación de la víctima y mediación penal. In: Martín Diz F, Carrizo González-Castell A (eds) Mediación en la Administración de Justicia: implantación y desarrollo. Andavira, Santiago de Compostela, pp 251–270

Carrizo González-Castell A (2018) El acceso a la justicia de las víctimas de violencia de género (reflexiones en torno a las propuestas contenidas en el Pacto de Estado de septiembre de 2017). In: Roca Martínez JM (ed) El acceso a la justicia. Tirant lo Blanch, Valencia, pp 104–125

Carrizo González-Castell A (2019) El acceso a la justicia de las personas en condición de vulnerabilidad: un reto pendiente para los derechos humanos. In: Sanz Mulas N, Gorjón Barranco MC, Nieto Librero AB (eds) Los Derechos Humanos 70 años después de la Declaración Universal. Tirant lo Blanch, Valencia, pp 287–310

Carrizo González-Castell A (2021) Justicia de menores y mediación penal en España ¿un derecho de la víctima o del menor infractor? In: Bujosa Vadell L M, Martín Diz F; González Pulido, I, Reifarth Muñoz, W Menores y justicia juvenil. Aranzadi-Thomson Reuters, Cizur Menor, pp. 191–215

Castillejo Manzanares R (2020) Nueva doctrina jurisprudencial sobre la dispensa del deber de declarar en violencia de género. Diario La Ley 9713:1–13

Castillo Roldán C (2020) Violencia de género. ¿Crisis de la justicia? Avanzar hacia la justicia restaurativa. Diario La Ley 9681:1–13

Christie N (1977) Conflicts as property. Br J Criminol 17(1):1–15

Crenshaw K (1989) Demarginalizing the intersection of race and sex: a black feminist critique of antidiscrimination doctrine, feminist theory and antiracist politics. Univ Chic Leg Forum 1:139–167

Cumbre Judicial Iberoamericana (2018) Brasilia Rules on access to justice for people in vulnerable situations. https://capacitacion.jusmisiones.gov.ar/files/material_curso/2019/Reglas_de_Brasilia_Centro_actualizadas.pdf

De la Herrán Ruiz-Mateos S (2020) A vueltas con la dispensa del deber de declarar de las víctimas de violencia de género a propósito de la Sentencia del Tribunal Supremos 389/2020, de 10 de julio. Revista de Derecho Penal y Criminología 3ª Época 23:45–66

Flores Prada I (2015) Algunas reflexiones sobre la justicia restaurativa en el sistema español de justicia penal. Revista Internacional de Estudios de Derecho Procesal y Arbitraje 2:1–45

Fuentes Soriano O (2018) Los procesos por violencia de género. Problemas probatorios tradicionales y derivados del uso de las nuevas tecnologías. Revista General de Derecho Procesal 44:1–39

García-Pablos de Molina A (2014) Tratado de Criminología. Tirant lo Blanch, Valencia

Gil P (2018) La perspectiva de la mujer víctima del sistema judicial ajeno al género. In: Martínez García E (ed) Análisis de la justicia desde la perspectiva de género. Tirant lo Blanch, Valencia, pp 229–248

González Monje A (2020) La declaración de la víctima de violencia de género como única prueba de cargo: últimas tendencias jurisprudenciales en España. Revista Brasileira de Direito Processual Penal 6(3):1627–1660

Guardiola Lago MJ (2009) La víctima de violencia de género en el sistema de justicia y la prohibición de la mediación penal. Revista General de Derecho Penal 12:1–41

Hanna C (1996) No right to choose: mandated victim participation in domestic violence prosecutions. Harv Law Rev 109(8):1850–1910

Herrero Álvarez S (2020) El ajetreo jurisprudencial sobre la dispensa del deber de declarar en procesos por violencia de género: la Sentencia 389/2020 de 10 de julio. Diario La Ley 9698:1–5

Huertas Martín MI (2017) Reflexiones sobre la prohibición de la mediación en violencia de género. In: Rodríguez Tirado AM (ed) Cuestiones actuales de Derecho Procesal Reformas procesales. Mediación y arbitraje. Tirant lo Blanch, Valencia, pp 379–412

Laurrari E (2022) Cinco reflexiones feministas en torno al proceso penal. InDret. Revista para el Análisis del Derecho 2:149–162
Magro Servet V (2020) La 'progresividad' de la declaración de la víctima en el proceso penal en el análisis de la alegación de contradicciones. Diario La Ley 9760:1–11
Marí Farinós E (2020) La STS 389/2020, de 10 de julio y el fundamento de la dispensa del derecho a no declarar del artículo 416 LECrim. La Ley Penal 147:1–10
Martínez García E (2018) Análisis de la justicia 'procesal' desde la perspectiva de género. In: Martínez García E (ed) Análisis de la justicia desde la perspectiva de género. Tirant lo Blanch, Valencia, pp 15–28
Montesinos García A (2017) Una breve aproximación a la justicia restaurativa. In: Montesinos García A (ed) Tratado de Mediación. Tomo II. Mediación Penal. Tirant lo Blanch, Valencia, pp 21–52
Ortiz Pradillo JC (2016) Estereotipos legales en la lucha contra la violencia machista: la irrelevancia jurídica de la voluntad de la víctima. Diario La Ley 8697:1–22
Pérez Rivas N (2017) Evolución histórica del estatuto jurídico de la víctima: especial referencia al derecho español. Revista General de Derecho Procesal 41:1–43
Quispe Remón F (2018) Acceso a la Justicia y Objetivos del Desarrollo Sostenible. In: Fernández Liesa CR, Díaz Barrado CM, Verdiales López DM (eds) Objetivos de Desarrollo Sostenible y Derechos Humanos: Paz, Justicia e Instituciones Sólidas/Derechos Humanos y Empresas. Instituto de Estudios Internacionales y Europeos Francisco de Vitoria de la Universidad Carlos III de Madrid, Madrid, pp 235–248
Rodríguez Álvarez A (2016) El dilema de la acusación: de nuevo a vueltas con la dispensa del deber de declarar en supuestos de violencia de género. Diario La Ley 8727:1–5
Rodríguez Álvarez A (2019) Dispensa del deber de declarar y violencia de género: el enésimo capítulo. In: Figueruelo Burrieza Á, Del Pozo Pérez M, Ramos Hernández P (eds) Retos actuales para la erradicación de la desigualdad y la violencia de género. Tirant lo Blanch, Valencia, pp 263–278
Rodríguez Álvarez A (2021) Claves de la reforma de la dispensa del deber de declarar *ex* Ley Orgánica 8/2021, de 4 de junio. Diario La Ley 9916:1–6
Rodríguez-García N (2017) Presente y futuro de la mediación penal. In: Rodríguez Tirado AM (ed) Cuestiones actuales de Derecho Procesal. Reformas procesales. Mediación y arbitraje. Tirant lo Blanch, Valencia, pp 269–310
Rodríguez-García N, Pahul Robredo MG (2022) Paz, justicia e instituciones sólidas: el ODS-16 y su proyección latinoamericana. Revista Criminalia 89(2):25–54
Sanz Mulas N (2019) Violencia de Género y Pacto de Estado. La huida hacia delante de una norma agotada (LO 1/2004). Tirant lo Blanch, Valencia
Sanz Mulas N (2021) Política Criminal. Ratio Legis, Salamanca
Tierno Barrios S (2022) El estado de la mediación penal en violencia de género en España: el debate de una prohibición. Revista General de Derecho Procesal 56:1–32
UN Women (2018) Turning promises into action: Gender equality in the 2030 Agenda for Sustainable Development. https://www.unwomen.org/sites/default/files/Headquarters/Attachments/Sections/Library/Publications/2018/SDG-report-Gender-equality-in-the-2030-Agenda-for-Sustainable-Development-2018-en.pdf
Vall Rius A (2019) Justicia Restaurativa y violencia de género. In: Soleto Muñoz H, Carrascosa Miguel A (eds) Justicia restaurativa: una justicia para las víctimas. Tirant lo Blanch, Valencia, pp 709–732

Right to Access a Lawyer for Victims of Domestic Violence: The Example of Italian Criminal Justice

Lucia Parlato and Marta Palmisano

Abstract The chapter aims to address the main issues concerning legal aid in Italian criminal proceedings related to domestic violence offences. Following an overall consideration of these offences, the chapter analyzes the specific possibilities for accessing free legal aid. In this regard, it examines critical points raised by the Italian legislative system, which concern eligibility for this benefit. The discussion focuses specifically on an important 2021 decision of the Italian Constitutional Court. In this context, the rationale underlying legal aid is also analyzed. After exploring some general criminal and procedural perspectives, the chapter offers an overview of supranational sources, including the Istanbul Convention, the European Convention on Human Rights and European Union Directives.

1 Introduction

This chapter commences with a brief analysis of domestic violence and its various manifestations. The challenge of precisely defining its boundaries is underscored by specific issues analyzed from both substantive and procedural criminal law perspectives, particularly concerning legal aid, which is contingent upon verifying offenses listed in Article 76(4 *ter*) of Presidential Decree no. 115 of 30 May, 2002.[1] In fact,

Lucia Parlato is the author of para. 5, 6, 7 and Marta Palmisano is the author of para.1, 2, 3, 4, 8.

[1] "Consolidated text of the legislative and regulatory provisions on legal expenses". Bianchi (2022) and Rossi (2022).

L. Parlato (✉) · M. Palmisano
University of Palermo, Palermo, Italy
e-mail: lucia.parlato@unipa.it

R. Erbaş (ed.), *Criminal Prosecution of Domestic Violence*, Ius Gentium: Comparative Perspectives on Law and Justice 128,
https://doi.org/10.1007/978-3-032-01202-9_8

this regulatory solution does not adequately satisfy the requirements set forth in Article 57 of the Istanbul Convention (IC), which states that "Parties shall ensure the right to legal assistance and free legal aid for victims under conditions established by their internal law". Indeed, the concept of "domestic violence crimes" is multifaceted, characterized by uncertain boundaries and constant evolution.

Additionally, the Italian criminal system lacks both a comprehensive list of these crimes and clear criteria for their identification. Consequently, some instances of domestic violence may fall outside the narrow list of offenses specified in Article 76(4 *ter*), leaving victims without sufficient protection. In this regard, starting with a reflection on whether an exhaustive list of offences is adequate to ensure effective protection for victims, we examine the potential to link legal aid to the concept of vulnerability. This approach is also supported by the new provisions in Law no. 168 of November 24, 2023 "Provisions for combating violence against women and domestic violence", which emphasizes a more inclusive understanding of victims, in line with the expectations set forth by the recent EU directive. To support this analysis, we examine the Italian Constitutional Court's ruling no. 1 of 11 January 2021, which clarifies the scope and rationale underlying legal aid benefits through fundamental constitutional principles. This ruling is now complemented by Law No. 168/2023 and Directive 2024/1385/EU of May 14th on "Combating Violence Against Women and Domestic Violence", which expands the legal framework for victim protection.

It further explores the relationship between domestic violence and legal aid through an analysis of the Istanbul Convention, the European Court of Human Rights (ECHR) and European Union Directives, including the new emphasis on data collection and monitoring of domestic violence cases as mandated by recent laws.

2 Domestic Violence in the Italian Legal System: Criminal Law Profiles and Main Norms on Legal Aid

The Istanbul Convention defines "domestic violence" as all acts of physical, sexual, psychological or economic violence occurring within the family or household or between current or former spouses or partners, regardless of shared residence (Article 3).[2] This definition is similarly reflected in the Italian legal framework under Decree Law 14.08.2013, no. 93 (Article 3(1)), converted[3] into Law 15.10.2013,

[2] With reference to the protection of minors see "the Lanzarote Convention" which aims to protect victims from the "violence" inherent in the trial process. Specifically, Article 31(3) states "Each Party shall ensure that victims have access, provided free of charge where warranted, to legal aid when it is possible for them to have the status of parties to criminal proceedings". However, he main issue is the requirement for victims to be classified as a "party" to access this benefit.

[3] "Conversion into Law, with Amendments, of Decree-Law No. 93 of August 14, 2013, which contains urgent provisions on security and combating gender-based violence, as well as civil protection and the management of provinces".

no. 119.[4] This broad definition encompasses various forms or patterns of violence, regardless of legally recognized biological or familial ties.[5] In this context, distinguishing domestic violence from relational conflicts and family quarrels can be challenging, especially when power differentials are not overtly visible.[6] In this regard, the IC identifies two main types of DV: violence between current or former partners and intergenerational violence.[7] DV may also manifest as situational violent behavior or systematic controlling behavior, characterized by an unbalanced gender relationship.[8] Additionally, DV may also manifest in less visible forms of psychological violence, such as denigration, intimidation, or persistent threats.[9]

The multifaceted nature of domestic violence presents challenges in identifying its various manifestations and the nature of the relationships involved. This complexity is compounded by overlapping categories of violence such as violence against women, domestic violence, gender-based violence, and sexual violence. It is also difficult to identify the crimes of DV within the contiguous category of crimes committed within the family, against life and individual safety, against personal and moral liberty. In this context, one also wonders what role the perception of the victim plays. This issue is also closely linked to the fact that there is no clear definition of family in Italian criminal law and that the concept of "domestic" appears elusive and lacks precise connotations and boundaries.[10]

As previously mentioned, these observations are further complicated by critical issues related to the application of legal aid provisions, which in Italian law are

---

[4] The definition is taken over, albeit with two differences; according to the national provision it must be serious or non-episodic acts and replaces the term 'partner' with 'persons bound by emotional relations. On the concept of "violence" in the penal system, recently, De Simone (2024).

Within the Italian legal framework, numerous legislative interventions have tackled domestic violence (DV). Among the most significant measures are: Law no. 154 of 5.4.2001, Law no. 38 of 23.4.2009, Law no. 77 of 27.6.2013 (implementing the IC), Law 15.10.2013, no. 119, Law 19.7.2019, no. 69 ("Red Code"), Law no. 134 of 27.9.2021, Law no. 168 of 14.11.2023. With specific reference to the protection of minors see also Law no. 269 of 3.8.1998, Law no. 38 of 6.2.2006, Law. no. 172 of 1.10.2012 (Ratification of the Lanzarote Convention) and Legislative Decree no. 39 of 4.3.2014.

[5] Recently, Cass., 12.1.2023, n. 809; Cass., 15.5.2023, n. 37978; Cass., 23.11.2023, n. 47121; Cass., 3.5.2024, n. 17656; Cass. 4.9.2024, n. 33653.

[6] Federal Department of Home Affairs FDHA, Swiss Confederation, Definition, forms and consequences of domestic violence (June 2020). See Farina and Pecorella (2018) p. 21 ff.

[7] The second type includes cases of minors witnessing violence between parents (Cass., Sec. VI, 23.02.2018, no. 18833); Explanatory Report of the Council of Europe Convention on Preventing and Combating Violence against Women and Domestic Violence, Istanbul, 11 May 2011, Council of Europe Treaty Series, no. 210, para. 41. However, it is pointed out that most victims of DV are women.

[8] Johnson (2008) and Gloor and Meier (2012).

[9] Dorothy and Parsons (2005), p. 34.

[10] *Ex multis*, Cass., Sec. VI, 19.05–2.08.2021, no. 30129; ECtHR, *Buturuga v. Romania* (56,867/15), 11.02.2020.

conditional on the verification of the occurrence of one of the offences expressly indicated by the legislation. These offences are listed in Article 76 (4 *ter*), of Presidential Decree no. 115 of 30 May 2002, "Consolidated Act of legislative and regulatory provisions on legal expenses". This regulatory solution, however, does not necessarily satisfy the requirements set forth in Article 57 of the IC.[11] In fact, there is no comprehensive list of DV offences in the Italian criminal system, a concept with uncertain boundaries. Moreover, the criterion adopted by the Italian legislator ties access to legal aid to well-defined requirements; however, it also raises further questions. In this regard, this raises questions about the validity of the selective criterion adopted, which also runs the risk of not taking due account of the evolution of the violent phenomena, of the social contexts and of the specific characteristics of the victims of such crimes.[12]

An additional factor deserves to be mentioned. Article 115 *bis* of Presidential Decree no. 115/ 2002, introduced by Law no. 36 of April 26, 2019 "Amendments to the Criminal Code and other provisions regarding self-defense" has a general value in relation to legitimate defense of the victim "at home", but can assume specific importance in relation to attacks in the frame of emotional relationships and in family contexts. This article introduced in fact a specific case of free legal aid that concerns individuals for whom dismissal, acquittal, or non-proceedings have been ordered due to acts committed in conditions of legitimate defense.[13] This system aims to prevent those who have acted in self-defense "at home" from being required to pay legal fees. In this context, in addition, the recent Directive 2024/1385/EU emphasizes the need for member states to ensure comprehensive protections for victims of domestic violence, including access to legal aid and psychological support, as well as the establishment of effective reporting mechanisms. This directive reinforces the obligations already set forth in the Istanbul Convention, urging Italy to enhance its legal framework to better align with these standards.

Particularly noteworthy is Recital 32 of the directive, which states "Member States can extend legal aid, including free legal aid, to victims when reporting criminal offences, where provided for by national law. When assessing the victim's resources for the purpose of deciding whether to grant legal aid, Member States should consider the victim's effective access to his or her financial resources". Indeed, domestic violence can manifest as economic control by the offender, and victims may lack effective access to their own financial resources.

[11] Article 57 of the IC "The Parties shall ensure that victims are entitled to legal aid and free legal aid under the conditions provided for by domestic law". The IC is transposed into Italian law by Law no. 77 of 27.6.2013.

[12] It is important to mention that recent legislative changes, particularly the Law no. 168/2023 and the legislative decree no 150, of *10.10.2022 ("Cartabia reform")*, emphasize the need for a more cohesive approach to addressing domestic violence, including improved access to legal aid and support services for victims.

[13] Moreover, the recent Law no. 168/2023 emphasizes the importance of training for operators who interact with victims and expands economic support for victims of violent crimes.

3 Offences for Which Legal Aid Is Provided and Some Problematic Aspects

The offenses for which victims are eligible for legal aid are set out in Article 76(4 *ter*) of Presidential Decree no. 115/2002.[14] In particular, pursuant to the aforementioned Article 76(4 *ter*), it is provided that individuals offended, by others, by the crimes referred to in Articles 572 (family maltreatment), 609 *bis* (sexual violence), 609 *quater* (sexual acts with a minor), 609 *octies* (group sexual violence) and 612 *bis* (persecutory acts, so-called *stalking*), as well as, where committed to the detriment of minors, the offences referred to in Articles 609 *quinquies* (corruption of minors) and 609 *undecies* (solicitation of minors) Criminal Code (CC), may be granted legal aid, exempting them from the income limits established by the decree.[15] This rule represents a significant advancement in the traditional rules on legal aid. In fact, legal aid was originally intended solely as a protection for those documented as indigent.[16] Conversely, the introduction of free legal aid for vulnerable victims addresses both economic barriers to justice and other social obstacles that may render the right to justice illusory.[17]

These two institutions, therefore, have different purposes and underlying principles. In the first case the constitutional source is found in Article 24(3) of the Italian Constitution (Const.), emphasizing the right to effective legal representation and defense; in the second case, this interpretation appears different. In this regard, the Constitutional Court's ruling no. 1 of 11 January 2021 states that the rationale "is to be found in a precise choice of political-criminal policy aimed at offering concrete support to the victims (the victim is presumed to be vulnerable due to the nature of the crime[18]) and at encouraging them to report and actively participate in the process of emergence of the truth". Read in this light, the provision of Article 76(4 *ter*) would find its basis in Article 3(2) Const., which seeks to eliminate social barriers

---

[14] Paragraph 4 *ter* was added by Article 4(1) of Decree-Law no. 11 of 23.2.2009 and finally was so amended by Article 2(3) of Decree-Law No. 93 of 14.8.2013. On the institution of legal aid see Gerosa (2021), p. 259 ff.

Other offenses listed in Article 76(4 *ter*) of Presidential Decree no. 115/2002 include: 583 *bis* (female genital mutilation practices), 600 (reduction to or maintenance in slavery or servitude), 600 *bis* (child prostitution), 600 *ter* (child pornography), 600 *quinquies* (tourist initiatives aimed at exploiting child prostitution), 601 (trafficking in persons), and 602 (purchase and sale of slaves).

[15] Generally, access to legal aid, which allows for legal representation at State expense, is available to those who do not have sufficient income to afford an adequate defense. The law specifies that the maximum taxable income threshold for eligibility for legal aid is EUR 12.838,01.

[16] In Italy, the terms "free legal aid" and "legal aid", though often used interchangeably today, actually refer to different systems. "Free legal aid" refers to the system established by Royal Decree no. 2627 of December 6, 1865, which assigned the task of defending those unable to afford legal services to the legal profession on an "honorary and obligatory" basis, without remuneration. In contrast, Presidential Decree no. 115/2002 introduced the concept of "legal aid", which shifts the responsibility for compensating legal representation to the public purse.

[17] Repetto (2006), para 3.

[18] On the subject Cass., Sez. VI, 25.7.2024, no. 30592.

that hinder the effectiveness of rights, in the perspective of achieving substantive equality.

The free legal aid for victims of the crimes referred to in Article 76(4 *ter*) thus represents the legislator's choice to "privilege" some victims over others on account of their fragility, determined by the violence of the crime suffered and the risk of consequent reluctance to file a complaint, not measured from an economic point of view.[19] Moreover, in order for the *ratio* of the rule, of encouraging victims to denounce and support them during the process, to appear worthy of appreciation and for this discipline to be an effective instrument of equality and not turn into an unjustifiable inequality of treatment, it could be important to identify the notion of "vulnerable victim".[20] In fact, the provision contains a catalogue of offences in respect of which the victims are deemed presumed to be vulnerable.[21] To overcome these problems, legislative intervention would also face challenges in identifying a general notion of vulnerability, which is challenging to anchor to objective categories.[22] In this regard, addressing this issue requires a nuanced understanding of each case's context and the victim's unique characteristics.[23] By enhancing the rationale of Article 76(4 *ter*) of Presidential Decree no. 115/2002 and avoiding the problems that an overly rigid selection of the offences identified therein could cause, a potential solution could involve permitting judges to assess vulnerability on a case-by-case basis rather than relying solely on a predefined list of offenses.[24] This would enable judges to evaluate whether a particular crime has a more severe impact on the victim based on specific circumstances. In this regard, it should be noted that Article 90 *quater* of the Code of Criminal Procedure (CPC) introduces a rule identifying vulnerable victims, leaving its concrete identification to the judge.[25] It may therefore

---

[19] Given this basis, however, it is necessary to reflect on the constitutionality of the rule regarding its non-application to victims of specific crimes who are in comparable situations of vulnerability to those for whom the rule does apply.

For example, minors who are victims of crimes such as enslavement or human trafficking are eligible for this benefit, whereas adult victims of the same crimes, as well as the mentally ill or the elderly, are not.

[20] For an in-depth analysis of the relationship between criminal law and victim vulnerability, see: Fiandaca (2021).

[21] Furthermore, it is essential to consider extending the scope of this provision to include all individuals in comparable situations; for this reasoning, Gerosa (2021), p. 265 ss.

[22] Gerosa (2021); Cendon (1988); Romanelli (2020); Trapella (2019); Cassibba (2014), p. 6.

[23] Trapella (2019), p. 3.

[24] For an analysis of the concept of vulnerability in the context of access to legal aid, refer to Cass. Pen., Sez. VI, Sent. no. 12345 del 2022. In doctrine, M. Russo (2023).

[25] Article 90 *quater* CPC "Victims with specific protection needs": "1. For the purpose of applying the provisions of this Code, a victim's specific protection needs shall be assessed not only based on their age and physical or psychological impairment but also in relation to the type of offence and the circumstances and details of the case at hand. The victim's specific protection needs shall be evaluated considering whether the offence involved violence or racial hatred, whether it constitutes organized crime or national or international terrorism, or involves trafficking in human beings, whether it was committed with discriminatory intent, and whether the victim is dependent on the offender emotionally, psychologically, or economically"; see Canestrini (2020).

On vulnerability in criminal proceedings, Bouchard (2019); Parlato (2021a), pp. 427–454.

be appropriate for eligibility for legal aid also to be assessed by the judge under Article 90 *quater* CPC. In this frame, it is significant to mention recent reforms, including Law no. 168 of 2023, that emphasize the importance of this assessment and the need for judges to consider the specific circumstances of each case.

This issue is closely tied to the previously highlighted challenges related to DV cases, ending up providing a solution also to the problems highlighted there. Indeed, vulnerability could serve as a criterion for delineating crimes eligible for legal aid, particularly concerning DV cases; vulnerability is in fact one of the features that characterize the people offended by crimes committed within the "domestic violence cases".

4 The January 2021 Italian Constitutional Court Ruling

The concept of "vulnerability" is also crucial in the context of domestic violence (DV), where individuals may require criminal protection due to their weakened status within the family. The Italian Constitutional Court's ruling no. 1 of 11 January 2021 emphasizes the importance of "vulnerability". The ruling addressed the constitutionality of Article 76(4 *ter*) of Presidential Decree No. 115/2002, which allows automatic admission to legal aid for victims of specific offences, regardless of income limits.[26]

The case arose from a sexual assault incident involving a woman, leading the Preliminary Investigations Judge (G.I.P.) of Tivoli to question the constitutionality of this automatic provision. The judge argued that it undermined judicial discretion and treated financially diverse situations uniformly, conflicting with Article 3 of the Constitution.[27] Concerns were also raised that this indiscriminate access could benefit individuals with significant economic means, potentially impacting public expenditure and raising legitimacy doubts under Article 24.[28] However, the Constitutional Court rejected these arguments, affirming that the provision does not violate the equality principle outlined in Article 3. The Court emphasized its role in supporting vulnerable victims and facilitating crime reporting.[29] It acknowledged that legal aid is not solely based on a presumption of poverty but is informed by victimological studies indicating that many victims lack financial resources.[30]

---

[26] It is important to note that the list of offences has been progressively expanded, particularly in response to the Lanzarote Convention and Directive 2011/36/EU. Some scholars have suggested reflecting on the advisability of including the new crime of coercion or inducement to marry, introduced by Law 69/2019 in Article 558 *bis* of the Italian Criminal Code, within this list of offences; see, on this subject, Dava (2021).

[27] It. Cost. Court, 11.1.2021, n. 1, para 1. On legislative automatisms, see Marcenò and Zagrebelsky (2018), p. 181. For an analysis of the compatibility relationship between legislative automatisms and the principle of equality, see Leone (2018).

[28] Ibid.

[29] It. Cost. Court, 11.1.2021, n. 1, para 5. In the substantive case law, in a conforming sense, Cass., Sec. IV, 15.2.2017, no. 13497; 10.10.2018, no. 52822; 15.4.2020, no. 12191.

[30] Ibid., n. 1, para 7.

Regarding concerns about Article 24(3), which safeguards the right to defense for economically disadvantaged individuals, the Court clarified that this does not prevent legislators from ensuring access to justice for other constitutionally relevant values.[31] Moreover, the G.I.P.'s comparison between protecting vulnerable victims and controlling state expenditure was deemed unreasonable.[32] It is noteworthy that similar exceptions to income-based legal aid are established in Italian procedural-criminal law under Article 76(4 *quater*) of Presidential Decree no. 115/2002, for unaccompanied foreign minors, and Article 10 of Law no. 206 of 2004, for victims of terrorism and related acts. Even in these cases, these exceptions are grounded in a "reasonable" foundation found in Article 3(2) of the Constitution, emphasizing substantial justice over existing social difficulties in accessing justice.[33] Indeed, this derogatory discipline assumes particular relevance with reference to gender violence and DV, which, inserted in a negatively connoted socio-cultural context, also represents a discriminatory phenomenon, since it mainly affects women, limiting their freedom of self-determination.

The ECtHR has echoed similar sentiments, recalling CEDAW's call for states to take positive action to restore substantive equality between men and women. CEDAW specifies that "Adoption by States Parties of temporary special measures aimed at accelerating *de facto* equality between men and women shall not be considered discrimination as defined in the present Convention" (Article 4).

The Istanbul Convention (IC) reinforces this perspective by valuing instances of substantive justice and stating that "Special measures that are necessary to prevent and protect women from gender-based violence shall not be considered discrimination under the terms of this Convention" (Article 4(4)).[34] Moreover, the IC includes an ad hoc provision in Article 57 dedicated to access to legal aid for women victims of violence. Therefore, the Court concluded that the legislative provision under review is neither unreasonable nor detrimental to equal treatment principles, when considering the vulnerability of victims and the need to ensure these crimes are reported.[35] It is therefore clear, the Court goes on to say, that "the *ratio* of the rules in question is to be found in a deliberate criminal policy choice to provide tangible

---

[31] Ibid., n. 1, para 8.

[32] The individual may therefore also be admitted to legal aid, bypassing the income limits set out in Article 76(4 *bis*); this implies that the application only needs to meet the requirements outlined in Article 79(1), letters a) and b), of Presidential Decree no. 115/2002, and does not require the submission of a declaration in lieu of certification (letter c)) attesting to compliance with the income limits prescribed by that article. On this subject see also Legal aid without income limits if ... (Cass. 16,272/22), in CanestriniLex, Criminal Cassation, 28.04.2022.

[33] Dava (2021), p. 3; Gerosa (2021), p. 265 f.

[34] Specifically concerning access to justice for women victims of male violence, it is worth recalling the Strasbourg Court's ruling—ECtHR, *Talpis v. Italy* (41,237/14), 2.03.2017—which condemned Italy for violating not only Articles 2 (right to life) and 3 (prohibition of inhuman or degrading treatment) of the Convention, but also Article 14 (prohibition of discrimination). The judgment harshly criticises the Italian judicial authorities for their failure to recognise and properly address the issue of violence against women.

[35] It. Cost. Court, 11.1.2021, n. 1, para 5.

support to victims, whose vulnerability is accentuated by the particular nature of the offences". Further purpose is to ensure the assistance of a professional, which is particularly important throughout the criminal proceedings.

These commitments are reinforced by Directive 2012/29/EU,[36] transposed into Italian law by Legislative Decree no. 212 of December 15, 2015, which guarantees extensive rights in criminal proceedings for victims of "[...] gender-based violence, violence in close relationships, sexual or hate-based violence or exploitation and victims with disabilities" (Article 22).[37] In this context, free legal aid enables victims to effectively exercise their rights in criminal cases, thereby applying the principles outlined in Article 24 of the Constitution and preventing secondary victimization—a significant barrier to reporting crimes.

Lastly, it should be noted that the perspective of the Judge for preliminary investigations (the s.c. *giudice per le indagini preliminari*, G.I.P.) "does not appear to be aimed at extending the scope of application of the benefit", but rather "at restricting the number of recipients of the benefit, to ensure equality *in malam partem*".[38] In other words, the doubt of unconstitutionality concerns a favorable discipline aimed at achieving substantive justice, as highlighted by the Constitutional Court.

The Constitutional Court's considerations were later echoed in substantive case law, particularly in a ruling by the Court of Cassation, section IV criminal, on April 28, 2022, no. 16272, which confirmed that producing an ISEE[39] certificate (an income assessment tool) is unnecessary for legal aid applications.[40] This reading is imposed by the *ratio* of the rule, which appears aimed at facilitating access to justice for the victims of the crimes identified by the legislator.

5 Article 57 of the Istanbul Convention and Further Council of Europe Sources

In the frame of the Council of Europe, several norms converge in establishing legal aid. They are the expression of an ongoing cultural and political evolution. The latter has been influencing the supranational legislative landscape, in order to give attention not only to the accused's rights but also to the victim's ones. Such a trend

[36] It should be noted that an ongoing Proposal aims to modify the contents of the Directive (COM(2023) 424 final, 12.07.2023).

[37] Cf. Almansi (2021), p. 4.

[38] Dava (2021), p. 5.

[39] Equivalent Economic Situation Indicator.

[40] Moreover, for several years, the Supreme Court has recognized the right of the person harmed by one of the offences listed in the law to access legal aid solely on the basis of their status as a victim, irrespective of their financial situation. Consequently, income conditions do not need to be declared or certified in accordance with Presidential Decree. no. 115 of 2002, Article 79(1) lett. c); see Cass., Sec. IV, 15.02.2017, no. 13497; Cass., Sec. IV, 10.10.2018, no. 52822.

has explicitly recognized the fundamental principle that victims' care represents a duty of social solidarity.

The Istanbul Convention (IC)[41] and the Lanzarote Convention (LC)[42] aim to protect victims and to shield them from the "violence" inherent to the trial itself. Victims might have both a passive and weak role or an active and strong one. On the one hand the offended may need assistance, information and support. On the other hand, they may want to take an active part in the proceedings. Both perspectives involve the topic of legal aid.

In particular, Article 57 IC requires the States Parties to guarantee the rights to legal assistance and to free legal aid in favor of victims of gender and domestic violence (GDV) "under the conditions provided by their internal law". The norm pertains to the sphere of victims' procedural protection and involves one of the so-called Four Pillars or "4 Ps" of the Istanbul Convention,[43] namely, protection. However, it also concerns the remaining three Pillars: prevention, prosecution and coordinated policy. Technical defense often represents a precondition of each of the four indicated fields. The norm is inspired by article 15(2), Council of Europe Convention on Action against Trafficking in Human Beings ("CATHB").[44]

Article 57 IC does not automatically grant victims the right to free legal aid. The States are entitled to establish the criteria to obtain this support.[45] However, GREVIO reports have highlighted a set of standards to be met to ensure that legal aid is guaranteed under domestic law and is actually accessible to victims. In particular, in GDV cases, victims must be afforded this right, in order to effectively access justice.[46]

GREVIO reports highlight good practices: in some States, bar associations are legally required to set up systems of duty lawyers specialized in GDV proceedings.[47] By contrast, several shortcomings have been identified in relation to the accessibility of legal aid because of long or complex procedures,[48] the inadequate consideration given to women's financial resources[49] and the poor quality of information about legal aid.[50] GREVIO has further pointed out that legal aid lawyers and

---

[41] Council of Europe Convention on preventing and combating violence against women and domestic violence, Istanbul, 11.05.2011.

[42] Council of Europe Convention on the Protection of Children against Sexual Exploitation and Sexual Abuse, 25.10.2007.

[43] Council of Europe (CoE), The four Pillars of the Istanbul Convention, in https://rm.coe.int.

[44] Council of Europe Convention on Action against Trafficking in Human Beings, 16.05.2005; GREVIO's (Baseline) Evaluation Report: Italy, GREVIO/Inf(2019)18,13.012020.

[45] Council of Europe (CoE), Explanatory Report (n 2), par. 295.

[46] Ibid., par. 294.

[47] GREVIO's (Baseline) Evaluation Report: Spain (n 3).

[48] GREVIO's (Baseline) Evaluation Report: Serbia, GREVIO/Inf(2019)20, 22.01.2020 and others.

[49] GREVIO's (Baseline) Evaluation Report: Italy (n 4), GREVIO's (Baseline) Evaluation Report: Malta (n. 9), and others.

[50] GREVIO's (Baseline) Evaluation Report: Andorra, GREVIO/Inf(2020)18, 30.11.2020; GREVIO's (Baseline) Evaluation Report: Montenegro, GREVIO/Inf(2018)5, 25.10.2018.

NGOs are not always trained as they should.[51] All these issues are emphasized in relation to legal aid in favor of asylum seekers.[52] Furthermore, GREVIO has highlighted the need to increase access to legal aid at the early stages of proceedings.[53]

A set of measures facilitates the exercise of the victim's rights to justice and to defense in criminal proceedings. In this regard, GREVIO has focused on a distinction, that can be detected in supranational and national sources: it has distinguished between primary legal aid (legal advice and relevant services) and secondary legal aid (specialized legal support).[54] The former is often mentioned by EU sources as "counselling" and represents a significant background to the actual legal aid guarantee. GREVIO has expressed satisfaction with the legal aid system of some States, where support services provided by public specialists effectively cover both primary and secondary aid.[55]

Article 57 IC is included in a panorama of legal sources that aim to guarantee the victim's right to defense. Some legislative tools of the Council of Europe deserve to be mentioned in this context. Resolution 77(27) concerns the compensation of victims of crime. The 1983 European Convention on the compensation of victims of violent crimes can be considered a development of this Resolution.[56] Recommendation (83)7, on participation of the public in crime policy, is one of the first legal sources reserved to victims. It is no coincidence that this Recommendation gives special consideration to legal aid and urges the States to set up "an efficient system of legal aid for victims so that they may have access to justice in all circumstances".[57] Recommendation (2006)8, on assistance to crime victims, establishes the victim's right to be informed of the availability of "legal aid, legal advice, or any sort of advice" and, if necessary, of the related costs.[58] The 2006 Recommendation was replaced by Recommendation CM/Rec(2023)2 on rights, services and support for victims of crime, adopted by the Committee of Ministers on 15 March 2023. Among other points, according to Art. 6, f) "Member States should ensure that victims are offered *ex officio*" information on "how and under what conditions they can access legal advice, legal aid and any other sort of advice". Moreover, Article 12 is titled

[51] GREVIO's (Baseline) Evaluation Report: Albania, GREVIO/Inf(2017)13, 24.11.2017, and others.

[52] Council of Europe, Mid-term Horizontal Review of GREVIO baseline evaluation reports, par. 569.

[53] GREVIO's (Baseline) Evaluation Report: Spain (n 3), GREVIO's (Baseline) Evaluation Report: Malta (n 9).

[54] GREVIO's (Baseline) Evaluation Report: Spain (n 3), GREVIO's (Baseline) Evaluation Report: Albania (14) and others.

[55] GREVIO's (Baseline) Evaluation Report: Andorra (n 13).

[56] Council of Europe, Committee of Ministers, Resolution 77 (27) on the Compensation of Victims of Crime, 28.09.1977 (whereas no. 2); Convention on the Compensation of Victims of Violent Crimes, Strasbourg, 24.XI.1983 (whereas no. 3).

[57] Council of Europe, Committee of Ministers, Recommendation of the Committee of Ministers to Member States on Participation of the Public in Crime Policy, 23.061983, 29.

[58] Council of Europe, Committee of Ministers, Recommendation Rec (2006)8 on assistance to crime victims, 14.06.2006.

"Right to legal aid". In the light of this Article "member States should ensure that victims have access to legal aid". It is noteworthy that this requirement arises "at least where" victims "have the status of parties to criminal proceedings". The States "are encouraged to ensure access to free legal aid for victims concerning all decisions where the interests of justice so require". However, "the conditions and procedural rules under which victims have access to legal aid should be determined by national law." All these sources express the goals of the European criminal policy, but they are not binding for the States.

Apart from the IC, further Conventions address the topic of victims' legal aid, attempting to protect specific categories of vulnerable victims. Article 15 of the above-mentioned CATHB imposes on the States the duty to include in their legislations a provision on victims' right to legal aid, "under the conditions provided by its internal law".[59]

In the Lanzarote Convention, Article 31 is dedicated to "general measures of protection". In general, this Article aims to assure victims effective protection not only during the proceedings, but also "from" the criminal trial itself. However, the LC shows a point of weakness that can be detected also in the Directives that will be considered as follows. The Lanzarote Convention binds the States to "ensure that victims have access, provided free of charge where warranted, to legal aid when it is possible for them to have the status of parties to criminal proceedings". It follows that the State is bound to provide legal aid to victims only if domestic legislation recognizes them the role of party. Another critical point of the Lanzarote and Istanbul Conventions is that the States have broad margin of maneuver in assuring the right to technical defense. This can result in uneven levels of protection in the different countries.

6 The Case-Law of the ECtHR

The ECtHR has been gradually recognizing the importance of the victim's role in criminal proceedings. A relevant case-law has been developing in the frame of the so-called "positive obligations". In this context, the Court of Strasbourg has repeatedly acknowledged the need to guarantee legal aid to the victim and their family members in order to assure their effective participation in investigations. This trend derives from several articles of the Convention and results in an evolution in favor of the victims' right to legal aid.

Further, the self-evident "negative obligation" to abstain from behaviors that violate the fundamental rights under Articles 2, 3, 4 and 8 ECHR, the ECtHR affirms that the States have "positive obligations" both in the substantial sphere and the procedural one. As far as the latter is concerned, it is mandatory for the States to

[59] Council of Europe (CoE), Explanatory Report to the Council of Europe Convention on Preventing and Combating Violence against Women and Domestic Violence, Istanbul, 11.05.2011, par. 295.

ensure the actual identification and punishment of perpetrators. State authorities are bound to conduct complete and effective investigations.[60] In this frame, the States must also guarantee to the victim and their close relatives the right to participate in the criminal proceedings, to be heard and to introduce evidence. At the same time victims need to be protected from the risk of "secondary victimization", which could result from the participation of the charged in the trial, or from the dynamics of the proceeding itself.

This case-law trend stresses the necessity of protecting the victim not only through the justice system, but also *from* it. Many ECtHR judgments are noteworthy in this regard, but only some of them—more directly pertaining to legal aid issues—will be taken under consideration here for lack of space. The European Court repeatedly confirmed a "positive obligation" for the States, namely a "obligation to do".[61] The Court of Strasbourg has invoked the above-mentioned articles to point out the duty of the States to carry out efficacious criminal proceedings in GDV cases.[62] Incidentally, it is useful to underline how the Committee of Ministers of the Council of Europe[63] stressed that member States should "have an obligation to exercise due diligence to prevent, investigate and punish acts of violence, whether those acts are perpetrated by the State or private persons, and provide protection to victims".

The considered interpretative current of the European Court is the very cornerstone of victims' protection. In this context, the ECtHR has affirmed the importance of granting victims free legal aid, as the latter plays a central role in enabling them and their close relatives to participate in the investigations and the trial. The Court has recognized several violations of Article 2 or Article 3 ECHR in the procedural sphere. In some cases, the ECtHR has stressed that the victim could not participate in the proceedings in a suitable and effective way, because they were not granted free legal aid.[64]

Some judgments are emblematic of this trend and deserve to be cited, even though they do not specifically concern cases of domestic violence. Among others, the *Savitzkyy v. Ukraine* judgment involved an alleged abuse by the police.[65] In relation to this case, the Court affirmed that the positive obligations of the State, deriving from Article 3 ECHR, include the duty to assure access to legal aid. Consequently, the ECtHR condemned Ukraine for failing to meet its positive obligations and to provide the applicant with free legal assistance, in order to ensure an effective participation in the proceedings. Similarly, the *Rantsev v. Cyprus and Russia* judgment recognized the violation of Article 2 ECHR and condemned the State of Cyprus for

[60] Marandola (2020) and Erbaş (2021).

[61] ECtHR, *Opuz v. Turkey* (33401/02), 9.6.2009; *Rumor v. Italy* (72964/10), 27.05.2014; *Talpis v. Italy* (41237/14), 2.3.2017; *Volodina v. Russia* (41261/17), 1.6. 2017: see now *Volodina v. Russia* (40419/19), 14.9.2021; *Tërshana v. Albania* (48756/14), 4.8.2020.

[62] Among others, see again ECtHR, *Y v. Bulgaria* (41990/18), 20.02.2020.

[63] Recommendation (2002)5 of 30.04.2002 on the protection of women against violence.

[64] ECtHR, *Savitskyy v. Ukraine* (38773/05), 26.07.2012; *Rantsev v. Cyprus and Russia* (25965/04), 7.1.2010.

[65] ECtHR, *Savitskyy v. Ukraine* (38773/05), 26.07.2012.

not conducting satisfactory investigations.[66] In this case, the State authorities did not provide legal aid to the father of a murder victim. It is true that the applicant did not carry out the right procedure to obtain legal aid, however the Court stressed the duty of the State to inform the people involved in the trial about the correct protocol, through the judicial authority. To conclude, it is significant to mention the *E.B. v. Romania* case, related to the alleged rape of a person considered particularly vulnerable because of her mental disability. The lack of legal aid was strongly stigmatized by the ECtHR,[67] pointing out the risk for the victim to experience further traumas during the proceedings. The Court took advantage of this case to clearly promote legal aid as a tool for victims' protection, in order to avoid "secondary victimization". The latter is the sufferance that proceedings themselves can cause to victims.

It is clear that the ongoing evolution of the ECtHR case-law aims to include victims' legal aid in the list of the States' procedural duties in criminal matters.[68]

7 Legal Aid and EU Sources: Directive 2012/29/EU and Further Directives

Legal aid issues are addressed also by EU sources. Directive 2012/29/EU on victims' protection outlines a general system of protection for all victims, regardless of their personal characteristics and of the type of crimes.[69] In the light of this Directive, legal aid can be traced back to the so-called service rights, which enable victims to effectively access justice. Victim support services range from emotional and psychological support to the arrangement of accommodation. Articles 8 and 9 of the Directive play a crucial role. Article 8 provides that "Member States shall ensure that victims, in accordance with their needs, have access to confidential victim support services, free of charge [...] before, during and for an appropriate time after criminal proceedings". Benefitting from these services is independent from a formal complaint lodged by the victim. Article 9 is relevant in establishing the State's duty to provide information to victims on the support services they are entitled to. Pro bono legal assistance, given by NGOs or others, is in line with Articles 8 and 9, although their activities are generally limited to providing victims with basic advice and information concerning legal procedures. Furthermore, whereas no. 38 is dedicated to specialized services to be offered to particularly vulnerable victims and also mentions, among the types of assistance, "legal advice".[70]

---

[66] ECtHR, *Rantsev v. Cyprus and Russia* (25965/04), 7.1.2010.

[67] ECtHR, *E.B. v. Romania* (49089/10), 19.03.2019.

[68] Parlato (2021a), p. 135 ff.

[69] Civello Conigliaro (2012); Bellender Todino and Morillo (2017); p. 3 ff.; Bargis and Belluta (2017), p. 15 ff.

[70] Parlato (2012), p. 215 ff.

Unlike services, legal aid is given little attention by Directive 2012/29/EU. Only meagre Article 13 is reserved to it: "member States shall ensure that victims have access to legal aid, when they have the status of parties to criminal proceedings". The norm also affirms that "the conditions or procedural rules under which victims have access to legal aid shall be determined by national law".

In an attempt to respect national diversity (whereas no. 20), the Directive has supplied very few practical indications on this point. After all, domestic systems are very different from one another. Some States consider the victim as a party in proceedings, while other ones—including Italy—define them as a simple "subject" (Article 90 CPC).

Article 13 is articulated on two different levels. On the one hand, it binds States to guarantee free legal aid only to victims who "have the status of parties to criminal proceedings". On the other hand, it entirely delegates to national legislations the crucial task to establish "the conditions or procedural rules" under which the right can be accessed. The provision follows in the wake of what was provided for by Article 6 Framework Decision 2001/220/JHA, but it further limits the protection scope. While in the Framework Decision the guarantee was ensured to victims as "possible" parties to the criminal proceedings, the Directive only refers to victims who "have" the party status.[71]

Article 14 of the Directive regulates the refund of expenses resulting from victims' participation in proceedings. The norm does not explicitly mention "legal aid" but, on a practical level, it originates an extension of the guarantee, in line with the trend followed by some national legal systems which incorporate the refund of legal costs into the concept of "legal aid". However, Article 14 shows weaknesses similar to those of Article 13. Under the former, the right to the reimbursement of procedural expenses is recognized "in accordance with their role in the relevant criminal justice system". Furthermore, Article 14 also entrusts the States with the task of establishing the conditions and methods to exercise the guarantee.

The provision seems to have broader scope than Article 7 of the 2001 Framework Decision: it protects victims regardless of their status as plaintiff or witness. However, the vagueness of the rule and the express reference to national legislations cast doubts on its actual ability to effectively bind the States. Furthermore, whereas no. 47 restricts the meaning of Article 14 because it establishes that procedural expenses "should only be covered to the extent that the victim is obliged or requested by the competent authorities to be present and actively participate in the criminal proceedings". As expressed by the Commission, the minimum extent of these costs should be identified in "travel expenses and loss of earnings".

Under this Directive, victims' legal aid risks to remain an empty formulation of principle. Moreover, the total lack of "remedies" to be activated in case of violation of the guarantee can compromise the effectiveness of the measures pursuant Articles 13 and 14, as well as the background of legal aid itself, namely information and advice services.

[71] Bargis and Belluta (2017), p. 38 ff.

Incidentally, it should be noted that an ongoing Proposal aims to modify the contents of the Directive (COM (2023) 424 final, 12.07.2023), providing access to specialized support services for vulnerable victims (such as free psychological support for as long as necessary depending on the victims individual needs). Moreover, the Proposal seeks to facilitate access to justice by ensuring victims are sufficiently assisted in Court and are empowered to challenge the criminal proceedings' decisions affecting their rights, independently of their status during these proceedings. Furthermore, from an economic perspective, the Proposal deserves to be mentioned specifically, because it tends to ensure effective access to compensation, both by guaranteeing it immediately after the judgment and by providing that the State should directly pay the sums to the victim, seeking reimbursement from the offender afterwards. However, a comparison can be drawn between a victim's legal aid and that of the accused, under Directives 2012/29/EU and 2016/1919/EU.

Both Directives have a common central core, namely the coverage of defensive expenses in criminal proceedings. Directive 2012/29/EU goes a step further, in granting victims with initial information and counseling services, legal support and assistance, together with a refund of the costs associated with their participation in the proceedings. However, Article 13 of Directive 2012/29/EU does not offer tools for strengthening the guarantee, whereas Directive 2016/1919/EU does.

Article 13 only recognizes the right to legal aid to victims who are "parties" in domestic criminal proceedings. If, according to the national system, the victim does not fill the role of "party", the norm is not binding for the State. Nevertheless, even if the internal discipline of State X attributes the role of "party" to the victim, the wide discretion granted to the States by Directive 2012/29/EU allows them to adopt a restrictive approach and to subordinate the access to the guarantee to very strict conditions. By contrast, Directive 2016/1919/EU protects free legal aid in favor of the accused more strongly, by regulating admission procedures, services quality and the "remedies" that can be activated if the right is denied.[72]

A further comparison concerns only the victim, involving the system of Directive 2012/29/EU and the one of ECHR. The European Union aims to guarantee a broader but weaker protection. This gap can be bridged considering that a victim's legal aid is clearly recognized by article 47(3), CFREU (Charter of Fundamental Rights of the European Union). The meaning of this provision has to be at least equal to the one established by the ECHR, pursuant article 52(3), and 53 CFREU. Both Articles preclude any interpretation that may jeopardize the level of protection established by the ECHR itself. All this implies that the margin of discretion given to the States by Directive 2012/29/EU should in any case comply with article 47(3), CDFUE and, consequently, with the ECtHR case-law.

Further EU Directives provide specific measures to safeguard and support the victims of particular types of crime (such as trafficking in human beings, sexual exploitation of minors and terrorism). In particular, three Directives deserve to be initially mentioned. First, Directive 2011/36/EU addresses trafficking in human

[72] Costa Ramos and Vidal Fernández (2020), pp. 39–55.

beings (THB) and aims to protect the victims of these crimes. This Directive has made several steps forward as compared to Directive 2012/29/EU. The former overcomes the debated limits of Directive 2012/29/EU, which excludes from legal aid the victims who are not "parties" to criminal proceedings. Moreover, Article 12(2), of Directive 2011/36/EU draws a distinction between legal counselling and legal representation: member States are required to ensure both guarantees (the second one "in accordance with the role of victims in the relevant justice system") without delay and cost-free ("where the victim does not have sufficient financial source").

The 2011 Directive was recently amended by Directive 2024/1712/EU, which underlines that Article 12 "shall apply in addition to the rights set out in Directive 2012/29/EU". In order to improve assistance support to victims of THB, the new source clearly aims to ensure that victims "have access to shelters and safe accommodation equipped to accommodate" their "specific needs" (whereas no. 16).

Secondly, Directive 2011/93/EU concerns the fight against sexual abuse and exploitation of children and child pornography. In this context, the victim has the right to access "without delay" legal counselling and legal representation, with—in the latter case—the usual limits that depend on national law (article 20(2), and whereas no. 32). A recast of this Directive is in progress and "Parliament insisted that victims of child sexual abuse should be provided with proper assistance and support, especially legal aid and psychological support" (Combating child sexual abuse: Revising Directive (2011/93/EU)—recast, 1st edition, 23.7.2024).

Thirdly, Directive 2017/541/EU concerns the fight against terrorism. In this frame, the protection of the right to legal aid does not differ much from the basic structure of Directive 2012/29/UE. However, Directive 2017/541/EU offers a stronger guarantee, through the States' duty to take into due consideration the "circumstances and [...] the seriousness of the criminal offense", in relation to the conditions of access to the guarantee, and to the procedural rule.[73] Victims' right to access to legal aid is guaranteed by para. 6 of Article 24, "where they have the status of parties to criminal proceedings". Article 25 clarifies that the provided measures are available not only in favor of terrorism victims, but also of "their family members".

The just mentioned Directives contain both substantial and procedural provisions. It is questionable whether these sources ensure greater protection than Directive 2012/29/EU, in the field of legal aid. If they did, they would prevail over the latter, when criminal conducts fall also under one of the categories they concern and not only within the sphere of domestic violence (it can happen above all for human trafficking or crimes against children). The answer seems to be positive in relation to the most central core of the guarantee, namely the coverage of the defensive expenses in criminal proceedings.

Moreover, a further specific source was adopted in 2024. The already cited Directive 2024/1385/EU is precisely dedicated to the protection of the victims of domestic violence. As anticipated, it provides for access to legal aid and psychological support, requiring the States to guarantee the establishment of effective

[73] Amalfitano (2017), p. 89 ff.

reporting mechanisms, too. According to Whereas no. 32 "member States can extend legal aid, including free legal aid, to victims when reporting criminal offences, where provided for by national law". As already stressed, in order to decide whether to grant legal aid, the States "should consider the victim's effective access to his or her financial resources". The provision aims to strengthen the guarantee of free legal aid in favor of DV victims, regardless of either their role as a party to the proceedings, or their apparent financial status.

8 Conclusions

> The promotion and protection of women's rights are fundamental requirements for building a true democracy[74]

In the Italian legal system, especially in recent years, there has been a growing tendency to implement measures aimed at ensuring a more effective response to crimes of domestic violence, which are increasingly seen as a social alarm. This shift reflects heightened cultural and legal awareness of violence against women and minors. Consequently, the is a desire to establish a more effective support system for victims, facilitating their involvement in the detection and emergence of criminal behavior; in this context, particular importance is assumed by Directive 2024/1385/EU of May 14th and Law No. 168 of November 24, 2023.

The benefit of legal aid under Article 47(3) of Presidential Decree no. 115/2002, reinterpreted in light of the Constitutional Court's judgment no. 1/2021, aligns with this logic. The rationale behind these rules, as reconstructed by the examined ruling, reflects a clear choice in criminal policy aimed at offering concrete support to victims whose vulnerability is heightened by the nature of the offences they endure. This approach encourages victims to report crimes and actively participate in the pursuit of truth. However, the Italian legal system, often characterized by fragmented legislation, does not always meet international and European standards for effectively combating domestic violence.[75]

Specifically, regarding legal aid, there has been ineffective transposition of the Istanbul Convention, which mandates that States guarantee the right to legal assistance and free legal aid for victims of domestic violence. This requirement is complicated within the Italian legal framework by challenges in defining domestic violence and identifying related crimes, leading to critical issues in developing effective proced2ural-criminal instruments for victim protection.

As a result, we have witnessed numerous rulings from the European Court of Human Rights condemning Italy for violating Articles 2, 3, 6, and 8 ECHR, due to the failure to provide effective protection for victims of domestic violence. Despite legislative attempts to enhance the legal framework through technical defense

[74] Recommendations to Italy by the CEDAW Committee, 2005.

[75] In a reform perspective, recently, Collica (2024).

measures, it remains essential to address social contexts and increase both cultural and legal awareness regarding victims' rights and their roles in criminal proceedings.

References

Almansi G (11 Mar 2021) Commento alla sentenza n. 1/2021 della Corte costituzionale. Il gratuito patrocinio in assenza di limiti di reddito della donna non è incostituzionale. Osservatorio Violenza sulle Donne

Amalfitano C (2017) La tutela delle vittime di reato nelle fonti dell'Unione europea diverse dalla direttiva 2012/29/UE e le misure di attuazione nell'ordinamento nazionale. In: Bargis M, Belluta H (eds) Vittime di reato e sistema penale. Giappichelli, Torino

Bargis M, Belluta H (2017) La direttiva 2012/29/UE: diritti minimi della vittima nel processo penale. In: Bargis M, Belluta H (eds) Vittime di reato e sistema penale. Giappichelli, Torino

Bellender Todino I, Morillo FF (2017) The victim's right directive: origins and expectations. In: Bargis M, Belluta H (eds) Vittime di reato e sistema penale. Giappichelli, Torino

Bianchi AM (2022) Le vittime di reato e l'assistenza legale in Italia: Un'analisi critica. Studi di Diritto Penale e Procedura Penale

Bouchard M (2019) Sulla vulnerabilità nel processo penale. Diritto Penale e Uomo 12:101–124

Canestrini N (2020) Italian Criminal Procedure Code. Canestrinilex.com

Cassibba F (11 July 2014) Oltre Lanzarote: la frastagliata classificazione soggettiva dei dichiaranti vulnerabili. Diritto penale contemporaneo. 1–10 https://archiviodpc.dirittopenaleuomo.org/upload/1404981476CASSIBBA_2014.pdf

Cendon P (1988) I diritti delle persone deboli. In: Violante L (ed) Storia d'Italia. Annali 14, Legge diritto Giustizia. Einaudi, Torino

Civello Conigliaro SC (22 Nov 2012) La nuova normativa europea a tutela delle vittime di reato. https://archiviodpc.dirittopenaleuomo.org/upload/1353580802CONIGLIARO%202012a.pdf

Collica MT (30 October 2024) La violenza sessuale tra law in the books e law in action: un intervento riformatore non più rinviabile. Archivio Penale

Costa Ramos V, Vidal Fernández B (2020) Access to a lawyer and legal aid/directives 2013/48 and 2016/1919. In: Arangüena Fanego C, de Hoyos SM, Lópex AH (eds) Procedural safeguards for suspects and accused persons in criminal proceedings. Springer, Cham, pp 39–56

Dava M (28 May 2021) Patrocinio a spese dell'Erario, a prescindere dalle condizioni di reddito, per le persone offese (tra l'altro) dai reati di violenza di genere: la Corte costituzionale ne ribadisce la ragionevolezza. Sistema Penale

De Simone G (12 November 2024) Il concetto di violenza nel sistema penale tra diritto interno e dimensione sovranazionale". Archivio Penale

Dorothy DW, Parsons S (2005) Domestic abuse of women and men in Ireland: report on the National Study of domestic abuse, stationery office. The National Crime Council in association with the Economic and Social Research Institute, Dublin

Erbaş R (2021) Effective criminal investigations for women victims of domestic violence: the approach of the ECtHR. Women's Stud Int Forum 86:1–12

Farina P, Pecorella C (2018) La risposta penale alla violenza domestica: un'indagine sulla prassi del tribunale di Milano in materia di maltrattamenti contro familiari e conviventi (article 572 c.p.). Diritto penale contemporaneo. 1–26. https://archiviodpc.dirittopenaleuomo.org/upload/2026-pecorellafarina2018a.pdf

Federal Department of Home Affairs FDHA, Swiss Confederation, Definition, forms and consequences of domestic violence (June 2020).

Fiandaca G (2021) Il diritto penale e la vulnerabilità della vittima. Rivista Italiana di Diritto e Procedura Penale

Gerosa A (6 April 2021) Il patrocinio a spese dello Stato per le vittime vulnerabili: un istituto soltanto di diritto processuale? Osservazioni alla sentenza della Corte costituzionale n. 1 del 2021. Associazione italiana dei Costituzionalisti

Gloor D, Meier A (2012) Evaluation du dégré de gravité de la violence domestique. Rapport de base du point de vue des sciences sociales, su mandato dell'Ufficio federale per l'uguaglianza fra donna e uomo UFU, Bern. https://www.ebg.admin.ch/dam/ebg/fr/dokumente/haeusliche_gewalt/bericht_schweregradhaeuslichegewalt.pdf.download.pdf/rapport_degre_degravitedelaviolencedomestique.pdf

Johnson PM (2008) Typology of domestic violence. Intimate terrorism, violent resistance and situational couple violence. Northeastern University Press, Boston

Leone S (2018) Automatismi legislativi, presunzioni assolute e bilanciamento. In: Apostoli A, Gorlani M (eds) Crisi della giustizia e (in)certezza del diritto. Atti del Convegno di Brescia, 24 novembre 2017. Editoriale scientifica, Napels, pp 223–252

Marandola A (22 Sept 2020) Reati violenti e Corte europea dei diritti dell'uomo: sancito il diritto alla vita e il "diritto alle indagini". https://www.sistemapenale.it/it/scheda/marandola-cedu

Marcenò V, Zagrebelsky G (2018) Giustizia costituzionale, Vol. I—Storia, principi, interpretazioni. Il Mulino, Bologna

Parlato L (2012) Il contributo della vittima tra azione e prova. Torri del Vento, Palermo

Parlato L (2021a) Domestic violence in light of the Istanbul convention: some procedural issues. In: Bonini V, Erbaş R (eds) The 10th anniversary of the Istanbul convention. Pisa University Press, Pisa, pp 129–146

Parlato L (2021b) Vulnerabilità e processo penale. In: Spangher G, Marandola A (eds) La fragilità della persona nel processo penale. Giappichelli, Torino, pp 427–454

Repetto G (2006) Assistenza giudiziaria ai non abbienti. Enc. giur. Treccani, Roma. Istituto dell'Enciclopedia Italiana, Rome. para 3

Romanelli B (2020) La persona offesa vulnerabile nel procedimento penale. EDUCatt Università Cattolica, Milan

Rossi FT (2022) L'accesso alla giustizia per le vittime di violenza domestica: Normativa e giurisprudenza. Rivista di Diritto e Procedura Penale

Russo M (2023) La Vulnerabilità delle Vittime e il Gratuito Patrocinio. Rivista di Diritto Penale e Processuale

Trapella F (2019) La tutela della vittima vulnerabile. Regole europee, prassi devianti, possibili rimedi. Archivio penale 3:1–39. https://archiviopenale.it/File/DownloadArticolo?codice=bf7f4778-b9b6-4abb-ad2c-ddf0e223b8fb&idarticolo=21753

Applicability of Restorative Justice in Cases of Domestic Violence-Case Study of Bosnia and Herzegovina

Ena Kazić-Çakar

Abstract Domestic violence, for various reasons, has been and still is a true challenge for the theory and practice of criminal law. Its nature makes it suitable to be part of the dark figure of crime and although national and international endeavors for its prevention exist and are visible, countries are still seeking an effective way to encourage victims to report this crime and with that to open the opportunity for punishment of perpetrators. This chapter aims to test whether a different approach to the perpetrator and victim, in the form of restorative justice (hereinafter RJ), would be suitable to be applied in cases of domestic violence and if its application would overcome the challenges of reporting and effectiveness in prosecutions of this type of criminal offense. To achieve that goal, the author will correlate the general concept of restorative justice with the nature of domestic violence, and *in concreto,* upon identification of types of restorative justice programs applicable in Bosnia and Herzegovina, through the analysis of relevant provisions of positive criminal codes applicable in that country, establishes whether this criminal offense fits under objective criteria of application of RJ.

1 Introduction

On May 20, 2015, defendant A.A. had an argument with his common-law wife, whom he lives with in a joint household. He hit her with the laptop charger cable in the area of the right eye and pushed her away. She fell on the bed and hit the wooden

The author uses the opportunity to thank the Federal Prosecutorial Office for the delivery of data about the application of restorative justice forms for the period 2017–2022. That data is of immense importance as they illustrate the authors' theoretical allegations.

E. Kazić-Çakar (✉)
International University of Sarajevo, Sarajevo, Bosnia and Herzegovina
e-mail: ekazic@ius.edu.ba

R. Erbaş (ed.), *Criminal Prosecution of Domestic Violence*, Ius Gentium: Comparative Perspectives on Law and Justice 128,
https://doi.org/10.1007/978-3-032-01202-9_9

part of the bed, which caused her minor physical injuries in the form of bleeding on the upper eyelid of the right eye and blood swelling in the area of the lower part of the abdominal wall. Before this critical event, the perpetrator took away the passport of the victim, who is a foreign citizen, to make sure that she would not leave him. As he was the only provider in the family, his denial of giving her a small amount of money for groceries was a common cause of further quarrels, which would often culminate in punching the victim in the region of her stomach, in front of their child. The perpetrator threatened the victim not to mention the arguments to anybody, and not to report him, since he knew everybody at the police, and because of this, she would have to leave Bosnia and Herzegovina (hereinafter B&H). For this continuous verbal, psychological and physical violence in the family, the perpetrator was sentenced conditionally, with a sentence of 6 months, which will not be executed unless he commits a new criminal offense within 2 years. In the justification of the verdict, it is pointed out that the reason for this sentence are the fact that the accused is the father of a minor child, his correct behavior before the court, and his previous lack of conviction. The victim did not file a property claim.[1]

The traditional criminal procedure that was used in this case was of that kind that within the verdict it cannot be determined with certainty whether or not the victim was taught of her rights—to file a property claim. Having a victim as a witness to testify and eventually file her property claim are the two most common activities within which the role of the victim is being consumed? in the traditional approach to criminal justice. The questions of the unsolved source of the conflict between the perpetrator and the victim, the question of victims' satisfaction with the verdict given or their opinion about the sanction, the certainty of application of the victims' right to property claim, the issue of the preventive purpose of the sanction given, and never-ending victims' question– "why this happened to me", "am I going to be safe" are all unsolved questions whose answers the applied traditional retributive approach cannot solve or simply are not of the priority.

Thus, it is socially and legally justified to wonder if another criminal justice approach, particularly RJ, would be more appropriate to be applied in these cases. The aim of this chapter is to determine whether RJ may be appropriate remediation in cases of domestic violence or not. The test is both theoretical and normative, as it will inspect the nature of RJ and its aims, and correlate it with domestic violence. Then the case study of B&H, will inspect the forms of RJ and normative, legal conditions to their application *in concreto*, for the criminal offense domestic violence. With that conclusion about the applicability of RJ in domestic violence cases *in concreto* will be made.

The chapter falls into four parts. The first and last parts are the introduction and concluding remarks. The second part aims to present the nature and sensitivity of this violence type and polarized opinions about the application of RJ in these cases, together with examples from the comparative law of its successful application. The third part is a case study of the applicability of RJ in domestic violence cases in

---

[1] See: Halilović (2019), pp. 53–66.

Bosnia and Herzegovina (hereinafter B&H), which offers the legal background to RJ and its forms in this country, the legal requirements of their application, and the test of their applicability to all forms of the criminal offense of domestic violence. Descriptive, comparative, and normative methods will be used, with the statistical analysis.

1.1 What Is Restorative Justice?

The introductory case illustrates the imperfections of the traditional, retributive justice approach, which is focused on the establishment of what had happened and the punishment of the perpetrator with an aim to accomplish special and general prevention goals. The State has been the guardian of that process, the perpetrator was accused, the state was the accusing party through the role of the prosecutor and the state was the decision-making party through the role of the court. The victim was left aside as a testimony provider, and its right to file a property claim was set to be such an irrelevant item, that is not described in the verdict whether it was filed.

It is exactly this situation, one of the fathers of RJ, *Nils Christie* had in mind when criticizing retributive justice and writing his criminal justice approach-changing article "Conflict as property",[2] in 1977. He stated that the state stole the ownership over the crime (if it is observed as a property) from the real property owner—victim. That is what had to be changed. This revolutionary thought was quite successful and well-received as the ground of an old-new[3] approach to criminal justice. The concept of restorative justice is well described by *Tony Marshall* who considers it as "a procedure in which all parties, or participants in a specific criminal offense, meet, in order to decide together on the resolution of the consequences of the criminal offense and its implications for the future".[4] Similarly, *Howard Zehr* in his "A Little Book of Restorative Justice[5]" perceives it as „...an approach that involves all the stakeholders... and addresses harms, needs, obligations, in order to heal and put things as right as possible".[6] *Zehr* establishes the aims of RJ as "putting key decisions into the hands of those most affected by crime, making justice more healing and, ideally, more transformative, and reducing the likelihood of future offenses".[7] Furthermore, he offers methods for the accomplishment of these aims through

[2] Christie (1977), p. 1.

[3] As a form of justice it is a new concept, but its core idea was conceived and practiced for centuries within traditional communities of New Zealand, South Africa, Canada. See: "The Origins of Restorative Justice", http://www.restorativeapproaches.eu/origins.

[4] Clark (2008), p. 339.

[5] Zehr (2002), p. 37.

[6] Ibid.

[7] Ibid., p. 37.

> ..[I]nvolving victims in the process and coming out of it satisfied, offenders understand how their actions have affected other people and take responsibility for those actions, outcomes help to repair the harms done and address the reasons for the offense, victim and offender both gain a sense of "closure".[8]

From the seventies onwards RJ, or "a new form and mechanism to deal with crime",[9] has emerged and many countries[10] decided to take and implement its ideas in their criminal justice system, separately from it or integrated into it.[11] Many international and regional documents encouraged countries on that path, such are the Economic and Social Council Resolution on *Basic principles on the use of restorative justice programs in criminal matters (ECOSOC Resolution 2002/12)*, which not only provides the main definitions about RJ and with that excludes *legal standards,* but also clearly sets principles such are "the use of RJ at any stage of the criminal justice system",[12] controlling the safety of all parties in any case and in conducting the RJ process, free willingness of parties, and many other. Important is the *Recommendation of the Council of Europe No. R (99) 19 to member States concerning mediation in penal matters*, which "recognized the legitimate interest of victims to have a stronger voice in dealing with the consequences of their victimization, to communicate with the offender and to obtain apology and reparation and established the importance of encouraging the offenders' sense of responsibility and offering them practical opportunities to make amends, which may further their reintegration and rehabilitation"[13] and strongly recommended mediation in criminal matters if there is a consent of the parties.[14] Then, the important role has the *Directive 2012/29/EU of the European Parliament and of the Council of 25 October 2012 establishing minimum standards on the rights, support and protection of victims of crime* which *Biffi* finds to be "the first binding and enforceable legal instrument at the EU level that defines restorative justice and provides the legal safeguards to protect victims of crimes informed about and participating in a restorative justice process".[15]

Next, *Recommendation CM/Rec(2018)8 of the Committee of Ministers to member States concerning restorative justice in criminal matters* established the potential benefits of using RJ and recognized "research evidence which indicates the effectiveness of RJ on a variety of metrics, including victim recovery, offender desistance and participant satisfaction".[16] The advocacy for RJ is present through

---

[8] Zehr (2002), pp. 37–38.

[9] Hargovan (2005), p. 49.

[10] Fifty-five countries by 2019 have codified restorative justice into their criminal justice system. See Maryfield et al. (2020), p. 2, quoting Gonsales.

[11] Ibid., p. 50.

[12] ECOSOC Resolution 2002/12, Sec. II, par. 6.

[13] Recommendation No. R (99) 19 of the Committee of Ministers to member States concerning mediation in penal matters, preamble.

[14] Ibid., Art. II, par. (3).

[15] Biffi (2016), p. 4.

[16] Recommendation CM/Rec (2018)8 of the Committee of Ministers to member States concerning restorative justice in criminal matters, preamble.

the scholastic work of many accomplished scholars such are *Chapman*, *Biffi*, *Ćorović*, *Pali* and *Marder*. *Hudson* particularly considers RJ appropriate in cases of intimate and sexual offenses,[17] and it may be identified in various programs: mediation, family conferences, and diversion programs.[18]

The recent *Directive of the European Parliament and of the Council on Combating Violence Against Women and Domestic Violence* (2024) does not explicitly focus on restorative justice. This important act widens the definition of domestic violence as it prescribes new criminal offenses that should be considered acts of domestic violence (par. 9) and gives procedural grounds for their prosecution and prevention of victimization. However, the Directive is victim-oriented, as it sets rules for the protection of victims, estimation of their best interest, and raising of awareness, which indirectly can be seen as elements of a restorative nature.

2 Domestic Violence Through the Restorative Justice Lenses

With all these recommendations, the support of the international community, practitioners, and scholars who all advocate for the application of RJ, why is then important to test the applicability of RJ in domestic violence cases? The first legal document that brought uncertainty in advocacy for RJ in domestic violence cases was the UN "Handbook for legislation on violence against women", which explicitly prohibited mediation in all cases of violence against women.[19] The reason for that is further explained through an understanding of RJ by the UN. Namely, it problematized RJ as "it removes care from judicial sensitivity, proves that both parties have equal bargaining power, reflects an assumption that both parties are equally at fault for violence, and reduces offenders' accountability", which naturally would not fit with domestic violence cases, as in many of these cases victims do not feel equal to their aggressors nor they have any fault for the violence.[20] However, this approach may be questionable for many, as they perceive RJ as a "philosophy that places emphasis on repairing harms, empowering a victim-driven process...",[21] however, it does reflect the particular nature of domestic violence and its true essence.

---

[17] Hudson (1998), p. 243.

[18] Maryfield et al. (2020), pp. 3–4.

[19] United Nations "Handbook for legislation on violence against women" (2009), p. 38.

Prior to bringing this document, the United Nations Office on Drugs and Crime (UNODC) in 2008 organized an expert group meeting in Vienna (Austria) to discuss good practices in legislation on violence against women. The encounter resulted in recommendations and examples of good practices related to the legislative framework on violence against women. See https://www.un.org/womenwatch/daw/vaw/v-handbook.htm.

[20] Drost et al. (2015), p. 9.

[21] Hopkins et al. (2004), p. 289.

2.1 *The Sensitive Nature of Domestic Violence*

Domestic violence is a generic term defined in the *Istanbul Convention*, for "all acts of physical, sexual, psychological or economic violence that occur within the family or domestic unit or between former or current spouses or partners, whether or not the perpetrator shares or has shared the same residence with the victim".[22] The positive criminal law of B&H, influenced by that definition, determines it as "act of endangerment of the peace, physical integrity or psychological health of a member of his family through violence, insolent or reckless behavior".[23] The sensitivity of its nature is visible at first from this definition, because it includes members of the family or domestic unit as the main subjects of crime. Their close relationship not only is an aggravating fact,[24] because family as a pillar of society and human life, should be the provider of care, security and peace, yet when it comes to domestic violence turns out to be quite opposite to it. As such, not only does the act of physical, sexual, psychological, or economic violence leaves its general and usual consequences, but it also brings deep emotional consequences of betrayal, insecurity, and despair for its victims.[25] Out of fear for their own life, but not rarely out of shame for it being perpetrated in the family/domestic background that is something to be cherished and kept far from the insight of others, victims very often decide to remain silent about it, so, criminal offense of domestic violence falls in the dark figure of crime.

The estimations of the WHO about the frequency of this criminal offense are that 30% of women in the world are victims of domestic violence (one in third women).[26] Those figures confirm that it is a challenging and burning legal issue for which many countries are trying to establish the best approach to be reduced and prevented in overall. Another issue that arises from the fact that domestic violence is being perpetrated within the family and home is the wrong perception that what happens at home is a private issue and officials, neighbors, family, and friends should not get involved into it.[27]

The above-mentioned recommendation not to apply RJ in cases of domestic and sexual violence emerged from the fact that passive subjects are victimized due to high levels of social, physical, economic, or gender inequality to their perpetrator and thus they cannot perceive themselves or cannot be perceived by their offender as equal parties who will have the significant role in the resolution of the case, what RJ implies. Many authors[28] argue the existence of status inequality between perpe-

[22] Art. 3 (b).

[23] Art. 222 (1) of the CCFBH.

[24] Art. 222 (2) of the CCFBH.

[25] Mušić (2018), p. 171; Cheon and Regehr (2006), p. 379.

[26] Domestic Violence, https://www.who.int/news-room/fact-sheets/detail/violence-against-women.

[27] Edwards and Sharpe (2004), p. 6. note that family plays an important role in prevention of domestic violence, as some countries are prone to be culturally tolerant to it.

[28] Ibid., p. 6; Mujezinović et al. (2020), p. 16 ff.

trator and victim and note it as a domestic violence risk factors (i.e. level of education, a history of exposure to child maltreatment, etc).[29] *Edwards and Sharpe* remind of the results of *Pelikans'* research who shows that RJ "is effective only when the victim has resolved to have a life without physical violence and has resources (money, qualification) to live independently.[30]

2.2 *Pros and Cons of Restorative Justice in Domestic Violence Cases*

Having in mind this particular nature of domestic violence and the sensitivity of passive subjects, many authors determined reservations and benefits from the use of RJ in domestic violence cases. Among reservations on this topic, Jokinen summarizes the feminist approach to the issue of the application of RJ in this violence type and finds that this movement does not believe in RJ in domestic violence at all, as they find "female victim is expected to put aside her needs and instead work for the wellbeing of the male offender".[31] In addition to that, *Fernandez*[32] reminds on their understanding of RJ as "... a "soft option"—perhaps even "cheap justice"—and concerns of reprivatizing gendered violence in ways that revictimize and are harmful to victims". *Drost* et al. name safety as an issue of *concern* for RJ, as in these cases there is a power imbalance that may result in re-victimization once the victim and offender are brought to the same place.[33] Therefore, overall it may be counterproductive for both parties. First, the perpetrator can give a manipulative, false apology. Second, victim may be concerned for safety, and thus can accept the apology just to escape from potential victimization.[34] *Hopkins* argues that this power imbalance can make victim be silenced and unable to speak the truth.[35] Furthermore, understanding RJ as a soft process,[36] with symbolic, no long-term implications is found to be concerning for this author. In addition to these, *Hopkins* finds that there is an overemphasis on reconciliation in RJ. Victims should not feel obliged to forgive, even if the apology takes place.[37] *Hopkins* et al. additionally potentiate the

---

[29] See: Violence against women. https://www.who.int/news-room/fact-sheets/detail/violence-against-women.

[30] Edward and Sharpe (2004), p. 6.

[31] Jokinen (2020), p. 44.

[32] Fernandez (2010), p. 10.

[33] Drost et al. (2015), p. 11.

[34] Ibid.

[35] Hopkins (2020), p. 342.

[36] *Hargovan* finds that the gravity of domestic violence demands judicial adjudication. Hargovan (2005), p. 50.

[37] Hopkins (2020), p. 342.

situation that due to the apology,[38] victims may feel they should be again engaged in the risky relationship.[39] *Castella et al*, although concluded that RJ has the potential as a means of addressing domestic violence, correctly suggest that "…DV [domestic violence] is not a homogenous phenomenon, but rather one that manifests in a wide range of offences…", so "…it is unlikely that a single approach will be suitable for all cases".[40] Finally, it is noteworthy that Istanbul Convention, within its article 48 prohibits taking „mandatory alternative dispute resolution processes, including mediation and conciliation, in relation to all forms of violence covered by the scope of this Convention". This provision is most certainly the result of all the above-mentioned fears and concerns related with the application of RJ in gender violence.

As for the *benefits* of the use of RJ in cases of domestic violence, most commonly they are established as a chance to change the relationship with the perpetrator (in the cases of non-aggressive perpetrators), meet the needs of victims, women's voice is to be heard,[41] offenders are taking the responsibility, safety is not an issue—as there is a contract of behavior that can be observed and controlled.[42] *Hopkins* finds very positive the fact that "public truth-telling serves a number of important functions for benefit of victim and society".[43] The same author argues that RJ is a component of victims' recovery, as human beings need to talk about harm and truth-telling has a healing impact. Acknowledgment of what happened may ameliorate the position of victims as a group. It can undercut the denial by police, prosecutors, judges and society[44] of the existence and harm of domestic violence. *Hopkins* views even benefit for society, as it can encourage the public acceptance of responsibility for intimate violence.[45] Finally, *Parosanu* reminds on statistical data, which shows that the use of RJ in domestic violence cases seems to be efficient when it comes to the prevention of crime, as "only in 11% of the cases within 3 years perpetrators re-offend".[46] Furthermore, the data indicate a "high level of victims satisfaction and empowerment" with the RJ.[47] Similar results offer *Luneman* who presents the results of research from 2015, which included 32 victims in five countries and states that most of the victims and offenders were satisfied with mediation as a form of RJ

[38] Brookes finds the question of apology to be problematic. If false, then the victimization will happen again and that circle has a tendency to be continuous. See more: Brookes (2019), p. 2.

[39] Hopkins et al., (2004), p. 303.

[40] Castella et al. (2011), p. 407.

[41] Hargovan finds this as an opportunity to put the victim in the center of the process, which may be satisfactory to the victim. See Hargovan (2005), p. 54.

[42] Drost et al., (2015), p. 13.

[43] Hopkins (2020), p. 320.

[44] Ibid., 328.

[45] Ibid.

[46] Parosanu (2016), p. 3.

[47] Ibid., p. 3.

applied in their cases.[48] Fernandez,[49] who conducted research on application or RJ in domestic violence concludes in her work which included qualitative research (interviews and data), that "it became amply clear that the victim-survivors of intimate partner violence longed for much more than a retributive legal conclusion of their domestic violence experiences. There was a palpable hunger for healing and closure that restorative justice principles could address".

2.3 A Few Examples of the Application of Restorative Justice in Domestic Violence Cases

Although a legally non-binding recommendation of the United Nations not to apply RJ in cases of sexual and domestic violence does exist, many scientists, as shown above, advocate its application noting its benefits. Many countries, carefully introduced RJ forms in domestic violence cases.

For the *United States of America*, *Kim* notes that RJ is mostly focused on juveniles and school conflicts, while it is very limited for domestic violence.[50] However, states have the jurisdiction to organize RJ programs. *Barocas* et al. find the USA to be the world's leader in combating domestic violence, through models that include community-coordinated responses (perpetrator interventions, victim counseling and support, child counseling and support).[51] They recognize the importance of "OHANA" Family Conferencing (Hawaii), that has been established in 1996. They bring together family members of both parties and lead them through 10 stages of conferencing so that family members and parties take responsibility in the problem-resolution process, create a future plan, and the plan is reviewed by the service provider.[52] Apart from this model, there are noteworthy programs developed in Minnesota. The "Family Group Decision" model, that has been established 20 years ago, aims to "engage parents in conversation about how their abusive behavior is impacting their children".[53] "Transitional Support Circles, a program that has been established in 1996, also in Minnesota, aims to motivate "the perpetrator of DV [domestic violence] to begin the repair the harm and to plan a non-violent life".[54] *Gavrielides* notes that victim-offender programs are successfully accepted throughout the USA, by both victims and offenders.[55] While victims state they reclaimed lives after only 18 months of completion of the program and find the program life-

[48] Lünnemann and Wolthius (2015), p. 23.

[49] Fernandez (2010), p. 15.

[50] Kim (2021), p. 169.

[51] Barocas et al. (2020), p. 319.

[52] Ibid.

[53] Ibid.

[54] Ibid.

[55] Gavrielides (2016), p. 70.

changing, offenders claim the programs helped them develop sympathy for victims and make them feel at peace with them.[56]

RJ is being applied in the *United Kingdom*, through various programs,[57] although views about its application are polarized. Sherman[58] reminds about results of research conducted in the UK, which shows "that there is growing interest among domestic abuse victims to have an opportunity to participate, with extended family members, in a police-led restorative justice conferences", which he deems to be effective. Apart from those, *Warwickshire DV Support* and *Family mediation* are just a few programs to mention. Their joint point is that they provide forms of RJ upon screening each case, and if they find it unsuitable, they offer an alternative to it.[59] In-depth, assessment is a condition *sine qua non* in another pioneer of the application of RJ in cases of domestic violence, *Finland*. Since the 1980's it applies it quite successfully for cases of domestic violence.[60] In order to check whether the case is suitable for mediation, frequency of violence, the seriousness of violence, whether the offender admits to his/her actions, whether the offender takes responsibility for the incident and whether the participation of a volunteer was ensured, are all the points that have to be checked.[61] Once that police or prosecutor indicates mediation, separate face-to-face meetings are held prior to the mediation itself.[62] After the meetings, a follow up plan is made for victim, and damage compensation is discussed and agreed.

Austria has a long experience in the application of RJ in domestic violence cases (21% of RJ cases), which dates back to 1992 and *Parosanu* illustrates the procedure.[63] It involves two facilitators, one male, and one female, each approaching the party of the same gender. They sit all together, but facilitators are the ones who talk and present the cases.[64] However, *Miller* (through *Lunneman* 2015) notes that Austria, in order to prevent potential negative outcomes of non-punitive remedies, additionally assesses offenders' dangerousness in terms of "escalation, reoffending, re-traumatization of victims with risk assessment tool that includes criteria such as a history of violence, weapons, financial dependency, threats",[65] which is a quite good and cautionary approach.

Belgium is one of the leaders of RJ practices and it even applies it in serious cases. It employs professional mediators who conduct the case screening. Mediation

---

[56] Ibid., p. 70.

[57] Ibid., p. 18.

[58] Sherman (2018), p. 460, calling on Nettleton and Strang (2018).

[59] Ibid.

[60] Ibid., p. 18.

[61] *Instructions for people considering mediation*. https://www.riku.fi/en/guides-and-instructions/instructions-for-people-considering-mediation/.

[62] Parosanu (2016), p. 15.

[63] Ibid.

[64] Parosanu (2016), p. 7.

[65] Miller (2020), p. 71.

and family meetings are successful forms of RJ applied traditionally in *Canada* and in *South Africa.*[66] In *Indonesia*, according to *Saraya*, RJ is present (as of 2004 and *Law No. 23* which enacted *legi speciali* for settlement in domestic violence cases), but was additionally confirmed with the by-law Regulation of the Indonesian National Police Number 8 of 2021 concerning the Handling of Crimes Based on RJ. Although RJ is applicable for domestic violence cases, the principle of voluntariness or dependence on the willingness of both parties to apply its forms is crucial.[67] "The application of RJ will lead to a shift in the direction of punishment and the purpose of sentencing that is punishing or revenge by taking responsibility for every act committed into a settlement that places more emphasis on efforts to heal/restore to its original state before the occurrence of a crime".[68]

Italy is one more country with the successful application of restorative justice. The latest legislative reform, in form of the *Legislative Decree No. 150/2022*, within articles 43 and 44 prescribes wide application of RJ in criminal law area regardless of the type of criminal offense or its gravity and sets principles of its application (confidentiality, voluntarism, consent, community participation, etc.). However, paragraph 4 of article 43, clearly states it should be limited in the cases where it may become dangerous for the victim. That implies that all the programs of RJ are applicable for all criminal offenses, including domestic violence, unless they may bring danger to the participants of RJ. According to article 53, "mediation, the restorative dialogue or any other dialogue program guided by mediators, carried out in the interest of the victim of the crime and the person named as offender" are accessible programs of RJ, thus they are applicable for domestic violence.

3 Restorative Justice and Domestic Violence—Testing it *In Concreto: A Case of B&H*

One of the aims of this chapter is to test whether RJ is applicable in cases of domestic violence in B&H or not. RJ in overall has been a part of the Bosnian criminal law system from 1998 and 2003 retrospectively when general criminal codes have been brought. Namely, due to the specific constitutional division of jurisdictions, the matters of criminal law are being regulated through four *legi generali*: *Criminal Code of B&H and Criminal Procedure Code of B&H* (2003), *Criminal Code of Federation of B&H (hereinafter CCFBH) and Criminal Procedure Code of Federation B&H* (2003), *Criminal Code of Brčko District of B&H (hereinafter CCBD)* and Criminal *Procedure Code of Brčko District BH* (2003) and *Criminal Code of RS (hereinafter CCRS)* (2017) and *Criminal Procedure Code of RS* (2003). However, RJ as a term has not been used in any of these codes, so in order to conclude if RJ is part of the

[66] Ibid., p. 15.

[67] Saraya (2022), pp. 1–10.

[68] Ibid., p. 10.

criminal system of this country one has to analyze institutes of those codes and by identifying their restorative nature that fits with the aims and mechanisms of RJ, may conclude the RJ exists. Apart from these *legi generali*, sources of RJ are *legi speciali* as Code on Protection and Dealing with Juveniles in Criminal Procedure (RS, FBH, BD), and many others.

According to *Ćorović*,[69] in the Bosnian criminal law system, RJ may be categorized into RJ applicable to juveniles and RJ applicable to adults. Situations "…when the victim submits a property claim for damages as a result of the offense, when requiring community service as an alternative to a prison sentence, and when requiring from the offender to fulfill certain obligations as a condition of probation" are identified as forms of RJ applicable for adults.[70] Arguments for that are seen in the establishment of a correlation between perpetrator and victim and potential for mediation in the first, and for inclusion of the wider community/work for its benefit in the last two. When it comes to juveniles, it may be recognized in "educational recommendations, police warnings, and educational measures (obligations of juvenile)".[71]

(a) *Mediation* in B&H is applicable in criminal cases only in situations when a victim files a property claim.[72] The court may propose mediation through a mediator to the victim and perpetrator, "if the court considers that the claim under property law is such that it would be purposeful to refer it to the mediation".[73] This solution is possible until the finalization of the main trial, for all types of criminal cases. When it comes to the number of the application of mediation in practice, they are not available. However, from the various indirect sources, it can be concluded that mediation is not applied in B&H in criminal law cases,[74] due to traditionalism, costs, and institutional factors.[75] Namely, judges are prone to continue with the criminal procedure and solving the damage compensation claims within the criminal procedure. The traditional approach is followed also by victims who usually file damage compensation through the traditional procedure. The costs may be an additional obstacle for using mediation, since at the moment of filing the request for mediation, the party which requests is obliged to pay for it in advance (advance pay). If the agreement is achieved, the costs of mediation fall under the amount to be compensated. If the agreement is not reached, the amount paid in advance will not

[69] Ćorović (2018), p. 56. Also see: Kazić and Ćorović (2018), pp. 171–180; Kazić and Ćorović (2019), pp. 81–82.

[70] Kazić and Ćorović (2018), pp. 171; Kazić and Ćorović (2019), pp. 84–85.

[71] Ibid.

[72] According to the OSCE (2011), p. 59, victims usually do not file the property claim in the cases of domestic violence.

[73] Criminal Procedure Code of FBH (2003), art. 212 paragraph (2).

[74] See: www.umbih.ba.

[75] Kazić et al. (2019), pp. 71–72.

be paid back.[76] The amount depends on the value of dispute and can go from 75–10,000 BAM (tax excluded). This may be a good indicator of why subjects of mediation sometimes decide not to request it.

(b) *Community service* holds restorative nature, as it implies that the perpetrator may be obliged to conduct a particular action in favor of the community. Namely, pursuant to Art. 44 of the Criminal Code of the Federation of B&H, the court may in the cases when determines and pronounces imprisonment up to 1 year, order substitution of that sanction with community service. The Code prescribes that application of this sanction is possible when it is not necessary to incarcerate the perpetrator to achieve the substance of the imprisonment, and also when convicting an individual to probation would not be sufficient.[77] This RJ form is applicable only for lenient criminal offenses. *Ćorović* offered the statistics for the period 2006–2015, and concluded that their frequency is very low, knowing that in Republika Srpska (here in after RS) there was only one case of its use/sanctioning, 16 in Brčko District BH, and 244 in Federation of B&H.[78]

(c) *Probation* is indirectly correlated with RJ. According to Art. 62 of the Federal Criminal Code, for the cases for which the court determines the criminal sanction of up to 2 years of imprisonment or monetary fine, the Court may decide not to apply it and instead suspend it with condition that in the probation period (1–5 years)[79] perpetrator does not re-offend. The obligation which correlates this sanction to RJ is monetary compensation to the victim.

(d) *Police warning* is a divertive, warning measure that can be issued to juveniles for the criminal offenses for which imprisonment of up to 3 years or a fine can be applied. However, in order to apply this measure, together with this objective condition, there are objective-subjective conditions for its application, and those are: the minor admits the criminal act; the recognition was given freely and voluntarily; there is sufficient evidence that the minor has committed a criminal offense; the minor has not previously been given a police warning, educational recommendation or criminal sanction.[80] According to *Ćorović*, police warning is extensively being used in RS (243 cases for the observed period), while not often in Brčko District (18) nor in the Federation of B&H (14).[81] Most recent data from the Federal Prosecutorial office, for the period

---

[76] Book of rules on costs of mediation (2015). https://www.umbih.ba/dokumenti/pravilnici/pravilnik_o_nagradi_i_naknadi.pdf.

[77] Art. 44. par (2) of the CCFBH and Criminal Code of Brčko District and Art. 70 of the Criminal Code of RS.

[78] Ćorović (2018), pp. 175–195.

[79] Art. 62 par (1) and (2) of CCFBH and Criminal Code of Brčko District, Art. 62 of the Criminal Code of RS. Note that in RS, objective condition that refers to the sanction is one, not 2 years of determined sanction, like it is in the other entity of B&H.

[80] Art. 23 par. (1) and (2) of the Code on Protection and Dealing with Juveniles in Criminal Procedure in Federation of B&H (2014).

[81] Ćorović (2018), p. 179; Kazić Cakar and Ćorović (2022), p. 162.

2017–2022 show that the number of police warnings has decreased in the Federation (from 35 in 2018 to 10 in 2020), but it has the tendency to grow (16 in 2021).[82]

(e) *Educational measures* are a type of criminal sanction for juveniles, and may be correlated to RJ only through one of its forms: measures of warning-special obligations.[83] One of those may be work for a humanitarian organization. With this obligation, a juvenile is establishing contact with the community and restores the relationship.

(f) *Educational recommendations* are alternative measures that may achieve the double goal: the perpetrator to take the responsibility for the act, and the victim to be satisfied, without imposing sanctions on a juvenile. More precisely, they "represent a form of alternative measures that prosecutors or judges, based on the principle of opportunity, apply to a minor perpetrator of a criminal offense, thereby making a diversion from the usual criminal procedure".[84] They can be applied if objective and subjective conditions are fulfilled: the criminal offense is punishable with a fine or imprisonment of up to 3 years (or even more than 3 years if it is proportionate to the circumstances and gravity of the criminal offense). In addition to that, cumulatively: the minor admits the criminal act, the recognition was given freely and voluntarily, there is sufficient evidence that the minor committed a criminal offense, the minor expresses in writing his willingness to reconcile with the injured party, the minor gives written consent to the application of the educational recommendation, and the younger minor also with the consent of the parents or guardian and the aggrieved party gives written consent in the event that this is required by law.[85] Six educational recommendations are prescribed by the law, and they may be recommended by either judge or the prosecutor, however, only two are having restorative nature: a personal apology to the victim and damage compensation. The numbers of educational recommendations in B&H are low. However, the most proactive in their application is Unsko-Sanski Canton, which issued a total of 48 educational recommendations of personal apology to a victim in the past 5 years. Other cantons either did not or in very low figures issued these measures.[86]

---

[82] Response per authors' data request No. A-583/22, from November 22, 2022.

[83] Art. 32 (1) b of Code on Protection and Dealing with Juveniles in Criminal Procedure in RS (2010) and Code on Protection and Dealing with Juveniles in Criminal Procedure in Federation of B&H (2014).

[84] Code on Protection and Dealing with Juveniles in Criminal Procedure in Federation of B&H (2014), Art.12 (p).

[85] Code on Protection and Dealing with Juveniles in Criminal Procedure in Federation of B&H (2014), Art. 24.

[86] There is no data from the Prosecutorial office about the damage compensation as an educational recommendation. Note from the Federal Prosecutorial Office A-583/22. Besides that, Kazić et al. (2019), pp. 66–67. established that in 5 years (2012–2017) no educational recommendation was applied in one of the most populated cantons-Canton Sarajevo. Similar data offers Ćorović (2018), p. 175 for the period 2006–2015.

Overall, it can be concluded that regardless of which type of criminal offense, RJ although *de iure* established in B&H, *de facto* is not often applied, and consequently, not (often) applied for domestic violence. Except for mediation that can be used in any case regardless of its gravity, because it is related only to the victims' property claim, other (indirect) forms of RJ have objective criteria that are related to the gravity of criminal offenses and in overall those are less grave ones. In our opinion, that is the correct legislative approach, as it is inclusive towards RJ and gives an opportunity for its usage for more lenient cases, but for the grave ones stays with the retributive approach. This confirms the co-existence of retributive justice and RJ in our legislation. In addition to that, that approach is not opposite to article 48 of the *Istanbul Convention*, which disables the usage of obligatory mediation in gender violence, since the mediation prescribed in the positive criminal codes in Bosnia and Herzegovina is not mandatory, it is sole potential for the victim, and it refers only to a damage compensation claim, not to merit of the criminal offense.

3.1 Is Restorative Justice Applicable to Domestic Violence Cases in B&H?

Apart from the polarized theoretical opinions about the challenges/concerns and benefits of the application of RJ in the cases of domestic violence, it is necessary to test its applicability on objective grounds. All the above-mentioned forms of RJ, apart from mediation are restricted by either established or prescribed sanctions for the criminal offense, so some of them are automatically excluded from its application. In order to establish if that is the case with domestic violence, it is necessary to analyze its legal regulation, particularly the part of the legal norm that refers to the sanction.

In B&H a fourth woman is a victim of domestic violence (18% of women).[87] Out of that number, 28% of women experienced some forms of domestic violence from the age 15.[88] Women and children are dominant profiles of victims.[89]

Domestic violence as a crime has been prescribed by the entity criminal codes in B&H and the District Criminal Code. According to Art. 222 of the Federal Criminal Code,[90] this crime consists of its basic form and five aggravating forms. In its basics, domestic violence is any "act of endangerment of the peace, physical integrity or psychological health of a member of his family through violence, insolent or reckless behavior". As this criminal offense falls in so-called "self-handed" criminal

[87] OSCE (2019), p. iii.

[88] Ibid. The Report also established that 36% of the victims experienced psychological, 28% sexual violence and 5% stalking.

[89] Mušić (2018), p. 182. Interestingly, most of the convictions are resolved with parole (71,2%). See: OSCE (2011), p. 59.

[90] Art. 218 (1) of the Criminal Code of Brčko District (2003).

offenses, whose perpetrators and victims may be only individuals who are in a particular relationship,[91] those are the essential elements of the body of this crime. As such, they can be only members of the family. As it affects the family, which is a pillar of society, and since perpetrators may be members of the family, the object of protection of this criminal offense is the family as an individual but also as a collective interest.

The legal analysis of the provision indicates that age or gender is not relevant for the existence of this criminal offense. The action encompasses acts of violence, insolent or reckless behavior. The consequence is in the form of endangerment of peace, physical integrity, or psychological health. Similarly, is described this criminal offense in RS, however, it together with the act of endangerment, additionally includes the act of threat to cause the above-mentioned consequences. The criminal sanction prescribed in Federal Criminal Code is an alternation of money fine and imprisonment for up to 1 year. In RS and Districs' Criminal Codes, the sanction is also an alternation of money fine and imprisonment, but the special maximum here is 3 years, which makes these codes stricter *in concreto.* Related to RJ, forms of RJ mentioned in the text above, in Federation are all applicable for the basic form of domestic violence, as the punishment falls into the scope of the sanction limits prescribed for each form of RJ. However, since in RS and Brčko District the sanction is heavier, it can be concluded that only community service would not be applicable if the judge determines the sanction up from a year of imprisonment, nor the probation since the prescribed sanction is 3 years of imprisonment while the objective criteria for probation are money fine or imprisonment up to 2 years.

The first aggravated form that is prescribed only in the Federal and District Criminal Codes exists if the act from the basic form of this criminal offense is perpetrated against a person from the same household.[92] In that case, the sanction is heavier, fine or imprisonment up to 3 years. For that reason, when observing the objective criteria of its application, applicable are community service if the judge establishes the sanction of imprisonment of 1 year in the particular case, police warning, educational measures, and educational recommendations.

Method of perpetration (use of a weapon, dangerous tools, or other means suitable for severely injuring the body or impairing the health) is what makes the next form of this criminal offense aggravating, with the imprisonment from 3 months to 3 years (prescribed in the Federal and District Criminal codes),[93] or from 6 months to 5 years according to the Republic Criminal Code.[94] While all forms of RJ are applicable for this second aggravated form (FBH and BDBH), mediation,

---

[91] Tomić (2007), p. 123.

[92] Art. 218 (2) of the Criminal Code of Brčko District (2003); Art. 222 (2) of the CCFBH (2003).

[93] Art. 218 (3) of the Criminal Code of Brčko District (2003)-partially, as it consumes two aggravated forms prescribed in Federal Code, Art. 222 (3) of the CCFBH (2003), Art. 190 (2) of the Criminal Code of RS.

[94] In Brčko, the additional element is that the criminal offence has been perpetrated in front of child. Art. 218 (3) of the Criminal Code of Brčko District (2003).

community service (if the court determines 1 year) and educational measures are applicable for this form according to the Republic Criminal Code.

The next aggravated form of this criminal offense is in the case of the existence of aggravating consequences (serious physical injury, severe impairment of health), or the criminal offense has been perpetrated against a child or minor, the perpetrator will be punished with imprisonment 1–5 years (Federation of B&H),[95] or 2–10 years (RS). Mediation, educational measures for both entities, and community service (only for the Federation), are applicable for this form of a criminal offense.

The death of a member of the family due to the violence is an aggravating circumstance of the next aggravated form of this criminal offense, which is punishable with imprisonment of two (three in Republika Srpska) to 15 years of imprisonment. In this case, only mediation regarding the property claim would be theoretically applicable, but *de facto* would arise the skepticism presented in cons to RJ in domestic violence cases.

The last aggravating form is differently prescribed in RS on one hand, and in Federation B&H and Brčko District, on the other. While RS criminalizes breach of protective measures, and prescribes fine and imprisonment of up to 3 years, the other two parts of the territory of B&H had criminalized the death of a person who was previously subject to domestic violence[96] and prescribed at least 10 years of imprisonment or long term imprisonment. While for the last, theoretically, but not practically the mediation may be only applicable, for the first all forms could be applicable.

4 Conclusion

The development and embracement of RJ appear most certainly as one of the most significant steps in the evolution of criminal law. It manages to overcome the flaws of traditional, retributive justice and may coexist with it or be its alternative. However, due to the devotion to the traditional approach, or because of the fear towards new and different (among many other reasons), and often with justified arguments, RJ is not being only challenged generally as a concept, but also more particularly—regarding its applicability for certain types of criminal offenses. This chapter demonstrated the main concerns and benefits of RJ applied in cases of domestic violence. Many of the concerns stated above can be overcome. For instance, the fear of trivialization of criminal offenses can be easily overcome with the fact that RJ may be applied in these cases together with retributive justice, as

[95] Art. 218 (3) of the Criminal Code of Brčko District (2003) and it is punishable from 3 months to 3 years, Art. 222 (4) of the CCFBH (2003), Art. 190 (2) of the Criminal Code of RS.

[96] The public was appalled by the case from 2015 in which mother, stepfather, grandfather, and grandmother abused the four-year-old boy S.Ć., who died after his mother punched him in the chest and threw him in the air. The murder was preceded by domestic violence. See: https://avaz.ba/vijesti/crna-hronika/184054/dosje-izivljavanje-koje-ni-odrastao-covjek-ne-bi-prezivio.

such any room for the trivialization of victimization or suffering does not come into being.

The concern related to the safety of the passive subject and revictimization can be overcome in a dual manner: First, through screening of every single case, the perpetrators character, characteristics of the victim, and objective criteria for application of RJ and only upon the results of the screening, the decision on whether or not to apply forms of RJ can be made. That subjective and objective screening is the key of the applicability of RJ in these cases and the avoidance of the potential revictimization risk. Second, the voluntaristic basis and engagement of professionals who are experienced in working in cases of domestic violence may serve as a guarantee of protection from re-victimization. In our opinion, RJ upon screening may empower victims, as it will place them in the decision-making position about the sanction and solution of the criminal case, but also the apology received, and the answers heard may provide healing for a victim.

As for the case of B&H, it has *de iure* embraced forms of RJ. Testing their applicability in this type of violence, for now, means testing the objective criteria, that are prescribed for those forms and which have an eliminatory impact. Domestic violence is criminalized through three criminal codes in B&H, which appear not to be harmonized regarding the prescription of the act and the sanctions. That results in different conclusions about the applicability of RJ forms in cases of domestic violence in Federation B&H, RS, and Brčko District.

Our testing showed that most of the forms of RJ are applicable to the basic form of domestic violence, while the aggravated forms differ. In our opinion *lege lata* should also prescribe obligatory screening (like the Austrian approach), which would include observation of *case + personality of perpetrator + personality of the victim*, even in those permissible cases, and with that, any potential for re-victimization of the victim may be overcome. Finally, the everlasting problem of unharmonized criminal laws in B&H should be overcome with its future harmonization, otherwise, the room for discrimination and lack of legal certainty of the citizens of B&H will continue to exist.

References

Barocas B, Avieli H, Shimizu R (2020) Restorative justice approaches to intimate partner violence: a review of interventions. Partn Abus 11(3):318–349. https://doi.org/10.1891/PA-2020-0010

Biffi E (2016) Practice guide to Rj services: the victims' directive: challenges and opportunities for restorative justice. EFRJ, Leuven

Brookes DR (2019) Restorative justice and domestic violence. https://papers.ssrn.com/sol3/papers.cfm?abstract_id=3756614

Cheon A, Regehr C (2006) Restorative justice models in cases of intimate partner violence: Reviewingthe evidence. Vict Offenders 1(4):369–394. https://doi.org/10.1080/15564880600934138

Christie N (1977) Conflicts as property. Br J Criminol:1–17

Clark JN (2008) The three Rs: retributive justice, restorative justice and reconciliation. Contemp Justice Rev 11:331–350

Ćorović R (2018) Restorativna pravda u sistemu krivičnog pravosuđa [Restorative Justice in the Criminal Justice System]-doctoral dissertation (Doctoral Thesis). University of Sarajevo, Sarajevo

De Castella K, Platow MJ, Wenzel M, Okimoto T, Feather NT (2011) Retribution or restoration? Anglo–Australian's views towards domestic violence involving Muslim and Anglo–Australian victims and offenders. Psychol Crime Law 17(5):403–420. https://doi.org/10.1080/10683160903292253

Drost L, Haller B, Hofinger V (2015) Restorative justice in cases of domestic violence best practice examples between increasing mutual understanding and awareness of specific protection needs. European Commission, London

Edwards A, Sharpe S (2004) Restorative justice in the context of domestic violence: a literature review. Mediation and Restorative Justice Center, Edmonton

Fernandez, M. (2010). "Restorative Justice for Domestic Violence Victims: An Integrated Approach to Their Hunger for Healing". Faculty Book Gallery. https://scholarcommons.scu.edu/faculty_books/421

Gavrielides T (2016) Repositioning restorative justice in Europe. Vict Offenders 11(1):71–86. https://doi.org/10.1080/15564886.2015.1105342

Halilović M et al (2019) Ponovno čitanje I analiza presuda za nasilje u porodici u Bosni I Hercegovini. Atlantska incijativa, Sarajevo. https://atlantskainicijativa.org/wp-content/uploads/Ponovno-citanje-i-analiza-presuda-nasilja-u-porodici-u-Bosni-i-Hercegovini-web.pdf

Hargovan H (2005) Restorative justice and domestic violence: some exploratory thoughts. Empowering Women Gender Equity 1:48–65

Hopkins CQ (2020) Tempering idealism with realism: using restorative justice processes to promote acceptance of responsibility in cases of intimate partner violence. Harv J Law Gend 35:312–353

Hopkins CQ, Koss MP, Bachar KJ (2004) Applying restorative justice to ongoing intimate violence: problems and possibilities. Saint Louis Univ Public Law Rev 22:289–313

Hudson B (1998) Restorative justice: the challenge of sexual and racial violence. J Law Soc:237–256

Jokinen H (2020) The limits of hospitality? Approaching. Religion 10(2):37–54. https://doi.org/10.30664/ar.91773

Kazić E, Ćorović R (2018) Restorative justice within legal system of B&H. In: Restorative approach and social innovation: from theoretical grounds to sustainable practices. University of Padua, Padua, pp 167–187

Kazić E, Ćorović R (2019) Is restorative justice an appropriate legal remediation for sexual violence. Rev Eur Comp Law XXXVIII:65–95

Kazić E, Dž M, Ljubović M (2019) Primjena odgojnih preporuka kao oblika restorativne pravde u Kantonu Sarajevo u periodu 2012–2017 [application of educational recommendations as a form of restorative justice in the Canton Sarajevo for the period 2012–2017]. International University of Sarajevo, Sarajevo

Kazić, E., & Ćorović, R. (2022). A Few Remarks About Challenges in Application of Restorative Justice: A Case Study of Bosnia and Herzegovina. Review of European and Comparative Law, 49(2), 153–172. https://doi.org/10.31743/recl.13478

Kim ME (2021) Transformative justice and restorative justice: gender-based violence and alternative visions of justice in the United States. Int Rev Victimol 27(2):162–172. https://doi.org/10.1177/0269758020970414

Lünnemann K, Wolthius A (2015) Restorative Justice in Cases of Domestic Violence. Verwey-Jonker Instituut. www.irks.at/assets. Accessed 10 October 2025

Maryfield, B., Przybylski, R., & Myrent, M. (2020). Research on restorative justice practices. Justice Research and Statistics Association. Web.

Miller SL, Hefner MK, Iovanni L (2020) Practitioners' perspectives on using restorative justice with crimes of gendered violence. Contemp Justice Rev 23(1):65–90. https://doi.org/10.1080/10282580.2019.1700372

Mujezinović J, Hodžić Lemeš M, Gutić Memić A, Mulić Čorbo D (2020) Nasilje u porodici. Osnovne informacije. EU, UNDP
Mušić S (2018) Nasilje u porodici kroz pravni okvir u Bosni I Hercegovini. Zbornik radova Pravnog fakulteta Sveučilišta u Mostaru:168–189. https://doi.org/10.47960/2637-2495.2018.26.168
Nettleton, C., Strang, H. (2018). Face-to-Face Restorative Justice Conferences for Intimate Partner Abuse: an Exploratory Study of Victim and Offender Views. Camb J Evid Based Polic 2, 125–138. https://doi.org/10.1007/s41887-018-0028-0
OSCE (2011). Krivična odgovornost i sankcioniranje počinilaca nasilja u porodici: Analiza i preporuke o krivičnopravnim sankcijama u predmetima nasilja u porodici u BiH.
OSCE (2019). Annual Report. https://www.osce.org/files/f/documents/0/9/449104_0.pdf. Accessed 10 October 2025..
Păroşanu A (2016) A Review of European Standards on Restorative Justice and Domestic Violence
Saraya S (2022) The Urgence of restorative justice in the police in the settlement of domestic violence cases. Int J Law Legal Ethics 3(2):1–13. https://ojs.udb.ac.id/index.php/IJLLE/article/view/2328/1755
Sherman LW (2018) Policing domestic violence 1967-2017: president's crime commission. Past Future Criminol Public Policy 17(2):453–465. https://doi.org/10.1111/1745-9133.12365
Tomić, Z. (2007) Krivično pravo II - posebni dio. Univerzitet u Sarajevu.
United Nations (2009) Handbook for legislation on violence against women
Zehr H (2002) The little book on restorative justice. Good Books, London

The Holistic Approach Towards Domestic Violence and the Urgent Need for Its Effective Implementation: The Case of Republic of North Macedonia

Besa Arifi and Arta Mero

Abstract This chapter provides an analysis of the legal approach towards domestic violence (DV) in the Republic of North Macedonia (RNM). The chapter intends to offer a holistic analysis of the position of the victims of DV from a penal, civil and victimological perspective, as well as to bring forth the need for a holistic approach by criminal justice authorities to addressing DV. The authors consider that collaboration among justice authorities and other State institutions is crucial, and they emphasize the importance of providing shelter for victims while prosecuting DV cases. The chapter analyzes the available data on the spread of DV cases in RNM and, more precisely, in the Polog region (Northwestern part of RNM). The chapter provides recommendations on implementing legal provisions and offering support to victims of DV.

1 Introduction

As a society, we are usually concerned with threats that are obvious and that bring devastation in our cities and countries; however, we are prone to overlook what is happening in our homes and how safe they feel for the family members. As noted by *Wolhuter* et al., "[t]he biggest domestic threat of terrorism is not on our doorstep but inside, beyond it".[1]

Domestic violence (DV), violence against women (VAW) and gender-based violence (GBV) are recognized today as general socio-political problems from which

[1] Wolhuter et al. (2009), p. 51.

B. Arifi (✉) · A. Mero
South East European University, Tetovë, North Macedonia
e-mail: b.arifi@seeu.edu.mk

R. Erbaş (ed.), *Criminal Prosecution of Domestic Violence*, Ius Gentium: Comparative Perspectives on Law and Justice 128,
https://doi.org/10.1007/978-3-032-01202-9_10

no one is completely immune.[2] *Black* indicates that DV "occurs between people of any social class, any race, religion, sexual orientation, and all age groups".[3] North Macedonia and the Western Balkan region are no exception in this regard. A report of the Ministry of Interior of RNM indicates that in the last quartile of the year 2022 (October to December), a total of 308 DV related criminal offences occurred, of which three were murders.[4] Furthermore, during the Sixteen Days of Activism Against VAW in 2022, two women were murdered in Kosovo within 1 week. Both victims had previously reported DV to the authorities.[5]

Discussing the commonness and spread of DV, *Strathern and Stewart* indicate that it is usually directed at women and children.[6] Moreover, *Erbaş* explores the challenging features and potential obstacles for investigating DV cases such as intimidated and threatened victims who are either not willing to report DV or are prone to withdraw their complaints for various reasons.[7] *Wollhuter* et al. explain that victims of DV and rape are often "objectified and subjected to traumatic cross-examination"[8] in criminal proceedings, which causes unwillingness to report such crimes. The problem with high dark figures in reporting DV cases is best summarized in the ECtHR judgement *Tërshana v. Albania*[9] as quoted by *Erbaş*: "...Violence against women was under-reported, under-investigated, under-prosecuted, and under-sentenced".[10] As *Erbaş* puts it, these four "under-s" call urgently "for the criminal justice system to adopt a particular approach" to addressing DV cases.[11]

In order to deal with these four "under-s," there is a need to look for a holistic approach towards prosecuting DV cases. The first postulate of that holistic approach is that State institutions must treat women's rights as human rights. This is an obligation that derives from the practice of the ECtHR, noticeable in the landmark case *Opuz v. Turkey*[12] which draws attention to the problem of the intimidation of victims, as well as addresses the fact that DV is not always a visible offence since it occurs in closed circuits. Another important ECtHR case that emphasized the need

---

[2] Simic (2021), conclusions.

[3] Black (2019), para 9.

[4] Ministry of Interior of RNM (2023), Open data on Domestic Violence. [Online] Available via: https://mvr.gov.mk/analiza/kriminal/66. RNM has a population of 1.836.713 inhabitants: Population Census (2021), RNM State Statistical Office. Available via: https://www.stat.gov.mk/OblastOpsto_en.aspx?id=31.

[5] Bami (2022), Kosovo Authorities Failed, Second Woman Murdered in Week. [Online] Available via: https://balkaninsight.com/2022/12/01/kosovo-authorities-failed-second-woman-murdered-in-week/. Kosovo has a population of 1.739.825 inhabitants: Population Census (2011), Kosovo Agency of Statistics. [Online] Available via: https://ask.rks-gov.net/.

[6] Strathern and Stewart (2008), p. 75.

[7] Erbaş (2021a), p. 2; Erbaş (2021b), pp. 110–111.

[8] Wolhuter et al. (2009), p. 73.

[9] *Tërshana v. Albania* (48,756/14), 04.08.2020, para. 156.

[10] Erbaş (2021a), p. 11.

[11] Ibid.

[12] *Opuz v. Turkey* (33,401/02), 09.06.2009.

for a gender-sensitive interpretation and application of ECtHR, "which takes in account the factual inequalities between women and men and the way they impact on women's lives,"[13] is *Valiuliene v. Lithuania*.[14] Thus, the first commitment that States should make while addressing DV cases is to address them in the light of core human rights obligations, where prohibition of discrimination based on gender should take the most important place. The second postulate of a holistic approach towards prosecuting DV cases is the need for better coordination of State institutions that regulate different areas of legislation and law enforcement. DV cases require a holistic interpretation of provisions of criminal law, criminal procedure law, family law, social policy and health. Thus, State institutions active in these fields need to work together and act in coordination when dealing with DV victims.

This chapter offers an analysis of the position of the DV victims from a penal, civil and victimological perspective. The methods used involve desk research and analysis of statistical data gathered from official reports as well as from State law enforcement institutions. The chapter intends to explain the need for a holistic approach towards DV by analyzing the legal provisions and the reporting of DV cases in RNM. Bearing in mind that Western Balkan States share a similar legal system and a similar approach towards DV cases,[15] the conclusions and recommendations of this chapter are applicable on a larger scale.

2 The Legal Approach Towards DV in RNM

Until 2004, DV was not addressed separately in the legislation of RNM and was largely considered a private matter among family members. The general opinion in earlier times was that violence among family members was a rare phenomenon, and it was believed that only mentally disabled persons were perpetrators of such violence.[16] The existence and spread of DV in RNM were first indicated by empirical studies in the years 1990–2000[17] that began to raise the awareness of the public, scholars and legislators which eventually resulted in amending the Law on the Family,[18] the Criminal Code,[19] and the Law on Social Protection.[20] Similar to the

13 *Valiuliene v. Lithuania* (33,234/07), 26.03.2013, Concurring opinion of Judge Pinto de Albuquerque.

14 *Valiuliene v. Lithuania* (33,234/07), 26.03.2013.

15 European Parliament (2019), Study for the FEMM Committee: Women's Rights in Western Balkans, https://www.europarl.europa.eu/RegData/etudes/STUD/2019/608852/IPOL_STU(2019)608852_EN.pdf, p. 7.

16 Gruesvka-Drakulevski (2013), p. 110.

17 Ibid.

18 Law on Amending the Law on the Family, Official Gazette of RM No. 33/2004.

19 Law on Amending the Criminal Code, Official Gazette, of RM No. 19/2004.

20 Law on Amending the Law on Social Protection, Official Gazette of RM No. 65/2004.

practice of other contemporary countries, DV was "reframed from a private family matter to a crime that the State has an obligation to address".[21]

These amendments developed two parallel systems for the protection of DV victims: the criminal law system concentrated on sanctioning the perpetrators, whereas the civil law system concentrated on protection measures for DV victims. Both systems are intended to be complementary to each other.

2.1 Provisions in the Law on the Family

The Law on the Family amended in 2004 provided numerous protection measures for DV victims. Parallel to this, amendments to the Law on Social Protection established a new service for DV victims—"temporary accommodation in Centers for DV Victims – Shelters".[22] These shelters have been established in six cities in RNM. However, the Polog region of northwestern RNM, a region with more than 300.000 inhabitants remains under-served. In a large city like Tetovo there is no shelter for DV victims,[23] while in Gostivar one was recently established.[24] This situation contributes to the underreporting of DV cases because the victims are not provided an alternative to leave the violent environment and find accommodation in a shelter.

The Law on Family amended in 2004 indicated numerous measures to assist DV victims.[25] These measures are now part of the specific Law on prevention, combatting and protection from DV and VAW adopted in 2021.[26]

2.2 DV in the Criminal Code of RNM

Prior to 2004, DV was not defined in the Criminal Code of RNM (CC),[27] nor was it considered an important problem in the country.[28] The first definition came with the CC amendments of 2004, in an explanatory article of the general part, as follows:

[21] Hightower (2010), p. 17.

[22] Islami et al. (2020), p. 130.

[23] Bilbilovska (2022), Жртвите на семејно насилство од Тетово се препраќаат во шелтер центар во Велес - Victims of domestic violence from tetovo are being sent to the shelter in Veles. [Online] Available via: https://telma.com.mk/2022/05/20/zhrtvite-na-semejno-nasilstvo-od-tetovo-se-preprakjaat-vo-shelter-centar-vo-veles/.

[24] Ministry of Labor and Social Policy (2022), МТСП: Отворен Центарот за жени жртви на семејно насилство во Полошкиот регион - MLSP: Opening of the Center for women victims of domestic violence in the Pollog Region. [Online] Available via: https://www.mtsp.gov.mk/pocetna-ns_article-mtsp-otvoren-centarot-za-zeni-zrtvi-na-semejno-nasilstvo-vo-poloshkiot-region.nspx.

[25] Law on the Family, Official Gazette or RM, nr. 153/2014, Art. 94-g.

[26] Law on VAW, Official Gazette or RNM, nr. 24/2021.

[27] Criminal Code, Official Gazette of RM nr. 37/1996.

[28] Gruesvka-Drakulevski (2013), p. 110.

"Family violence shall refer to abuse, rude insults, safety threats, inflicting physical injuries, sexual or other mental or physical violence which causes a feeling of insecurity, threat or fear towards a spouse, parent or child or towards other persons who live in a marriage or civil partnership or in a joint household, as well as towards a former spouse or persons who have a child together or have close personal relations".[29]

In the context of acknowledged partnerships, this definition offers protection for victims regardless of their marital status. As such, victims can be married spouses, persons living in a civil partnership, persons who have a child together (regardless of whether they share the same household), or persons who have close personal relations. Regarding family relations, this definition offers protection for persons suffering DV in the capacity of a spouse, a parent, a child, or other persons who live in a joint household.[30] This broad definition attempts to offer protection to every person who may experience violence within a household or within family relations, irrespective of the living venue. For families in RNM—where large households with multigenerational families are also present—legislation providing protection for an extensive number of situations is important. Despite the broad definition, some family members may still be unprotected from DV. For instance, in case КЖ-111/20, the Court of Appeals in Bitola ruled that sisters do not fall under the definition of domestic violence unless they reside in the same household. In this particular case, since the sisters do not live together, the act was not considered DV.[31]

Before the 2004 amendments, the criminal law legislation in RNM treated DV cases as a private matter, meaning that the offender could be charged only through a private charge, and not by prosecutorial indictment. Instead, the CC of 1996 included a group of criminal offences against marriage, family and youth such as "Abandoning a helpless child (Art. 200); "Neglecting and maltreatment of juvenile persons" (Art. 201); "Refusal to pay alimony" (Art. 202); and "Violation of family obligations" (Art. 203). However, these were crimes against marriage, family, and youth, and thus, they were never seen as acts which specifically discriminate against women. Instead, the subject of protection was the family and the marriage, not the equality between genders. With the amendments of 2004, DV was specifically defined in the general provisions of the CC; yet this definition still lacked the element of recognizing the problem as a severe form of discrimination against women. Although DV was no longer considered a private matter between family members and became a State problem, the most common offence which includes acts of DV (Bodily injury, Art. 130) still requires a proposal from the victim to be prosecuted.

Islami et al. rightly point out that the incrimination of DV was not carried out through the introduction of a specific criminal offense. Instead, it was done by introducing aggravating circumstances for existing criminal offenses when they contain

[29] Criminal Code, Official Gazette of RM, no.37/1996, Art. 122, para. 21, translation by the author.
[30] Islami et al. (2020), p. 133.
[31] Case КЖ-111/20, Court of Appeals Bitola, 18.02.2022.

DV elements, including psychological, physical, and sexual violence.[32] For example, the basic crime of Murder is punished with 5–20 years of imprisonment. When murder is committed as an act of DV, it becomes an aggravated crime and it is punished with minimum 10 years of imprisonment or life sentence.[33] Other crimes that become aggravated when committed as acts of DV include: Bodily injury (Art. 130), Severe bodily injury (Art. 131), Coercion (Art. 139), Unlawful arrest (Art. 140), Endangering of security (Art. 144), Sexual act with misuse of status position (Art. 189) and Intermediation in committing prostitution (Art. 191). Additional crimes were added to this list with the amendments of the CC from February 2023, such as Female genital mutilation (Art. 129-a), Sexual harassment (Art. 190-a), Stalking (Art. 144-a) etc.[34]

The CC amendments that entered into force in February 2023 were adopted with the aim to ensure the proper implementation of the Istanbul Convention in RNM. These amendments make a clear distinction between DV, VAW, and violence against children, by providing separate comprehensive definitions for all three concepts. The definition of DV now additionally includes economic violence, a category which was not previously mentioned in the CC.[35] The newly adopted definition of VAW in the CC is directly incorporated from the Istanbul Convention.[36]

A very important novelty adopted with the amendments of the CC from February 2023 is the new definition of the crime Sexual assault and Rape which identifies lack of consent as the main element of sexual assault, whereas the use of force is regarded as an aggravating circumstance, not as a constitutional element of the crime.[37]

Activists have argued that psychological violence is not well defined in the CC of RNM, since the definitions of the crimes Coercion and Endangering of security are not compatible with psychological violence as a form of DV. As explained in the *Shadow Report of CSO-s on the implementation of the Istanbul Convention in RNM*: "The object of protection in the crime of Coercion is the freedom to form a will for a certain action, while the COE's Convention requires protection of the psychological integrity of the person",[38] whereas the crime Endangering of security fails "to link the threat to its outcome – the violation of mental integrity".[39] The amendments of the CC from 2023 indicate that when these crimes are committed as acts of GBV they will be punished more severely, same as in DV cases. However, these amend-

[32] Ibid., p. 129–130.

[33] Criminal Code, Official Gazette of RM, no.37/1996, Art. 123.

[34] Law on amending the Criminal Law, Official Gazeette of RNM, no. 36/2023.

[35] Ibid Art. 5, referring to Art. 122 of CC.

[36] Ibid.

[37] Ibid., Art. 20, referring to Art. 186 of CC.

[38] Association ESE, Coalition MARGINS, Association Open Gate, Edinburgh International Justice Initiative (EIJI), (2022), Shadow Report on the Implementation of CoE Convention on Preventing and Combating Violence Against Women and Domestic Violence in Republic of North Macedonia. Skopje. p. 52.

[39] Ibid.

ments do not provide new definitions for those crimes, therefore, the concerns of the activists remain relevant.

A major concern regarding the crime of Bodily injury (Art. 130) is that being the only DV crime which is prosecuted *ex officio* upon a proposal from the victim. All other DV crimes are prosecuted *ex officio* without requiring a proposal from the victim. This requirement puts the victim in a difficult position and often results in the withdrawal from charges, therefore, activists request that DV Bodily injury is prosecuted directly *ex officio.*[40]

Prior to the CC amendments of 2023, one could argue that not all forms of sexual violence were included in DV related incriminations. Arts. 186 and 188 of the CC, which defined the crimes of Rape and Sexual assault against a child under 14 years of age, did not include an explicit aggravating circumstance when they were committed as DV acts.[41] Research shows that victims of marital rape experience harsher consequences and trauma in comparison to victims of stranger rape, since marital rape can be recommitted over longer periods of time.[42] Activists in RNM had requested several times that marital rape and sexual assault of underage children by family members should become separate offences.[43] With the amendments of 2023, marital rape became incriminated,[44] however, the amended crime Rape of a child under the age of 15 years still lacks an aggravating circumstance when committed as a DV act.[45]

DV is mentioned in the CC of RNM in two additional contexts:

- Art. 125 defines the offence "Momentary homicide" as homicide committed when the offender (the DV victim) has been brought without his/her fault into an aggravated mental situation—a situation of affect… by the victim (the DV perpetrator) that was committing domestic violence which has resulted in the DV victim killing the DV perpetrator.[46] "Momentary manslaughter" is sentenced more leniently (1–8 years of imprisonment) in comparison to regular, unmitigated murder (5–20 years of imprisonment).[47] Similarly, "Momentary severe

[40] Association for Emancipation, Solidarity and Equality of women—ESE (2020), Report on Court Monitoring of Criminal and Civil Cases of Domestic Violence, Skopje.

[41] Criminal Code, Official Gazette of RM, no.37/1996, Arts. 186 and 188.

[42] Martin et al. (2007).

[43] Stevkovska (2021), НЕ треба да значи НЕ!—„Нетипичните"жртви на силување во Македонија не можат да го пријават и да го докажат делото (No must mean no! Atypical victims of rape in Macedonia cannot report and prove this crime). [Online] Available via: https://meduza.mk/fem-101/ne-treba-da-znachi-ne-netipichnite-zhrtvi-na-siluvaње-vo-makedonija-ne-mozhat-da-go-prijavat-i-da-go-dokazhat-deloto/.

[44] Law on amending the Criminal Law, Official Gazette of RNM, no. 36/2023, Art. 20, referring to Art. 186 of CC.

[45] Ibid. Art. 22, referring to Art. 188 of CC.

[46] Criminal Code, Official Gazette of RM, no.37/1996, Art. 125.

[47] For more information on the legal approach towards "Momentary homicide" see articles authored by McQuigg (2013) and Fitz-Gibbon et al. (2017). An interesting case in RNM is that of Pale Ilovska who killed her partner while he was physically abusing her. The prosecutor requested a

bodily injury" is sentenced more leniently when committed under similar circumstances.[48]

- While defining the responsibilities of the person who is subjected to probation, the CC enumerates attending a counseling program for persons convicted of DV related crimes.[49]

The new Draft Criminal Code (DCC)[50] that is still in an inclusive process of preparation will continue implementing the requirements of the Istanbul Convention which were already enacted with the amendments of the CC from February 2023. In addition to the offences: Female genital mutilation, Stalking and Sexual harassment, which are already incriminated,[51] the new DCC will also include the offences: Forced marriage (Art. 259), and Harassment in the workplace (Art. 214). The new DCC will hopefully provide a better definition of psychological violence; erase the requirement for a proposal from the victim to prosecute the crime of Bodily injury; and separately define Rape of a child under 15 years of age as an act of DV.

2.3 *Protecting DV Victims in Criminal Procedure*

The Criminal Procedure Code (CPC) 2010[52] (entered into force in December 2013) defines the victim of a crime as "any person who has suffered harm, including physical or mental harm, emotional suffering, material loss or other harm or endangering of their rights and interests as the result of a crime".[53] The CPC 2010 was revolutionary regarding the protection of victims since it dedicated an entire chapter to the crime victim and their rights. This was not the case in previous criminal procedure laws. However, the implementation in practice of these provisions remained a challenge.[54]

"guilty" verdict for "Momentary homicide", however, the court found her innocent based on self-defense. She had previously reported the abuses of her violent husband who worked as a police officer: Georgievski (2022), Court in North Macedonia acquits victim of domestic violence who killed her torturer. [Online] Available via: https://meta.mk/en/court-in-north-macedonia-acquits-victim-of-domestic-violence-who-killed-her-torturer/.

[48] Criminal Code, Official Gazette of RM, no.37/1996, Art. 130, para. 6.

[49] Ibid., Art. 56, para. 1, point 3.

[50] The Criminal Code currently in force was adopted in 1996 and since then it has been amended more than forty times. Codifying all amendments in one place is one of the reasons for drafting a new CC, since frequent amendments of the current code resulted in difficulties for legal practitioners and created a situation of legal uncertainty (Ministry of Justice or RNM (2017) Strategy for Reforms of the Judicial Sector for the period 2017–2022 with Action Plan, p. 33).

[51] Law on amending the Criminal Law, Official Gazeette of RNM, no. 36/2023, Arts. 8, 16 and 23.

[52] Criminal Procedure Code, Official Gazette of RM, nr. 150/2010.

[53] Ibid., Art. 21, para. 4. On the categorization of rights of victims of crime see Arifi (2016).

[54] On the issue of access to justice for women victims of DV in RNM, see Netkova (2013).

The law differentiates between" the basic rights of all victims and additional rights for victims of specified offences and vulnerable categories of victims".[55] Thus, there are four categories of victims' rights in this chapter:

(a) the rights of victims of all crimes (participation in criminal procedure; protection against secondary victimization; and professional assistance)[56];
(b) the rights of victims of severe crimes[57] (free legal representation and compensation of damages provided by a public fund).[58]
(c) the rights of vulnerable victims (this category includes children,[59] persons under risk of attack,[60] and especially delicate victims.[61] Their rights include the right to witness' and victims' protection measures)[62]; and
(d) the rights of victims of crimes against sexual freedom (measures to ensure privacy).[63]

One task of the National Strategy for Reforms in the Judicial Sector[64] is the adoption of a new Draft Criminal Procedure Code (DCPC), which is currently being drafted.[65] The new DCPC enlarges the scope of general rights of the victim of a crime[66] and regulates them with clearer provisions and better opportunities for their implementation.[67]

Protecting DV victims from secondary victimization is crucial for the successful investigation and prosecution of such cases. CPC 2010 specifically indicates the obligation of the police, prosecution, and the court to carefully address the victims and their needs.[68] This is particularly important for DV victims, considering that fear from ill-treatment during such proceedings is usually one of the reasons

[55] Arifi (2016).

[56] Ibid., Art. 53, para. 1.

[57] Ibid., Art. 53, para. 3. Crimes that are punished with a minimum of 4 years of imprisonment.

[58] Ibid., A special Law on the compensation of victims of violent crimes was recently adopted in November 2022 and entered into force in May 2023 (Official Gazzette of RNM No. 247/2022).

[59] Criminal Procedure Code, Official Gazette of RM, nr. 150/2010, Article 54: Persons under 18 years of age.

[60] Ibid.: Persons who could put themselves or their close family in danger while giving testimony related to the crime.

[61] Ibid.: Persons who, due of their age, the nature of the crime, physical or mental disability or other evident health condition, social and cultural history, family circumstances, religious beliefs or ethnicity, or relation to the defendant, could have negative consequences on their psychological or physical health or negatively could affect the quality of their testimony.

[62] Ibid., para. 1–6.

[63] Ibid., Art. 55, para. 1.

[64] Ministry of Justice of RNM (2017) Strategy for Reforms of the Judicial Sector for the period 2017–2022 with Action Plan.

[65] Ministry of Justice, Draft Criminal Procedure Code (DCPC).

[66] Ibid., Art. 53, para. 1.

[67] Ibid., Art. 55.

[68] Criminal Procedure Code, Official Gazette of RM, nr. 150/2010, Article 53, Paragraph 2.

identified for the underreporting of cases of domestic violence.[69] However, although the law provides certain rights for all victims of crime, it does not provide for any strong mechanism for their application.[70] The law merely obliges the officers and the institutions "to take care for the rights of the victim, to treat them with respect and to counsel them about their rights",[71] however, "it does not indicate how the victim can respond to the violation of these obligations."[72] There are neither established policies nor competent institutions that would "specifically deal with the protection of the rights of the crime victim."[73] This concern is also raised by studies which monitor DV related criminal and civil court cases. Those studies indicate that women living in rural areas are not well aware of the procedural rights available to them; they are not duly informed about the right to a counselor as provided by the CPC; criminal proceedings in DV cases are often delayed; and secondary victimization of DV victims is often evident in court, since victims are required to testify multiple times in different stages of criminal proceedings.[74] Another shadow report emphasizes the disturbing testimony of a DV victim who tried to report her case at the police station and was advised by a policeman as follows: "Go back home and don't come here again. Don't you know who you are reporting? Don't you know your report will magically disappear? It is best if you shut up and make peace with him. Your anger will pass, you'll forget".[75]

Introducing comprehensive and elaborate provisions in material and procedural criminal codes is not sufficient to effectively address DV and VAW. Therefore, there is an urgent need for a holistic approach towards this problem, which will include raising the awareness not only of victims but also of legal practitioners, law enforcement officers and institutions. Attractive laws that are not implemented in practice provide no protection for DV victims.

2.4 Law on Prevention, Combating and Protection from VAW and DV, 2021

Despite the numerous changes in the criminal legislation, the need for adopting a *lex specialis* in this field was evident.[76] In 2014, the Government of RNM adopted the first Law on Prevention, Combating, and Protection from DV. In 2015, the

[69] Erbaş (2021a).

[70] Arifi (2016).

[71] Ibid.

[72] Ibid.

[73] Ibid.

[74] Association for Emancipation, Solidarity and Equality of women—ESE (2019) Is Domestic Violence being Sanctioned? Do the Perpetrators of Domestic Violence get the Deserved Sentence? Skopje.

[75] Gender Equality Platform (2022) Shadow Report on the Implementation of the Council of Europe Convention on Preventing and Combating Violence against Women and Domestic Violence in North Macedonia, Skopje. p. 4.

[76] Islami et al. (2020), pp. 130–132.

Government established the National Coordination Body against DV.[77] After the ratification and entry into force of the Istanbul Convention, a National Action Plan (NAP 2018–2023) for the implementation of the Convention was adopted, followed by the adoption of a new Law on Prevention of, and Protection Against, VAW and DV (Law on VAW) in 2021.[78] This Law defines the concepts of VAW and GBV, under the provisions of the Istanbul Convention. It stipulates the *due diligence* principle in Article 4, which obliges the State institutions to act "urgently with due attention to the interests and needs of the victim".[79] The Law postulates important principles that need to be taken into consideration by State authorities for prevention and protection against VAW and DV, such as: non-discrimination; prohibition of victimization; protection and care for vulnerable women; adoption of measures for women with disabilities; gender responsible policies; and empowering women who have suffered violence.[80] An important characteristic of the Law lies in viewing VAW and DV as discrimination against women which restrict them in fulfilling their rights and freedoms in equal opportunities as compared to men.[81]

The Parliament and the Government of RNM are enumerated as State authorities that are eligible to prevent and combat VAW and DV.[82] The National Coordinative Body established with this law includes representatives from the General Secretariat of the Government; the Ministries of: Labor and Social Policy; Internal Affairs; Health; Education and Science; and Justice; local government units; and institutions that carry out activities in these fields.[83] These institutions need to take measures to protect victims from, and to prevent, GBV and DV.[84]

The Law on VAW provides protection measures for victims of DV and VAW which are issued by the Centers for Social Works which include: temporary accommodation; health protection; psycho-social intervention and treatment; continuous education for the child of the victim; counseling; legal assistance and representation; initiation of court procedure; etc.[85] Moreover, the courts can issue certain prohibitions to the offender which include: prohibition to directly or indirectly communicate with a member of the family; prohibition to approach the residence, school, working place of another member of the family; eviction regardless of ownership, prohibition of possession of a firearm or its confiscation; etc.[86] These measures are important steps towards protecting DV victims as well as implementing

[77] Decision published in the Official Gazette or RM, nr. 72/2015.

[78] Law on VAW, Official Gazette or RNM, nr. 24/2021.

[79] Ibid. Arts. 1 and 4.

[80] Ibid. Arts. 5–10.

[81] Ibid. Art. 5.

[82] Ibid. Arts. 13 and 14.

[83] Ibid. Art. 15.

[84] There is a lack of studies and a literature gap in RNM regarding the effectiveness of the measures to protect victims from recurring DV. Generally, on the effectiveness of such remedies see Ferstman (2021).

[85] Law on VAW, Official Gazette or RNM, nr. 24/2021, Art. 46.

[86] Ibid. Art. 58.

the requirements of the Istanbul Convention in RNM. However, numerous shadow reports from local organizations indicate a large gap between what is written in the legal provisions versus their implementation in practice, signaling that although the temporary measures of protection (TMP) have been a part of RNM legislation for 20 years, they "faced serious implementation gaps and [have] not really come to life in practice".[87] Nevertheless, there are cases in the court practice of RNM that show that those measures are being implemented. Temporary measures under the Law VAW were upheld in case ГЖ-2308/19 by the Court of Appeals in Skopje, prohibiting the perpetrator from insulting, harassing, or contacting the victim, and from approaching her residence within 100 meters.[88] Similarly, in case ГЖ-1319/21, the Court of Appeals in Bitola confirmed legal grounds for imposing measures to prevent the perpetrator from threatening or harassing the victim, as outlined in the Law on VAW.[89]

The spirit of the Istanbul Convention is best incorporated into the Law on VAW, and this should be reflected in other legal provisions as well. Not all criminal law provisions that were mentioned in previous sections of this chapter offer very restrictive and limited definitions of crimes that consist in VAW and DV, and often they do not make a strong link between the prohibition of discrimination against women and the acts of VAW or DV. Legal definitions of crimes that are committed as acts of VAW or DV need to clearly state that these are forms of severe discrimination based on gender which obstruct women from enjoying the same rights as men, and thus fulfil the first postulate of the holistic approach towards DV. The adoption of the new Law on VAW and DV illustrates clearly the holistic approach that RNM has in its legislation regarding DV and VAW, however, this will be insufficient if efforts are not made to implement its provisions in practice; to raise the awareness of institutions, of law enforcement officers, and of the victims; and to provide effective legal and social protection for them in the name of due diligence obligations as required by the Istanbul Convention.

3 Reported DV Cases in RNM

Researchers have indicated the importance of comprehensive and accessible data on the spread of DV cases.[90] There exists a system of data gathering in RNM regarding DV cases which was distinctly improved over the years, particularly in 2022, when more detailed data became publicly accessible, as required by the new Law on

87 Association ESE, Coalition MARGINS, Association Open Gate, Edinburgh International Justice Initiative (EIJI), (2022), Shadow Report on the Implementation of CoE Convention on Preventing and Combating Violence Against Women and Domestic Violence in Republic of North Macedonia. Skopje. p. 67.

88 Case ГЖ-2308/19, Court of Appeals Skopje, 26.02.2019.

89 Case ГЖ-1319/21, Court of Appeals Bitola, 11.08.2021.

90 Mills et al. (2013), p. 56.

Table 1 Reporting of domestic violence cases in the territory of RNM 2019–2022

	October–November 2019	2020	2021	2022	October 2019–December 2022
Total DV criminal offences	279	992	1056	1117	3444
Total offenders	290	1025	1097	1154	3566
Offenders—men	258	930	988	1061	3237
Offenders—women	32	95	109	93	329
Total victims	294	1052	1155	1191	3692
Victims—men	57	212	266	249	784
Victims—women	237	840	889	942	2908

The data presented in the figure are taken from: SIA Tetovo RNM

VAW.[91] The data gathered from the Sector for Interior Affairs in Tetovo RNM (SIA Tetovo)[92] shows an increase in reporting DV cases in recent years. Table 1 shows an overall total of reported DV cases in the territory of RNM. The data were gathered for four consecutive years. For the year 2019 SIA Tetovo had available data only for the months of October and November. For the years 2020, 2021 and 2022 the data cover the entire year.[93] The data show the total number of DV reported cases and the total number of offenders and victims, which are distinguished by offenders' and victims' gender. These data were collected by the authors exclusively for the purpose of this chapter and in order to provide a comparative view on the reporting of DV cases in recent years.

Figure 1 below presents a slight increase of DV reporting in recent years. Bearing in mind that 2020 and 2021 were also years when measures of isolation related to the Covid-19 pandemic were implemented throughout the State, it is important to note the increase in DV cases during that period. Authors *Krishnakumar and Verma* conclude that changes in everyday activities "during the COVID-19 lockdown provided more opportunities to the perpetrators of domestic violence."[94]

Figure 2 below shows that men are most reported as DV offenders. On the other hand, it is interesting to see an increase in the reporting of women as DV offenders.

Figure 3 below shows that women are most reported as DV victims. However, an increased reporting of men as DV victims is noticed, which shows that men in RNM have begun to overcome the taboo of reporting DV committed against them.[95] An interesting case at the Court of First Instance in Sveti Nikole (K.бр.22/22) involved

[91] Law on VAW, Official Gazette or RNM, nr. 24/2021, Arts. 28–32.

[92] SIA Tetovo replied positively to the official request of the authors of this chapter to provide statistical data on DV cases for the years 2019–2022. Tetovo is the largest city in the Polog region reporting DV data for the entire region for the state statistics for DV crimes.

[93] Complete data for the year 2022 are found in the Open Data source of the Ministry of Interiors in RNM as it is shown in Table 2.

[94] Krishnakumar and Verma (2021), p. 19.

[95] Underreporting of domestic violence cases where victims are male is a common issue, see Dutton and White (2013).

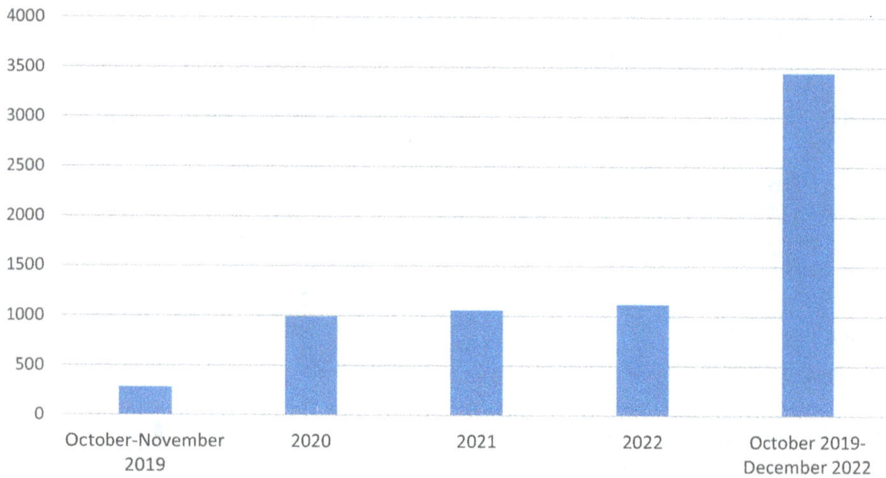

Fig. 1 Total criminal offences 2019–2022. (The data presented in the figure are taken from: SIA Tetovo RNM)

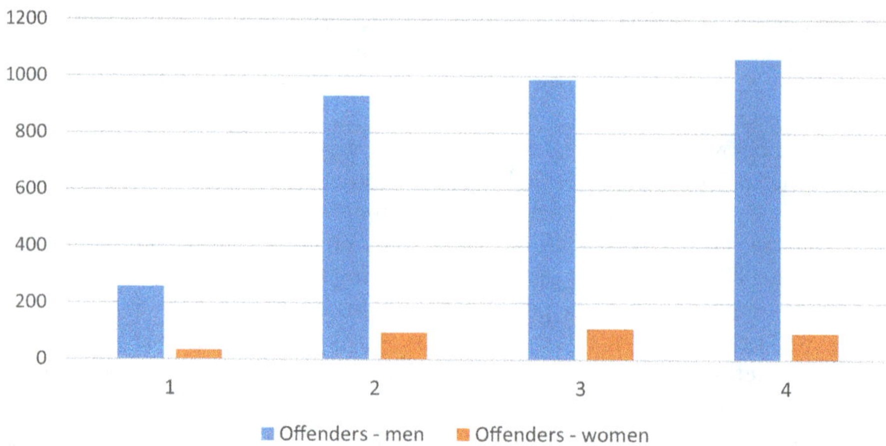

Fig. 2 Offenders by gender 2019–2022. (The data presented in the figure are taken from: SIA Tetovo RNM)

a former wife being found guilty of psychological domestic violence against her ex-husband and sentenced to parole.[96] In earlier years, it would have been very uncommon to have over 200 reported male DV victims in RNM.

The most represented DV offences are Bodily injury and Endangering of security.[97] Fig. 4 below presents these two offences committed as DV acts in the last years

[96] Case K.бр.22/22, Court of First Instance Sveti Nikole, 1.6.2022.

[97] Data provided by the SIA Tetovo (2022).

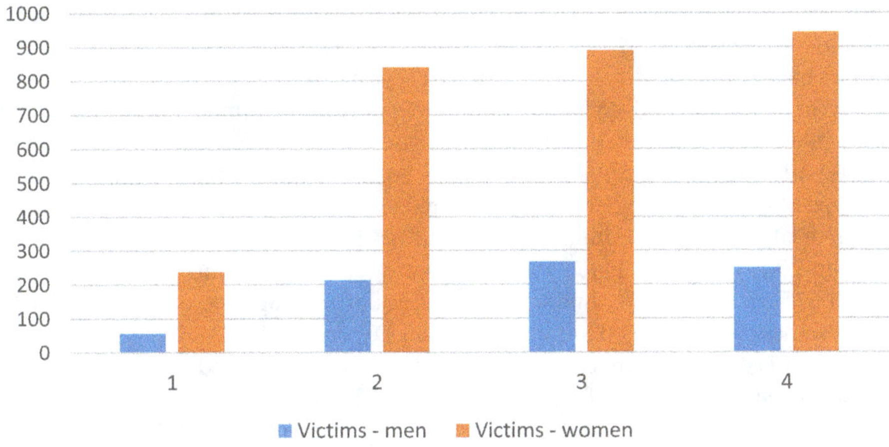

Fig. 3 Victims by gender 2019–2022. (The data presented in the figure are taken from: SIA Tetovo RNM)

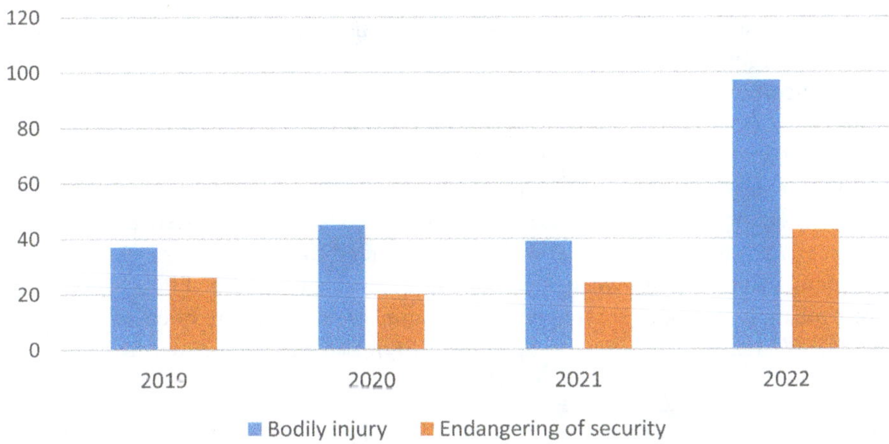

Fig. 4 Structure of domestic violence offences in the region of Tetovo, 2019–2022. (The data presented in the figure are taken from: SIA Tetovo RNM)

in the region of Tetovo, which covers an area populated by around 200,000 inhabitants. From 2019 to 2022, there were a total of 331 reported DV cases, of which 218 were Bodily injury and 113 were Endangering of security.[98] Bodily injury refers to physical violence, whereas Endangering of security refers to psychological violence. The data clearly show the preference of victims to report physical abuse as opposed to psychological abuse which is usually more common but underreported.

[98] Ibid.

In 2022 three additional types of DV crimes have been reported in the Tetovo region: 2 Murders, 1 Severe bodily injury and 1 Coercion.[99] No DV cases of sexual violence have been reported in this region for the last 4 years.

Starting from 2022, the Ministry of Interiors of RNM has implemented a specific data gathering mechanism (Open Data database on DV) which now provides more precise information about the regional spread of DV offences throughout the country, type of offences, number of offenders and victims, as well as data on the family status of offenders and victims. Thus, based on these publicly available statistical data, in 2022 a total of 1117 DV crimes were reported in police stations, out of which 675 cases of Bodily injury and 389 cases of Endangering of security which again shows that these two are most reported DV crimes in RNM.[100] Likewise, in 2022 most DV crimes were committed by men (1061) as opposed to women (93).[101] These data are organized in four yearly quartiles. Table 2 below shows reported DV cases on specific crimes in all SIA-s in RNM on the last quartile of 2022.[102]

It can be noted that sexual violence remains underreported in RNM. It is expected that the 2023 amendments of CC will provide more opportunities to report DV sexual offences if appropriate measures are taken to raise the awareness for reporting these crimes.

A report conducted by the Office of the Ombudsperson in RNM for the year 2019 finds a substantially lower number of persons convicted of DV cases in basic courts throughout RNM as opposed to DV cases reported to the police.[103] Even more concerning are the sentences issued to the offenders, most of which are probation sentences, and very few are incarceration sentences.[104] This is indicated as a major concern by the Office of the Ombudsperson in the conclusions of the report.[105]

Other reports also indicate that although criminal provisions sanction all forms of DV, psychological violence is less reported compared to physical violence, and sexual violence is not reported at all; DV victims often tend to withdraw their proposal for prosecuting Bodily injury when committed as a DV act; sentences of incarceration are rare, probation sentences are frequent; DV criminal procedures are often delayed; and female DV victims are re-victimized while testifying in a criminal procedure.[106]

---

[99] Ministry of Interior of RNM (2023), Open data on Domestic Violence. [Online] Available via: https://mvr.gov.mk/analiza/kriminal/66.

[100] Ibid.

[101] Ibid.

[102] Ibid.

[103] Office of the Ombudsperson of the Republic of North Macedonia (2021). Special report on the research on the situation with domestic violence conducted for the year 2019 and for the period January–May 2020, Skopje.

[104] While it is important to ensure incarcerating sentences in DV cases, it is also important to not completely exclude the effective and appropriate use of restorative justice: see Mills et al. (2013), p. 56.

[105] Report of the Ombudsperson in RNM (2021) p. 71.

[106] Association for Emancipation, Solidarity and Equality of women—ESE (2019) Is Domestic Violence being Sanctioned? Do the Perpetrators of Domestic Violence get the Deserved Sentence? Skopje.

Table 2 DV crimes committed in October–December 2022, separated by regional Sectors for interior affairs

TYPE OF DV OFFENCE	TOTAL NUMBER OF OFFENCES	SIA SKOPJE	SIA BITOLA	SIA VELES	SIA KUMANOVO	SIA OHRID	SIA STRUMICA	SIA TETOVO	SIA SHTIP
Murder	**3**	1	1					1	
Attempted murder	**0**	–	–	–	–	–	–	–	–
Bodily injury	**179**	39	33	12	14	11	16	36	18
Severe bodily injury	**8**	3		1				2	2
Coercion	**5**	3		1				1	
Endangering of security	**113**	27	24	7	2	11	7	21	14
Unlawful arrest	**0**								
Sexual act with misuse of official position	**0**								
Facilitation in committing rprostitution	**0**								
TOTAL	***308***	***73***	***58***	***21***	***16***	***22***	***23***	***61***	***34***

The data presented in the figure are taken from: DV Open Data, Ministry of Interiors, RNM

Important improvements have been made in data gathering at police stations, however, publicly available, and easily accessible data on prosecution and sentencing of DV crimes are still lacking. *Mantler and others*, emphasize the importance of creating a "comfortable environment for women to disclose at their own discretion."[107] Furthermore, the EU Directive on Combating Violence Against Women and Domestic Violence highlights that victims should be able to report such crimes easily, without facing secondary or repeated victimization.[108] However, media in RNM expresses concerns that DV court cases take too long to resolve, with perpetrators often receiving parole sentences and victims remaining unsafe during the proceedings.[109] Thus, in case K-17/20 at the Court of First Instance in Bitola, a man was found guilty of 17 incidents of DV against his wife, including Endangering security, Bodily injury, and Non-implementation of court decisions, nevertheless, he was sentenced to 5 years of parole.[110]

4 Requirements for a Holistic Approach Towards DV

The most important international document addressing the issue of VAW and DV is the Istanbul Convention[111] which demands a holistic response to the actions required.[112] In comparison with earlier documents, such as the CEDAW,[113] the Istanbul Convention does not use general and abstract definitions, but rather specific and comprehensible requirements from State parties. The Convention demands a holistic approach towards VAW and DV, as indicated in the provisions that oblige States to show due diligence regarding this problem. They are required to amend their legal provisions by foreseeing criminal sanctions for concretely defined crimes; ensuring measures of protection for the victims; and by obliging State institutions and civil organizations to engage in identifying cases by gathering measurable data and acting upon information related to VAW and DV. The Convention requires

[107] Mantler et al. (2021), Conclusions.

[108] Directive (EU) 2024/1385 of the European Parliament and of the Council of 14 May 2024 on combating violence against women and domestic violence, paragraph (29).

[109] According to a study by Jordanovska and Janevska (2024), the Criminal Court in Skopje issued 198 parole sentences, 58 supervised parole sentences, and 88 incarceration sentences for DV cases between 2020 and May 2024. Jordanovksa and Janevska (2024), Семејно насилство: Од ќотек до пресуда поминале шест години, насилникот одамна е во бегство (Family violence: Six months elapse from the assault until the verdict is reached, the perpetrator remains a fugitive). [Online] Available via: https://meta.mk/semejno-nasilstvo-od-kjotek-do-presuda-pominale-shest-godini-nasilnikot-odamna-e-vo-begstvo/.

[110] Case K-17/20, Court of First Instance in Bitola, 11.02.2020.

[111] Council of Europe Convention on preventing and combating violence against women and domestic violence (CETS No. 210) 11.05.2011.

[112] Bonini (2021), p. 74.

[113] Convention on the Elimination of All Forms of Discrimination against Women, UN General Assembly resolution nr. 34/180 of 18 December 1979.

internal as well as international coordination of State bodies and other agencies for the fulfillment of these aims. It envisages thorough research and effective addressing of this problem.

As a new document, the Directive (EU) 2024/1385 establishes minimum rules to prevent and combat violence against women and domestic violence across the European Union.[114] It includes provisions for criminal offences, victim protection, support services, data collection, prevention measures, and cooperation among Member States. The Directive aims to ensure a higher level of protection for victims, empower competent authorities to take immediate action in emergency situations, and promote gender equality and non-discrimination. EU candidate countries, including RNM, are not bound by the provisions of Directive (EU) 2024/1385 on combating violence against women and domestic violence. However, as part of the EU accession process, candidate countries are expected to align their national legislation with EU standards, including those related to gender equality and the protection of women from violence. Therefore, while not obligated to comply with the Directive at present, candidate countries are encouraged to work towards meeting its objectives and principles as part of their accession preparations.

RNM signed the Istanbul Convention in 2011 and ratified it in March 2018. The Convention entered into force in July 2018.[115] The first State Report was submitted in April 2022, whereas additional reports were submitted by civil society organizations.[116] As explained in this chapter, the Istanbul Convention influenced the amendments of both criminal and civil legal provisions in RNM as well as the adoption of a *lex specialis* on VAW. A holistic approach is evident in legal amendments; however, certain concerns remain regarding the effective implementation in practice of these provisions:

- Lack of precise data on the spread of DV. There is evident progress in collecting structured data in police stations when DV related crimes are reported. However, publicly accessible data on civil and criminal proceedings on DV cases remain insufficient. Lack of data on indictments and court decisions on DV cases makes it difficult for State institutions to provide detailed statistics for DV and VAW.
- Lack of coordination between the authorities authorized to address DV. Law enforcement agencies need to work together, particularly abiding by the same principles and postulates when it comes to tackling DV and VAW.
- Raising awareness is needed not only for the victims of DV and VAW but also for law enforcement officers to tackle the underreporting of such crimes, as well as to prevent the secondary victimization of victims.

[114] Directive (EU) 2024/1385 of the European Parliament and of the Council of 14 May 2024 on combating violence against women and domestic violence.

[115] Council of Europe, 2022. Country Monitoring - North Macedonia. Available via: https://www.coe.int/en/web/istanbul-convention.

[116] Ibid.

5 Conclusion

Domestic violence is a complex phenomenon that cannot be handled solely with criminal law mechanisms; hence, a holistic approach is crucial. RNM legislation has adopted a multisectoral approach towards DV, providing mechanisms of prevention in the Law on the Family; the Law on Social Protection; the Criminal Code; the Criminal Procedure Code; the Law on the VAW as a *lex specialis*; as well as in bylaws of the Ministry of Labor and Social Policy. These legal provisions offer comprehensive and inclusive definitions on the most relevant concepts related to DV, VAW, and GBV, ensuring adequate protection for victims.

However, despite having elaborate legal provisions for numerous situations, certain improvements can be made, such as ensuring a better legal definition of DV cases of sexual violence against a child under the age of 15. Additionally, the provisions that sanction psychological violence are not specific enough, and are difficult to prove in criminal procedures, which results in an underreporting of cases of psychological violence. Finally, removing the requirement for a proposal by the victim and prosecuting DV Bodily injury fully *ex officio* is essential.

Another major problem is the lack of holistic evidence and statistical data on DV in RNM. It is exceedingly difficult to obtain accurate data on all stages of addressing of DV cases, since apart from the Ministry of Interiors, other State institutions do not use a joint system for reporting of DV cases, which means that the gathered data are not always precise. A better system of gathering and analyzing data related to DV should be established not only in police stations but also at the public prosecution offices and courts. A national system of gathering and structuring data regarding age, gender, types of violence with clear indications of the provided civil and/or criminal measures, is essential for gaining a better perspective about the spread of this phenomenon and the measures taken for its prevention and combating.

There is a holistic legislative basis and a rather broad regulation of the legal approach towards DV in RNM. Many laws have already been amended to accommodate the obligations that derive from the Istanbul Convention. However, writing good laws is not sufficient for providing a healthy and secure environment for victims of DV.

Attention is drawn to the urgent need for establishing shelters for DV victims in all regions in RNM. There are large areas, such as the Tetovo region with more than 200,000 inhabitants, with no nationally established shelters for victims of DV. Leaving larger parts of the population without an official shelter is an unacceptable situation which requires an urgent solution. To contribute to reporting DV cases, the State needs to provide alternatives for victims and opportunities for them to leave a violent environment and find accommodation in shelters.

Ensuring a legal approach which considers VAW and DV as severe forms of discrimination on the basis of gender should be the main concern of State institutions, substantiated in legislation, legal practice and State policies. A holistic and inclusive approach towards dealing with DV is the best way to ensure that victims can overcome this situation, that offenders can invest in their own rehabilitation, and that society can prosper.

References

Arifi B (2016) Categorization of crime victims: comparing theory and legislation. Temida 19(3–4):493–515. https://doi.org/10.2298/TEM1604493A

Black IS (2019) Chapter 32 - domestic violence: take a stand against violence. In: Fennelly L (ed) Handbook of loss prevention and crime prevention, 6th edn. Butterworth-Heinemann, Oxford, pp 405–412

Bonini V (2021) The Istanbul convention's values and its implementation in Italy. In: Bonini V, Erbaş R (eds) The 10th anniversary of the Istanbul convention. Pisa University Press, Pisa, pp 69–84

Dutton DG, White KR (2013) Male victims of domestic violence. New Male Studies Int J 2(1):5–17

Erbaş R (2021a) Effective criminal investigations for women victims of domestic violence: the approach of the ECtHR. Women's Stud Int Forum 86:1–12. https://doi.org/10.1016/j.wsif.2021.102468

Erbaş R (2021b) Evidentiary challenges to an effective criminal investigation for domestic violence: an introduction. In: Bonini V, Erbaş R (eds) The 10th anniversary of the Istanbul convention. Pisa University Press, Pisa, pp 101–118

Ferstman C (2021) Do guarantees of non-recurrence actually help to prevent systemic violations? Reflections on measures taken to prevent domestic violence. Netherlands Int Law Rev 68:387–405. https://doi.org/10.1007/s40802-021-00204-8

Fitz-Gibbon K, Vannier M (2017) Domestic violence and the gendered law of self-defence in France: the case of Jacqueline Sauvage. Fem Leg Stud 25:313–335. https://doi.org/10.1007/s10691-017-9358-8

Gruesvka-Drakulevski A (2013) Domestic violence in the Republic of Macedonia. Macedonian Rev Criminal Law Criminol 20(1):109–162

Hightower J (2010) Chapter 2 - abuse in later life: when and how does gender matter? In: Gutman G, Spencer C (eds) Aging, Ageism and Abuse, 1st edn. Elsevier, London, pp 17–29

Islami H, Selmani-Bakiu A, Zendeli E, Mehmeti S (2020) The impact of the COVID-19 pandemic on domestic violence-psychological consequences, the legal framework and its treatment in the Republic of North Macedonia. SEEU Rev 15(1):121–141

Krishnakumar A, Verma S (2021) Understanding domestic violence in India during COVID-19: a routine activity approach. Asian J Criminol 16:19–35. https://doi.org/10.1007/s11417-020-09340-1

Mantler T, Jackson KT, Shillington K et al (2021) Factors influencing rural women's disclosure of intimate partner violence: a qualitative study. SN Soc Sci 1:19. https://doi.org/10.1007/s43545-020-00027-z

Martin EK, Taft CT, Resick PA (2007) A review of marital rape. Aggress Violent Behav 12(3):329–347

McQuigg RJA (2013) The Canadian supreme court and domestic violence: R v Ryan. Fem Leg Stud 21:185–193. https://doi.org/10.1007/s10691-013-9236-y

Mills LG, Barocas B, Ariel B (2013) The next generation of court-mandated domestic violence treatment: a comparison study of batterer intervention and restorative justice programs. J Exp Criminol 9:56–90. https://doi.org/10.1007/s11292-012-9164-x

Netkova B (2013) Access to justice for women victims of domestic violence in the Republic of Macedonia. Int Rev Law 2013:5. https://doi.org/10.5339/irl.2013.dv.5

Simic A (2021) Feeling safe and secure from gender-based violence: highly educated, middle-class Indian women migrants' gendered understandings of integration in the UK. J Int Migr Integr 22:69–86. https://doi.org/10.1007/s12134-019-00721-9

Strathern AJ, Stewart PJ (2008) Anthropology of violence and conflict, overview. In: Kurtz L (ed) Encyclopedia of violence, peace, and conflict, 2nd edn. Academic, Cambridge, pp 75–86

Wolhuter L, Olley N, Denham D (2009) Victimology: victimisation and victims' rights. Routledge-Cavendish, Oxon

The ECtHR's Perspective: Positive Obligation and State's Intervention in Domestic Violence

The State's Duty to Protect Domestic Violence Victims from a Gender Perspective: Brief Reference to the Jurisprudential Developments of the European Court of Human Rights Jurisprudence

Raquel Borges Blázquez

> *"Under general international law and specific human rights covenants, States may also be responsible for private acts if they fail to act with due diligence to prevent violations of rights or to investigate and punish acts of violence, and for providing compensation".*
>
> *CEDAW. Committee General Recommendation 19, paragraph 9.*

Abstract Nowadays the idea that the liberal State not only has to avoid the violation of fundamental rights, but also protect our rights from the possible attacks of other citizens is widely spread. Furthermore, the enforcement in substantive law is not enough. In order to achieve effectiveness, the legislator has the obligation to

This Chapter has been written within the framework of project PID 2021-123170OB-I00. I would like to thank Assoc. Prof. Rahime Erbaş for encouraging me to write in English, making me overcome my fears and insecurities to express myself in a foreign language.

This Chapter develops some of the reflections from my Doctoral Thesis. More information : Borges Blázquez R (2020) ¿Cumple España con los estándares internacionales y europeos en materia de obligaciones positivas con perspectiva de género? Revista General de Derecho Procesal 51: 1-29; Borges Blázquez R (2021) Obligaciones estatales positivas con filtro morado o perspectiva de género. La Ley Penal 148:1-22; Borges Blázquez, R. "European Judicial Cooperation and Protection of Gender-Based Violence Victims, Fact or Fiction?". Journal of Penal Law and Criminology 8 (2020): 95–115.

R. B. Blázquez (✉)
Department of Administrative and Procedural Law, Faculty of Law, University of Valencia, Valencia, Spain
e-mail: Raquel.Borges@uv.es

R. Erbaş (ed.), *Criminal Prosecution of Domestic Violence*, Ius Gentium: Comparative Perspectives on Law and Justice 128,
https://doi.org/10.1007/978-3-032-01202-9_11

create a real and effective protection within the procedure. In the case of gender violence victims, the ECtHR is, little by little, acknowledging the responsibility of States for not having fulfilled their duties to protect their citizens. The chapter aims to identify the potential obstacles that may find women victims of gender and domestic violence in their national procedural criminal systems. Among these pages we will study different cases where the ECtHR had the opportunity to indicate the deficiencies in national criminal procedural laws that failed to prevent, investigate, or condemn. To do so, the chapter is divided in a theoretical part and a practical part. Finally, the chapter provides conclusions.

1 Introduction

> Violence against women was under-reported, under-investigated, under-prosecuted, and under-sentenced.[1]

The editor of this book starts a brilliant article with a reflection that struck me due to the fact that it was really similar to the reflection I made comparing the different motivations during trial procedure between a victim of a car robbery and a victim of intimate partner violence.[2]

> Assume that a man breaks into a house, takes jewelry from the home and manages to escape. The police catch the perpetrator. The prosecutor collects fingerprints as evidence from the surfaces the perpetrator touched at home, determines the act of taking another person's belongings as defined in the code, and submits the indictment to the Court accordingly. As for domestic violence, imagine a woman frequently experiences defamations, threats and bodily harms. (…) Because she went to hospital several days after injury, the biological evidence appears less valuable. Besides, she suffers from re-victimization and lives in fear for her children's well-being who also witnessed the repeated instances of violence at home. The police arrest the husband. However, she withdraws her complaint soon after her husband released from custody. How is criminal law supposed to respond to that case, then?.[3]

As *Erbaş* points out in case of Balsan v. Romania, in some cases domestic violence[4] is not even a criminal matter, and the courts impose an administrative fine on the perpetrator. The judgment itself indicates that "both at the investigation level and before the courts the national authorities considered the acts of domestic violence as being provoked and regarded them as not being serious enough to fall within the scope of the criminal law".[5] Without intending to advance reflections, we can affirm

---

[1] *Tërshana v. Albania* (48,756/14), 04.08.2020, par. 156.

[2] Borges Blázquez (2021), pp. 558–559.

[3] Erbaş (2021), p. 1.

[4] I would like to state that during this article I am going to analyze cases of gender violence within the partner, and, in some cases, children will be involved as long as they are also victims of the violence that suffers their mother. Therefore, even though during the chapter I will address to gender-based cases, children will be collateral or indirect victims of this violence.

[5] *Balsan v. Romania* (49,645/09), 23.5.2017, par. 67.

that both international legislations and supranational courts are agents of the paradigm change. The Istanbul Convention positions itself in Article 5 in the same way as General Recommendation 19 did on Paragraph 9. Both rules establish that the State could incur in responsibility for the criminal actions committed inside its territory in the case of not fulfilling due diligence obligations. Moreover, a review of the most recent case-law of the ECtHR and CJEU Jurisprudence show us how these Courts are little by little including State responsibility for not fulfilling the obligation to protect and gender perspective. Both Courts are correcting slopes between the conviction and performance of the EU and the internal lack of commitment from the EU member States. However, "ratifying the ECHR and being part of the ECtHR can indicate only a promise of the States. In fact, the concept of positive obligation was established through the case- law by the ECtHR".[6]

2 The Feminist Jurisprudence

> We will be told that our approach [...] is not neutral. But existing laws, and existing social reality, are already not neutral. The question is, on what side is no neutrality going to fall: to maintain inequality or to promote equality? The choice is between existing law – which is neutral from the standpoint of the advantaged and nonneutral from the standpoint of the disadvantaged – and the alternative, which, written from the viewpoint of the disadvantaged, may be considered nonneutral from the advantaged standpoint. The question is whether you want the problem of inequality solved. You can't solve the problem of disadvantage from the standpoint of dominance. You can solve it from the standpoint of the disadvantaged. In a hierarchical situation, neutrality really is not available.[7]

Judging with a gender perspective allows us to transform the practices of application and interpretation of the law and to act in a comprehensive manner on the legal conflict.[8] Law is not neutral and its egalitarian application in cases where one of the parties is in a subordinated position may result in a new discrimination, this time from the judicial system.[9] Judging with a gender perspective implies making the right to equality a reality. It responds to a constitutional (Article 9.2 Spanish Constitution) and supranational (Article 10.2 Spanish Constitution) obligation to combat discrimination through procedural law in order to guarantee equal access to justice and to remedy, in the specific case, asymmetrical situations of power.[10] According to *Fletcher*, "the legal system justifies its capacity to oblige individuals to act in a certain way, *e.g.*, pay a fine, by claiming objectivity and neutrality in its application of rules to people. Judges are expected to be impartial in their determination of cases, and law itself is expected to rise above subjective personal interests.

[6] Erbaş (2021), p. 3.

[7] MacKinnon (2017), p. 124.

[8] Gutierrez-Solana Journoud (2018), pp. 837–838.

[9] Barona Vilar (2018), p. 60.

[10] Martínez García (2018a), p. 44.

Law is said to lose its legitimacy if it is shown to favor one person's wishes over another. In the abstract, such adherence to objectivity and neutrality seems fair and proper (…) But feminists among others have argued that the legal ideals of objectivity and neutrality are in fact a major problem for those seeking to represent groups which have been discriminated against historically."[11]

Martínez García exposes that the interest of the so called "feminist thought" in law led to the birth of *Feminist Jurisprudence*[12] or *Feminist Legal Theory*[13] in the 1960–1970s. Its object of study was precisely to study the law from a feminist analysis with a gender perspective. The *Feminist Jurisprudence* used the data to denounce that Law is masculine (the law sees and treats women in the way that men see and treat women), that it has a sex (it does not take into account the experiences and needs of women. For example, the way in which the penal types related to sexual crimes were historically constructed: instead of protecting the sexual integrity of the woman it protected the honor of the family) and it is gendered (the unequal power relations existing in society are reflected in the law, considering rules such as the diligence "of a good father of a family/ Reasonable men").[14] Even though there is no single school of feminist jurisprudence, the diversity of voices is essential.[15]

As *Rodrigo- Piñero* states, since gender violence became a matter of public interest affecting human rights, the ECtHR could not continue to understand it as a private matter that did not affect the human rights protected by the ECHR. The Court, thus, begins to recognize the responsibility of States that allow, tolerate, or fail to prevent individuals from violating such rights.[16]

3 The Interpretation of Positive State Obligations by the ECtHR

The obligations of criminal protection of human rights are manifestations of the positive obligations deriving from the general duty of Article 1 ECHR to "secure" the rights recognized by the ECHR.[17] When firstly ECHR was drafted, the positive obligations were not thought. Positive obligations were developed through the case law of the Court.[18] The foundational idea is that the obligation to respect fundamental rights has two sides: negative and positive. The negative duty regarding the

[11] Fletcher (2002), p. 135.

[12] https://www.law.cornell.edu/wex/feminist_jurisprudence.

[13] Lacey (1989), pp. 388–389.

[14] Ibid., p. 29–30 and Smart (1992), pp. 29–44.

[15] Charlesworth et al. (1991), p. 613.

[16] Rodríguez-Piñero y Bravo-Ferrer (2018), pp. 2–3.

[17] Akandji-Kombe (2007).

[18] Ashworth (2015), p. 198. See also Erbaş (2020), p. 231.

authorities implies that they should restrain themselves from any conduct that is potentially harmful to individuals. The positive aspect involves States making sure that they protect these rights against possible aggressions by third parties[19]: Therefore, State obligations include prevention, investigation, and punishment. The duties to prevent and punish would be included within the substantive obligations. On the other hand, the duty to investigate is part of the procedural obligations.[20] This duty confronts the public/private distinction. "The distinction implies that the private world is uncontrolled"[21] and, therefore, women and children become more vulnerable in the place where they should feel safest: their own home.

3.1 *The State's Duty to Protect the Citizens*

The non-compliance of the State's duty to protect citizens and its obligation to prevent crimes are the *leitmotiv* from which a wide variety of consequences have been drawn in concrete applications. Among others, the dominant German doctrine explicitly uses this argumentation to support the assignment of a position of guarantee to police officers by which they can be held liable for commission by omission for failing to prevent a crime.[22] In the case law of the ECtHR the limits of State duties were outlined in *Osman v. United Kingdom.*[23] However, nowadays "there is no general definition of what is an effective or ineffective criminal investigation as settled but the case-law of the ECtHR".[24]

The Osman case involved a lawsuit filed by the widow and son of Mr. Osman, who was murdered by a teacher who had developed an unhealthy obsession with his son and his son's classmate. The teacher murdered the minor's father, wounded the minor, murdered one of the minor's schoolmates and wounded his father.[25] Before murdering the child's father and his schoolmate, who was also one of his students, he had already shown clear signs of irregular and suspicious behavior.[26] The parents had contacted the police numerous times, but the fatal outcome was not prevented. When he was arrested by the police, he asked them why they not arrested him before committing the murders, if he had given signs that anticipated the killings: *"Why didn't you stop me before I did it, I gave you all the warning signs?"*[27]

---

[19] Viganò (2012), p. 314.

[20] De Luis (2019), p. 499.

[21] Charlesworth et al. (1991), p. 627.

[22] Tomás-Valiente Lanuza (2016), p. 4.

[23] Osman v. The United Kingdom (97/1997/871/1083) 28.10.1998.

[24] Erbaş (2020), p. 223.

[25] Osman, par. 10.

[26] Ibid., paras. 49, 118, 119.

[27] Ibid., par. 57.

The Strasbourg Court states that, theoretically, there is a positive duty of the State to prevent the infringement of citizens' rights and, consequently, the right of the citizens to have the State comply. However, in practice it outlines it in a restrictive way. In order to appreciate this violation, the Court must be convinced that the authorities knew or should have known that one or more individuals were under real and immediate threat to their lives by criminal acts of a third party at the time of the facts and, even so, did not take those measures within the framework of their powers that from a reasonable point of view would have alleviated the risk.[28]

In other words, the need to respect the rights of the citizens must be considered, as well as the difficulties that the police have in exercising their functions in contemporary societies and the unpredictability of human behavior.[29] This obligation must be interpreted without imposing an unbearable and excessive burden on the authorities.[30] Any alleged threat to life cannot oblige the authorities to take concrete measures to prevent its realization. In this regard, the Court concludes that Articles 2 (right to life) and 8 (right to respect for family and private life) were not violated, but that Article 6 (right to a fair trial) ECHR was violated.[31] The ECtHR considers that the State cannot be held responsible for the deaths because, although there was an irregular and threatening behavior, the Court considers that the police could not have foreseen the outcome since it entailed a great escalation of violence between 1) the graffiti, the destruction of furniture, the hanging around the children's houses and 2) the murder of two people.[32] However, the reality is that the police did not properly assess the risk and therefore the victims' families should be entitled to an effective remedy under the conventional law of Article 6 of the Convention.

3.2 *The Use of Criminal Law to Protect Human Rights*

"The criminal sanction is at once prime guarantor and prime threatener of human freedom. Used providently and humanely it is guarantor; used indiscriminately and coercively it is threatener".[33] If we affirm that the obligation of States to "secure" human rights also includes the "duty to protect" these rights through criminal law, either preventively (criminalization of harmful conduct) or reactively (exercise of

---

[28] Tomás-Valiente Lanuza (2016), p. 42.

[29] Osman, par. 116.

[30] Ibid.

[31] Ibid.

[32] Judgement ECtHR Osman v. The United Kingdom, n. 97/1997/871/1083, 28 October 1998 paragraph 119 as: "In assessing the level of knowledge which can be imputed to the police at the relevant time, the Court has also had close regard to the series of acts of vandalism against the Osmans' home and property between May and November 1987 (…) It observes firstly that none of these incidents could be described as life-threating and secondly that there was no evidence pointing to the involvement of Paget-Lewis".

[33] Packer (1968), p. 366.

ius puniendi against the perpetrator of the aggression),[34] this idea implies a radical change in the function of human rights in the criminal discourse. Traditionally, human rights were limits to the punitive power of the State, thus protecting the accused through guarantees of due process and the convicted by prescribing standards of humanity in the enforcement of sentences. The victims' human rights would act as an engine of expansion, forcing the State to exercise its *ius puniendi.*[35]

The ECtHR made its first reference to positive obligations in the case of X and Y v. The Netherlands of 26 March 1985: "Although the object of Article 8 is essentially that of protecting the individual against arbitrary interference by the public authorities, it does not merely compel the State to abstain from such interference: in addition to this primarily negative undertaking, there may be positive obligations inherent in an effective respect for private or family life (...) thee obligations may involve the adoption of measures designed to secure respect for private life even in the sphere of the relations of individuals between themselves".[36] The Court denounced a gap in Dutch legislation in cases involving victims of sexual abuse with a mental impairment and the State's obligation to protect the right to respect private and family life under Article 8 ECHR.[37] This pronouncement generated different positions in academia.[38] I position myself with *Prof. Tomás-Valiente* arguments: citizens renounce the self-protection inherent in the state of nature in exchange for receiving it from the State. It is the theory of the HOBBES' leviathan, also present in Enlightenment thought, early liberalism and European and North American constitutionalism.[39]

These positive obligations do not necessarily imply (but may imply) the duty to protect the fundamental right at stake under criminal law. In *the X and Y case*, the Court concluded that the only appropriate measures to protect the right to privacy of the mentally handicapped victims were of a criminal nature, since a purely civil remedy such as compensation would be insufficient[40]: "Effective deterrence is indispensable in this area, and it can be achieved only by criminal-law provisions".[41] This case remained isolated until the end of the 1990s, when the ECtHR began to multiply rulings in which it recognized violations of the Convention because the State did not criminally protect the victim's right.[42] As *Tulkens* summarizes as "in short, human rights have both a defensive and an offensive role, a role of both neutralizing and triggering the criminal law. If this is indeed a paradox and not just a contradiction, an attempt must be made not to resolve it but to come to terms with

[34] Karsai (2013).

[35] Viganò (2012), pp. 311–312.

[36] X and Y v. The Netherlands (8978/80), 26.03.1985, par. 23.

[37] Viganò (2014), pp. 444–448. See e.g. Erbaş (2020), p. 224.

[38] Ashworth (2015), pp. 199–200.

[39] Tomás-Valiente Lanuza (2016), p. 3.

[40] Viganò (2012), p. 314.

[41] *X and Y v. The Netherlands* (8978/80), 26.03.1985, par.27.

[42] Viganò (2012), p. 314.

it, whilst being aware of the complexity of the ensuing consequences, and to clarify it in the light of the requisite balance between its component parts".[43] It pronounces herself in the same way *Erbaş* when she ask the reader whether Criminal Law comes as prima ratio or ultima ratio when "human rights forces criminal law to take an (effective) action".[44]

The A. v. United Kingdom case is very illustrative in the area of children fundamental rights within the home.[45] The broadness of the English criminal system regarding "*reasonable chastisement*" or "*ius corrigenda*" was questioned. This created a risk of impunity for serious injury to the physical and moral integrity of children in the name of their upbringing.[46] In this case, the stepfather allegedly hit his stepson repeatedly with a gardener's cane to punish him for his behavior, but he benefited from the common law reference to "*reasonable chastisement*".[47] The ECtHR was able to establish the responsibility of the State in the absence of punishment of the act that led to the violation of the right under Article 3 ECHR, *i.e.,* to be free from inhuman and degrading treatment.[48] It further condemned the United Kingdom for the insufficient protection of abused children by stating that "the old patriarchal thought of duty-based and duty-infused rights continued to languish in only one corner of the legal order: family law (…) However, even in family law, legal guarantees were increasingly introduced to ensure that husbands and parents exercised their rights properly (…) In family law, too, the transformation of duty infused rights into self-serving rights and into duties that benefit third parties was under way".[49]

4 The ECtHR and the Gender Perspective

The recognition of the phenomenon of domestic and gender-based violence as acts against human rights and, consequently, their necessary conventional protection is relatively recent.[50] The ECtHR could not remain oblivious to this new approach to gender violence.[51] The doctrine of indirect horizontal effect emerges precisely in order to make directly responsible the State even though the fact interfering with human rights was done by a non-State actor.[52] States must be held accountable for

[43] Tulkens (2011), p. 579.

[44] Erbaş (2020), p. 222.

[45] *A. v. The United Kingdom* (100/1997/884/1096), 23.09.1998.

[46] Viganò (2012), p. 316.

[47] *A. v. The United Kingdom*, paras. 14 and 23.

[48] Viganò (2012), p. 449.

[49] Radbruch (2020), p. 676.

[50] Hasselbacher (2010), p. 192.

[51] Rodríguez-Piñero y Bravo-Ferrer (2018), p. 3.

[52] Lane (2018), p. 26.

serious human rights violations that occur to their citizens.[53] In a situation of indirect horizontal effect the victim brings the claim against the State instead of the responsible.[54] Otherwise, they send a message to the public that certain conduct goes unpunished. This has long been the case for victims of domestic violence. Interest and concern about the violations of basic rights that occur when the doors of homes are closed is relatively recent. *Erbaş* makes the personal political when she states "patriarchy grows in family or private relationships".[55] As *Dempsey* states "symbolic value is perhaps the most widely recognized intrinsic value discussed in the literature regarding the criminal justice response to domestic violence cases".[56]

In the case of C.R. v. United Kingdom,[57] the ECtHR did not accept the arguments of an English citizen who claimed that Article 7 had been violated by being punished for an act that was not a crime at the time it was committed.[58] During their separation proceedings, and with his ex-wife living at her parents' home, he took advantage of her being home alone to force her to have sexual intercourse with him. He claims that he cannot be convicted for wanting to have sexual intercourse within marriage.[59] Neither the English judges nor the ECtHR consider that his right has been violated by being convicted for acts that at the time were not criminal because forcing your ex-partner to have sexual intercourse without her consent is in fact a crime.[60]

In Kontrová v. Slovakia case,[61] the Court found violations of Articles 2 and 13 ECHR. The first complaint was withdrawn by the victim because it was suggested by the police.[62] After this her husband murders their two children and commits suicide.[63] In this case, given that the police knew about the family situation, the fact that they did not carry out an investigation to clarify the facts or report them to the judicial authority means that they failed in their obligation to protect the lives of the two common children, minors, and the direct consequence was their death.[64] The judgment also found a violation of the right to a legal remedy under Article 13 ECHR because the mother could not obtain financial compensation for the damages suffered.[65]

---

[53] For example, "prosecutors can condemn patriarchy through actions of deciding what kinds of evidence to submit at trial and what kind of theory of the case to argue to the jury", Dempsey (2007), p. 928.

[54] Lane (2018), p. 26.

[55] Erbaş (2021), p. 4.

[56] Dempsey (2007), p. 914.

[57] *C.R. v. The United Kingdom* (20,190/92), 22.11.1995.

[58] Ibid., par. 51.

[59] Ibid., par. 54.

[60] Ibid., par. 62; Brownmiller (1975) and Russell (1975).

[61] *Kontrová v. Slovakia* (7510/04), 24.09.2007.

[62] Ibid., par. 9.

[63] Ibid,. par. 14.

[64] Ibid., paras. 52, 53 and 54.

[65] Ibid., par. 62.

In Bevacqua and S. v. Bulgaria,[66] Article 8 ECHR is violated by the failure to adopt precautionary measures.[67] This cannot be considered a civil or private matter.[68] In this case, as in many other cases of gender violence, the violence takes place in front of the minor son. The child is afraid of his father.[69] Although the Court recognizes that the authorities were not entirely unmoved by the abuse, due diligence is also diligence without delay.[70] Treating domestic violence against women as a private matter is incompatible with the right to respect family and private life in Article 8 ECHR.

In Branko Tomasic et al. v. Croatia[71] the perpetrator is a partially unimpeachable subject.[72] A violent man convicted for continuous death threats directed at his partner and daughter.[73] For these threats his sentence is 5 months' imprisonment and a security measure of compulsory psychiatric treatment because of the personality disorder he suffered and diminished, but did not annul, his capacity of decision and responsibility.[74] Although the court initially established that the measure should last, if necessary, even after the prison sentence, the appellation court limited the duration of the treatment to the same duration as the prison sentence. Neither was any treatment plan formulated after his release.[75] Within weeks of his release he killed his wife and daughter. Then he committed suicide.[76] The ECtHR finds the Croatian State responsible for many factors, including the lack of diligence in the administration of treatment or the failure to check the inmate's level of danger prior to his release.[77] Reference is also made to the domestic regulatory framework on the execution of the treatment measure which is described as deficient.[78] Article 2 ECHR was violated because the perpetrator carried out his threat to kill his wife and daughter and then committed suicide. The State had failed to prevent the deaths. It had failed to investigate and in consequence the police officers who had knowledge of the facts were investigated and punished because of not investigating even though they were aware of the danger.

[66] *Bevacqua and S. v. Bulgaria* (71127/01), 12.09.2008.

[67] Ibid., par. 82.

[68] Ibid., par. 83.

[69] Ibid., par. 33.

[70] Ibid., par. 70, "The evidence is, however, that the District Court did not treat the matter with any degree of priority and, during the first six months, ignored the issue of interim measures."

[71] *Branko Tomasic and others v. Croatia* (46,598/06), 15.04.2009.

[72] Ibid., par. 7.

[73] Ibid., par. 8.

[74] Ibid.

[75] Ibid., par. 9.

[76] Ibid., par. 10.

[77] Ibid., paras. 54 to 60.

[78] Tomás-Valiente Lanuza (2016), pp. 51–52.

In Opuz v. Turkey,[79] the ECtHR considered there was a violation of Articles 2, 3 and 14 ECHR in the Turkish authorities' failure to protect the applicant and her mother (killed by the applicant's ex-partner) from the acts of domestic violence they both suffered, and which were known to the authorities.[80] Both had repeatedly complained and withdrawn the complaints due to their fear of retaliation by the plaintiff's ex-partner.[81] Violence is tolerated by the authorities and society and domestic remedies do not work. There was a risk, and the victims repeatedly warned the authorities of the existence of that risk. In addition, the penalty for murder was lowered because it was considered an honor killing.[82] In this case, the ECtHR focused mainly on the existence of discrimination because she was a woman.[83] Article 42 of Istanbul Convention stress the importance of legislative or other measures to ensure that those who commit the so-called "honor" crimes according to culture, custom, religion or tradition do not find justification in the criminal procedure. On the other hand, in the successive judgments, when imposing the need for prevention and State repression of domestic violence, it focuses mainly on the violation of specific rights depending on the result generated by the violence. It is from each of these offenses that the positive obligations of the States are deduced. It thus assumes the due diligence principle of the Istanbul Convention, both for law enforcement and judicial authorities.[84]

In the E. S. et al. v. Slovakia case,[85] the ECtHR considered that Articles 3 and 8 ECHR had been violated. Despite having filed for divorce because her husband beat and sexually abused the applicant and her minor daughter the aggressor had no obligation to leave the family home.[86] As a result, it was the victim and her children who were forced to leave their home, family, school and friends to escape the abuse.[87]

Article 8 ECHR is also violated in A. v. Croatia.[88] The perpetrator suffers from post-traumatic stress disorder (PTSD) since he suffered tortures during the war.[89] It is proven that the children were aware of the mistreatment. The ECtHR recognizes that the authorities acted well because they never suggested the plaintiff to withdraw the complaint and settle their disagreements in private but an apparently neutral policy can turn into discrimination because of the specific circumstances of the vulnerable group.[90]

---

[79] *Opuz v. Turkey* (33,401/02), 9.09.2009.

[80] Ibid., par.118.

[81] Ibid., par.154.

[82] Ibid., par. 121.

[83] Ibid., par. 200.

[84] Rodríguez-Piñero y Bravo-Ferrer (2018), p. 5.

[85] *E.S. and others v. Slovakia* (8227/04), 15.09.2009.

[86] Ibid., par. 33.

[87] Ibid., par. 36.

[88] *A. v. Croatia* (55,164/08), 14.10.2010.

[89] Ibid., par. 6.

[90] Ibid., par. 77 and 94.

In the Hajduová v. Slovakia case[91] the authorities' inaction caused them to fail to comply with the mandate of Article 8 of the Convention. The perpetrator repeatedly threatens to kill his wife and others.[92] There is an escalation of violence encouraged by State inaction.[93] The courts were aware that the aggressor was a danger because there were expert reports that corroborated this. The aggressor suffered from a bipolar disorder that could have been alleviated if he had followed the appropriate treatment.[94] It was the State inaction that allowed him to continue to threaten his wife and his wife's lawyer. The authorities knew or should have known there was a risk and failed to protect the endangered. The consequence of this is that the victims keep living with fear.[95] We witnessed the same situation in Volodina v. Russia[96] and Volodina v. Russia (no. 2).[97] The authorities are aware of the facts, the facts are criminalized, but the authorities refuse to investigate because they consider that they do not meet the minimum threshold.

In the Eremia et al. v. Republic of Moldova case[98] a violation of Article 3 was recognized for not adopting effective measures against the husband and there was another violation of Article 8 regarding the daughters because they were psychologically affected by the abuse due to the fact that they had to observe the violence exercised by their father against their mother in the family home without measures being taken to prevent the repetition of such conduct.[99] There are protective measures that he violates. In addition, there is a violation of Article 14 because there is discrimination against the wife on the part of the authorities and the police even suggested that she should withdraw her complaint.[100]

In Bljakaj et al. v. Croatia,[101] a man with a criminal background and mental problems who is going through a divorce tells a bank employee that he is going to commit suicide and to do something that people will talk about.[102] The bank employee alerts the police and they come to his house.[103] When they arrive to his house, he tells them that he has taken out the money for his funeral from the bank because he has decided to commit suicide one of these days and there is nothing the authorities can do to prevent it.[104] After this statement the policemen let him stay in his home

[91] *Hajduová v. Slovakia* (2660/03), 30.11.2010.
[92] Ibid., par. 3 and 7.
[93] Ibid., par. 52.
[94] Ibid., par. 43.
[95] Ibid., par. 49.
[96] *Volodina v. Rusia* (41,261/17), 1.07.2017.
[97] *Volodina v. Russia (No. 2)* (40,419/19), 14.09.2021.
[98] *Eremia v. The Republic of Moldova* (3564/11), 28.05.2013.
[99] Ibid., par. 60.
[100] Ibid., par. 17.
[101] *Bljakaj and others v. Croatia* (74,448/12), 18.09.2014.
[102] Ibid., par. 14.
[103] Ibid., par. 15.
[104] Ibid., par. 19.

without any precautionary measures. He returns to the bank demanding to know who alerted the police and that same morning he goes in search of his wife, shoots her and tries to kill her.[105] After that, he goes to the office of the lawyer who is handling his wife's divorce and shoots her in front of several witnesses causing the lawyer's death.[106] The underlying legal issue is the positive State duty to protect society against the possible violent acts of a person with a perceptible mental disturbance. Using the Osman test, the Strasbourg Court concludes that there was a real and immediate risk which the authorities knew or should have known about. If the authorities had ordered a forced entry that morning, making use of the possibility available to them under domestic law, the outcome would have been entirely different.[107]

The risk in this case was real and imminent. The police had sufficient information to investigate and make use of a precautionary measure. The police officers did not give the bank employee's call any importance. Proof of this is that they later falsify the reports of the day of the events because no action was taken between the visit to the victimizer's house and the attempted murder of his ex-wife and the murder of his ex-wife's lawyer.[108] On that day they had several opportunities to arrest him: they went to his house after the call from the bank employee and shortly after the victimizer appeared at the police station to ask who had informed them of his intention to commit suicide. In addition, the statements of those who were at the bank mention that he was "disturbed", "totally unstable", "crazy" and "mentally disturbed".[109] The Court finds a violation of the rights contained in Articles 2 and 13 ECHR because the civil actions for damages have not been satisfactory either.

In Kurt v. Austria[110] the applicant's partner goes to her children's school and shoots her son, leaving her daughter alive. He then commits suicide in the car. The authorities find a suicide letter in which he explains that he is going to kill his children and then kill himself because after the separation he has been deprived of what he loves most in life. There was a restraining order, but it was not enough. In addition, after this case Austria amended the legislation to give greater protection to minors in cases of domestic violence.[111] Despite the tragic outcome, using the Osman test, the Court finds that the State acted with due diligence and that the outcome was not foreseeable.[112] The Court held: "The scope of the positive obligation

[105] Ibid., paras. 21 and 22.

[106] Ibid., par. 23.

[107] Ibid., par. 122.

[108] Ibid., par. 20.

[109] Ibid., par. 117.

[110] *Kurt v. Australia* (62,903/15), 4.07.2019.

[111] "The Government submitted, however, that the legislator should not be blamed for having introduced these improvements in connection with the incident in question", ibid., par. 61.

[112] "For such a positive obligation to arise, it must be established that the authorities knew or ought to have known at the time of the existence of a real and immediate risk to the life of an identified individual from the criminal acts of a third party and that they failed to take measures within the scope of their powers which, judged reasonably, might have been expected to avoid that risk" par. 65.

must be interpreted in a way which does not impose an impossible or disproportionate burden on the authorities. The Court is fully conscious of the difficulties encountered by the domestic authorities when deciding, as in the instant case, whether or not to issue a barring order against a suspect or even arrest him or her, on the basis of limited information available, often under time pressure and by nonetheless carefully balancing the rights of the person who poses a threat on the one hand, and the rights of the victim(s) on the other. It is therefore most relevant to recapitulate what was known to the authorities at the time when they decided which measures to take in respect of E., taking into account the competencies accorded to them by the law and a certain discretion offered by this law".[113] The time lag between reports without attempts on the lives of minors, coupled, in this case, with the rapid action of law enforcement agencies following each report, means that the risk was not foreseeable by the authorities.[114] In addition, the Court notices that "after the murder, the domestic authorities conducted a comprehensive investigation into the circumstances of A's death and the events leading up to it".[115] With regard to "imminent risk" the concurring opinion is interesting because it considers that the Osman test should not be applied in cases of domestic violence, as it arose in a different context.[116]

Ultimately, we will refer to the Rumor v. Italy and Talpis v. Italy cases.[117] In Rumor v. Italy[118] the Italian State had rejected the claim of a woman victim of domestic violence who felt threatened by her ex-partner. The Court ruled that the abuse should have reached a minimum level of seriousness, according to the circumstances of the case, in order for the State to ensure protection against ill-treatment by private individuals for acts of which it knew or should have known.[119] I endorse the words of *Mc Quigg*: "The recent case of Rumor serves to highlight the limitations of human rights law when applied to the issue of domestic violence. Even with a sophisticated doctrine of positive obligations, there are limits to how far human rights law can reach to protect individuals from violations occurring in the private sphere, such as domestic violence. Even though the ill treatment that the applicant had suffered was certainly 'inhuman and degrading', no breach of the ECHR was found, as it was held that the State had fulfilled its obligations in the matter".[120] The Court recognizes that the applicant was a vulnerable person and that she had probably been mistreated.[121] However, it considers that the authorities did not remain passive in the face of that ill-treatment because her partner had been

---

[113] *Kurt v. Australia* (62,903/15), 4.07.2019, par.69.

[114] Ibid, par. 72.

[115] *Kurt v. Australia* (62,903/15), 4.07.2019, par. 75.

[116] Concurring opinion *Kurt v. Austria*, par. 20.

[117] Rodríguez-Piñero y Bravo-Ferrer (2018), pp. 7–11.

[118] *Rumor v. Italy* (72,964/10), 27.05.2014.

[119] Ibid., par. 57.

[120] McQuigg (2015), p. 1024.

[121] *Rumor v. Italy* (72,964/10), 27.05.2014, par. 60.

arrested and convicted earlier.[122] Furthermore, it takes into consideration the existence of an exchange of e-mails between the applicant and her former partner after the conviction.[123]

In the Talpis v. Italy case,[124] the victim was a Moldovan immigrant with two children of a former marriage. Before arriving to Italy, she had already been assaulted by her alcoholic husband.[125] In Italy she and her daughter were again abused, and she notified the police. This abuse was repeated on several occasions. The plaintiff is interrogated for the first time by the police 7 months after her first complaint. At that time, she modified her initial statements about the seriousness of the facts, stating that she did not know Italian well and was unable to express herself correctly.[126] A little over a year later, the police receive a new call. When they go to the apartment there are clear signs of violence but they accept without further ado the statements of the plaintiff, who says that she called because her husband needed a doctor.[127] The husband is taken to the hospital and, that same night, the police find him in the street in a drunken state, identify him and let him return home where he tries to assault the plaintiff with a knife.[128] The son gets in the way to try to prevent the assault. His father stabs him three times and he die. The woman tries to escape, but her husband follows her down the street and stabs her several times but does not kill her.[129]

This judgment highlights the importance of protective measures against dangerous situations in cases of domestic violence. The authorities did not take measures to protect the victims even though they were aware of the violence suffered. It is the absence of reasonable measures that could have changed the course of events or attenuated the harm caused that provides the ECtHR with a sufficient basis for imposing liability on the State.[130] This judgment has been the subject of two dissenting opinions, partially dissenting, because insufficient reasons are given to reach a conclusion contrary to that of the Rumor case. Among these, Judge Spano, applying the test of the Opuz judgment on the proven existence of a real and immediate risk to the life of an identified person, considers that the lapse of time between the first aggression and the final aggression resulting in death (14 months) did not allow to determine that the authorities could have known the imminent nature and the reality of the risk.[131]

---

[122] Ibid., par. 64.

[123] Ibid., par. 70.

[124] *Talpis v. Italy* (41,237/14), 2.03.2017.

[125] Ibid., par. 9.

[126] Ibid., par. 30.

[127] Ibid., par. 38.

[128] Ibid., paras. 39, 40 and 41.

[129] Ibid., par. 42.

[130] Ibid., par. 149.

[131] Partly dissenting opinion of Judge Spano, par. 5.

5 Conclusion

The study on the jurisprudence of the ECtHR shows us a change in the way to approach violence against women and children in the home is dealt with by international and national legislations. Gender-based violence is not only a public issue, but also a State issue. We can affirm that a backtracking or minimization of the disvalue of these behaviors is not possible in the European space. Gender Equality Strategy (2025) that implies equal treatment legislation, integration of the gender perspective into all other policies and specific measures for encouraging women.[132]

In recent times we are witnessing the use and abuse of criminal law to educate and raise awareness in society. We are observing how criminal law is expanding to take on functions that do not correspond to it. The preventive and communicative effect that criminal law has, useful and required, does not have the ability to solve the problem of gender violence neither was it created to do so. As *Erbaş* states, this could mean a reversal from the *ultima ratio* to the *prima ratio*. It is important to repeat once again that society will change with education and that punitivism will not end gender and domestic based violence. When criminal law arrives, we are too late.[133] In all these cases we saw as Criminal law failed the victims. It was necessary the use of Criminal Law because of the fundamental rights involved but the main problem remains. Our legislators think that we can change a social problem only using criminal law. To fight against gender and domestic violence, we need to think outside the box and realize that only a transversal solution involving legal and extra-legal knowledges will be able to solve it. However, this reflection cannot lead us to underestimate the significant contribution by the case-law of the ECtHR in the fight against violence against women and children. The Court has succeeded in bringing a type of violence that for centuries has been silenced and relegated to the private sphere into the public sphere.

I would also like to refer to EU Directive 2024/1385 on combating violence against women and domestic violence. Although the ECtHR has a wider scope than the Union itself, the criminalization of gender-based violence at European level will have an impact on the future pronouncements of the ECtHR. Spanish legislation already covers the forms of gender-based violence included in the Directive, and few major legislative changes are foreseen because of the Directive. Furthermore, I believe that the Directive has missed a great opportunity to show a firm and decisive commitment against gender-based violence and has opted for general definitions without legislating on the most problematic issues.[134] This issue could be the subject of a new article, but it needs to be highlighted.

---

[132] https://commission.europa.eu/strategy-and-policy/policies/justice-and-fundamental-rights/gender-equality/gender-equality-strategy_en.

[133] Van de Watering (2013), pp. 52–54; Van Der Aa and Ouwerkerk (2011), p. 268.

[134] Borges Blázquez (2023).

References

Akandji-Kombe J (2007) Positive obligations under the European convention on human rights. A guide to the implementation of the European convention on human rights. In: Akandji-Kombe J (ed) Human rights handbooks no. 7. UNHCR, Geneva

Ashworth A (2015) Positive obligations in criminal law. Hart Publishing Limited, Oxford

Barona Vilar S (2018) La necesaria deconstrucción del modelo patriarcal de justicia. In: Martínez García E (ed) Análisis de la Justicia desde la perspectiva de género. Tirant lo Blanch, Valencia, pp 29–70

Borges Blázquez R (2021) In: Barona Vilar S (ed) Violencia de género y mediación penal, ¿condenadas a entenderse? Meditaciones sobre mediación (MED+). Tirant lo Blanch, Valencia, pp 549–573

Borges Blázquez R (2023) La ¿creación? del delito de violencia de género en la Unión Europea y su posible incidencia en la Directiva 2011/99/UE sobre la orden de protección europea. Revista General de Derecho Europeo 59:69–108

Brownmiller S (1975) Against our will. Men, women and rape. Ballantine Books, New York

Charlesworth H, Christine C, Wright S (1991) Feminist approaches to international law. Am J Int Law 85(4):613–645

De Luis GE (2019) El Derecho a una investigación efectiva en la jurisprudencia del TEDH. Revista Boliviana de Derecho 27:494–515

Dempsey MM (2007) Towards a feminist state: what does "effective" prosecution of domestic violence mean? Modern Law Rev 70(6):908–935

Erbaş R (2020) Effective criminal investigations in combating domestic violence and the ECtHR: *prima ratio* v. *ultima ratio*? In: Stradella E (ed) Gender based approaches to the law and *juris dictio* in Europe. Pisa University Press, Pisa, pp 221–240

Erbaş R (2021) Effective criminal investigations for women victims of domestic violence: the approach of the ECtHR. Women's Stud Int Forum 86:1–12

Fletcher R (2002) Feminist legal theory. In: Banakar, Travers (eds) An introduction to law and social theory. Hart, London, pp 135–154

Gutierrez-Solana Journoud A (2018) La invisible perspectiva de género del TJUE en asuntos que afectan exclusivamente a las mujeres: generalidad frente a especificidad. In: Etxebarría Estankona K, Ordeñana Gezuraga I, Otauza Zabala G (eds) Justicia con ojos de mujer. Cuestiones procesales controvertidas. Tirant Lo Blanch, Valencia, pp 829–843

Hasselbacher L (2010) State obligations regarding domestic violence: the European court of human rights, due diligence and international legal minimums of protection. Northwest J Int Hum Rights 8(2):190–215

Karsai K (2013) Ultima ratio and subsidiarity in the European criminal law. Juridpol:53–63

Lacey N (1989) Feminist legal theory. Oxf J Leg Stud 9(3):383–394

Lane L (2018) The horizontal effect of international human rights law in practice. Eur J Comp Law Governance 5:5–88

MacKinnon CA (2017) Butterfly politics. Harvard University Press, Cambridge

Martínez García E (2018a) Análisis de la justicia procesal desde la perspectiva de género. Proyecto de investigación, Segundo ejercicio de Cátedra inédito. Dissertation, University of Valencia

Martínez García E (2018b) Análisis de la justicia "procesal" desde la perspectiva de género. In: Martínez García E (ed) Análisis de la Justicia desde la perspectiva de género. Tirant lo Blanch, Valencia, pp 15–28

McQuigg RJ (2015) Domestic violence as a human rights issue: rumor v. Italy. Eur J Int Law 26(4):1009–1025

Packer HL (1968) The limits of the criminal sanction. Paolo alto. Standford University Press, California

Radbruch G (2020) Law's image of the human. Oxf J Leg Stud 40(4):667–681

Rodríguez-Piñero y Bravo-Ferrer M (2018) El Tribunal Europeo de Derechos Humanos y la violencia doméstica. La Ley 1730:1–12

Russell D (1975) The politics of rape. The victim's perspective. iUniverse, Bloomington
Smart C (1992) The woman of legal discourse. Soc Leg Stud 1:29–44
Tomás-Valiente Lanuza C (2016) Deberes positivos del Estado y Derecho penal en la jurisprudencia del TEDH. Indret:1–72
Tulkens F (2011) Paradoxical relationships between criminal law and human rights. J Int Criminal Justice 9:577–595
Van De Watering EJE (2013) Criminal Protection Orders: Effective legal remedies or False promises to victims? An explorative research on the effectiveness of criminal protection orders
Van Der Aa S, Ouwerkerk J (2011) The European protection order: no time to waste or a waste of time? Eur J Crime Criminal Law Criminal Justice 19:267–287
Viganò F (2012) Sobre las obligaciones de tutela penal de los derechos fundamentales en la jurisprudencia del TEDH. In: Mir Puig S, Corcoy Bidasolo M (eds) Garantías constitucionales y derecho penal europeo. Marcial Pons, Madrid, pp 311–382
Viganò F (2014) La arbitrariedad del no punir. Sobre las obligaciones de tutela penal de los derechos fundamentales. Polít Crim 9(18):428–476

Post-Talpis Reflections: Reassessing and Redefining ECHR Standards and Italy's Approach to Domestic Violence

Vittorio Cama

Abstract *Talpis v. Italy* still offers the interpreter a privileged vantage point on the subject of States' obligations to protect victims of domestic violence. In particular, it gives the opportunity to bring into clearer focus some recurrent issues connected to the violations of Articles 2, 3 and 14 ECHR and to the parameters used by the European Court of Human Rights to address them. Nevertheless, in the course of the Court's analysis, one gets the impression that something is missing. The same perception arises with reference to the most recent interventions of the Italian legislature, adopted in response to the critical issues underlined by the Court not least in *Talpis*, as well as to the emotional thrust of tragic news events. Above all, it is the excessive reliance on measures in the sphere of substantive and procedural criminal law that appears unsatisfactory from a perspective that demands criminal law to be the *ultima ratio* of State intervention. The plethora of subsequent legislative interventions, the Court's further pronouncements on the subject and, most importantly, the persistently alarming statistics on gender-based violence in Italy collectively warrant the search for the missing piece in the Court's reasoning. Consequently, this chapter endeavors to conceptualize a complementary, rather than alternative, approach to addressing domestic violence, through the valorization of a complex of normative positive responses consisting in measures of an economic, social and cultural nature.

1 Introduction

On 25 November 2013, the night of the International Day for the Elimination of Violence Against Women, a man attempts to kill his wife, who manages to escape from the attack. The same fate, however, does not befall his son who, in an attempt

V. Cama (✉)
University of Trento, Trento, Italy
e-mail: vittorio.cama@unitn.it

R. Erbaş (ed.), *Criminal Prosecution of Domestic Violence*, Ius Gentium: Comparative Perspectives on Law and Justice 128,
https://doi.org/10.1007/978-3-032-01202-9_12

to defend his mother, loses his life. Before this tragic event, a first episode of violence occurred in June 2012, when both the woman and her daughter suffered injuries from battery. In this case, the authorities merely recorded Mr. Talpis' state of intoxication, without filing formal charges. This event is followed by a further episode in August, when the woman was threatened with a knife by her husband who ordered her to follow him in order to engage in sexual relations with him and his friends. Although some vagueness as to what happened next exists, it is certain that the woman was hospitalized, and that the episode of violence resulted only in the man being fined for illegally carrying the knife.

Subsequently, in an attempt to distance herself from her husband, the woman found shelter in an anti-violence center run by an NGO. However, she was forced to leave shortly thereafter due to funding shortages on the part of the Udine social services who informed her that they were unable to arrange alternative care. In September, she filed a complaint for injuries, ill-treatment, and threats, but retracted it seven months later (April 2013) during her first and only hearing before the authorities, leading to the dismissal of the case. Finally, on 25 November 2013, a first fight broke out. In the course of these events, the man was identified and transported to hospital in an intoxicated state. Later discharged, he was found again by a patrol car drunk and, despite the long record of episodes of violence and the quarrel, was allowed to return home where he struck his wife and, fatally, his son.

The picture outlined by the facts in *Talpis v. Italy*[1] takes on the contours of a script that has been played out too many times in the context of domestic violence. In such cases, there is often the risk of assessing the facts with the benefit of hindsight. In fact, the impression arises that the authorities could have intervened on too many occasions, before the night of the events, by taking preventive measures. On the contrary, the only measures taken against the man were two purely pecuniary penalties for unlawfully carrying a knife and causing injury. Similarly, there are reasons to believe that the woman's forced departure from the shelter due to inadequate funding was a decisive factor in the tragic outcome of the case.

The ruling of the ECtHR deserves attention for a number of reasons. First and foremost, only a few years earlier, the Court, in *Rumor* (2014),[2] had found the Italian framework consonant with the obligations stemming from the ECHR. In 2022, the Court reached the same statement in *Landi*[3] and *M.S.*[4] This begs the question of what changes *Talpis* has triggered in Italy. Moreover, the judgment offers the interpreter a privileged perspective on recurrent issues related to domestic violence, on the positive obligations incumbent on States under Articles 2, 3 and 14 of the European Convention of Human Rights ("ECHR") and on the integrated use of sources such as the Istanbul Convention.[5]

---

[1] *Talpis v. Italy* (41,237/14), 02.03.2017.

[2] *Rumor v. Italy* (72,964/10), 27.05.2014.

[3] *Landi v. Italy* (10,929/19), 07.04.2022.

[4] *M.S. v. Italy* (32,715/19), 07.07.2022.

[5] De Vido (2017b).

The first part of the chapter is devoted to a recapitulation, primarily of the doctrine of positive obligations and the *Talpis* case, with an analysis of the violations of the ECHR addressed by the Court. Building on this background, the second part addresses the critical aspects of the Court's analysis and, in particular, the excessive reliance on criminalization measures, and the lack of assessment of possible further obligations of a general nature. In this respect, we will consider whether this jurisprudential approach is to be regarded as immutable or whether there is room for an evolutionary interpretation of the rights protected by the ECHR. Finally, the third part assesses the direction in which the measures adopted by the Italian Legislature and Government are moving, in order to verify whether they can be considered to be steps forward or, possibly, backward towards an effective protection of women's rights and an effective prevention of their violation.

2 The Positive Obligations of States Under the ECHR: An Overview

The protection of fundamental rights entrusted to the ECHR operates from a dual perspective. By virtue of the general obligation to respect set forth in Article 1,[6] State parties are obliged not only to refrain from conduct that might infringe upon the rights and freedoms protected by the Convention (negative obligations), but also to proactively take steps to adopt measures of a positive nature and to implement a general legislative framework that ensures a real and effective protection against actions carried out by third parties (positive obligations).[7] At this stage of the analysis, it should be observed that these principles are the result of the developing case law of the ECtHR.[8] As such, they are neither to be regarded as permanently established nor as free from possible shortcomings.[9]

Positive obligations can, then, be sub-categorized into three further types of obligation of substantive, preventive and procedural nature.[10] Firstly, States may (if not must) provide criminal rules of a substantive character. The purpose of such rules lies essentially in preventing and "deterring", through the imposition of an effective

[6] The source of positive obligations to protect is found in both Article 1 and the individual articles of the Convention. See Akandji-Kombe (2007), Buscemi (2017), Klatt (2011) and Mowbray (2004).

[7] Clapham (1993) pp. 200 ff, Lemmens (2018), pp. 11 and Schabas (2015) pp. 90–91.

[8] The leading judgment in this regard is *X and Y v. the Netherlands* (8978/80), 26.03.1985. For previous attestations, see *Marckx v. Belgium* (6833/74), 13.06.1979, *Airey v. Ireland* (6289/73), 09.10.1979. See also *A. v. UK* (25,599/94), 23.09.1998 and *M.C. v. Bulgaria* (39,272/98), 04.12.2003. For an analysis on the application and development of positive obligations, see Xenos (2013), pp. 57–142. See also Tulkens (2011).

[9] See, for instance, Xenos (2013), p. 28 ff.

[10] Kamber (2020).

penalty, conducts that infringe upon the rights protected in the ECHR.[11] This obligation is complemented by the duty "to take preventive operational measures to protect an individual whose right is at risk from the criminal acts of another individual"[12]; once such a violation inevitably occurs, it is necessary for the State to provide appropriate procedural mechanisms aimed at ascertaining it and effectively prosecuting it.[13]

Although the Convention does not mandate that the measures for the protection of rights take the form of penal provisions, the ECtHR's case law reveals a tendency to treat criminal law as the *prima ratio* for the protection of the rights enshrined in the ECHR.[14] Consistently with this perspective, those States (such as Italy) that recognize the value of the doctrine of positive obligations,[15] tend to base the measures adopted (see paragraph 5) primarily, if not "exclusively",[16] on the introduction of new criminal offences and the tightening of penalties attached to pre-existing ones.

This approach, however, risks neglecting the potential of economic, social and cultural measures that, as will be discussed below, could lead to effective prevention.[17] Attention to these aspects, in fact, paves the way for the full realization of substantive and relational equality between men and women[18] which constitutes a formidable means to prevent and counter gender-based violence.[19] For instance, from a social perspective, the allocation of additional resources and funding to shelters has been identified as a measure capable of ensuring more effective protection of potential victims, especially at the first signs of domestic violence; an element which could have been decisive in *Talpis*. With respect to the cultural realm, particular attention has been devoted to the importance of dismantling gender stereotypes, the patriarchal culture and the widespread belief that what happens in the family sphere is to be considered purely private (a misconception that also affects the judiciary).[20] Finally, from an operational aspect, the lack of cooperation in the collection of evidence[21] has been noted as a structural weakness that could be countered by allocating more funds to improve the instruments at the disposal of the

[11] Tulkens (2011), pp. 584–585. See also the case law cited by the Author. For instance, as regards Art. 2 ECHR, *Kiliç v. Turkey* (22,492/93), 28.03.2000, par. 62. As concerns Art. 3, *A. v. UK*, par. 22; and, above all, *M.C. v. Bulgaria*, par. 186.

[12] Ashworth (2013), p. 198.

[13] For a thorough analysis of positive protective obligations and rulings made against Italy, see Montagna (2019).

[14] For a commentary on the issue and, in particular, the relationship between the contrast against domestic violence and the principle of *ultima ratio*, see Erbaş (2020, 2021a).

[15] On the issue see Erbaş (2020), p. 232; (2021a), p. 3.

[16] Bonini (2021), p. 80.

[17] On the issue, see Cingari (2021) and, as cited there, Basile (2021), Bertolino (2021) and Vitarelli (2021).

[18] For a comprehensive analysis of the constructs that prevent the achievement of substantive equality, please refer to D'Amico (2020a, b, c). See also Pellizzone (2021) and Lorenzetti and Pezzini (2020).

[19] Pellizzone (2021), p. 46.

[20] Erbaş (2020), pp. 3 ff.

[21] Erbaş (2021a), p. 5; (2021b).

inquiring authorities, by entrusting investigations to a special prosecutorial bureau (also for better cooperation),[22] and by effectively implementing appropriate training courses for the authorities.[23]

It is worth noting that the Istanbul Convention covers most of these obligations. For instance, from the social perspective, on the one hand, the Convention requires the adoption of measures to effectively implement policies of equality between women and men and the empowerment of women. On the other hand, from the economic perspective, Article 8 already calls for the allocation of "appropriate financial and human resources for the adequate implementation of integrated policies". Moreover, the Convention, as a cultural, and not merely a legal, instrument,[24] requires "measures to promote changes in the social and cultural patterns of behavior of women and men with a view to eradicating prejudices, customs, traditions and all other practices which are based on the idea of the inferiority of women or on stereotyped roles for women and men" (Article 12) as well as awareness-raising campaigns (Article 13).[25] Finally, from an operational viewpoint, Article 15 requires the implementation of appropriate training for all officers involved in gender-based violence.

Arguments in favor of the importance of such obligations can be found also in the Convention on the Elimination of All Forms of Discrimination Against Women, as supplemented by the 1992 General Recommendation No. 19 of the UN Committee on the Elimination of Discrimination Against Women ("CEDAW Committee"), and the Declaration on the Elimination of Violence Against Women adopted by the United Nations in 1993.[26] Indeed, all these instruments call on States to specifically address the "situations of disadvantage or marginalization in which this phenomenon thrives".[27]

3 Recurrent Issues on the Topic of Domestic Violence in the Light of Talpis

Once the framework of positive obligations arising from the ECHR has been briefly clarified, it is necessary to examine their relevance in the context of domestic violence. In this respect, the importance of the obligations stemming from Articles 2, 3 and 14 ECHR is evident in the ECtHR pronouncements concerning the phenomenon of domestic violence in Italy, among which *Talpis* stands as a particularly illustrative example.[28]

---

[22] Erbaş (2020, 2021a), p. 6. See also Bonini (2021)

[23] Cingari (2021).

[24] Bonini (2021).

[25] Ibid., p. 74.

[26] Pellizzone (2021), pp. 46–47.

[27] Ibid. The translation was made by the Author.

[28] For a helpful commentary, see De Vido (2017a, b).

Since the very beginning of its reasoning in *Talpis*, the First Section of the ECtHR emphasizes the importance of positive obligations by stating that the provisions of the ECHR shall "be interpreted and applied so as to make its safeguards practical and effective."[29] In reiterating its case law, and especially the judgment rendered in *Opuz*,[30] the Court clarifies that where the rights of vulnerable groups (such as women and children) are at stake, it is particularly important for the State to put in place a system that ensures effective deterrence (prevention) and an efficient and independent judicial system, as well as expeditious investigations,[31] which guarantee prompt and effective detection and punishment (repression) in order to ensure the effective implementation of the Convention.[32] Thus, these obligations substantiate the general duty to provide an "adequate legal framework affording protection against acts of violence."[33]

Furthermore, in the context of "due diligence" obligations, the State is called upon to take "preventive operational measures".[34] A violation of this particular obligation emerges whenever it is "established that the authorities knew or ought to have known at the time of the existence of a real and immediate risk to the life of an identified individual from the criminal acts of a third party and that they failed to take measures within the scope of their powers which, judged reasonably, might have been expected to avoid that risk."[35] The core of this test, referred to as the *Osman* test,[36] is the parameter of the "real and immediate risk."[37] In this regard, however, it should be noted that the general trend tends towards the abandonment of this benchmark in favor of one which, in the presence of a vulnerable group, is based on a simply "present (but not yet imminent)" risk that imposes an anticipated duty

[29] *Talpis v. Italy*, par. 96. Some first important attestations of this formula can be found, inter alia, in *Artico v. Italy* (6694/74), 13.05.1980, par. 33; *Soering v. UK* (14,038/88), 07.07.1989, par. 87 and *Rantsev v. Cyprus and Russia* (25,965/04), 07.01.2010, par. 275.

[30] *Opuz v. Turkey* (33,401/02), 09.09.2009. For a commentary of the *Opuz* case, see Erbaş (2020) and Londono (2009). See also Viviani (2009).

[31] *M.C. v. Bulgaria*, par. 151.

[32] On the effectiveness of criminal law measures, *M.G. v. Turkey* (646/10), 22.03.2016, par. 80.

[33] *Talpis v. Italy*, par. 100. For previous attestations of this principle, see *Bevacqua and S. v. Bulgaria* (71,127/01), 12.06.2008, par. 65; *Janković v. Croatia* (38,478/05), 05.03.2009, par. 45; *A. v. Croatia* (55,164/08), 14.10.2010, par. 60.

[34] *Talpis v. Italy*, par. 101. See also *Tomašić and Others v. Croatia* (46,598/06), 15.01.2009, par. 50; *Opuz v. Turkey*, par. 128; *Kaya v. Turkey* (22,535/93), 28.03.2000, par. 85; and *Kılıç v. Turkey*, par. 62.

[35] Ibid. See *Keenan v. UK* (27,229/95), 03.04.2001, paras. 89–90; *Gongadze v. Ukraine* (34,056/02), 08.11.2005, par.165; and *Opuz,* cited above, paras. 129–30. On the ECtHR's approach to risk assessment and positive obligations, see Stoyanova (2018a, b).

[36] The test was designed by the ECtHR in *Osman v. UK* (87/1997/871/1083), 28.10.1998, paras. 115–22. On the so-called *Osman* Test and recent developments related to it, see De Vido (2017a, b), pp. 7–15. Regarding a comparative perspective, it bears noting that the Inter-American Court of Human Rights has resorted to the *Osman* test, See Ebert and Sijniensky (2015). pp. 343–368.

[37] See *Osman v. UK*, par. 116.

of prevention and protection as the reverse side of a context of widespread abuse and violence already known to State authorities.[38]

The Court then notes the fundamental limits on the operability of the obligations analyzed. In particular, it is necessary that "an impossible or disproportionate burden"[39] is not imposed on the authorities in light of "the difficulties involved in policing modern societies, the unpredictability of human conduct and the operational choices which must be made in terms of priorities and resources."[40] In addition to this limitation, there is, as remarked by *Judge Spano* in his separate opinion, the need for the "fight" against domestic violence to be carried out "within the boundaries of the law, not outside them"[41] and therefore in full respect of the rights of the alleged perpetrator (especially Articles 5 and 8 of the Convention).[42]

3.1 Violation of Article 2, Right to Life

When it comes to domestic violence, the right to life, as enshrined in Article 2 ECHR, obviously acquires particularly prominence. While this right is usually identified as protection from unlawful killing by State authorities,[43] in the context of positive obligations, it is configured as protection of the victim from acts perpetrated by third parties and thus in a horizontal and relational perspective.[44] As evidenced by the *Talpis* ruling, for a violation of the right to life to emerge it is not necessary for the conduct of the third party to result in the death of the victim. In this regard, inherently life-endangering actions in the face of which the authorities are called upon to take preventive measures or, *in extremis*, lethal force,[45] are deemed sufficient.[46]

The factors considered by the Court are various. Prominent among them is the fact that the applicant had not been "heard" by the police for seven months from the time of the complaint (June to April).[47] In this context, "by failing to act rapidly after

---

[38] Judge Pinto de Albuquerque's opinion in the *Valiulienė* case, is considered the first formulation of such a test. See Concurring Opinion of Judge Pinto de Albuquerque, *Valiulienė v. Lithuania* (33,234/07), 26.03.2013, p. 31. On this topic, see De Vido (2017a).

[39] This formula was used before in *Osman v. UK*, par. 115. An early prototype of the formula can be found in *Kelly*, where the Court refers to the "obstacles and difficulties" associated with effective investigations. See *Kelly and Others v. UK* (30,054/96), 04.08.2001, paras. 96–98.

[40] *Talpis v. Italy*, par. 101 and *Osman v. UK*, par. 116.

[41] Partly Dissenting Opinion by Judge Spano, *Talpis v. Italy*, par. 15.

[42] *Talpis v. Italy*, par. 101, *Osman v. UK*, par. 116, and *Opuz v. Turkey*, par. 129.

[43] *L.C.B. v. UK* (23,413/94), 09.06.1998, par. 36; *Makaratzis v. Greece* [GC] (50,385/99), 20.12.2004, paras. 49–55.

[44] *L.C.B. v. UK, ibid.*

[45] *Talpis v. Italy*, par. 109.

[46] *Camekan v. Turkey* (54,241/08), 28.01.2014, par. 38, and *Talpis v. Italy*, 110.

[47] *Talpis v. Italy*, par. 114.

the applicant had lodged her complaint, the national authorities deprived the complaint of any effectiveness, creating a situation of impunity conducive to the recurrence of A.T.'s acts of violence against his wife and family."[48] Specifically, at the moment when the risk to the applicant's life had reached its peak, the authorities had failed to intervene, ignoring both the existence of investigations against the offender and the past incidents of violence, thereby giving rise to a form of State co-responsibility.

3.2 *Violation of Article 3, Prohibition of Inhuman or Degrading Treatment*

Equally significant in the context of domestic violence are the obligations deriving from Article 3 ECHR, which prohibits inhuman and degrading treatment. In this perspective, the Court has ruled that "the violent acts perpetrated against the applicant, manifesting themselves in physical injuries and psychological pressure, are sufficiently serious to be classified as ill-treatment within the meaning of Article 3 of the Convention."[49] In this case, unjustified delay in the investigation carried out to ascertain such acts not only diminishes the chances of success, but also risks casting doubt on the good faith of the authorities, to the point where a situation of judicial complacency, and thus co-responsibility, may arise with respect to the suppression of conducts that violate Article 3.

According to the Court, two aspects should be highlighted. First, the protection of victims of domestic violence is brought back to the protection of "vulnerable persons".[50] Article 3, which is also often used with reference to other vulnerable groups, thus serves as a catalyst for the special protection that certain categories require through the prism of human dignity. The second aspect worth noting is the systematic interpretation given by the ECtHR with respect to the State's protection obligations.[51] This, in fact, highlights that, in the case of domestic violence, the need for "diligence" not only "due", but even "special", derives not only from the ECHR and Article 3, but also from the obligations undertaken by States under the Istanbul Convention.[52]

---

[48] See *Kılıç v. Turkey*, par.99.

[49] *Talpis v. Italy*, par.126.

[50] *A. v. UK*, par. 22.

[51] On this topic, see Pitea (2013).

[52] *Talpis v. Italy*, paras. 129–30. On the Istanbul Convention and the relationship with criminal law, see Bonini (2021), Cingari (2021) and Erbaş (2021b). For an analysis of the positive obligations descended from the Istanbul Convention, see Grans (2018).

3.3 Violation of Article 14, Prohibition of Discrimination

A further and final dimension of the analysis concerns the violation of Article 14 of the ECHR.[53] The difference with the examination of violations of Articles 2 and 3, lies in the circumstance that the finding of a violation of the prohibition of discrimination disengages from the facts of the specific case and rather impinges on the entire legislative system of a State in order to assess its possible discriminatory nature against certain groups.

To this end, violations of Articles 2 and 3 may be relevant in the sense of shedding light on systemic deficiencies in the Italian legal system as a whole. In fact, he passivity or complacency of the authorities in a specific case may be symptomatic of a "general and discriminatory judicial passivity"[54] that consequently creates a "climate" that is "conductive to domestic violence."[55] However, in order to prove a systematic discrimination, a procedure of logical inference from the specific case is not sufficient. For these reasons, the examination of Article 14 violations revolves around the ascertainment of data and statistics that demonstrate the inadequacy of the system of protection set up by a State as a whole. In this regard, the Conclusions of the Special Rapporteur on violence against women, its causes and consequences, following his official visit to Italy, those of the CEDAW Committee, and those of the National Statistics Institute have assumed a special relevance in *Talpis*.[56] In this regard, the *prima facie* evidence emerging from the violation of Articles 2 and 3, supported by reliable documents, showed "that domestic violence primarily affects women and that, despite the reforms implemented, a large number of women are murdered by their partners or former partners (femicide) and, secondly, that the socio-cultural attitudes of tolerance of domestic violence persist."[57]

4 Critical Issues in the Court's Examination

4.1 The Excessive Reliance on Measures of a Penal Nature

As mentioned above, when values and rights such as human life and physical and psychological integrity come into play, the protection offered by the ECHR is embodied in obligations of a positive nature. Considering, however, that the protection of the right to life first and foremost consists in the protection against "violent death", criminal law – and, in particular, the norms that criminalize various forms of homicide – is deemed the primary and principal framework for the protection of

---

[53] On the Court's approach to Article 14 of the ECHR, see Fredman (2016).

[54] *Talpis v. Italy*, par. 141; see also *Opuz v. Turkey*, par. 191 ff.

[55] Ibid.

[56] *Talpis v. Italy*, par. 145.

[57] Ibid.

victims.[58] Unsurprisingly, the Court itself aknowledges that an effective protection of the rights covered in the provisions of the ECHR, "may, and under certain circumstances must, include recourse to the criminal law."[59] However, the emphasis consistently placed by the Court on the necessity of an "effective deterrence"[60] reveals that criminal law is regarded not merely as a last resort for extreme cases, but as the *prima ratio* of the legislative intervention.[61] Although this perspective may offer an adequate response in cases involving grave violations of women's right to life and physical integrity, it cannot leave the observer completely satisfied in the context of an effective prevention of such conducts.

Firstly, if we consider criminal law as the *ultima* (or *extrema*) *ratio* of state intervention in the sphere of citizens' freedoms and rights, measures with equal effectiveness that impinge less on them should be favored.[62] This is also because of the necessary orientation of punishment to the promotion of human dignity and thus to the resocialization[63] of the offender and to the principle of proportionality. These principles collide with a perspective hinging only on deterrence (usually in a symbolic and populist manner).[64] Furthermore, as correctly pointed out, criminal sanctions are not only "insufficient in terms of prevention of violence", but also risk becoming "harmful for the victim" in light of "the high risk of secondary victimization during criminal proceedings."[65]

It is true that, also considering the paradoxical relationship between human rights and criminal law[66] – whereas the former can act both as a limit and a *stimulus* for the latter –[67] once human rights such as those enshrined in Articles 2 and 3 ECHR are harmed and violated, criminal law can be configured as the *prima ratio*. Yet, the principle of *ultima ratio* does not entail a wholesale rejection of criminal responses or their complete replacement with civil or administrative remedies. Indeed, in this

---

[58] Schabas (2015), p. 127.

[59] *Railean v. Moldova* (23,401/04), 05.01.2010, par. 27; *Cioban v. Romania* (dec.) (18,295/08), 24.02.2015.

[60] *Öneryıldız v. Turkey* [GC] (48,939/99), 30.11.2004, paras. 89–90; *Krivova v. Ukraine* (25,732/05), 09.11.2010, par. 44.

[61] Erbaş (2020) and Erbaş (2021a, b). For a critique of this trend, see Lazarus (2012), who argues that the rhetoric of "protective duties" often masks the imposition of "coercive duties" on the State, thereby legitimizing an expansion of criminal law without sufficient regard for countervailing rights. See also the contributions in Lavrysen, Mavronicola (2020) and Pinto (2023).

[62] On the topic of criminal law as an *ultima ratio*, albeit in Italian, see Bricola (1997), p. 101 ff.

[63] In this respect, see *Viola v. Italy* (77633/16).

[64] In this regard, see, for example, Husak (2008). See also, with similar conclusions, Cingari (2021) and also Basile (2021), Bertolino (2021) and Vitarelli (2021).

[65] Bonini (2021), p. 81. In this regard, the insufficiency of a prevention based only on criminal sanction seems to be confirmed by the real increase of gender-based crime, despite the introduction of the Red Code (paragraph 5). As concerns the situation in Italy, see Italian Ministry of Internal Affairs (2021).

[66] See Tulkens (2011) and Maugeri (2013).

[67] On the issue, see Erbaş (2021b), p. 227 and, as cited by the Author, Roxin, Greco (2020) and Tulkens (2011).

sense, the risk of underuse of criminal law would indeed be at least as great as that of its overuse.[68] On the contrary, the principle of the *ultima ratio* demands that before resorting to criminal sanction and prior to the materialization of harm, the State must take all measures at its disposal to prevent such harm through the adoption of economic, social and cultural measures. Indeed, the recourse to criminal sanctions implies, *per se*, the failure – and thus a form of co-responsibility – of the State to protect potential victims of violence, since criminal protection can be activated, beyond deterrence, only once the violation to the victim's rights actually occurs.

Finally, it bears noting that it is one thing to argue that the State is called upon to supplement the criminal protection of human rights with non-criminal measures, and another to dwell on the serious procedural deficiencies in the effective investigation and prosecution of human rights violations.[69]

4.2 By Contrast: The Lack of Emphasis on Obligations Pertaining to the Economic and Social Spheres

In light of the foregoing, it may be suggested that the answer to effective prevention should not be found primarily in the area of criminal law and criminal procedural law, but rather in a different sphere of action[70] through "a complex of normative responses"[71] consisting, for instance, in strong investments in socio-economic and, therefore, welfare measures.[72] This perspective, which promotes a minimalistic approach to criminal law,[73] implies that criminalization should be seen as the "last resort"[74] and that other fields of law and forms of social control should take precedence over it.[75] In fact, violence against women is only the "tip of the iceberg".

[68] Erbaş (2021b), p. 230.

[69] Erbaş (2021b), p. 239; see also Bonini (2021), p. 80.

[70] On this point, Bricola's reflections are particularly useful. See Bricola (1997), p. 101 ff.

[71] See Cavaliere (2018), p. 15. This approach is also known, in Italy, as "positive garantism".

[72] On this point see, as cited by Buscemi (2017), *Integration of the Human Rights of Women and the Gender Perspective: Violence against Women*, paras. 15 and 47. Similarly, Concurring Opinion of Judge Pinto de Albuquerque, *Valiulienė v. Lithuania*, p. 28.

[73] The idea of a "minimum criminal law" is found, in Italian doctrine, in the work of Ferrajoli and Baratta (where the concept is built on criminology), and from a comparative point of view, in Ashworth. See Ashworth (1995), p. 33, Baratta (1986), p. 443 ff., Baratta (1998), p. 24 ff, Baratta (2004), pp. 35–36, Ferrajoli (2011) and Ferrajoli (2014), p. 129 f. See also Cavaliere (2018), p.1 ff. For a reference in the context of domestic violence, see Karsai (2013), p. 53 ff. In the context of organized crime, see Moccia (1999), pp. 153 and 173. In the context of corporate wrongdoing, see Ashworth (2013), pp. 23–24.

[74] Jareborg (2004), pp. 524–526.

[75] Ashworth (1995), p. 33.

Before getting to the tip, gender stereotypes, hierarchization and discrimination against women in all fields of life should be addressed.[76]

As mentioned earlier, cultural and socio-economic measures such as the allocation of adequate funds for shelters can prove of paramount importance in ensuring the protection of victims of domestic violence.[77] In particular, the latter aspect was crucialin *Talpis* since the victim had initially found temporary shelter through an NGO. As previously noted, despite this first moment of protective relief, thehe municipality of *Udine* soon informed the applicant that it lacked the resources either to provide alternative accommodation or to continue covering the costs of the shelter arranged by the NGO. Both the Court and dissenting opinions are silent on the issue, despite the obligation under the Istanbul Convention to "support at all levels, the work of relevant non-governmental organizations and of civil society active in combating violence against women."[78]

In the same preventive vein, socio-economic measures should also address individuals at "risk" of becoming perpetrators of such violence, for instance by investing in initiatives aimed at protecting mental health both in the context of a relationship and in, for example, the workplace where frustration can arise and subsequently spill over into the family environment. Further, given the dismal association between violence and alcohol and drug abuse, investments in support and rehabilitation programs might be required.[79] Nor should the impact of additional factors, ranging from the low education attainment and economic hardship experienced by perpetrators, the exposure, even during adolescence, to violence in the domestic context, and the persistence of gender-inequitable social norms – especially those that associate notions of manhood to dominance and aggression – be underestimated.

An integrated socio-economic perspective is all the more necessary if one considers that the group labelled as "women" does not constitute a monolithic category and it is therefore possible that vulnerabilities linked to gender constructs are compounded by other forms of intersectional discrimination which are often connected to social and economic factors.[80] In this sense, for instance, it has been argued that economically or socially disadvantaged women face a more complex and difficult path out of violence.[81]

---

76 For a discussion on this model, see Henn (2019), p. 23 ff.

77 See, for instance, CEDAW Committee (2017a), par. 32(1)(iii); CEDAW Committee (2017b), par. 28; Special Rapporteur on Violence Against Women (2012), paras. 90–94; and Di.Re (2018).

78 Article 9 of the Convention. See De Vido (2017a), p. 14. On this point see also Buscemi (2017).

79 WHO (2012).

80 For a thorough analysis, please see Lorenzetti (2021), p. 57 ff. The Author also emphasizes the importance of a correct conceptualization of the very notions of vulnerability, marginality, weakness and minority.

81 Pellizzone (2021), p. 50.

Along similar lines, it is worth noting that such vulnerabilities have been exacerbated by the Covid-19 Pandemic and the subsequent economic crisis.[82] In greater detail, during the Pandemic the constant cohabitation with perpetrators of violence turned homes into prisons and drastically decreased recourse to the competent authorities.[83] The very call to "stay at home" made it clear how social and economic conditions can make confinement ineffective or, in the case of domestic violence, even dangerous.[84] In this particular context, "the simultaneous action of several conditions of marginality has in fact shaped unprecedented forms of vulnerability".[85]

4.3 *The ECtHR Approach on Socio-Economic Rights: A Possible Evolutionary Interpretation*

The incorporation of socio-economic and cultural measures into the positive obligations of States, with a view to addressing the root causes of domestic violence, does not appear to be inherently irreconcilable with the nature of the ECHR as an instrument for the protection of civil and political rights. As mentioned, the subject of positive obligations is the result of ECtHR case law and is constantly evolving. Likewise, while the ECHR has, traditionally, been regarded as an instrument inherent, primarily, to civil and political rights of the individual,[86] the ECtHR, since *Airey v. Ireland* and *Marckkx v. Belgium,* has increasingly tended towards the recognition of certain socio-economic rights.[87] From this viewpoint, Article 3 plays an essential role. Through the prism of human dignity,[88] it can serve as a catalyst for an evolutionary interpretation of the Convention[89] that considers the rights of the individual as indivisible.[90] Such indivisibility also emerges from the jurisprudence of the ECtHR, which considers indifference on the part of authorities[91] as an essential

[82] Pellizzone (2021), pp. 46–47 and Lorenzetti (2021), p. 57 ff. See also D'Amico (2020b) and D'Amico (2020c).

[83] Pellizzone (2021).

[84] Lorenzetti (2021), pp. 58–59.

[85] See Ibid., p. 57. The translation was made by the Author.

[86] *Airey v. Ireland*, par. 26.

[87] Ibid., and *Marckx v. Belgium*. See Leijten (2018); see also Scheinin (2011). For critical views on this trend, see for example, Judge Sajò's partially concurring and partially dissenting opinion, *M.S.S. v. Belgium and Greece* [GC] (30,696/09), 21.01.2011, par. 103. See also *D.H. and Others v. the Czech Republic* [GC] (57,325/00), 13.11.2007, and *Horváth and Kiss v. Hungary* (11,146/11), 29.01.2013, reported by Buscemi (2017)

[88] O'Cinneide (2020).

[89] Prebensen (2000).

[90] According to O' Cinneide, *N v. UK* demonstrates a formal adherence to the universalist approach to social and economic rights. O'Cinneide (2020), p. 57.

[91] *M.S.S. v. Belgium and Greece* (GC), par. 263.

step in the finding of socio-economic obligations,[92] thereby contributing to bridging the gap between the two spheres of state intervention.

The principle of the indivisibility of rights becomes even more significant when the ECHR is read systematically together with its counterpart in the sphere of socio-economic rights, the European Social Charter ("ESC").[93] In this regard, the conclusion of the European Committee of Social Rights in *FIDH v. France*, is of pivotal importance: "due to their universality, indivisibility, interdependence and interrelation, the rights enshrined in the ESC are to be considered connected to the right to life."[94] In the same sense and in addition to Article 3, the right to life (Article 2 ECHR) can also be understood to give rise to a borader set of positive obligations especially when read in relation to the obligations that flow from the ESC. Similarly, many other rights, such as the right to respect for private and family life, could support such an expansion.

A similar outcome may also derive from the identification of victims of violence as a "particularly underprivileged and vulnerable population group in need of a special protection."[95] , This would, in turn, activate the additional safeguard offered by the prohibition of non-discrimination under Article 14 ECHR, which is being increasingly relied upon to argue for the existence of positive obligations[96] and, at times, even obligations in the socio-economic sphere.[97] Indeed, the prohibition allows – in a trend that is increasingly present in the Court's pronouncements – to bring to the attention of States a notion of equality (non-discrimination) that is not only formal but also substantive, one that duly takes account of the social context and the relationships that form its bedrock.[98] Against this background, the relevance accorded in *Talpis* to the possibility of even indirect, unintentional violations of the prohibition, namely practices that disproportionately and negatively affect a certain group, is significant as it hints at the recognition of deeper structural and systemic inequalities which, even when covert or indirect, lie at the root of discriminatory patterns.[99]

Despite these tentative openings, the Court's jurisprudence still demonstrates a self-restraining, particularly deferential attitude toward States in this field.[100] Budgetary and political interests have crystallized the sphere of socio-economic adjudication as still deeply anchored in the full sovereignty of the latter.[101] In

---

[92] Leijten (2018).

[93] Khaliq, Churchill (2008). On this issue, see also Cama (2021).

[94] *International Federation of Human Rights Leagues (FIDH) v. France*, Complaint No. 14/2003, European Committee of Social Rights. See Georgopoulou et al. (2018).

[95] On the subject of migrants, see *M.S.S. V. Belgium and Greece*, par. 215.

[96] Salerno (2016).

[97] *D.H. and Others v. the Czech Republic* and *Horváth and Kiss v. Hungary*.

[98] See Arnardóttir (2014) and Fredman (2016).

[99] Buscemi (2017).

[100] Clements, Simmons (2008), p. 418.

[101] Bossuyt (2012), pp. 232–233. See also Mantouvalou (2011), pp. 85–171.

contrast, it should also be emphasized that, with reference to social welfare services, the CEDAW Committee has reminded that the failure to provide such services cannot be justified solely on the basis of financial contingencies.[102] In line with this broader perspective, further guidance may also be drawn from the Istanbul Convention (and the other relevant international instruments, see paragraph 2), which, within the framework of its four pillars (prevention, protection, prosecution and coordinated policies), places a marked emphasis on measures that go beyond criminal repression at the substantive and procedural levels.

5 The Relationship Between the Notion of Vulnerable Group and the Prohibition of Discrimination

As a further piece of this evolving mosaic, *Talpis* is particularly relevant in identifying victims of domestic violence as a category of "vulnerable persons" deserving of "special protection". In this respect, it bears noting that the vulnerability of a given group also and above all emerges from the systemic discrimination of that group, whether intentional or, more frequently, unintentional, by a given legal system. In this sense, the relationship between the positive obligations flowing from Articles 2 and 3 of the Convention and those flowing from the prohibition of discrimination is bidirectional insofar as violations of the former may also serve as a basis for establishing a violation of the latter. On a more general level, it can, in fact, be observed that "on the one hand, gender-discrimination facilitates gender-based violence. On the other hand, gender discrimination is reinforced by gender-based violence."[103] In light of this, a particular link emerges between the notion of vulnerability and the prohibition of discrimination in Article 14 of the Convention, since "an individual's situation of particular frailty is in fact often the result of discriminatory practices that affect a certain social group that is the bearer of special needs."[104]

Building on this connection, the notion of vulnerability has come to occupy an increasingly prominent place in the Court's jurisprudence.[105] This, as noted,[106] results in the imposition of more intense obligations of protection on States and diminishes the so-called margin of appreciation.[107] It has also been argued that the case law of the ECtHR shows that when "persistent forms of stereotyping, prejudice and/or stigma, which results in social marginalization," are involved, the Court's

[102] Buscemi (2017) and CEDAW Committee (2017b), par. 9.

[103] Tiroch (2010), p. 398, the quote is reported by Buscemi (2017). In the same vein, see also Concurring Opinion of Judge Judge Pinto de Albuquerque, *Valiulienė v. Lithuania*, p. 31.

[104] Buscemi (2017), p. 10.

[105] Timmer (2016), pp. 145 and 169–70. Please refer to Arnardóttir (2014) for a comprehensive analysis of the case law. See also Buscemi (2017).

[106] Buscemi (2017).

[107] On the notion of vulnerability see Peroni, Timmer (2013), pp. 1056–1085 and Zimmermann (2015), pp. 539–562.

analysis “should be conscious of how structural patterns of social disadvantage and exclusion function to keep marginalized groups in the margins” and that therefore “the object and purpose of eliminating such structures, or at least minimizing their effect on individuals.”[108]

Finally, in the same vein, it may be suggested that in situations of double or multiple marginality (see paragraph 4.2), where several competing and overlapping factors of vulnerability converge, the corresponding obligations should become even more stringent.

6 Recent Developments in the Italian Legislative Framework

In 2019, approximately 2 years after *Talpis*, the Italian Legislature enacted the so-called Red Code.[109] The legislation primarily focused on criminal measures, introducing new crimes in the context of domestic violence and enhancing penalties for existing ones. It is also noteworthy that the Red Code introduced procedural innovations with the aim of facilitating the intervention of public authorities, and in particular prosecutors, in a more expeditious manner. According to the Code, upon acquiring the report of the crime, the judicial police are required to immediately refer it to the prosecutor, even orally. The prosecutor is then obliged to obtain information from the aggrieved party or the individual who reported the crime within 3 days of the crime report being entered. These measures can be considered, at least in part, intended to address the issue of delayed responsiveness by authorities, as highlighted in the *Talpis* case.

Furthermore, in response to the *impetus* provided by tragic news events and the alarming number of ‘femicides’ in Italy, on 24 November 2023, almost precisely 10 years after the events of *Talpis*, the Italian Legislature adopted Law No. 168 of 2023, which enacted further provisions for combating violence against women and domestic violence. Key innovations include expanding the crime of violating restraining orders to encompass breaches of civil protection orders, introducing deferred arrest *in flagrante delicto* for domestic violence and stalking, allowing public prosecutors to urgently remove individuals from the family home even outside cases of *flagrante delicto*, and broadening the range of individuals subject to preventive measures under Legislative Decree No. 159 of 2011.

In the middle, The so-called “Cartabia Reform”[110] also introduced some relevant changes, such as excluding crimes under the Istanbul Convention from the application of non-punishability for particularly minor offences. The reform also controversially expanded the requirement for a victim’s complaint to prosecute various crimes in this area and failed to coordinate new alternative sentences with recent

[108] Arnardóttir (2014), pp. 664–665.

[109] Law No. 69 of 19 July 2019.

[110] Law Decree No. 149 and 150 of 10 October 2022.

rules requiring participation in programs for abusers as a precondition for benefits, seemingly prioritizing the goal of reducing criminal justice times over some previous value choices in combating gender-based violence.[111] The same reform also and notably introduced measures to avoid secondary victimization in civil cases.

With regard to measures that are not strictly criminal in nature, some positive developments must be taken into account, such as the 017–2020 and 2021–2023 Plans[112] about the allocation of funds specifically dedicated to issues related to gender violence, awareness-raising campaigns, and the implementation of the important National Guidelines "Educating for Respect: for gender equality, prevention of gender-based violence and all forms of discrimination" (dating back to 2015) to be adopted in schools. In addition, the Red Code itself provides for mandatory training courses for authorities and the possibility that a person convicted of one of the crimes be placed on probation in therapeutic paths to be carried out with NGOs in the field. Mention should also be made of Law No. 53 of 5 May 2022, which seeks to regulate the collection of data and information on gender-based violence against women, with the objective of effectively monitoring the phenomenon and developing appropriate prevention and counteraction policies.

Most notably, in response to the global pandemic, the Prime Minister at the time introduced the 'freedom income' scheme. It consists of a monthly allowance, which can be combined with other forms of financial assistance, designed to support women who have experienced violence. The allowance is intended to provide a minimum of 400 euros per month for a maximum period of 1 year. The beneficiaries are women with minor children or without children, followed by an officially recognized anti-violence center and in economic need. Recently, the measure has been secured by the allocation of funds until 2026. This economic measure, although open to improvement and provided it is maintained and strengthened, is to be cautiously applauded as a means of bolstering independence from the economic vulnerabilities that contribute to the perpetuation of domestic violence.

Despite these improvements, as pointed out by the shadow report and communications prepared by Di.Re,[113] with reference to these aspects, as well as many others, there are still many shortcomings. These include the lack of involvement of NGOs in policy-making, the insufficient allocation of funds (including those directed to shelters and anti-violence centers), the absence of adequate monitoring and accountability mechanisms regarding the allocation of these funds, the insufficient aggregation of real data, and the failure to include assessments pertaining to women with disabilities or to assess the additional vulnerability experienced by these and migrant women. The GREVIO report itself recommends, at present, the

[111] For an assessment of the impact of the Reform, see Dova (2024).

[112] The "National Strategic Plan against Male Violence against Women" defines the overall strategy to implement the Istanbul Convention through a shared pathway between all institutional and non-institutional actors. Pending the adoption of the 2025–2027 plan, the 2021–2023 plan has been extended.

[113] Di.Re (2018, 2023, 2024). See also the Report by "Italian civil society organizations for CEDAW" of January 2024.

adoption of complementary measures.[114] This report is still particularly important because it emphasizes that "the full realization of due diligence standard depends on investing equally in the necessary prevention, investigation, punishment, reparation, and protection […] starting with the transformation of patriarchal gender structures and values that perpetuate and root violence against women".[115]

In this context, as a provisional assessment, it may be argued that, in light of the shortcomings highlighted, not least by GREVIO, the obligations stemming from the Istanbul Convention offered the ECtHR – especially from the perspective of a systematic and integrated interpretation of the rights enshrined in the ECHR that also accords due weight to other international sources – the opportunity to place greater emphasis on measures pertaining to the social, economic and cultural spheres. In this respect, while a self-restraining approach may be understandable from the perspective of avoiding the jurisprudential creation of additional burdens on States with reference to Articles 2, 3 and 14, in this case, the existence of the *ad hoc* Convention and specific obligations on States could have justified a greater emphasis on obligations pertaining to the socio-economic sphere. On the other hand, what emerges — particularly from the most recent measures adopted in Italy — is still an excessive reliance on criminal repression,[116] driven by penal populism and resulting in over-criminalization, both through the introduction of new criminal offences and a tightening of the sanctions already provided for in a perspective of pure and symbolic "deterrence", which is—as said—incompatible with a criminal law understood as an *ultima ratio*, with the principle of resocialization of the convict and with the principle of proportionality in all its dimensions.[117]

Similarly, although the Red Code has indeed provided for new forms of training for the Italian authorities, the allocation of funds for this purpose appears inadequate.[118] This shows that, even in the criminal repression realm, the core issue is the absence of sufficient resources (and therefore economic measures) to support effective investigations by the authorities.

In spite of these critical issues, the ECtHR, which was called upon to rule again on the subject in *Landi* and *M.S.*,[119] notes that "since 2017 and the adoption of the aforementioned *Talpis* judgment, Italy has taken steps to implement the Istanbul Convention, thus demonstrating its genuine political will to prevent and combat violence against women."[120] According to the Court, the reforms implemented since 2008, have, in fact, created "a broad set of rules and mechanisms to strengthen the ability of authorities to match their intentions with concrete actions to end

[114] GREVIO (2020)

[115] Kuş (2021), p. 216.

[116] Bonini (2021), p. 80.

[117] Cingari (2021), p. 94.

[118] Cingari (2021), p. 97. See also Basile (2021), p. 13 and Bertolino (2021), p. 69.

[119] The translation of the reported passages of the judgments was made by the Author.

[120] *Landi v. Italy*, par. 103 and *M.S. v. Italy*, par. 160.

violence."[121] Despite these improvements, however, the Court finds a violation of Articles 2 and 3 of the Convention. Similar conclusions are also reached in *De Giorgi*[122] and *Scavone*.[123] Overall, the aforementioned pronouncements, the multitude of additional legislative measures, and the alarming statistics on gender-based violence in Italy collectively demonstrate the persistent presence of structural deficiencies and systemic criticalities within the Italian framework.

Instead of seeking to remedy these deficiencies, the described over-criminalizing trend peaked with the recent Senate's approval of a bill (23 July 2025) establishing the autonomous offence of femicide (DDL No. 1433 on the "introduction of the offence of femicide and other legislative measures to combat violence against women and to protect victims"). Far from addressing the problem's social and cultural roots, the new provision doubles down on an over-criminalizing strategy, raising serious constitutional challenges to the principles — among others — of rehabilitation and equality while entrenching the system's punitive nature by extending a web of aggravating circumstances to other offences.

It should finally be noted that the European Commission adopted a new Strategy on victims' rights (2020–2025).[124] Although the strategy will have to be re-evaluated in the future, some innovations are worth mentioning. These include the plan to implement awareness-raising campaigns on domestic violence victims' rights, the provision of safe places for victims, and, above all, the intention to finance, through the new multiannual financial framework for 2021–2027, victim support organizations for the implementation of EU rules, and the integration of victims' rights measures in the context of EU funding programmes for safety, health, and education. Within this framework, particular consideration must also be given to the EU's landmark Directive (2024/1385) on combating violence against women, which should serve as a key reference point for reassessing the adequacy of Italy's predominantly criminal-law oriented approach.[125]

While these developments demonstrate a certain *impetus* to address the problem of domestic and gender-based violence, in summary, it may be concluded that the goal of effective equality still seems far from full realization, which would require structural interventions in the social fabric and continued economic support for anti-violence centers.[126]

---

[121] *M.S. v. Italy*, par. 160.

[122] *De Giorgi v. Italy* (23,735/19), 16.06.2022.

[123] *Scavone v. Italy* (32,715/19), 07.07.2022.

[124] European Commission (2020).

[125] For a thorough analysis of the last developments in the Italian framework, please refer to Fiano (2023), pp. 30–59.

[126] See Ibid. pp. 56–59.

7 Conclusions

The *Talpis* case has provided an opportunity to analyze some of the recurrent issues that authorities and courts, and first and foremost women, face in the context of domestic violence. These issues, according to the Court's analysis in the most recent cases concerning Italy, have been solved thanks to the intervention of the Italian legislator and the so-called Red Code. Yet, statistics and facts show that, despite the introduction of new criminal measures, very limited progress has been made.

In light of the aforementioned considerations, it may be appropriate to question the necessity for a change of perspective on the part of the Court in its theorization of positive obligations. Such a transition should be achieved, first and foremost, through the proper realization of the principle of *ultima ratio*. As explained, an accurate interpretation of this principle requires a shift in focus from criminal repression and prevention through criminalization to positive general prevention on the part of both the ECtHR and the Italian legislature and government. At the same time, an effective prevention should imply the enhancement of economic, social and cultural measures aimed at solving the problem of domestic violence at its roots, thus preventing the script read in *Talpis* from being recited again and again.

Prospective studies should therefore address how, in the realm of criminal law, the need not to overburden State finances can be combined with an effective prevention of conduct detrimental to the rights to life, physical and mental integrity. In fact, as this chapter attempted to explain, the refrain from imposing obligations on States in the socio-economic sphere is not an immutable or incontrovertible solution according to the ECHR. In this sense, the Court's typical deferential attitude on this point could be overcome, by enhancing: (a) the jurisprudence of the ESCR concerning the interconnection between (and indivisibility of) civil and political and socio-economic rights; (b) the notion of vulnerability of a given group with a view to granting it stronger protection thanks to the imposition of more intense obligations on States especially in cases of intersectional discrimination; (c) the implementation of the numerous socio-economic and cultural obligations contained in the Istanbul Convention, in the light of a systematic interpretation, that has already proven to be of particular value to the Court in the criminal law realm; (d) the emphasis placed by GREVIO on the need to invest in prevention with the aim of cutting the cultural and social roots of domestic violence and, thus, fully realize the due diligence standard.

Among these possibilities, particular emphasis should be placed on the implications of recognizing the vulnerability of a particular group and the possible role that the principle of human dignity, which permeates the entire text of the ECHR, could assume in a real expansion of the individual's guarantees. It should not be forgotten, in fact, that whenever criminalization is chosen in place of structural solutions, not only is there a potential cost lying in the sacrifice of the alleged perpetrators' rights, but, above all, the State abdicates, *in apicibus*, its duty and (co)responsibility to protect victims by conceding that it can only intervene after their rights have been harmed and thus violated.

A further question that deserves attention in the future is whether such an approach can be espoused not only with reference to domestic violence, where the presence of an instrument such as the Istanbul Convention gives it a stronger foothold, but more generally with reference to criminal law obligations with regard to any form of offence that interferes with the rights enshrined in the ECHR.

References

Akandji-Kombe J (2007) Positive obligations under the European convention on human rights. A guide to the implementation of the European convention on human rights. In: Akandji-Kombe J (ed) Human rights handbooks no. 7. UNHCR, Geneva

Arnardóttir OM (2014) The differences that make a difference: recent developments on the discrimination grounds and the margin of appreciation under article 14 of the European convention on human rights. Hum Rights Law Rev:647–670

Ashworth A (1995) Principles of criminal law. Clarendon law series. Oxford University Press, Oxford

Ashworth A (2013) Positive obligations in criminal law. Hart Publishing Limited, Oxford

Baratta A (1986) Il diritto penale minimo. La questione criminale tra riduzionismo e abolizionismo. ESI, Napoli

Baratta A (1998) La politica criminale e il diritto penale della Costituzione. Nuove riflessioni sul modello integrato delle scienze penali. In: Canestrari S (ed) Il diritto penale alla svolta di fine millennio. Giappichelli, Torino

Baratta A (2004) Il Corpus Juris e la cultura giuridico-penale europea. In: Moccia S (ed) Ambito e prospettive di uno spazio giuridico-penale europeo. ESI, Napoli

Basile F (2021) La tutela delle donne dalla violenza dell'uomo: dal Codice Rocco... al Codice Rosso. Diritto Penale e Uomo

Bertolino M (2021) La violenza di genere e sui minori tra vittimologia e vittimismo: notazioni brevi. Diritto Penale Contemporaneo

Bonini V (2021) The Istanbul convention's values and its implementation in Italy. In: Bonini V, Erbaş R (eds) The 10th anniversary of the Istanbul convention. Italian—Turkish conference Pisa, 18th June 2021. Pisa University Press, Pisa, pp 69–84

Bossuyt M (2012) The court of Strasbourg acting as an asylum court. Eur Const Law Rev:203–245

Bricola F (1997) Politica criminale e scienza del diritto penale. Il Mulino, Bologna

Buscemi M (2017) La protezione delle vittime di violenza domestica davanti alla Corte europea dei diritti dell'uomo. Alcune osservazioni a margine del caso Talpis c. Italia. Osservatorio sulle fonti

Cama V (2021) The phenomenon of Caporalato in the context of the Covid-19 pandemic. In: Staiano F, Ciliberto G (eds) Labour migration in time of Covid-19: inequalities and perspectives for change. CNR Editore, Roma

Cavaliere A (2018) Il diritto penale minimo in Alessandro Baratta: per un'alternativa alla "cultura del penale". Archivio Penale

CEDAW Committee (2017a) General recommendation No. 35 on gender-based violence against women. Available via https://www.ohchr.org/en/documents/general-comments-and-recommendations/general-recommendation-no-35-2017-gender-based

CEDAW Committee (2017b) Concluding Observations on the Seventh Periodic Report of Italy. https://www.ohchr.org/en/documents/concluding-observations/cedawcitaco7-concluding-observations-seventh-periodic-report

Cingari F (2021) Criminal law and contrast to violence against women. In: Bonini V, Erbaş R (eds) The 10th anniversary of the Istanbul convention. Italian—Turkish conference Pisa, 18th June 2021. Pisa University Press, Pisa, pp 85–100

Clapham A (1993) The "drittwirkung" of the convention. In: Macdonald R, Matscher F, Petzold H (eds) The European system for the protection of human rights. Nijhoff, Dordrecht

Clements L, Simmons A (2008) European court of human rights: sympathetic unease. In: Langford M (ed) Social rights jurisprudence: emerging trends in international and comparative law. Cambridge University Press, Cambridge, pp 409–427

D'Amico M (2020a) Una parità ambigua. Costituzione e diritti delle donne. Raffaello Cortina, Milano

D'Amico M (2020b) Emergenza, diritti, discriminazioni. Rivista del Gruppo di Pisa:16–42

D'Amico M (2020c) I diritti fondamentali alla prova dell'emergenza sanitaria da Coronavirus: prifli costituzionali. BioLaw Journal Rivista di BioDiritto:31–52

De Vido S (2017a) States' Positive Obligations to Eradicate Domestic Violence: The Politics of Relevance in the Interpretation of the European Convention on Human Rights, ESIL Reflection

De Vido S (2017b) The ECtHR Talpis v. Italy Judgment. Challenging the Osman Test through the Council of Europe Istanbul Convention?. Ricerche Giuridiche. Edizioni Ca' Foscari, Venice

Di.Re (2018) Shadow report, Implementation of the Istanbul Convention in Italy: Report of Women's NGOs. https://www.direcontrolaviolenza.it/wp-content/uploads/2018/11/GREVIO.Report-inglese-finale.pdf

Di.Re (2023) Communication by Di.Re on the group of cases: Talpis v. Italy application n. 41237/14 and J.L. v. Italy application n. 5671/16. https://www.direcontrolaviolenza.it/wp-content/uploads/2023/11/31.07.2023_Talpis-group-and-J.L.-v.-Italy-by-D.i.Re_.pdf

Di.Re (2024) Osservazioni conclusive sull'ottavo rapporto periodico dell'Italia. https://www.direcontrolaviolenza.it/wp-content/uploads/2024/02/CEDAW_C_ITA_CO_8_57560_E_-ITA.pdf

Dova M (2024) La riforma Cartabia e il contrasto alla violenza contro le donne. Sistema penale

Ebert FC, Sijniensky RI (2015) Preventing violations of the right to life in the European and the inter-American human rights systems: from the Osman test to a coherent doctrine on risk prevention? Hum Rights Law Rev:343–368

Erbaş R (2020) Effective criminal investigations in combating domestic violence and the ECtHR: *prima ratio* v. *ultima ratio*? In: Stradella E (ed) Gender based approaches to the law and juris dictio in Europe. Pisa University Press, Pisa, pp 221–240

Erbaş R (2021a) Effective criminal investigations for women victims of domestic violence: the approach of the ECtHR. Women's Stud Int Forum 86:1–12

Erbaş R (2021b) Evidentiary challenges to an effective criminal investigation for domestic violence: an introduction. In: Bonini V, Erbaş R (eds) The 10th anniversary of the Istanbul convention. Italian—Turkish conference Pisa, 18th June 2021. Pisa University Press, Pisa, pp 101–118

European Commission (2020) EU Strategy on victims' rights (2020–2025). https://eur-lex.europa.eu/legal-content/EN/TXT/?uri=CELEX%3A52020DC0258

Ferrajoli L (2011) Diritto e ragione : teoria del garantismo penale. Laterza, Roma

Ferrajoli L (2014) Cos'è il garantismo? Crim:129–141

Fiano N (2023) Le recenti novità in tema di protezione delle donne vittime di violenza. Un'analisi alla luce del diritto costituzionale. Federalismi:30–59

Fredman S (2016) Emerging from the shadows: substantive equality and article 14 of the European convention on human rights. Hum Rights Law Rev:273–301

Georgopoulou A, Schrempf TA, Venturi D (2018) Putting things into perspective: the added value of the ICRMWs substantive provisions. In: Desmond A (ed) Shining new light on the UN migrant workers convention. Pretoria University Law Press, Pretoria, pp 129–150

Grans L (2018) The Istanbul convention and the positive obligation to prevent violence. Hum Rights Law Rev:133–155

GREVIO (2020) Baseline Evaluation Report: Italy. https://rm.coe.int/grevio-report-italy-first-baseline-evaluation/168099724e

Henn EV (2019) International human rights law and structural discrimination. Springer, Berlin

Husak DN (2008) Overcriminalization: the limits of the criminal law. Oxford University Press, New York

Italian Ministry of Internal Affairs (2021) Dossier Viminale. Un anno di attività del Ministero dell'Interno. https://www.interno.gov.it/it/dossier-viminale-2021-anno-attivita-ministero-dellinterno

Jareborg N (2004) Criminalization as last resort (ultima ratio). Ohio State J Criminal Law 2:521–534

Kamber K (2020) Substantive and procedural criminal law protection of human rights in the law of the European convention on human rights. Hum Rights Law Rev:75–100

Karsai K (2013) Ultima ratio and subsidiarity in the European criminal law. Forum: Acta Juridica et politica 3:53–63

Khaliq U, Churchill RR (2008) The European Committee of Social Rights Putting Flesh on the bare bones of the European social charter. In: Langford M (ed) Social rights jurisprudence: emerging trends in international and comparative law. Cambridge University Press, Cambridge, pp 428–452

Klatt M (2011) Positive obligations under the European convention on human rights. Heidelberg Journal of International Law:691–718

Kuş (2021) The due diligence standard and combating violence against women. In: Bonini V, Erbaş R (eds) The 10th anniversary of the Istanbul convention. Italian—Turkish conference Pisa, 18th June 2021. Pisa University Press, Pisa, pp 205–220

Lavrysen L, Mavronicola N (2020) Coercive Human Rights: positive duties to mobilise the criminal law under the ECHR. Hart Publishing, Oxford

Lazarus L (2012) Positive obligations and criminal justice: duties to protect or coerce? In: Zedner L, Roberts J (eds) Principles and values in criminal law and criminal justice: essays in honour of Andrew Ashworth. Oxford University Press, Oxford, pp 135–156

Leijten I (2018) Core socio-economic rights and the European court of human rights. Cambridge University Press, Cambridge

Lemmens K (2018) Chapter I—general survey of the convention. In: Van Dijk P, Van Hoof F, Van Rijn A, Zwaak L (eds) Theory and practice of the European convention on human rights. Intersentia, Cambridge, pp 1–78

Londono P (2009) Developing human rights principles in cases of gender-based violence: Opuz v Turkey in the European court of human rights. Hum Rights Law Rev:657–667

Lorenzetti A (2021) Genere e condizioni di vulnerabilità nell'emergenza: l'inesorabile emersione di una doppia marginalità. In: Catelani E, D'Amico M (eds) Effetto Covid. Donne: la doppia discriminazione. Il Mulino, Bologna, pp 57–71

Lorenzetti A, Pezzini B (2020) La violenza di genere dal codice rosso al codice Rocco. Un itinerario di riflessione plurale attraverso la complessità del fenomeno. Giappichelli, Torino

Mantouvalou V (2011) In support of legalisation. In: Gearty CA, Mantouvalou V (eds) Debating social rights, 1st edn. Zed Books, London, pp 85–169

Maugeri AM (2013) Fundamental rights in the European legal order both as a limit on punitive power and as a source of positive obligations to criminalise. New J Eur Criminal Law:374–408

Moccia S (1999) Criminalità organizzata e risposte ordinamenti : tra efficienza e garanzia. ESI, Napoli

Montagna M (2019) Obblighi convenzionali, tutela della vittima e completezza delle indagini. Archivio penale

Mowbray A (2004) The development of positive obligations under the European convention on human rights by the European court of human rights. Bloomsbury, Oxford

O'Cinneide C (2020) Migrants with irregular status in Europe: Evolving conceptual and policy challenges. In: Spencer S, Triandafyllidou A (eds) Migrants with irregular status in Europe evolving conceptual and policy challenges. Springer International Publishing, Cham, pp 51–71

Pellizzone I (2021) La violenza: impatto delle misure restrittive sulle donne e sui minori in una prospettiva di diritto costituzionale. In: Catelani E, D'Amico M (eds) Effetto Covid. Donne: la doppia discriminazione. Il Mulino, Bologna, pp 45–56

Peroni L, Timmer A (2013) Vulnerable groups: the promise of an emerging concept in European human rights convention law. Int J Const Law:1056–1085

Pinto M (2023) Coercive human rights and the forgotten history of the Council of Europe's Report on Decrminalisation. Mod L Rev:1108–1133

Pitea C (2013) Interpreting the ECHR in the light of "other" international instruments: systemic integration or fragmentation of the rules on treaty interpretation? In: Boschiero N, Scovazzi T, Ragni C, Pitea C (eds) International courts and the development of international law. Essays in honour of Tullio Treves. Springer, The Hague, pp 545–559

Prebensen S (2000) Evolutive interpretation of the European convention on human rights. In: Ryssdal MP (ed) Protection des droits De L'homme: La perspective Européenne: mélanges À La Mémoire De Rolv Ryssdal = protecting human rights: the European perspective: studies in memory of Rolv Ryssdal. C. Heymann, Köln, pp 1123–1137

Roxin C, Greco L (2020) Strafrecht Allgemeiner Teil Band 1: Grundlagen. Der Aufbau Der Verbrechenslehre. 5. Auflage. C.H. Beck, München

Salerno ME (2016) To what extent has the construction of article 14 ECHR evolved from a 'negative' to a 'positive' right? Giurisprudenza Penale Web

Schabas W (2015) The European convention on human rights. A commentary. Oxford University Press, Oxford

Scheinin M (2011) Economic and social right as legal rights. In: Eide AC, Krause C, Rosas A (eds) Economic social and cultural rights: a textbook second revised edition, 2nd edn. Martinus Nijhoff, Dordrecht, pp 29–54

Special Rapporteur on Violence Against Women (2012) Report on Italy. https://www.ohchr.org/sites/default/files/Documents/HRBodies/HRCouncil/RegularSession/Session20/A-HRC-20-16-Add2_en.pdf

Stoyanova V (2018a) The disjunctive structure of positive rights under the European convention on human rights. Nordic J Int Law:344–392

Stoyanova V (2018b) Causation between state omission and harm within the framework of positive obligations under the European convention on human rights. Hum Rights Law Rev:309–346

Timmer A (2016) A quiet revolution: vulnerability in the European court of human rights. In: Fineman M, Grear A (eds) Vulnerability: reflections on a new ethical foundation for law and politics. Routledge, London, pp 147–170

Tiroch K (2010) Violence against women by private actors: the inter-American court's judgment in the case of Gonzalez et Al. ('cotton field') V. Mexico. Max Planck Yearb United Nations Law 14:371–408

Tulkens F (2011) The paradoxical relationship between criminal law and human rights. J Int Criminal Justice:577–595

Vitarelli T (2021) Violenza contro le donne e bulimia repressiva. Diritto penale contemporaneo, Rivista trimestrale

Viviani A (2009) Violenza domestica, discriminazione e obblighi degli Stati per la tutela delle vittime: il caso Opuz dinanzi alla Corte europea dei diritti umani. Diritti Umani e Diritto Internazionale

WHO (2012) Understanding and addressing violence against women: intimate partner violence. https://apps.who.int/iris/bitstream/handle/10665/77432/WHO_RHR_12.36_eng.pdf

Xenos D (2013) The positive obligations of the state under the European convention of human rights. Routledge, London

Zimmermann N (2015) Legislating for the vulnerable? Special duties under the European convention on human rights. Revue suisse de droit international et européen:539–562

Concluding Remarks: Common Problems and Core Solutions in Prosecuting Domestic Violence

Rahime Erbaş

Abstract This last chapter offers a comparative analysis to establish common problems and to generate core solutions from different jurisdictions in Europe, as such, to reach a holistic solution on how to tackle the issue of ineffective criminal prosecution. It shows some core areas as follows: (1) under and over-use of criminal law in conjunction with the State's positive obligation; (2) the multi-causality of violence vs. mono-causal risk analyses; (3) breaking down the public/private dichotomy; (4) equal access to justice: secondary victimization and procedural rights; (5) a need to change the lenses also for domestic violence; and (6) a holistic approach and an effective co-operation as an urgent need. Finally, it provides conclusive remarks.

1 Under and Over-Use of Criminal Law: Positive Obligation

This book stems from the concerns on impunity in domestic violence cases, which implies under-use of criminal law. To cope with impunity, the State's positive obligation in shaping the approach of criminal justice system to domestic violence has paved the unique way for the Council of Europe members.[1] Therefore, we can consider the creation and adopting of positive obligation by the case law of the ECtHR as the European equivalent of what the feminist movement[2] in the USA in 1970s

[1] See further Erbaş (2020), p. 221 ff.

[2] See Chara Chioni-Chotouman in this volume.

R. Erbaş (✉)
Faculty of Law, Istanbul University, Istanbul, Türkiye
e-mail: rerbas@istanbul.edu.tr

R. Erbaş (ed.), *Criminal Prosecution of Domestic Violence*, Ius Gentium: Comparative Perspectives on Law and Justice 128,
https://doi.org/10.1007/978-3-032-01202-9_13

served.[3] Both served the same function: being a catalyst for transition of this violence from a private to public issue from an outside look into the criminal justice system.[4] The creation of positive obligation was a product of a supra-national perspective and, respectively, a supra-national conceptualizing.[5] Further, this was a new expectation from States which was not envisaged when the ECHR was opened to signature in 1950, with Ashworth raising objection against this new role.[6]

Today, any study addressing criminal law dimension of domestic violence takes its roots from the concept of the State's positive obligation. Therefore, the book has a special part, titled as "The ECtHR's Perspective: Positive Obligation and State's Intervention in Domestic Violence." As a matter of fact, reaching positive obligation represents an improvement on the one side. We observe this in most of the contributions in this book because it offers both a theoretical and practical basis: "All steps towards an effective investigation originate in that core concept from the point of view of the ECtHR.".[7] If a State does not recognize or not fully adopt this concept into its national system, an improvement in combatting domestic violence becomes more difficult.[8] Chapter "The State's Duty to Protect Domestic Violence Victims from a Gender Perspective: Brief Reference to the Jurisprudential Developments of the European Court of Human Rights Jurisprudence" by Raquel Borges Blázquez and Chapter "Post-Talpis Reflections: Reassessing and Redefining ECHR Standards and Italy's Approach to Domestic Violence" by Vittorio Cama demonstrate the development of this concept throughout the jurisprudence of the ECtHR through theoretical and practical explanations.

Approaching domestic violence and, respectively, violence against women from a gender-based discrimination is another improvement. In that regard, *Opuz v Türkiye (2009),*[9] as a breakthrough, was the first clear recognition that domestic violence and, respectively, violence against women was a gender-based discrimination and thus violation of Art. 14 of the ECHR. Further, gender may appear as a vulnerability factor within the criminal justice system as ensuring equal access to justice, e.g., criminal procedural rights and evidentiary process become more difficult in terms of vulnerable groups, as we will discuss under the heading "equal access to justice."[10] The core problematic thus arises as to whether the existing law, either substantive or procedural, ignores the existing gender-based discrimination by standing as neutral. Put differently, a core problematic of combatting domestic violence may stem from what the law presumes. This brings us to recognize sub-

[3] "Feminist theory has heightened our national consciousness about domestic violence and has provided the impetus for law reform effort," Hanna (1996), p. 1855.

[4] Hanna (1996), p. 1869.

[5] Erbaş (2020), p. 226. See also Chara Chioni-Chotouman in this volume.

[6] Ashworth (2013), p. 209.

[7] Erbaş (2021a), p. 3.

[8] Ibid.

[9] *Opuz v Türkiye* (33401/02), 09.09.2009.

[10] See also Selena Tierno Barrios in this volume.

layered problematics of domestic violence that can be resolved under the general concept of positive obligation. In other words, this time over reliance upon positive obligation may camouflage diverse façades of domestic violence. Therefore, Chapter "The State's Duty to Protect Domestic Violence Victims from a Gender Perspective: Brief Reference to the Jurisprudential Developments of the European Court of Human Rights Jurisprudence", by Borges Blázquez, suggests education as a preventive measure. At first impression, this suggestion may not sound a novelty. However, looking again, it discloses a core problematic: over-use of criminal law is equally problematic just as under-use of criminal law, as discussed below.

It is noted that the State's positive obligation as the European equivalent with the feminist movement in the USA in the 1970s. The same parallelism happened regarding the later outcomes: how at the beginning the feminist movement in the USA it served as useful, but then relying on it as the sole basis created more problems.[11] The same is true for over-reliance on positive obligation. Overreliance upon positive obligation turns out as over-reliance on criminal law. This is shown in Chapter "Post-Talpis Reflections: Reassessing and Redefining ECHR Standards and Italy's Approach to Domestic Violence" by Cama, which analyzes the case law of the ECtHR in terms of the *Talpis*[12] case, as the most recent case concerning Italy. Consequently, it demonstrates the reflection of the Italian legislator, known as the so-called Red Code. It proves that very limited progress has been made upon the introduction of new criminal measures. As such, it reaches the point that it is high time to question the need for a change of perspective on the part of the Court. This change will serve as a transition through the proper realization of the principle of *extrema ratio*.

Extrema ratio application of criminal law represents a manifestation of populism and, as such, punitive paternalism as Elisa Simó Soler illustrates in Chapter "Domestic Violence in Spain from a Gender Perspective: Risk Assessment and Analysis". The bottom line is that sole and over-reliance on criminal law remains as a mono-causal look into the multi-causal nature of domestic violence. The hidden driver of extreme resorting to criminal law, even if it is a mono-causal look, the outcomes of violent acts, death, injured, or harmed, falls under criminal law, although the predecessors of such violent acts in a domestic setting occurs in a multi-causal factors. As a matter of fact, Chapter "The Holistic Approach Towards Domestic Violence and the Urgent Need for Its Effective Implementation: The Case of Republic of North Macedonia", by Besa Arifi and Arta Mero, looks at the position of the victims of domestic violence from a penal and civil as well as victimological perspective and reaches the conclusion that it is impossible to handle this violence type solely with criminal law mechanisms as it is a complex phenomenon.[13] Further, Chapter "Punitive and Preventive Measures against

[11] "Yet leaving the choice of prosecution to the victim - and rationalizing that decision on the basis of feminist theory - creates more problems than it solves,"Hanna (1996), p. 1909.

[12] *Talpis v Italy* (41,237/14), 02.03.2017.

[13] See Besa Arifi and Arta Mero in this volume.

Domestic Violence in Italy: A Critical Assessment", by Lara Ferla, calls on an interdisciplinary approach as an appropriate response to this type of violence cannot be reached through the simple application of a criminal sanction.[14]

2 The Multi-Causality of Violence vs. Mono-Causal Risk Analyses: Scientific Reference

The private sphere as a domestic setting in cases of violence creates another disadvantage for women victims: the multi-causality of domestic violence. Indeed, domestic violence is also categorized as relationship-based crime.[15] The escalating effects of violence in domestic settings have been a concern. As is seen in the introductory example of Chapter "The Role of Police and Prosecutorial Bodies in Resolving Cases of Domestic Violence: The Example of Serbia", by Mina Zirojevic, finds the risk assessment and analysis is not sufficiently integrated in the criminal justice system. As the chapter addresses, the irreplaceable role of police in risk assessments and analyses should be highlighted. Because the police, as a first contact point of the victims in most of the cases, occupy a very central position. As such, it is the police who bring risk assessments and analysis points to the prosecutors and judges. The dependency of the prosecution and the court on the data brought by the police is obvious in risk assessments and analyses as well as in many areas.

Risk assessment and analysis comes as a novelty in addressing domestic violence at the early stage of criminal prosecution to avoid further harm. However, the significant role of such analyses was not yet entirely captured by the ECtHR just as it appears in the case of *Kurt v Austria*[16] where the applicant's son was murdered by her violent husband who had acted in compliance with the restraining order. In so doing, the progressive role of the Court in the case of *Opuz v Türkiye* is not observed in in the case of *Kurt v Austria*. Chapter "Punitive and Preventive Measures against Domestic Violence in Italy: A Critical Assessment" by Ferla and Chapter "Domestic Violence in Spain from a Gender Perspective: Risk Assessment and Analysis" by Simó Soler deal with the *risk assessment and analysis* in domestic violence.

Chapter "Punitive and Preventive Measures against Domestic Violence in Italy: A Critical Assessment" tackles the difficulty of reliably predicting dangerousness human behavior and the escalation effects of violent acts within personal relationships. It analyzes considerable difficulties in guaranteeing prompt, proportionate and effective measures of protection for individuals exposed to violent contexts which are linked to the choice of the right moment in which public intervention is to be addressed. Chapter "Punitive and Preventive Measures against Domestic

---

[14] See Lara Ferla in this volume.

[15] Tidmarsh et al. (2021), p. 1 ff. See also Peterson and Bialo-Padin (2012), p. 103 ff; Erbaş (2021b), pp. 105–106.

[16] *Kurt v Australia* (62,903/15), 4.07.2019.

Violence in Italy: A Critical Assessment" advocates a prognostic assessment which implies the feasibility of a specific "prognosis" regarding the future possible behavior of a perpetrator, their dangerousness, and the risk of reoffending in family relationships. In doing so, Chapter "Punitive and Preventive Measures against Domestic Violence in Italy: A Critical Assessment" demonstrates the transition in the Italian penal law from a strict and predefined profile, which was a prevailing approach in the twentieth century, to the probabilistic assessments, which is the emerging approach today. It discusses the probabilistic elements applied in the Italian case-law in predicting the risk of reoffending as the parameters as follows: "criminal capacity," "character," "conduct" and "condition of personal, family and social life" of the perpetrators. Although the transition in the Italian penal law from a strict and predefined profile to the probabilistic assessments implies the development, it criticizes that these parameters are generally assessed without reliable scientific reference. The need in approaching prediction of further violence in domestic settings through probabilistic assessments and reliable scientific reference brings us to the role of technology.

Risk assessment and analysis implies an improvement in the matter. However, using technological developments in risk assessment and analysis in case of domestic violence appears as a novelty. Chapter "Domestic Violence in Spain from a Gender Perspective: Risk Assessment and Analysis", by Simó Soler, presents Integral Monitoring System for Gender-based Violence Cases (VioGén) as technological progress which was established in Spain to proper risk prediction and management by police, judges, and other professionals involved in victims' protection. Considering the multi-causality of domestic violence requires a risk prediction and management as fundamental axes, it concludes that such risk assessment and analyses cannot be achieved through mono-causal analyses. Most importantly, it emphasizes that an incomplete response places women in positions of greater vulnerability. As Chapter "The Vulnerability of Domestic Violence Victims from A Gender Perspective in Spanish Criminal Proceedings: Challenges and Proposals against the Phenomenon of Secondary Victimization", by Selena Tierno Barrios, further explains, this is an exposure of the victim to the effects of secondary victimization.[17]

3 Breaking Down the Public/Private Dichotomy

Extrema ratio application of criminal law through the positive obligations in ECtHR's case law should be avoided. Albeit, positive obligation has played a role as breaking down the public/private dichotomy which historically disadvantaged the development of women's human rights.[18] The first point in the book is focused on

[17] Selena Tierno Barrios in this volume.

[18] Charlesworth (1988-1989), p. 197, Hasselbacher (2010), pp. 191-192; Erbaş (2021a), p. 4.

the initiation of prosecution. Accordingly, Chapter "Prosecuting Domestic Violence: Balancing the Public and the Private Interest: The Example of Greek Legislation", by Chara Chioni-Chotouman, thus questions how to balance the public and the private interest and as such, how *to initiate the prosecution of domestic violence case.* It deals with the tension between liberal theory and State intervention approach and concludes for the need for impetus in Greece by showing a historical and philosophical background of the problematic. The same conclusion for Turkish law is shared by Rahime Erbaş, Hazel Ateş Sarıdağ and Ramazan Zeyrek *in* Chapter "How to Initiate the Criminal Prosecution of a Domestic Violence Case, *ex officio* or *ex parte*?: The Example of Turkish Law", which takes on more legislative approach and constitutional aspect on whether domestic violence case is prosecuted *ex officio* or *ex parte*. Chapter "Prosecuting Domestic Violence: Balancing the Public and the Private Interest: The Example of Greek Legislation" and "How to Initiate the Criminal Prosecution of a Domestic Violence Case, *ex officio* or *ex parte*?: The Example of Turkish Law"complete each other on how to initiate the criminal prosecution regarding domestic violence.

Both chapters imply the tension between sending a message to society that State does not tolerate the violence in domestic settings where women's human rights are disadvantaged due to the public/private dichotomy while respecting the autonomy of the women victims. This brings us to decide on the question whether we need a dosage or impetus for the prosecution of domestic violence. Greek and Turkish examples demonstrate that a dosage approach may fail, rathere there is a clear need for impetus. The presumption behind this conclusion is that a dosage approach may fail in breaking down the public/private dichotomy. The underlying concept this rests on is the prevailing of a patriarchy as a power imbalance based on gender in a given society. The Greek and Turkish examples indicate that the stronger the patriarchy the more intense the need for impetus emerges. As a matter of fact, Chapter "Punitive and Preventive Measures against Domestic Violence in Italy: A Critical Assessment", by Ferla, in an Italian example, emphasizes that domestic violence appears to be a "manifestation of power."

The second point of the book concerns the role of the police as first contact by the judicial authorities. The attitude of the police toward domestic violence victims at the early stage of criminal prosecution has been crucial. It may be encouraging or discouraging for victims. In the Opuz case, the ECtHR states that "police officers often believe that their duty is to encourage women to return home and 'make peace' and fail to investigate the women's complaints."[19] The first inherent problem lies in the prevailing of patriarchy as a power imbalance based on gender through the eyes of police officers in a given society.[20] Chapter "The Role of Police and Prosecutorial Bodies in Resolving Cases of Domestic Violence: The Example of Serbia", by Zirojevic, demonstrates the research showing that the way police react, act and behave depends to a large extent on the personal attitudes, prejudices and

---

[19] *Opuz v Türkiye* (33,401/02), 09.09.2009, par.102.

[20] See for China example, Li et al. (2021).

stereotypical views of police officers, as the rules of operational work, even if strict, give the police a wide margin of discretion.

The second inherent problem, as Chapter "The Role of Police and Prosecutorial Bodies in Resolving Cases of Domestic Violence: The Example of Serbia" further addresses, is the organizational weaknesses within the police structure and the police's collaboration and inter-working with prosecutors and courts. The chapter analyzes the legal and organizational solutions in Serbia in comparison with other parts of the world, especially the EU and the countries of the region. It concludes that the victims of domestic violence are easily dismissed and inadequately treated because many perpetrators report false victims, and the prosecutors are not trained enough to recognize and protect the real victim. It is necessary for there to be training in gender perspective of all legal operators of criminal justice systems.[21] This proves that "domestic violence cases entail some challenging features and potential obstacles for criminal investigation authorities."[22]

4 Equal Access to Justice: Secondary Victimization and Procedural Rights

The role and rights of victim in criminal procedure have been limited in comparison with the suspect and accused. Therefore, the victim has stood as the "great forgotten one" of the criminal procedural system for centuries.[23] It is noted that the ECtHR has been gradually recognizing the significance of the role of victim in criminal procedure.[24] Indeed, as for the victim of domestic violence, forgottenness deepens through the vulnerability and the obstacles faced by women victims throughout the criminal justice system *vulnerability,* and one of the core ramifications in the criminal justice system, *secondary victimization*, stand as an impediment to equal access to justice for women victims of domestic violence. Equal access to justice, with the purpose of transforming the world, relies on the 2030 agenda of the UN as the Goal 16 for Sustainable Development, adopted through Resolution of 25 September, 2015. Chapter "The Vulnerability of Domestic Violence Victims from A Gender Perspective in Spanish Criminal Proceedings: Challenges and Proposals against the Phenomenon of Secondary Victimization", by Tierno Barrios, presents the European attention of the UN agenda as well as Brazilian Rules on the matter.

By virtue of the lack of adequate mechanism for victims of domestic violence within the criminal justice system, the phenomenon of secondary victimization inevitably occurs. First, as domestic violence against women implies gender-based violence, the evidentiary problem arises. The process related to evidence may

[21] See also Selena Tierno Barrios in this volume.

[22] Erbaş (2021a), p. 2.

[23] See also Selena Tierno Barrios in this volume.

[24] See Lucia Parlato and Marta Palmisano in this volume.

generate concern in criminal proceedings for gendered violence crimes as Tierno Barrios elaborates in Chapter "The Vulnerability of Domestic Violence Victims from A Gender Perspective in Spanish Criminal Proceedings: Challenges and Proposals against the Phenomenon of Secondary Victimization". It analyzes the victim statement as the only incriminating evidence in criminal proceedings for gendered violence crimes under two points: the scarcity of evidentiary material and changes in statements made by victims during the course of proceedings. Most importantly, Chapter "The Vulnerability of Domestic Violence Victims from A Gender Perspective in Spanish Criminal Proceedings: Challenges and Proposals against the Phenomenon of Secondary Victimization" provides the Spanish Supreme Court's parameters to the international audience. Further, it emphasizes the utmost importance of the exemption from the duty to testify regarding gender-based violence through the Spanish Organic law.

In achieving equal access to justice, "anchoring the use of legal aid to the concept of vulnerability" is critical as Lucia Parlato and Marta Palmisano consider in Chapter "Right to Access a Lawyer for Victims of Domestic Violence: The Example of Italian Criminal Justice". Accordingly, ensuring women with the right to access a lawyer mitigates the obstacles faced by the women victims of domestic violence by facilitating their involvement into criminal proceedings. Chapter "Right to Access a Lawyer for Victims of Domestic Violence: The Example of Italian Criminal Justice" analyzes the right to access a lawyer for victims of domestic violence by EU directives and the Istanbul Convention through their journal in the Italian criminal justice system. As such, Chapter "Right to Access a Lawyer for Victims of Domestic Violence: The Example of Italian Criminal Justice" provides genuine insights into the case-law of the Italian Constitutional Court in providing women victims free legal aid. We observe ensuring women with the right to access a lawyer especially for women living in rural areas as discussed in Chapter "The Holistic Approach Towards Domestic Violence and the Urgent Need for Its Effective Implementation: The Case of Republic of North Macedonia" by Arifi and Mero.[25]

5 A Need to Change Lenses Also for Domestic Violence?

Considering the multi-causal nature of domestic violence and the concerns on the impossibility of the criminal justice system to provide the women victims of domestic violence with an adequate protection and respectively on secondary victimization, it creates a tendency toward the application of restorative justice in domestic violence. Chapter "Applicability of Restorative Justice in Cases of Domestic Violence-Case Study of Bosnia and Herzegovina", by Ena Kazić-Çakar, demonstrates the main discussions as well as some application examples of jurisdictions before presenting the example of Bosnia and Herzegovina. In other words,

[25] See Besa Arifi and Arta Mero in this volume.

restorative justice in domestic violence appears as a new way to diversify the look of criminal justice system through the changes of lenses as Howard Zehr suggests.[26] Further, Chapter "The Vulnerability of Domestic Violence Victims from A Gender Perspective in Spanish Criminal Proceedings: Challenges and Proposals against the Phenomenon of Secondary Victimization", by Tierno Barrios, examines challenges and proposals against the phenomenon of secondary victimization in terms of vulnerability of domestic violence victims from a gendered-based discrimination perspective in Spanish criminal proceedings. Chapter "The Vulnerability of Domestic Violence Victims from A Gender Perspective in Spanish Criminal Proceedings: Challenges and Proposals against the Phenomenon of Secondary Victimization" considers restorative justice as a mechanism to prevent secondary victimization and to contribute to the empowerment of women. Prohibition of domestic violence implies an absolute mistrust.[27]

Whether domestic violence and, respectively, violence against women, is suitable to be addressed within the restorative justice or not has been a controversial topic and jurisdictions' approaches vary. Remarkable amount of works in this topic has been carried out in the literature so far. Chapter "Applicability of Restorative Justice in Cases of Domestic Violence-Case Study of Bosnia and Herzegovina", by Kazić-Çakar, pays attention to the sensitive nature of domestic violence. The new lenses for domestic violence also have pros and cons as well. Safety concerns, power imbalance and secondary victimization appear as concerns of the applications of restorative justice and female empowerment as well as meeting the needs of victims. After showing statistical data and some jurisdictional examples, Chapter "Applicability of Restorative Justice in Cases of Domestic Violence-Case Study of Bosnia and Herzegovina"embraces the application of restorative justice in domestic violence. It provides a case study of Bosnia and Herzegovina in order to come up with a new contribution to the field, just as Chapter "The Role of Police and Prosecutorial Bodies in Resolving Cases of Domestic Violence: The Example of Serbia" does.

6 Avoiding Chaos and Embracing a Holistic and Integrated Approach

In avoiding a mono-causal view and embracing the multi-causality of domestic violence, it brings us to approach domestic violence through a holistic and integrated approach. The Istanbul Convention in Art. 7 calls on *an effective co-operation* among all relevant agencies, institutions and organizations. This is another peculiarity of prosecuting domestic violence. Chapter "The Holistic Approach Towards Domestic Violence and the Urgent Need for Its Effective Implementation: The Case

[26] Zehr (2015).

[27] Selena Tierno Barrios in this volume.

of Republic of North Macedonia", by Arifi and Mero, displays this urgent need for a holistic approach and provides the case of the Republic of North Macedonia. They analyze mechanisms of prevention in the Law on the Family; the Law on Social Protection; the Criminal Code; the Criminal Procedure Code; the Law on the violence against women as a *lex specialis*; as well as in bylaws of the Ministry of Labor and Social Policy.

The prevention of domestic violence and the protection of victims require measures taken by both criminal justice and administrative authorities. That being said, in Chapter "Punitive and Preventive Measures against Domestic Violence in Italy: A Critical Assessment", Ferla first highlights that various stages of the criminal proceedings provide some set of occasions to evaluate the personality and attitude of the individuals who are under the suspicions of commission of a crime. It secondly highlights the role of administrative authorities in social prevention and also gathering evidence for criminal procedure in terms of the Italian case.

We profoundly observe the urgent need for a holistic approach in domestic violence regarding the role of the police, which has many dimensions, as represented by Chapter "The Role of Police and Prosecutorial Bodies in Resolving Cases of Domestic Violence: The Example of Serbia" by Zirojevic. It brings to light where the police, as a first contact point of the victims in most of the cases, occupy a very central position. It is the police who bring risk assessments and analysis points to the prosecutors and judges. Chapter "The Role of Police and Prosecutorial Bodies in Resolving Cases of Domestic Violence: The Example of Serbia" highlights the inter-sectoral cooperation between the police, prosecution and the court, data collection, the treatment facilities and social centers.

Chapter "The Holistic Approach Towards Domestic Violence and the Urgent Need for Its Effective Implementation: The Case of Republic of North Macedonia", by Arifi and Mero, first demonstrates domestic violence is already reflected upon by diverse law in a diverse manner. Ensuring adequate protection for victims can be only possible in applying a holistic and integrated approach by avoiding disorganization among law provisions. Secondly, it urges an effective cooperation of all operators of the justice system to be able to effectively respond to the multi-façades and peculiarities of domestic violence for risk assessment and analyses as an urgent need. Therefore, an effective co-operation appears as an inevitable method to effectively address domestic violence through the punitive sanctions, preventive and precautionary measures and individual treatment as significant strategies as a part of an integrated response.

7 Conclusion: The Way Forward

This edited book aims to demonstrate common problems and core solutions in prosecuting domestic violence mostly in Europe. Nine chapters from seven jurisdictions — Bosnia and Herzegovina, Greece, Italy, North Macedonia, Serbia, Spain, and Türkiye— addressed the main obstacles of prosecuting a domestic violence case, from initiation to finalization of the prosecution through its journey in the criminal justice system. Through the critical analysis of various obstacles, the chapters are mostly focused on the pre-trial phase of criminal prosecution in which the police and public prosecutors are mainly competent authorities. This firstly stems from peculiarities of domestic violence cases as is explained in this chapter under heading four, challenges on penal policy and comparative study on domestic violence. Secondly, this is because of the increasing role of pre-trial actions by the police and public prosecutor in today's criminal procedure.

This book tackles the violence committed in the domestic settings, the sphere, requiring particular attention of criminal justice authorities to prevent the perpetrators from enjoying impunity or receiving lenient punishment for their violence at home. This chapter summarizes core areas as follows: (1) under and over-use of criminal law in conjunction with the State's positive obligation; (2) the multi-causality of violence vs. mono-causal risk analyses; (3) breaking down the public/private dichotomy; (4) equal access to justice and as such secondary victimization and procedural rights; (5) a need to change the lenses also for domestic violence; and (6) a holistic approach and an effective co-operation as an urgent need.

This chapter provides some core solutions which may contribute to effectively addressing domestic violence in the criminal justice system. First, it is high time to rethink the role of criminal justice system in domestic violence. Secondly, the criminological nature of domestic violence should be considered in the criminal justice system just as the German criminal law scholar, Hans-Heinrich Jescheck, aptly put that "without criminology, criminal law is blind; even without criminal law, criminology is endless."[28] In so doing, the multi-causality and multi-façades of domestic violence can be recognized. This brings us to the third point: the adaptation of a holistic approach and carrying an effective co-operation among judicial authorities. As such, systemic barriers in both society and the criminal justice system for victims of domestic violence can be eliminated and the impunity in domestic violence can be avoided.

References

Ashworth A (2013) Positive obligations in criminal law. Hart Publishing Limited, Oxford

Charlesworth H (1988–1989) The public/private distinction and the right to development in international law. Australian Yearb Int Law, 12:190–204

Erbaş R (2020) Effective criminal investigations in combating domestic violence and the ECtHR: *prima ratio* v. *ultima ratio*? In: Stradella E (ed) Gender based approaches to the law and juris dictio in Europe. Pisa University Press, Pisa

Erbaş R (2021a) Effective criminal investigations for women victims of domestic violence: the approach of the ECtHR. Women's Stud Int Forum 86

[28] Jescheck (1988), p. 36.

Erbaş R (2021b) Evidentiary challenges to an effective criminal investigation for domestic violence: an introduction. In: Bonini V, Erbaş R (eds) The 10th anniversary of the Istanbul convention. Italian—Turkish conference Pisa, 18th June 2021. Pisa University Press, Pisa

Hanna C (1996) No right to choose: mandated victim participation in domestic violence prosecutions. Harv Law Rev 109(8):1849–1910

Hasselbacher L (2010) State obligations regarding domestic violence: the european court of human rights, due diligence, and international legal minimums of protection. Northwestern Univ J Int Human Rights 8(2):190–215

Jescheck HH (1988) Lehrbuch des Strafrechts- Allgemeiner Teil. Duncker & Humblot, Berlin

Li L, Sun IY, Lin K, Wang X (2021) Tolerance for domestic violence: do legislation and organizational support affect police view on family violence? Police Pract Res 22:1376–1389. https://doi.org/10.1080/15614263.2020.1866570

Peterson RR, Bialo-Padin D (2012) Domestic violence is different: the crucial role of evidence collection in domestic violence cases. J Police Crisis Negotiations 12:103–121

Tidmarsh P, Sharman S, Hamilton G (2021) The effect of specialist training on sexual assault investigators' questioning and use of relationship evidence. J Police Crim Psych:1–10. https://doi.org/10.1007/s11896-021-09446-x

Zehr H (2015) Changing lenses: restorative justice for our times. Herald Press, Harrisonburg

www.ingramcontent.com/pod-product-compliance
Lightning Source LLC
Chambersburg PA
CBHW071417281025
34632CB00003B/24
9783032012012